The English Economy
from Bede to the Reformation

This book consists of a collection of articles on social and economic themes which range from a discussion of the social scene in the seventh century into which Bede was born, to an appraisal of the letters written by Henry VIII's uncle, Lord Lisle, and an analysis of the inevitable limitations of farming development in the sixteenth century. There is an article which attempts, yet again, to shed more light upon what contemporaries expected Domesday Book to reveal; and others which tackle problems raised by the workings of the manor in the twelfth and thirteenth centuries. The beneficent consequences of the Black Death upon the fortunes of those who lived in town and country are considered in a short series of articles which analyse such problems as economic conditions before the Black Death; the extraordinary failure of the Black Death to make any serious impact upon the economy for a generation after its arrival; the far greater importance of incomes policy than the Poll Taxes in bringing about the Peasants' Revolt; the unprecedented prosperity of ordinary villagers once the incubus of over-population had been lifted; and the thriving of the towns as numbers fell in the kingdom but individual incomes rose. There are, in addition, some shorter pieces on a variety of themes.

A. R. BRIDBURY taught at the London School of Economics, where he ran the medieval section of the economic history department for many years. He is the author of several books on medieval themes in addition to the articles collected here.

The English Economy
from Bede to the Reformation

A. R. BRIDBURY

THE BOYDELL PRESS

This collection first published 1992 by The Boydell Press, Woodbridge

The Boydell Press is an imprint of Boydell & Brewer Ltd
PO Box 9, Woodbridge, Suffolk IP12 3DF, UK
and of Boydell & Brewer Inc.
PO Box 41026, Rochester, NY 14604, USA

ISBN 0 85115 305 4

British Library Cataloguing-in-Publication Data
Bridbury, A. R.
    English Economy from Bede to the
    Reformation
    I. Title
    330.942
    ISBN 0–85115–305–4

Library of Congress Cataloging-in-Publication Data applied for

The paper used in this publication meets the minimum requirements
of American National Standard for Information Sciences –
Permanence of Paper for Printed Library Materials, ANSI Z39.48–1984

Printed in Great Britain by
St Edmundsbury Press Ltd, Bury St Edmunds, Suffolk

Contents

Acknowledgements

The following articles, included in this collection, have previously been published as indicated below.

'The Dark Ages', *Economic History Review*, 2nd ser., vol. xxii, no. 3 (1969)

'Domesday Book: A Re-interpretation', *English Historical Review*, vol. cv (April 1990)

'The Farming Out of Manors', *Economic History Review*, 2nd ser., vol. xxxi, no. 4 (1978)

'Thirteenth-Century Prices and the Money Supply', *Agricultural History Review*, vol. 33, part i (1985)

'Before the Black Death', *Economic History Review*, 2nd ser., vol. xxx, no. 3 (1977)

'The Black Death', *Economic History Review*, 2nd ser., vol. xxvi, no. 4 (1973)

'The Hundred Years' War: Costs and Profits', *Trade, Government and Economy in Pre-Industrial England*, ed. D. C. Coleman and A. H. John (Weidenfeld and Nicolson, London, 1976)

New Introduction to B. L. Manning, *The People's Faith in the Time of Wyclif* (Harvester Press, Hassocks, Sussex, 1975)

'Markets and Freedom in the Middle Ages', *The Market in History*, ed. B. L. Anderson and A. J. H. Latham (Croom Helm, London, 1986)

'English Provincial Towns in the Later Middle Ages', *Economic History Review*, 2nd ser., vol. xxxiv, no. 1 (1981)

A Reply to S. H. Rigby on 'Late Medieval Urban Prosperity: the evidence of the lay subsidies', *Economic History Review*, 2nd ser., vol. xxxix, no. 3 (1986)

'The Lisle Letters', *Economic History Review*, 2nd ser., vol. xxxv, no. 4 (1982)

'Sixteenth-Century Farming', *Economic History Review*, 2nd ser., vol. xxvii, no. 4 (1974)

Introduction[1]

The articles in this collection, written over a period of twenty years, reflect an attempt to re-think the significance of certain key events in medieval English history and to revise accepted interpretations of certain key documents. With the exception of the first and fourth of these articles all have been published before. No single theme binds them together, though manorial problems dominate those that examine issues which are contentious in earlier centuries just as the Black Death dominates those that examine issues which are contentious in later centuries. And it is inevitable that this should be so; for the manor raises difficult problems during its centuries of emergence; and the Black Death is still deplored, despite all the evidence to the contrary, as an unqualified disaster for the social and economic life of medieval England, or if not an unqualified disaster, then a disaster upon which one may reasonably dwell at length, with qualifications which one may dispose of in a sentence or so.

The origins of the manor seem to be irrevocably lost. When we first come across a social institution with the familiar lineaments of the manor, in the very sparse records that survive from Anglo-Saxon England, it appears to be fully operational. In Ine's laws we find a clause which deals with the problem encountered by a man who takes a parcel of land as a tenant.[2] We are not told how he pays his rent. He may pay in kind or in money or in both. All we know is that he does not pay any part of his rent in service; or perhaps we should say that when he takes up his tenancy he does not expect to have to pay in service: for the tenancy lacks living-quarters for the farmer. It is some meadowland perhaps, or strips in an open-field. Evidently once he is installed as a tenant his landlord demands service. Presumably his landlord demands service in addition to the rent already agreed. But that is not the issue. The tenant does not complain of an unwarrantable increase in rent but of an uncovenanted change in its character. The grievance is widespread enough to be brought to the attention of the king. The law needs to be re-stated or clarified; and that is what the king does. He declares that tenants are liable for service only when they take up a homestead as well as land. To put the matter another way, what the king does is to distinguish between those who take up tenancies which are in fact fully-equipped farms and those

---

[1] This introduction will only be lightly annotated because it confines itself to discussing matters which are more thoroughly documented in the articles that follow.
[2] F. L. Attenborough, *The Laws of the Earliest English Kings* (Cambridge, 1922), p. 59: Ine, 67.

who merely acquire parcels of land with which to augment the resources of their farms. So far as the law is concerned current practice in Ine's Wessex is clearly stated by implication: a farm-tenancy may or may not be a service-tenancy; but tenancy of parcels of farm-land emphatically is not.

Here we have agrarian society organising its labour supply in a way in which it was organised upon many medieval manors. The medieval lord of the manor, with a substantial demesne and a numerous retinue of servile tenants, normally farmed his demesne by requiring his servile tenants to discharge part of their obligations of rent by providing some of the labour upon which the demesne depended. So it seems did certain Anglo-Saxon lords in Ine's Wessex. We cannot possibly tell how widespread service-tenancy was in those early years of Anglo-Saxon settlement. Ine's response to the problem with which he was asked to deal certainly suggests that service-tenancy was a familiar element in the early Anglo-Saxon agrarian scene. Was it even more familiar to the medieval agrarian scene? Norman terminology has done its best to make us think so by calling every Anglo-Saxon estate a manor and thus conveying the entirely false impression that an institution with an immense variety of forms was nevertheless, in essential respects, uniform. But nobody who has heeded the lessons that Maitland admonished us to learn from Domesday Book and Kosminsky urged us to draw from the Hundred Rolls, or who has absorbed the conclusions of much brilliant work on regional variations in manorial structure, can ignore the fact that manorial types were endlessly various and that the classical manor, with its ample demesne lands and copious reserves of servile labour, was no more than *primus inter pares* even in parts of the country where it is still regarded as the commonest manorial type. Manors abundantly endowed with demesne and servile tenures were everywhere rivalled and often eclipsed by manors with more demesne than servile tenures with which to support it; or more servile tenures than the demesne could possibly employ even if every living-in servant and wage-earning labourer were to be dismissed in their favour; or by manors altogether bereft of demesne or servile tenures or even of both.

What does this multiplicity of forms mean? Does it mean that the medieval manor, as we see it in the records, has degenerated from some early perfection of form? Did the classical manor express that early perfection and should we therefore point to the cryptic allusions of Ine's laws as our best evidence for this early perfection? If so, then when we come across what look like woefully impaired, incomplete, stunted or warped specimens of the manor, in the records of the thirteenth and fourteenth centuries, we are bound to conclude that what we are examining is not the culminating phase of manorial development but the cumulative havoc wrought upon a symmetrical institution by centuries of depredations. Some very distinguished writers have certainly taken this view, if only implicitly. When Kosminsky, for example, was looking for an explanation of why so many classical manors were to be found, in thirteenth-century Midland England, upon estates owned by the most ancient ecclesiastical foundations, he turned naturally to an explanation that linked the antiquity of the foundations with the integrity of the manorial structure. Continuous possession by one owner, he argued, had preserved them from disruption.[3]

But this explanation will not answer to the facts because the most ancient ecclesiastical foundations of all, and also some of the biggest, were to be found in Kent where service-tenancies were so unusual that it would be no more than an exaggeration to call them anomalous.

When we look back to the earliest laws we find that they offer no comfort or support to the suggestion that the classical manor of the thirteenth century was a fortuitous survivor. Nor do they encourage us to believe that it was a masterpiece of evolutionary social engineering. Instead the laws invite us to see the problem of manorial development from a somewhat different point of view. They tell us about lordship and they tell us about service-tenure. But they do not link the two. Nor is there any reason why they should. Law deals with particular problems which raise general concern or affect influential sections of the community. Evidently whatever link there may have been called for no legislative action. In these early laws, however, lordship seems to have involved jurisdiction because lords collected fines and were expected to discipline their own dependents. Lordship also implied a military role. Lords who answered a summons to military service rode to the point of assembly armed and armoured. They also brought a retinue; for the obligation to answer a summons to military service extended to quite ordinary people. Some of these people may very well have been their lords' service-tenants. And it is not without significance, in this context, that lordship conferred other powers. Ine forbade anyone to leave his lord by going elsewhere without express permission. No doubt this clause was inserted for practical military reasons. But everyone appears to have had a lord in Ine's Wessex, even a poor illegitimate baby; and a clause which may have been intended to guarantee the tally of fighting men and their supporting contingents was not without value to the demesne farmer. The bond of lord and dependent cannot fail to have strengthened the bond of landlord and tenant. In centuries to come the rituals and symbolism inspired by these relationships will culminate in a network of social inter-dependence familiar to us as feudalism. But the active ingredients are very obviously at work at the earliest moment for which there are records which could possibly vouchsafe us a glimpse of their fermentation.

We are not justified, however, in concluding that what we find in the earliest laws is evidence of the classical manor merely in embryo. What we find is an estate governed by a lord with judicial powers and military functions who farms land upon which some of his men do service in part payment of rent and who is allowed by law to control the comings and goings of everyone who acknowledges his lordship. These relationships may not be

---

[3] E. A. Kosminsky, *Studies in the Agrarian History of England* (Blackwell, 1956), p. 116. See also p. 138, *et seq*.

caparisoned in the resplendent panoply of feudalism. They may be, therefore, no more than proto- or even crypto-feudal. But the medieval manor had little enough to add to an institution which is to be found, so far as we can tell, virtually as soon as the English Settlements had penetrated and subdued deep into the west country.

What we can also discern in the earliest laws are intimations of that variety of manorial types which is so clear later. To be more exact what the laws reveal is absence of restrictions upon the initiative of ordinary yeoman-farmers, and hence a presumption that 'tenurial heterogeneity' was far from being uncommon.

In short, if we examine the earliest laws without teleological bias, without expecting to find in the distant past no more than the rudiments of an institution which will not achieve maturity for centuries to come, then what we shall actually find is the medieval manor in full working order, lacking only in those fine points of doctrine and symbolism that conferred upon the manor of medieval times its unique characteristics. Nor should that surprise us. Service-tenure is, after all, merely barter applied to matters other than the exchange of goods and as such is presumably as old as farming itself. And the power to control those who submitted themselves to the conditions that regulated service-tenure varied inversely with the power of the state. Power flies to the periphery when the grip at the centre slackens. The early Anglo-Saxon estate, like the Roman colonate and the medieval manor, reflect variations of the terms upon which the state had to treat with those who increasingly took charge locally when its power faltered or who exploited its immaturity in periods before it had grown to full strength.

When we look deeper, however, the manor in all its protean re-incarnations must strike us as a strange solution to problems of agrarian labour supply. Providing the landlord with services as a condition of tenure may be one way in which to solve the problem of securing a labour force. But it is surely a paradoxical solution. In the abstract, service-tenure has every appearance of being a system designed to tie men to the land when labour is scarce. When labour is abundant it is superfluous because landlords can take their pick of the men on offer without inflicting upon themselves the cost in bureaucracy and litigation that such a system entails. Experience has always taught that, in the last analysis, scarcity of material resources, expressed as competition for work, will reduce the remuneration of labour to the lowest point compatible with survival. In such circumstances landlords can be quite sure of being able to extract the maximum return from their tenancies by rack-renting them and from their labour force by paying wages at the market rate. Many landlords found that to be true at times of labour surplus in the Middle Ages; and none of those who ran their estates without benefit of servile labour appears to have found that dependence upon the market for supplies of labour instead of upon the clumsy mechanisms of agrarian feudalism made their farming any less profitable than it might have been otherwise.

Landlords clearly need service-tenure only when labour is scarce. But when labour is scarce landlords are no longer masters of the situation. If they pay badly they will be served badly, if at all. If they pay well, they will hardly make ends meet. If they bully and threaten, their men will melt away knowing that a warm welcome and easier terms of employment await them elsewhere with no questions asked, landlord solidarity being as much of a chimera as the solidarity of the workers.

In the Middle Ages neither law nor intimidation could hope to maintain serfdom as a way of securing a labour supply when market forces were resolute for its destruction. The classic demonstration of their impotence is to be found in later medieval England where the seigneurial reaction to the emptying of the countryside by the Black Death failed abysmally and manorialism as a system of farming the land with the help of dependent labour came to an end. What makes the English example classic is the strength of the resistance offered by the landowning classes to the threat of change. The most powerful and highly-organised government in Europe allied to the most formidably cohesive landed classes were comprehensively defeated as a result of the individual and unco-ordinated decisions of myriads of English farmworkers and artisans, none of them men of any particular substance or public influence, unanimously resolved to make the most of unprecedented opportunities.[4]

How are we to resolve this paradox? Service-tenure is either unnecessary or unenforceable and yet we find it all about us in the medieval record even though it may be dominant only here and there. We must not expect an obvious explanation in terms of efficient resource allocation for what we find. Service-tenure was evidently more a form of conspicuous consumption than a thrifty use of assets. In normal circumstances, when labour was neither desperately scarce nor a drug in the market, it clearly suited the demesne farmer to make secure provision for some part of his labour supply by engaging men on permanent contracts whose binding force was the conditional grant of land. And there were incalculable but profoundly significant social advantages in doing so. The retainer was a tangible symbol of his lord's status and a visible expression of his lord's power over men. Lordship without a substantial following of retainers of all degrees was lordship bereft of dignity and magic; and the service-tenant was a humble assistant in that pageant.

Service-tenancy, however was not without its special risks. In some ways these were perhaps greater in medieval times than they had been in the kingdoms of the earliest English laws. Any tenancy involves the landlord in committing his property to the stewardship of someone about whom he usually knows very little until it is too late. But the risks of a leasehold are limited by the term of the lease. Servile tenancy in the Middle Ages was a

---

4 For examples of the contrary view, that servile status could be maintained by government diktat, see T. H. Aston and C. H. E. Philpin, eds, *The Brenner Debate* (Cambridge, 1985). For some comments of mine on this debate, see *Journal of Economic History*, Sept. 1986.

commitment without formal term. Even when, by some lucky chance, his tenant came to him with an exemplary record as a farmer, the medieval landlord could know nothing about his tenant's heir, though generally speaking he was committed to his tenant's heir once he had committed himself to the tenant. Moreover he, like his Anglo-Saxon forbear, rarely had an effective choice in the matter. His service-tenants came with the farm and, to all intents and purposes, were as much part of its fixed assets as its barns and fields. When a tenant turned out badly he was always, at any period, hard to remove and a risk to replace; and a bad tenant could be a bad influence as well as a thoroughpaced nuisance. A service-tenant had two separate spheres of activity in which to show his worth or lack of it. He was a farmer on his own account as well as a labourer on his lord's. An adequate farmer should have made an adequate labourer and no doubt often did. But there was no reason why he should have worked as conscientiously for his landlord as he did for himself. Often enough he saw no reason why he should work for his landlord at all and sent others to do the work that was expected of him. When he did so we can hardly believe that he always sent his best man rather than someone whose services he could most readily dispense with; and when he hired someone to take his place on the lord's demesne we can hardly believe that he always hired the best man he could get, rather than someone who was cheap because he was not worth more than he was paid.

Labour problems such as these were inherent in any system of service-tenure, whether medieval or Anglo-Saxon. The best that can be said for such a system is that the work the service-tenantry was called upon to do was, as a rule, so obviously confined to the kind that could be adequately done by anyone brought up in farming that a service-tenantry answered as well as anything to the need for a body of men who could carry out the laborious work of the farm whilst all the specialist jobs were being done by others.

Work that called for more skill than the general run of tenants could be expected to offer or more continuous attention than they were under contract to provide was generally done, in the Middle Ages as at the time of Aethelberht, by a *corps d'élite* of living-in servants whose work was very likely supplemented in Aethelberht's time and unquestionably supplemented later by that of men and women who were usually paid by the task. The demesne farmer in fact found himself reproducing on his estate a type of staffing structure with which everyone was very familiar in another context. It was a structure within which the service-tenant had a socially recognised place: for it was the structure to be found in the Anglo-Saxon as well as the feudal army. Led by its aristocratic commanders such an army consisted of a *corps d'élite* of retinues of picked men and battle-hardened mercenaries reinforced by bands of conscript reservists drawn from the partially-trained ranks of the peasantry. It is not difficult to appreciate how easily the service-tenant fitted into a scheme of things in which he himself was numbered, however humbly, in the ranks of his lord's retainers, his work having every appearance of being the agrarian equivalent of compulsory military service.

Wherever we find demesne farms sufficiently well-stocked with service-tenants to be able to make use of them we find them being used. In every age for which we have evidence, from the time of Ine's laws until servile tenancy was extinguished as a source of labour, but not as a badge of status, in the later Middle Ages, demesne farms, wherever they approximated to the structure of the classical manor, were run by a *corps d'élite* of specialists supported by service, or after the Conquest, servile tenants. When they were leased out, the lessee took over a going concern; and leasing out demesne farms was a commonplace of management policy in every period of early and medieval history of which we have any knowledge. A particular landlord might wish to reserve the jurisdiction of the court, or perhaps some meadowland, or the mills, for his own purposes, when he conveyed his demesne interests to a lessee. But reservations such as these apart, the lessee got the farm with all its working assets; and these included the services of the tenants. Indeed a demesne farm leased out was indistinguishable, as a working unit, from a demesne in hand. It was run in the same way. Its tenants answered to the reeve for services and other dues as they had done when the demesne was in hand. The manor court dispensed justice and imposed fines as it had done before the leasing of the demesne. The one and only item of administration to differentiate the demesne farm on lease from the demesne farm in hand was the destination of its earnings. When the farm was leased out these earnings went to the lessee instead of to the lord's accountant; and he, in due course, received from the lessee or from the bailiff of the manor whatever sum of money or supply of produce the lessee had agreed to pay in rent.

When Lennard declared that 'the bailiff and the lessee represent two essentially different kinds of estate management' he was betrayed into committing himself to an outrageously false antithesis.[5] He might just as well have said that 'the chef and the restaurant represent two essentially different kinds of catering arrangements'. The bailiff was as essential to demesne farming, whoever got its proceeds, as the chef is to any form of catering, wherever the diners sit or whatever arrangements they make about paying. The lessee who did not himself assume the responsibilities of the bailiff's office was obliged to appoint someone to do the supervisory work of the bailiff or suffer the consequences of his failure to do so. The medieval manor was locked into a system of working sanctioned and sustained by a network of customary usages which gave an innovator very little scope for change. Nor was the lessee, with his simple occupational lease, within his rights to do anything more than run the manor he had taken over, to the best of his

---

5 R. V. Lennard, *Rural England 1086–1135* (Oxford, 1959), p. 143. Prof. Du Boulay, quoted with approval by Dr Miller, is surely equally in error when he declares that 'the reeve and bailiff manorialism, so often regarded as typical of the Middle Ages and as agriculture's best medieval manifestation, was hardly more than a substantial interlude in an age-long system of leasehold farming'. F. R. H. Du Boulay, *The Lordship of Canterbury* (New York, 1966), p. 197. Cited by E. Miller, 'England in the Twelfth and Thirteenth Centuries: An Economic Contrast?', *Economic History Review*, 2nd ser., vol. xxiv (1971), p. 14.

ability, for the stipulated term of his tenure, returning it to the landlord at the end of that term in the same condition as it was when he received it.

The leasing-out of demesne farms is not only something that we find at all periods for which we have evidence of estate management: it is also something that we should expect to find. Sometimes demesne farms were better let than run because they were too far from the main concentration of estate farms for easy supervision. Sometimes they were let on beneficial terms as rewards for services rendered. Sometimes they went to relatives or friends or to those whom it was imprudent to alienate or advantageous to favour. But the demesne farmer whose main purpose in leasing was to procure for himself a dependable and trouble-free income by devolving his management responsibilities upon a lessee for an agreed period of time and for a rent which might not vary during the term of the lease but was certainly subject to review upon renewal, had in effect decided to turn his demesne farm into a fixed-income bearing asset. It was perhaps a decision much like the one taken centuries later by those who chose to put their capital into medium and long-dated government stock. And it was a decision with much to be said for it. Bad weather, disease which often desolated flocks and herds, farming mishaps of every description, not to speak of the incalculable repercussions of incompetence and mismanagement, were, as they still are, the bane of farming life; and any demesne farmer with better things to do than devote time and energy to the thankless task of supervising supervisors. inevitably looked about for lessees to whom these laborious responsibilities might be delegated.

Not everyone recognised by historians as a lessee was a lessee in fact. When an ecclesiastical corporation appointed a senior member to superintend the running of a particular manor or group of manors the chosen member was called a *firmarius*. And that is what he certainly was; for he returned a fixed and ascertainable income to the corporation. When he returned it in kind, as he was often required to do, it supplied a particular recurrent need. When he returned it in cash it was ear-marked for a particular recurrent expenditure. But that was not the end of the matter. The *firmarius* was not quit, as a leaseholder would have been, once he had fulfilled his fixed obligations There might be surpluses. These surpluses were not profits, as they were for leaseholders, with which the ecclesiastical *firmarius* could line his own pockets. The *firmarius* was the custodian of property whose income was dedicated to certain spiritual purposes. Any surpluses that accrued in times of plenty properly belonged to the body of which the *firmarius* was merely an executive limb. Consequently much scandal was caused when it transpired that some *firmarius* had so far forgotten his vows and his duty as to dispose of surpluses for his own ends. Despite the superficial resemblances between the obligations of leaseholder and ecclesiastical *firmarius*, the *firmarius* was not simply a leaseholder. At bottom he was the landlord's agent or steward. And when he was displaced by another kind of manager, the change is not properly to be understood as a change from leasehold to direct control. The control exercised by the *firmarius*, in such cases, was as direct as control could be; and the profits of demesne farming, in such cases, were enjoyed, in the absence of fraudulent conversion, by the corporation whose senior dignitary was lord of its manors.

The lessee of a demesne farm, when he was not something more or something less than a lessee, could be anyone substantial or plausible enough to be entrusted with a valuable assemblage of agrarian assets who, for reasons of his own, wanted to assume the management responsibilities that the lessor was content to relinquish. We can only speculate as to what such men were like. A farmer who takes a farm on lease is in effect managing another man's farm; and a farm-manager is someone who is making do with second-best. His preference, if he is a man of calibre, is for a farm of his own. It may be that he cannot afford a farm of his own however modest in size or value. But it may be that he cannot afford a farm of the size or value that he knows he can manage. A man who leases a substantial demesne farm on commercial terms may very well be someone who prefers managing a big farm to owning a smaller one. For such men farm-management is a career; and the prospect of taking charge of some important demesne farm on terms which might advance his career as well as rewarding his skills doubtless attracted many an able and ambitious farm-manager mature in judgement if not in years.

Many leases, then as now, were carelessly drafted.[6] They were imprecise as to the term for which the lease was to run or made no provision or hopelessly inadequate provision for rent reviews. Well-publicised examples of such grossly deficient legal instruments have made historians deeply suspicious of the medieval lease; and some historians have gone so far as to perceive the onset of hard times in any apparent increase in the readiness with which demesne farmers were prepared to lease out their farms, as if leasing out were something they did as a hedge against risks only when the portents were unfavourable. But that is to take disparagement of the lease to absurd lengths. The evidence that demesne farms were let out on lease when times were very far from being bad is so general that it is hard to understand how such an idea ever gained the currency it still enjoys. Moreover it was surely when times were really bad that demesne farmers encountered their greatest difficulty in recruiting men who were skilled, experienced and reliable, to take up their proffered leases. Prospective lessees of any calibre and substance knew better than to involve themselves in nightmarish problems when deflation, civil war, or devastating epidemic disease, threatened to compound the normal every-day vicissitudes of farming. There were always men who were willing to take a chance; but their terms for doing so were likely to have made leasing out an even less attractive prospect for many landlords than the risks of soldiering on as before.

Nevertheless, by adjusting the terms of the leases he offered so as to suit prevailing conditions, a demesne farmer could always secure a reputable

---

6 There was once, however an immense archive of properly drafted leases in duplicate and triplicate. Lennard, *op. cit.*, p. 165.

tenant even when conditions were very serious indeed. And that was as true for inflation as for deflation. Prices which seemed to be rising more than they fell, thus taking the market well beyond the familiar cycle of good and bad years, simply called for a fresh look at the terms of the lease. They did not in the least call for the comprehensive abandonment of leasing as a way of administering an estate. The words of the author of the *Dialogus de Scaccario* to the effect that leases were called farms because they were 'firm and immutable' went far beyond the meaning of the word *firma* and have made too deep an impression upon the minds of historians.[7] Firm does not imply immutable. What is fixed for a term can be changed when that term has ended. And when prices rise landlords can take them in their stride by shortening the terms of leases and by providing for the payment of a premium which would enable them to capitalise the annual increments foregone between reviews.

When it came to a question of bringing into full cultivation land which had been unused or under-used hitherto, a demesne farmer with such land within his estate boundaries but beyond his working fields and woods, did not have to manage it himself in order to get it brought up to farming standards. If economic conditions warranted its full exploitation, beneficial leases could do the rest. Applicants for tenancies attracted and encouraged by rents set at artificially low levels whilst they were establishing themselves could be expected to turn unimproved land to such good use that when they had done everything they might reasonably have been expected to do to it they would then be able to pay a rent which reflected the market value of the farms they had created on it. Much European agrarian development was sustained and rewarded in this way.

There was very little call in medieval England, however, for leases which told the tenant how he was to farm the land with which he had been entrusted; and that was so because very little was done to improve the performance of medieval demesne farming by increasing yields rather than by extending the margins of cultivation.[8] When the climate of opinion changed and markets were more favourable to reform, as happened in due course, progressive landlords wrote specific operational requirements into the leases they granted and made sure by inspection that the terms of their leases were kept. But wherever we look in the medieval record we find that demesne yields remained incorrigibly and devastatingly low. Medieval demesne managers were not unaware of what they had to do in order to mend matters. Dr Campbell and others who have worked upon these problems have made it perfectly clear that medieval demesne managers were very well

---

7 C. Johnson, ed., *Dialogus De Scaccario* (Nelson, 1950), p. 30.
8 F. L. Farmer, 'Crop Yields, Prices and Wages in Medieval England', *Studies in Medieval and Renaissance History*, vol. vi (1983); 'Grain Yields on Westminster Abbey Manors 1271–1410', *Canadian Journal of History* (1983), pp. 331–48.

aware of how to improve agrarian performance by raising yields.[9] They knew that they could enormously improve performance by having the land weeded more thoroughly, or manured more heavily, or seeded more generously, or planted more intensively with nitrogen-enriching legumes than custom or local usage commonly prescribed. Nor was this knowledge the privileged secret of some closed college of estate managers working exclusively for the richest and most powerful landlords in the kingdom. Dr Campbell has shown that some of those who ran quite small estates knew and practised a husbandry as progressive as that of any to be found on the biggest.[10]

If knowledge of what to do was widespread that was surely because it was, in a sense, obvious. Everyone could see that weeds choke, that dung enriches, that thickly-seeded land will do better than land which has been only lightly- sprinkled with seed, that water drowns and even that some crops actually do the soil good. Nevertheless if there is one conclusion which we may confidently draw from modern studies of medieval estates it is that agrarian progress, defined in terms of the yield of grain, signally failed to affect the practice of the average medieval English demesne farm.

Demesne farmers who failed to respond to the example set by their progressive contemporaries were not necessarily embodiments of the obstructive forces of perversity and inertia. The classical manor ought perhaps to take some share of the blame for their apparently wilful neglect of best practice; for its structured regimen of usages left an enterprising farmer with very little room for manoeuvre. But the greater part of the land given over to demesne farming was not subject to manorial restrictions which were anything like as intractable and comprehensive as those of the classical manor. If demesne farming was unprogressive in the Middle Ages we are surely driven to the conclusion that it was so because the results of progressive farming did not justify their costs; and that those who experimented with progressive methods did so in the spirit exhibited by those who run model farms in all ages and do so in defiance of costs and heedless of returns.

The evidence of the price material seems to bear out this conclusion. The thirteenth century is the first for which we have statistical evidence of prices. Of these prices by far the most important from the point of view of estate management were the prices obtained for grain. In Postan's felicitous phrase, the bigger estates were 'federated grain factories'. Grain sales and rents paid out of grain sales made up the bulk of the revenue upon which the finances of the bigger estates depended. Fortunately the records of grain prices are the most voluminous and reliable of all. That does not mean that the index of grain prices constructed by historians of prices is altogether satisfactory. But it is by now based upon research which is very nearly exhaustive and has produced conclusions upon which the leading historians in the field concur.

[9] B. M. S. Campbell, 'Agricultural Progress in Medieval England', *Economic History Review*, 2nd ser., vol. xxxvi (1983), pp. 26–46.
[10] Dr Campbell also notes the importance of peasant productivity. *Op. cit.*, p. 39.

The chief conclusion of their work is that, contrary to the sedulously propagated belief that the thirteenth century was one of rising prices during which the demesne farmer had things all his own way, the thirteenth century was in fact a time when grain prices sat first upon one plateau and then upon another for very nearly the entire span of the century. Such prices, if we consider them in isolation, could neither reward enterprise with easy profits nor assuage failure by soothing misfortune or mismanagement with the emollient of rising returns.

Times would have been easier for demesne farmers if the remuneration of labour had fallen. In the absence of a steady inflation of grain prices which, by running ahead of costs, handed a welcome bounty of profitability even to the most shiftless demesne farmer, only the remorseless pressure of an economic force acting upon the remuneration of labour could have achieved similar results. It is generally believed that there was such a pressure in the thirteenth century; a pressure which took the form of a serious problem of over-population. Had there been such a pressure, the remuneration of labour would certainly have fallen.

We have, however, no reason to believe that over-population forced the remuneration of labour down. The behaviour of grain prices is inimical to any such belief. People could not survive without grain; and grain was in fact the chief product of the soil. It was, therefore, the most sensitive index of medieval population growth we could hope to possess. Any pressure upon the land was bound to have raised grain prices even if it had not originated with an increasing demand for grain. And in the thirteenth century there was actually just such a pressure. It drew its strength from the spectacular expansion of Flemish and Italian clothmaking whose demands for English wool rose so prodigiously that towards the end of the century exports were running at an annual rate of about 27,000 sacks.[11] This means that by mid-century at the latest the export trade required the wool of between five and seven million sheep.[12] Unless home consumption had been very drastically curtailed in the meantime, this means that the foreign demand represented a substantial additional call upon the resources of the countryside at a time when we are told that those resources were already under pressure as a result of population growth.

To some extent this increase in the national flock was accomodated within the arable routine; and to some extent it was accomodated upon land which was not suitable for arable. Unfortunately, however, the best wool came from districts which were equally suitable for both arable and grazing. Moreover sheep have to be over-wintered; and fodder demands exerted pressure on the arable even when the sheep themselves apparently did not.

---

[11] A. R. Bridbury, *Medieval English Clothmaking* (1982), Appendix E.
[12] Assuming 364 lb of wool per sack and 1½ to 2 lb per fleece. For wool yields see D. Postles, 'Fleece Weights and the Wool Supply c.1250–1350', *Textile History*, vol. 12 (1981); also M. J. Stephenson, 'Wool Yields in the Medieval Economy', *Economic History Review*, 2nd ser., vol. xli (1988).

Fully exploiting hitherto unused or under-used land would undoubtedly have enabled farmers to increase output without raising prices. But it is very doubtful whether there was much usable land left to colonise by this time. As a rule, the evidence is of widespread but negligible gains, often at the margins of cultivation.[13] And even if we make the most generous allowance for exploitable reserves of land, it is unlikely that such reserves could have done more than compensate for the unparalleled growth in the demand for grazing land for sheep.

If we are to postulate pressure of population as the force that bore down upon the remuneration of labour in the thirteenth century, then this is the context within which we must consider it. So far as grain prices are concerned, they certainly did rise in the thirteenth century. They rose at the beginning of the century and again towards the end of its third quarter. But they rose, at such moments, so swiftly and briefly that, however we explain their behaviour, we cannot possibly attribute it to demographic forces or even to the encroachment of sheep upon land that did or could grow food. Population simply cannot expand so suddenly as to overwhelm the resources of the land and then stop expanding equally suddenly so that grain supplies are returned to a trendless cycle of good and bad years until the next eruption, many decades later, repeats the experiences of the one before. Nor is it likely that a sudden expansion of the national flock could have had a corresponding effect upon land values.

When we turn to the statistical records we find that wage material is very hard to come by and even harder to interpret. For the greater pert of the century we are dependent for information upon the estate accounts of the bishopric of Winchester. These accounts are highly suspect, where wages are concerned, because they record rates of remuneration which were unchanged for decades and, in some instances, for very nearly sixty years. If we assume that Winchester labourers got no more than the accounts said they got then living-in servants who were paid in cash and kind lost something whenever the purchasing-power of the money they earned depreciated as a result of inflation and gained something as the value of the grain with which they were paid increased. It would be difficult to demonstrate, from these meagre indications, that the remuneration of living-in servants employed by the bishops of Winchester reflected the growing impoverishment of the population of thirteenth-century England. Others who were paid wholly in money were less fortunate, according to the Winchester evidence. In the third quarter of the century, however, we begin to find alternatives to the Winchester evidence; and these show that elsewhere wages were being raised, presumably to compensate for the depreciation in the value of money.[14]

[13] B. F. Harvey, 'The Population Trend in England Between 1300 and 1348', *Transactions of the Royal Historical Society*, 5th ser., vol. xvi (1966), p. 31.
[14] H. E. Hallam, ed., *The Agricultural History of England and Wales, vol. 2, 1042–1350* (Cambridge, 1988), chapter 7.

Dr Farmer, who has done most to enlighten us about thirteenth-century wages, believes that the compensation was incomplete. According to his cost-of-living index, the purchasing-power of wages deteriorated sharply after the burst of inflation that took grain prices to a higher plateau in the 1270s. Some delay in the adjustment of wages to higher prices, creating a temporary disparity between the two, is a familiar element of inflationary experience. But this sudden eruption of bad times for farm workers, reflecting a permanent change in the relative scarcity of resources, is hard to credit. Its onset happens to have coincided with a short burst of inflation. The inflation soon ended in a flattening-out of grain prices at a higher level than before. But wages, according to Dr Farmer, did not recover their lost ground for two generations. A sudden worsening of standards of living, inaugurated by inflation and then stabilising at a lower level for a protracted period, is not something that it is easy to explain or justify. It is the pressure of population argument examined above expressed in terms of wages instead of prices and has all the shortcomings of that argument.

Whatever the truth about the behaviour of real wages in the last three decades of the thirteenth century may be, and we have every reason to be sceptical of the conclusions offered to us by those who know the evidence best, we are bound to return a verdict of not proven upon the indictment of the thirteenth century which claims that, taking the century as a whole, it was one in which, according to the statistical evidence, the living standards of the majority fell substantially, if not catastrophically.

Living standards may not have fallen; but that does not mean that we are entitled to assume that they were high or, in some sense, adequate. We may have good reason to suspect that they did not change very much. But we do know that when the Black Death started making inroads into the population the occupancy-rate of tenements did not fall markedly for a generation. If the villages of England were so full of people that there was usually someone to fill every vacancy when pestilence was making so many tenancies vacant, we cannot expect to find that standards of living in the thirteenth century were anything but low. How low they were we cannot possibly tell. But we cannot assume that they were abysmal. Grain yields on farms run by the big corporations were, as a rule, sensationally low. Historians generally assume that small farmers with fifteen or thirty acres did at least as badly, if not worse. By measuring ascertainable facts about the size of ordinary servile holdings and the liabilities incurred by those who held such holdings against pessimistic assumptions about their yields, historians have found it easy to demonstrate that ordinary farmers with average holdings were stretched to the limit of endurance and beyond for much of the thirteenth century.[15]

So great, however, was the sheer weight of obligations that small farmers incurred and in due course discharged regularly if not uncomplainingly that we are bound to ask how any but the luckiest of them managed to survive at

15 Kosminsky, op. cit., chapter iv reviews the discussion.

all if the assumptions commonly made about the deficiencies of their farming were true. They paid rents as well as dues and did service for their holdings. They paid fines for permission to do all the ordinary things that everyone expected to be able to do. They paid enormous amercements for petty offences. They paid taxes as onerous as their amercements. And they paid tallage. At Islip, for example, 43 tenants between them paid 100 shillings per year in tallage, and did so according to bye-laws promulgated a decade after the Peasants' Revolt when we might have supposed that conditions, even formal conditions, had eased.[16] They even found cash for their lords when their lords did not happen to want their services. And they paid tithe to the Church which, in addition, found innumerable other ways in which to play its part in emptying their purses by pursuing them for breaches of discipline, fancied as well as genuine, and for uncovenanted offerings which they dared not refuse.

Outgoings such as these were only part of the liabilities that small farmers had to meet. In addition they had to maintain the resources of their farms and provide for their families. Common rights and other subsidies contributed something towards the defraying of all these charges; and the family did what it could to help. But on the assumption that yields on small farms were generally as low as they were on most big ones, a handful of arable acres and some grazing constituted an exiguous basis for survival, if not a recipe for disaster. Why, however, should we make any such assumption? What had to be done in order to raise yields was simple enough. On the lands of the big corporations these things were very obviously not being done. For all the sophistication of their book-keeping, for all the complexity of their systems of control, these big corporations were, from a farming point of view, disastrous failures. Their crops were miserably and incorrigibly inadequate. They supplied such a meagre share of the commercially-traded produce of the kingdom that, according to Dr Farmer, wherever they unloaded their surpluses on to the market they did so without making any impact upon the level of prices.[17]

It is true to say, in their defence, that the big estates had to pay more for everything that was done for them than small farmers did. The small farmer's family could be made to work until its work was no longer worth doing on its own account because the small farmer's family took no more than its keep out of the family budget and had to be kept whether it worked or not. The big estates could only employ staff whose work was worth more than it cost or, in the case of servile labour, were obliged to accept whatever was offered. This undoubtedly weakened demesne husbandry because what counted then, as always, was the quality of the work done and the assiduity with which it was done. The small farmer and his family had every incentive to work

---

[16] Barbara F. Harvey, ed., *Custumal and Bye-Laws of the Manor of Islip*, Oxfordshire Record Society, vol. 40 (1959).

[17] Farmer, *Agricultural History*, as above, p. 742.

harder and more conscientiously than anyone who was merely employed by some remote institution or who was merely discharging some obligation of rent by working for such an institution. Even if we assume that the medieval farm-worker saw the authority of his remote employer or landlord in the person of the local bailiff or reeve in whom that authority reposed, as like as not it reposed in someone who was busily engaged in feathering his own nest and who was, therefore, the last person to inspire the loyalty or industry of those whom he was appointed to manage.

The whole question of productivity in farming turns upon this problem of incentive.[18] We can see how little success the big estates had by examining the yields they got from the land. But the big estates farmed only a part of the land. The ordinary demesne was often the biggest farm on the manor. But the manor usually consisted of a very large number of farms and small-holdings. In aggregate these farms and small-holdings, run by the tenantry, far surpassed the demesne lands in size and hence in importance. Unfortunately their records, if the tenants kept any, have not survived. Consequently we cannot tell how the greater part of the land of medieval England was farmed. By a curious convention, however, we assume that what was done on the lord's farm reflected best practice, or at any rate the best practice to be found locally, and that the rest of the land was farmed by tenants who either aspired to achieve the standards set by the manorial lord and usually fell short of their aspirations, or who, to put the matter as moderately as possible, were content with much less ambitious objectives.

We make the assumption that demesne productivity was comparatively high, in the Middle Ages, despite the devastating evidence that demesne yields were, on the whole, very nearly as low as they could be; and we reinforce our assumption by arguing that demesne farmers enjoyed many advantages denied to their tenants. High on this list of advantages comes the right to fold the animals belonging to their tenants upon their demesne acres. The tremendous expansion of wool exports in the thirteenth century ought to have given that right an importance never contemplated by those who initiated it. But it utterly failed to do so. The grain-yield evidence tells

[18] Recent studies of this problem have increasingly emphasised the importance of labour management in questions of productivity. Dr Farmer's words are particularly well-chosen: 'It must be stressed that grain yields, calculated from the quantities ultimately threshed, reflect a great many things other than the declining or improving fertility of the soil. They show also the effects of weather during the growing season and especially during the harvest, and perhaps of long-term climatic changes as well. They show something of the competence of the bailiff and the skill of the labourers in the fields and on the threshing floor, the quality of the seed and the density of sowing, the competition from thistle and couch-grass, and the losses to mildew and rust and theft and fraud, to birds eating the broadcast seed and the maturing ear and to rats and mice in the granary.' Farmer, 'Crop Yields', p. 122. See also W. Harwood Long, 'The Low Yields of Corn in Medieval England', Economic History Review, 2nd ser., vol. xxxii (1979), pp. 459–69; and E. Searle, Lordship and Community (Toronto, 1974), chapter 2, part 4.

us unequivocally that if the growing national flock of sheep contributed to the productivity of arable farming it did not contribute to the productivity of the demesne acres farmed by bailiffs and reeves on behalf of the big estates. Where did all this precious dung go? There were prodigious quantities of it; for tenant-farmers were responsible for the greater part of the wool produced in medieval England; and wherever tenants were servile manorial lords could legitimately demand rights of folding.[19] Had they done so as a matter of course the grain-yield figures would surely have reflected something of the effect of so much enrichment even though other important things had to be done to the soil if the crops rather than the weeds were to get the full benefit of the added fertility. That the yield figures so plainly reflect none of this enrichment argues that the dung was either wasted by those who were entitled to receive it or spirited away for their own benefit by those who were under obligation to provide it. Wasting on such a scale is as incomprehensible as failure to invoke rights of folding where they were due. We are left with misappropriation as the only possible explanation of the failure of folding rights to make any perceptible impression upon the otherwise dismal record of demesne achievements in arable husbandry. Since the courts were not crowded with miscreant tenants paying dearly for breaches of folding rights we are also left with the reflection that there were more ways of depriving a manorial lord of his folding rights than flagrantly defying the rules.

If productivity rose in the course of the Middle Ages everything conspires to suggest that tenant-farmers were more successful than manorial lords in raising it, not less. Nor can we doubt that productivity did rise. In the twelfth and thirteenth centuries markets proliferated, towns multiplied and ex-

---

[19] See below, 'Before the Black Death', for the analysis upon which this statement is based. Postan argued forcefully, on many occasions, that the peasantry was increasingly starved of livestock in the thirteenth century. His evidence for this contention is to be found in his 'Village Livestock in the Thirteenth Century', *Economic History Review*, 2nd ser., vol. xv (1962). This study depends almost entirely upon two taxation records. One is the Thirteenth of 1283 for the Hundred of Blackbourne, Suffolk, which he regarded as 'the most important of the assessments to be tested' (p. 220). This assessment Dr Langdon has recently described as 'probably the worst of the early assessments in regard to reliability'. J. Langdon, *Horses, Oxen and Technological Innovation* (Cambridge, 1986), p. 185. The other is the Fifteenth of 1225 for the rural deanery of Chalke, Wiltshire. This return tells us about the demesne lands and villeins of the religious with property in that area. See F. A. and A. P. Cazel, eds, *Rolls of the Fifteenth*, Pipe Roll Society, vol. lxxxiii, new ser., vol. xlv (1976–7), p. viii. Consequently it tells us nothing about the free tenants of the religious. Nor does it tell us about the possessions of the laity whether lords or tenants. It is impossible therefore to derive any sort of aggregate figure for village livestock from this return. We can certainly tell how many sheep were kept on certain demesne lands and by certain villeins, if we can trust what the record says. But 1225 is early days for the wool export trade, whose effect upon the national investment in sheep Postan wholly ignores. We should be seriously misled if we were to base any generalisation about village livestock upon such evidence as Postan has offered us here.

panded, industries throve and developed. Meanwhile pressure built up on the land, if not as a result of population growth then as a consequence of the demands of the wool trade. And all this came about without raising grain prices except at odd moments and in odd ways. Colonisation of immediately accessible and readily exploitable land would certainly have provided the resources necessitated by so much economic activity. But if we insist that yields on tenant-farms were, as a rule, no better than on demesne farms, then we shall be obliged to postulate the existence of immense stretches of unoccupied or under-used land to which twelfth and thirteenth-century farmers could turn for low-cost development. There were, however, no such reserves of land. The spacious days of uninhibited expansion were over. By the thirteenth century, if not before, increasing the quantity of land in any particular use meant drawing it away from less urgent uses or striking into areas where, however productive the land might prove to be in the long run, making it available imposed costs which would inevitably have had to be recovered in higher prices.

In short everything points to the conclusion that the fundamental reason why output rose without raising grain prices must be sought down on the farm, where the virgates were being made to yield bigger crops. An increase in yields, however, meant a greater investment of time, resources and management skills. If the big demesne farmers had been the ones getting the bigger crops that would have meant higher costs and hence higher prices. But, with exceptions, the demesne farmer was the laggard in this movement. It was the tenantry which must be presumed to have led the way. And for the ordinary tenant-farmer, as we have seen, time and even skill were not priced even though, strictly speaking, they had their cost. If we are to account for stable grain prices in a century of land pressure when demesne farmers were very far from leading the way in matters of husbandry and additional land could be had only at a price, then we are bound to turn to the ordinary virgator for the progressive management we cannot find elsewhere and hence for the higher real incomes which can alone explain the economic buoyancy for which the century is famous.

When we look at the accounts prepared for the big corporations in the thirteenth century we get an altogether misleading impression that they were enjoying a period of financial and commercial success. When we look closer, however, we may very well find that income rose, on particular estates, because the estates themselves had got bigger. Patronage and marriage, followed at a distance by purchase and reclamation, did infinitely more for the financial health of these estates than anything they did for themselves in the way of improving their husbandry. Sometimes we find an isolated year, or perhaps a run of years, during which the income of some big estate rose decisively above the average for the period. When that happens, as it does once or twice during the otherwise uneventful financial history of Canterbury Cathedral Priory, we may be sure that there is someone in charge who is enforcing higher standards of management efficiency than before by collecting arrears more diligently, by imposing neglected rights, by rack-renting farms hitherto assigned on negligent terms, and perhaps by levying harsher tallages and claiming higher dues. So much could be accomplished simply by performing the most ordinary duties more or less as they should be performed; and the difference it made is some measure of the laxity of normal standards of administration.[20]

There can be little doubt, however, as to the main reason for the general impression of financial buoyancy that we get from studies of the bigger thirteenth-century estates. When money incomes rise but yields do not; when there is no property acquisition or administrative reform to account for the financial improvements that take place; then we are bound to look for some extraneous factor like inflation to explain the changes we find. And an inflationary factor is to hand. Grain prices may have sat upon one plateau or another for most of the century; but they had to rise in order to get where they were destined to settle. Each rise was inevitably followed by an adjustment which spread its inflationary repercussions throughout the economic system. Accordingly the impression of financial prosperity conveyed by the accounting records of so many of the bigger estates is perhaps explicable in terms of this purely monetary adjustment.

The net income of the bishops of Ely, for example, doubled between 1171/2 and 1256/7 and then increased by a quarter between 1256/7 and 1298/9.[21] These are only isolated assessments of income giving no more than a general notion of the trend. Some part of this trend is attributable to reclamation and other acquisitions of land. But it is difficult to resist the conclusion that inflation was responsible for a good deal of the rest. On the bishop of Worcester's estates, which were not much more extensive at the Reformation than they had been at the time of Domesday, income nevertheless doubled between 1211/12 and 1266 and doubled again by 1299.[22] Once more these are isolated figures which merely serve to light up the trend. But they are particularly interesting figures because by 1299 we can see that cash provided the bishop with well over 75% of his income. This was nothing new in 1299. Four-fifths of the land of the bishop's manors consisted of tenants' land, not demesne.[23] And this means that the Worcester records provide us with an excellent example of an estate whose very substantial improvements of income of necessity owed much more to the adroit management of leases and other rents than to assiduous attention to demesne husbandry. And there is something more to be said about the Worcester figures. If the bishop's income grew at anything like the pace indicated by these isolated figures, we cannot reasonably ascribe the whole of the gain to inflation. We are left, therefore, with a strong presumption that the bishops of Worcester were able to raise their incomes so spectacularly, not because

20 M. Mate, 'The Farming Out of Manors', *Journal of Medieval History*, vol. 9 (1983), p. 336.
21 E. Miller, *The Abbey and Bishopric of Ely* (Cambridge, 1951), p. 94.
22 C. Dyer, *Lords and Peasants in a Changing Society* (Cambridge, 1980), p. 53.
23 Dyer, *op. cit.*, pp. 72–3.

the husbandry of their demesne lands had conspicuously improved, but because they were able to take advantage of improvements made by their tenants by raising their rents to a higher level than they would have been able to do if inflation had been their sole excuse.

Not every big estate managed to surmount the difficulties created by inflation as successfully as Ely or Worcester did. Indeed some of the biggest and most famous corporations were dismal failures financially. Between Domesday and 1274, for example, the archbishop of Canterbury's income scarcely varied by more than the normal fluctuations caused by the fortunes of farming.[24] This meant that the archbishop got poorer, in real terms, every time inflation raised the general level of prices. The Cathedral Priory fared even worse than the archbishop. Its income actually fell at times in the course of the thirteenth century.[25] It is impossible to say how much extra money-income was needed by particular institutions in order to offset the effects of inflation. To judge by how much extra income the more successful estates succeeded in acquiring it would seem, however, that an income which grew somewhat sluggishly, or failed to grow at all, indicated a management incapable not only of swimming with the inflationary tide but also of exploiting, as Worcester very likely did, whatever gains their tenants may have won from the soil. We must conclude, therefore, that the thirteenth century was not a good one, so far as business management is concerned, for two of the wealthiest and most venerable ecclesiastical foundations in the kingdom.

We should not, however, attempt to judge these huge conglomerates by purely commercial standards. Those who presided over them were princes of the Church and lay magnates of comparable power and influence. Some were immersed in politics and administration; others were gentlemen of leisure and members of collegiate societies. All were prominent and often distinguished local or national figures. They were not farmers. They valued their estates for the retinues they could support and the income they could reliably generate. They entertained no extravagant notions about the untapped potentialities of their estates. They knew that farming was a treacherous gamble, not least because their agents were often flagrantly dishonest; and that every sort of material and social advancement was to be sought elsewhere than in the sodden wind-swept fields upon which their peasants toiled. The ecclesiastical *firmarius* epitomised the objectives of farming from their point of view; and the manorial account gave these objectives tangible form.

The *firmarius*, as we have seen, was given a simple directive. He supplied an ascertained and unvarying need. His job was done when his obligations had been discharged. Nobody bargained for surpluses or anticipated deficits. Such matters were dealt with as they arose. Manorial accounts strikingly

---

[24] F. R. H. Du Boulay, *The Lordship of Canterbury* (New York, 1966), p. 243.
[25] M. Mate, *op. cit.*, pp. 334–6.

reflect this attitude of mind. They were compiled to check the work done on the farm. But they were drawn up in such a way that they could not readily be used for any other purpose. The manifest intention of those who administered the ordinary instruments of manorial control was to minimise losses by fraudulent conversion. Ingeniously and laboriously handled in conjunction with other records, the accounts were sometimes used for calculations of profit and loss, though a modern accountant might find medieval ideas as to what constituted profit and loss distinctly curious.[26] But they were not designed to reveal faults of planning, to suggest ways in which resources might be concentrated on profitable lines, or to indicate how output might be expanded or costs lowered.

Indeed the fixity of income which is supposed to have been the bane of the leasehold system turns out to have been the goal of demesne management. Manorial bailiffs and reeves were required to discharge certain obligations. They were penalised if they failed, but neither encouraged nor rewarded if they exceeded expectations. It was a system which put a premium upon that low cunning which gets the knowing stockroom-keeper out of trouble without contributing anything to the positive achievements of the business. And it was a system which gave more senior managers not the least help in assessing the commercial choices that lay before them. But making positive contributions to the achievements of the business or clarifying choices were not the purposes for which the system was designed. The intensely bureaucratic administrative machines that controlled the larger conglomerates may have stifled initiative and discouraged enterprise. But that was evidently thought to be the price that had to be paid for making sure of a moderate return from the demesne farms by keeping fraudulent conversion within reasonable bounds.

What then are we to conclude as a result of this somewhat prolix discussion of manorial matters? The manor, or rather the estate which the Normans will later call the manor, makes its debut in the earliest laws. In these laws it is virtually identical in structure and function with the manor we encounter many centuries later. There was, apparently, little scope for change and indeed little call for change in all that long period between its first appearance in seventh-century records and its disintegration as a farming unit in the late fourteenth century. How it originated, or how prevalent it was when we first catch a glimpse of it in the early laws, are questions we cannot answer. Sometimes the landlord manages his own manors. The tenor of Ine's laws is such as to suggest that he often does. When a lord grants a dwelling-house to his tenant, runs a famous clause, it is he rather than someone who stands in his place who is authorised to require service from

---

[26] E. Stone, 'Profit and Loss Accountancy at Norwich Cathedral Priory', *Transactions of the Royal Historical Society*, 5th ser., vol. 12 (1962). See also D. Postles, 'The Perception of Profit Before the Leasing of Demesnes', *Agricultural History Review*, vol. 34 (1986); and C. Noke, 'Accounting for Bailiffship', *Accounting and Business Research*, vol. 11 (1981).

that tenant. And when a lord goes away from his land, it is he not some tenant who is said to be under obligation to leave it sown not fallow. Sometimes, however, the lord conveys his land to a tenant in return for rent. We soon enough get plenty of evidence of the use of the lease and of the levy of food rents; and there can be little doubt that lords soon began to make those nice calculations as to the relative benefit to themselves of taking all the responsibilities of farming upon their own shoulders or of deputing these responsibilities to others in return for a rent which was firm, that we find them so often making in later centuries.

These, however, were minor problems of internal policy. Each lord had his own particular needs and circumstances to take into account before deciding whether to manage his own estate or to let someone else manage it as his tenant. There were doubtless fashions in such matters as there are in everything: compulsive feelings that, whatever the calculus of self-interest may recommend, what must be done is what the smart set is doing. Usually there was little enough to choose between managing and leasing. When times were good, managers returned surpluses which still reflected badly upon demesne husbandry; and when times were bad, leaseholders, however satisfactory their testimonials may have been, could hardly avoid defaulting on their rents notwithstanding the fixity of the obligations to which they had subscribed.

But whatever was decided made no difference in the villages and on the land. We must not allow ourselves to be so bemused by modern surveys of medieval management policy as to visualise the medieval English country scene as being in a state of perpetual upheaval with demesne land being by turns farmed by its manorial lords in accordance with the prescriptions of the contemporary treatises on husbandry and then consigned to lessees empowered to do with it we know not what. In fact the village and the land it farmed scarcely knew the difference when lessees took over from landlord or landlord repossessed from lessees. How could things have been otherwise? The lessees took over a working estate for a stipulated period with the obligation to hand it back as it was when he received it. The fixed and working capital with which the estate was equipped presupposed an established routine of farming; and the labour force was inured to working habits which it would have found intolerably irksome to change. The switch from direct management to lease is, for us, a switch from light to darkness; from a time when we can see what is happening to a time when we cannot. But the change is only in the lighting, not in the functioning of the estate. And when the lord of the manor reserved the court, leasing out only the land with its labour and other appurtenances, the medieval villager who saw familiar faces presiding over the courts would have been hard put to it to be able to recognise any changes at all.

In the twelfth century, for which we have only got a meagre stock of estate records, we can see that demesne farmers leased-out some of their interests and managed others directly. Historians commonly agree that twelfth-century demesne farmers leased-out their demesne interests more often than they managed them personally or with the help of stewards. They do so partly because they think of the ecclesiastical *firmarius* as a lessee which, as we have seen, he was not; and partly because Professor Harvey has tentatively concluded, from his scrutiny of the Pipe Rolls, that Exchequer policy changed over the years so that estates which were restored to the king in the twelfth century were more often found to have been leased-out by their latest occupiers than managed directly and that those restored to the king in the early thirteenth century were more often found to have been managed directly than leased-out.[27]

Professor Harvey lists 42 cases in support of his conclusion. But of these there are only 12 in which the Exchequer had more than one opportunity to manage the same estate; and of these 12 cases only two support his conclusion unequivocally. The archbishopric of Canterbury and the Abbey of Sherborne both had most of their manors leased-out in the late twelfth century and in hand by the early thirteenth. Elsewhere the story seems to have been one of management decisions varying endlessly in accordance with the perceived needs of particular institutions and families. The bishopric of Lincoln put out most of its manors to lease at all times in this period. The Honour of Haughley had part of its tally of manors on lease in 1170 and again in 1211/12 with everything on lease in 1184/5 and everything in hand in 1207. The archbishopric of York pursued a policy, if such it can be called, which was similarly pragmatic, managing most of its manors in 1186/7 and putting nearly half of them on lease in 1212/15. At Durham the bishops and at Ramsay the abbots kept some manors in hand and let others to tenants, as it suited them to do, there being no more evidence of a trend or pattern in their choice than in that of others who presided over the estates studied by Professor Harvey.

But there is another reason, at first sight an altogether deeper and more impressive reason, why historians believe that twelfth-century demesne farmers leased-out their demesne interests more often than they managed them. It is to Postan's fertile scholarship that we owe the idea that there was a chronological sequence in this matter of leasing or managing and that this sequence is clearly explicable in economic terms. According to Postan the twelfth century was a period when demesne farmers hedged their risks and stabilised their incomes by passing their demesne interests over to tenants. They did so because the twelfth century was one of exceptionally serious political disturbance when it was unusually hard for demesne farmers to make a satisfactory living from the land. As soon as the political problems were settled, agrarian prospects cheered up and the economy, so Postan claimed, passed from the gloom and distress of the twelfth century into the sunlight and buoyancy of the thirteenth. Meanwhile, however, in the twelfth

[27] P. D. A. Harvey, 'The Pipe Rolls and the Adoption of Demesne Farming in England', *Economic History Review*, 2nd ser., vol. xxvii (1974).

century, demesne farmers were compelled to resort to extreme measures in order to make themselves financially secure.

When they leased-out their demesne farms they did not do what demesne farmers had done as a matter of course for centuries. They did not merely delegate their responsibilities to a lessees who took over whatever there may have been in the way of demesne interests with the intention of running them as the demesne farmer himself had run them when they were directly managed by himself and his stewards. If that is what demesne farmers had done in the twelfth century there would have been nothing for Postan to say about it all. Postan's contention, however, was that demesne farmers did something altogether different in the abnormally disruptive conditions of the time. He contended that they broke up their demesne farms into parcels so as to turn them into a series of plots small enough to suit the means of ordinary peasants; for such peasants were always keen to acquire more land, even in bad times, provided they could afford it. These were undoubtedly desperate measures; but according to Postan these were desperate times: for the evidence to be found in a large sample of manors, that demesne farms were being broken up, testified, according to Postan, to a contraction of the commercial fortunes of many big estates and reflected a more general reduction of economic activity. The argument has a disquieting circularity about it which is not our immediate concern.

Postan expounded his findings in a lecture which he presented as a summary of results.[28] When it was published, Postan indicated in a footnote that there was a book on manorial profits forthcoming. The lecture therefore merely outlined his argument and supported it with a sample of evidence. His audience, and later his readers, had every reason to believe that the evidence he produced in the lecture was the best he had. With an hour at his disposal and a radical argument to propound he had no time in which to discuss evidence of doubtful provenance or to prove that equivocal or apparently contentious pieces of evidence in fact supported his case. His readers had every reasonable expectation that difficult matters would be explained in the forthcoming book. The lecture must be presumed therefore to have demonstrated the validity of his case by displaying some of the strongest supports upon which it depended.

The book never materialised; but the lecture has had so profound an effect upon scholarly thinking that distinguished scholars are still unable to emancipate themselves from its influence. The stark contrast, however, between the twelfth and thirteenth centuries raised questions which Postan's analysis did not readily answer. Nobody doubted what Postan had said; but so many pieces of evidence did not seem to fit that by 1971 Dr Miller felt that the

---

[28] M. Postan, 'The Chronology of Labour Services', *Transactions of the Royal Historical Society*, 4th ser., vol. xx (1937), pp. 169–93. So influential has Postan been, wherever he has intervened in medieval studies, that his work calls for comprehensive scrutiny. This scrutiny is being undertaken by Cameron Barnes of the University of New England, Armidale, NSW Australia.

time had come to attempt a squaring of the circle by accepting Postan's thesis as incontestibly established and then concluding that 'both centuries, despite short-term periods of dislocation, were centuries of economic expansion.'[29] Where did this judgement leave Postan, who had found demesne farmers desperately fragmenting their estates because times were so bad in the twelfth century that there was nothing else to be done with them? Dr Miller declared his belief that there was 'a real and substantial contrast between the twelfth and thirteenth centuries; but there is much to suggest that it is one rooted in the policies and attitudes of landlords rather than in the basic economic situation.' With these words Dr Miller had, in effect, relegated Postan's thesis to the status of an awkward but immoveable obstruction with which every reputable attempt to explain twelfth-century economic fluctuations was henceforth condemned to cope as best it might.

But what if Postan's thesis, with its seemingly impressive buttressing of evidence and its intimation of massive scholarship in reserve, should turn out to be, not a formidable triumph of knowledge and insight, but a fantasy, a mere fabrication wrought by a man who was resolved to make the evidence speak, not for itself, but as he dictated? The article on 'The Farming-Out of Manors', reprinted below, explains in detail how Postan contrived to manipulate the sources to suit his own purposes. Inconvenient but vital dates were arbitrarily changed to conform to the exigencies of his argument. The incontrovertible findings of scholarship were set aside without explanation when they contradicted the conclusions to which he required the evidence to point. Extracts from critically-important documents were neatly pruned so as to convey the impression that they meant the opposite to what they plainly said. Postan even attempted to pass off as genuine a document which, if it had been genuine, would have materially assisted his case. But it was not genuine as printed. It was a conflation of two separate and unrelated documents. The discovery that it was such a conflation was made by R. V. Lennard. His findings had been published in the *English Historical Review* only a matter of months before Postan gave his lecture.[30] Postan, however, blithely ignored them. His famous lecture was reprinted several times. On each occasion Postan had the opportunity to correct over-sights, revise misstatements and clarify remarks which might have been mis-understood. But Postan chose neither to justify nor to retract anything. He, at least, was well-content with what he had done.

The contrast between the twelfth and thirteenth centuries is now itself a matter of history. And that is so not simply because, with respect to economic conditions and demesne management policy, the twelfth century was much more like the thirteenth than Postan allowed it to be; it is also because the thirteenth century was, in certain respects, more like the twelfth as

[29] E. Miller, 'England in the Twelfth and Thirteenth Centuries', p. 12.
[30] R. V. Lennard, 'An Unidentified Twelfth-Century Custumal of Lawshall', *English Historical Review*, vol. li (1936), pp. 104–7.

Postan depicted it. Features of demesne management policy in the thirteenth century which we have been inclined to treat as anomalous can now be seen as rational adherence to tried and proven ways of doing things. Canterbury Cathedral Priory, for example, maintained many of its food-rents throughout the thirteenth century.[31] Food-rents are generally discountenanced in thirteenth-century conditions as bizarre remnants of another age. But they were inflation-proof; and they supplied needs which would have had to be met in other ways if food-rents had been abolished. On these grounds they cannot be faulted. They may have been products of high-cost farming. When they were the products of the demesne farms of the bigger corporations they very likely were. In such cases essential supplies of food and other farm products would have been more cheaply bought. But senior managers who had to rely on written accounts could not tell, by scrutinising the information conveyed to them in that way, whether their costs were excessive or not. And those who knew that their costs were high, because they had compared market prices with the prices at which they would have had to sell in order to meet ordinary outgoings, might very well have decided to persevere with a policy of self-sufficiency for any number of reasons, including security of supply and long-term stability of costs.

Other thirteenth-century policies with a twelfth-century look about them give historians an uneasy feeling that twelfth-century anxieties, as concocted for them by Postan, had returned, if that is the right word to use, to plague thirteenth-century managers. Towards the close of the thirteenth century, for example, several big ecclesiastical corporations can be seen releasing parcels of demesne to tenants. Outstandingly it was Winchester that did so; for Winchester shed, not small plots and a virgate or so, but thousands of acres.[32] Historians with Postan's apocalyptic words ringing in their ears fear the worst. But nothing in the prevailing economic climate foreshadowed trouble to come. Grain prices were as good as ever, in the sense that they were as stable as they had been for many years, once inflation had raised them to the level they then maintained for a generation. The wool trade was thriving. And whatever may be the truth about the growth of the population, nobody could possibly argue that labour was getting scarcer and hence dearer. Nor can we blame the political situation, which was anything but chaotic and disruptive domestically, for the agrarian policy that Winchester, and to a lesser extent others, seem to have adopted. Something else had motivated this change of direction; and by investigating the Winchester manor of Taunton we may perhaps find out what that motivation was, or at least what it was not.[33]

Between 1248 and 1311 the demesne farm of Taunton manor shrank by nearly 1,000 acres. At the same time the population of the manor increased

[31] M. Mate, 'The Farming Out of Manors', p. 334.
[32] J. Z. Titow, English Rural Society 1200–1350 (1969), p. 53 and p. 52 note 27.
[33] J. Z. Titow, 'Some Evidence of Thirteenth-Century Population Increase', Economic History Review, 2nd ser., vol. xiv (1961), pp. 218–23.

to such an extent that if everyone on the manor had been obliged to subsist upon what the manor's farms produced there would scarcely have been more than two acres per head upon which to live. Moreover entry fines soared. But Taunton was the seat of a borough as well as the site of a manor. In the course of the thirteenth century three of the tithings of the Hundred were drawn into the borough.[34] Many who lived within the jurisdiction of the manor obviously depended neither for sustenance nor livelihood upon what the manor could provide. The close proximity of a borough to a manor doubtless gave an altogether exceptional boost to rents and wages. But it also gave exceptional opportunities to agrarian enterprise. Elsewhere, at Exeter, for example, or Battle, demesne farming seems to have been invigorated and fortified by urban markets. At Taunton, however, Winchester chose a policy of disengagement notwithstanding. It was clearly a policy which conformed with what had been decided at the highest level for manors all over the estate. It was evidently not a policy dictated simply by conditions at Taunton. And the decision to let rather than to farm large stretches of Winchester demesne tells us that, in the considered opinion of Winchester's senior managers, local farmers at Taunton and elsewhere on the estate could make better use of Winchester's demesne land than they could; or to put the matter in the least favourable terms, could do no worse than they had done, whilst saving them all the trouble of farming the land for themselves. And this was clearly the measured and deliberate decision of Winchester's managers at a time when conditions were as good and prospects as fair as they had been for generations.

What seems to have been decided appears, on the face of it, to reverse Postan's dictum that when market prospects improve, as Postan thought they did in the thirteenth century, demesne farmers will resume control of their demesne lands as soon as they can. There are, it is true, exceptions to every rule. But that is not the lesson to be drawn from the Winchester decision to let rather than to farm the Taunton demesne lands. The lesson of Taunton is surely that, given the low level of productivity on most demesne farms, there was rarely, if ever, a clear commercial advantage in farming the land rather than leasing it out to tenants, even when that land stood in close proximity to a thriving borough. When we see demesne farms in hand we should, therefore, look for the influence of other considerations than purely commercial ones; or at least we should not treat it as axiomatic that every highly bureaucratised corporation was bound to manage its farms more efficiently and profitably than its tenants could manage them when they were given the chance to take them over as lessees.

If we are keen to find some element of dynamism in the manor it seems unlikely that we shall find it by looking for evidence of evolution in its structure or, with a shorter perspective in mind, for evidence of comprehens-

---

[34] T. J. Hunt, *The Medieval Customs of the Manors of Taunton and Bradford on Tone* (Frome, 1962), p. xl. I am indebted to Cameron Barnes for this reference.

ive changes, at particular periods, in demesne management policy. The manor had no culminating moment of maturity. Manors varied in structure and everywhere changes abounded; but none produced a new or more sophisticated type. And management policies differed to the extent that none seems to have swept the board. Indeed when we survey the evidence, from the time of the earliest laws until the final dissolution of the demesne farm in the late fourteenth century, what must strike us most forcibly is how stable manorial forms remained and how narrowly restricted was the range within which management was compelled to operate.

Whenever manorial managers were able to prove their metal they did. Assized rents were often surcharged, for example, but labour services were only rarely increased. The difference in treatment accorded to these two essential elements of the manorial system merely shows that manorial lords, or those who advised them, grasped the fact that labour services were inflation-proof and cash payments were not. But this awareness of the vulnerability of cash payments went beyond that simple point; for many dues were paid in cash. At Ely cash dues comprised 57% of income in 1299; and Ely was very far from being exceptional in this respect.[35] Inflation played havoc with the real value of such payments; and any manorial lord who failed to take measures to compensate himself for losses of real value soon found himself making unsolicited gifts of income to his tenants. Manorial lords seem to have reacted energetically to what might have become a serious wastage of assets by levying tallages at what might seem to be penal rates and pursuing those who failed to pay other cash dues with what looks like vindictive implacability. At any rate we ought to bear in mind that what we may be disposed to construe as examples of the ferocious exploitation of a helpless peasantry may very well represent an attempt to maintain income intact by recovering on one account what had been lost on another.

But doing more than maintaining income intact was beyond the capacity of the big demesne farmers; for even in the thirteenth century, when conditions for demesne farming are generally thought to have been particularly favourable, grain yields remained abysmally low on the great majority of demesne farms. In an economy such as that of the thirteenth century, with a growing demand for land and hence increasing pressure upon the food supply, only rising grain prices could have enabled demesne farmers to prosper at the expense of other classes. But, as we have seen, grain prices remained more or less stable for most of the thirteenth century; and demesne farmers could improve their relative positions, therefore, only at one another's expense. In the absence of a really precipitous fall in the remuneration of labour, for which there is not a scrap of evidence, there can be only one explanation for what we find. We are bound to assume that arable productivity was being substantially improved in thirteenth-century England and that,

---

[35] Miller, *Ely*, p. 94, Table II. Some of these dues were readily adjustable to changing circumstances but many were not.

since we cannot look for such improvements in the demesne sector, we must conclude that it is peasant productivity, using that term very broadly, which is mainly responsible for the rising output of grain and its stable price.

From all this it follows that the increasing aggregate income of the period, of which the expansion of trade and industry and the growth and multiplication of towns and markets are the most conspicuous features, owes more to what was happening in the peasant sector than to the much-vaunted changes and developments taking place higher up the social hierarchy.

Between the splendours and miseries of the thirteenth century, as depicted by modern orthodoxy: splendours for the socially ascendant, miseries for the rest; and the leaden gloom of the later Middle Ages, there lies a transitional period when famine, war, pestilence and death, brought the retribution foretold by St John the Divine. According to modern orthodoxy it was retribution not for sin but for over-population; and its attendant chastisements were not the byzantine torments set forth in the Book of Revelations but soil exhaustion.

The Black Death administered a blow to traditional relationships on the land so devastating that its repercussions were felt throughout the social system. After so many centuries of active life, servile tenure was struck dead by it. The manor was never the same again. It survived as a land registry. It continued to collect its increasingly antiquated dues. It enacted and enforced bye-laws. As a social force it retained an influence which was remarkably little impaired by the extinction of its strictly agrarian functions. Nevertheless feudalism atrophied at its roots once servile tenure had come to an end.

Historians who shrink from a cataclysmic view of affairs look for antecedent causes of this extraordinary transformation of a central institution of society. They look for signs of portentous shifts and ominous cracks in the social structure in the half-century or so before the Black Death began its work. Some historians believe that the arable acreage shrank before the Black Death because the soil had been exhausted by over-cultivation. Those who proclaim the exhaustion theory are generally the first to deplore the low productivity of the soil under medieval management techniques; and it is difficult to understand how farmers who got so little out of the soil could be said to have done so much damage to it. The statistical material adduced in support of the soil-exhaustion theory does not sustain it;[36] though the behaviour of grain prices was undoubtedly consistent with the view that the arable acreage had contracted. The fourteenth century was, until about 1370, a period when grain prices were usually much higher than they had been in the thirteenth century. But historians who postulate a shrinking acreage also argue that the famines of the second decade of the fourteenth century

[36] J. Z. Titow, *Winchester Yields: A Study in Medieval Agricultural Productivity* (Cambridge, 1972). On this see D. L. Farmer in *Agricultural History of England*, pp. 721–2 and more generally in his articles cited in note 8 above. I should like to thank Prof. M. Desai of the London School of Economics for allowing me to see his unpublished critique of the statistics gathered by Dr Titow.

seriously reduced the size of the population. And the behaviour of grain prices is not at all consistent with that hypothesis. Fewer people farming a smaller acreage should not force grain prices to rise, except perhaps in the disorganised aftermath of such climatic disasters as Europe then experienced.

Nor does the course of money wages point the way to a solution of the problem of explaining the behaviour of grain prices in terms of soil exhaustion and population loss. Money wages, if they do anything at all in the half-century before the Black Death, appear to follow grain prices whether these prices rose or fell; for grain prices certainly fell at times despite their high level when they rose. They fell in the 1330s and 1340s, and when they fell so did money wages. It is significant that money wage-rates should follow grain prices down on those occasions; for it indicates that there could have been no shortage of man-power in the economy a generation after the famines. Such a shortage would have raised wages and, as a corollary, depressed grain prices, thus reflecting the comparative abundance of land. That is what happened at the end of the century. If circumstances had been remotely similar in earlier decades that is what ought to have happened then. The price material strongly suggests that the fall of population, which undoubtedly occurred as a result of the famines, and any loss of land there may have been, which is highly problematical in any case, were not heavy enough to upset the established balance of resources.

With the arrival of the Black Death the medieval world braced itself for the melodramatic fulfilment of the scriptural prophecies; and modern historians have excelled themselves in their graphic treatment of this lugubrious theme. But however terrible it may have been to witness or endure, the Black Death's first visitation in 1349 failed to inflict upon the countryside that comprehensive desolation for which it was feared and reviled by contemporaries. Deserted tenancies were soon re-occupied; vacant livings were swiftly filled despite the frightful toll the Black Death took of parochial incumbents; apprentices were replaced; families re-formed; urban hierarchies were renewed; the potter's wheel turned once more; the smithy fire was re-kindled; soldiers marched off to resume the war with France; wool merchants consigned record cargoes to Flanders; and the clothmakers of England set about evicting the last of their foreign rivals from the domestic market as they began to compete with them in those markets abroad in which English cloth was soon to become famous and sometimes dominant.

The statistical conclusions drawn by Prof. Phelps-Brown from the material published by Thorold Rogers show, with incontestible clarity, that the purchasing-power of the money wages earned by building workers scarcely changed for a generation after this first visitation by the Black Death. They show, in fact, that however hard the community may have been hit, the economy was scarcely affected. That is certainly what the records of town and country, of trade and industry, seem to tell us. And when the evidence of purchasing-power confirms that a sample of working men, some skilled, some not, were no better off when the Black Death had dealt the country its first blow than they had been before it struck, we must surely take such evidence very seriously. Statistical backing for historical arguments is always suspect: so much can go wrong with the selection, manipulation and interpretation of the evidence. When arguments built on statistical evidence turn upon the discovery of very slight changes in output, income, price, quantity and the like, we do well to treat them with some scepticism. But the Phelps-Brown index is not like that. It bears out what we ought to have known from other evidence. And when it does reveal changes it does so by registering prodigious, indeed unexampled, changes in average standards of living that, again, we ought to have picked up for ourselves from other evidence. Statistical evidence is most credible when it confirms what we knew already, or when it draws attention to what we ought to have known already and, by concentrating our attention upon it, forces us to look again at what we thought we perfectly well understood. That, for all its obvious short-comings, is what the Phelps-Brown index has done for medieval studies.

Standards of living may not have risen, or risen very much, in the aftermath of the Black Death's first visitation. But money-wages shot up. The king, or those who advised him, were panic-stricken. An Ordinance to check the rise in wages was issued whilst the Black Death was still spreading through the kingdom. The Ordinance was followed by a Statute as soon as Parliament could be safely convened. Courts of law were set up to try accused persons and punish offenders. More legislation followed. It is not too much to say that historians have been deluded by all this evidence of wage increases and wages policy into thinking that the labour force was being better paid than ever before as a result of the Black Death. But there were other prices than the price of labour. In particular, grain prices also shot up after the Black Death. Indeed the prices obtained for grain, for a generation after the first appearance of the Black Death, were almost without precedent in the recorded history of such prices. We hear little or nothing about these prices in modern accounts of the Black Death and its consequences. But they were of fundamental importance in the agrarian history of the period. High grain prices enabled those estates to thrive which were more or less dependent upon wage rather than servile labour when they might otherwise have been bankrupted by the high wages they were forced to pay. They made very many demesne farmers, and others, careless of the size of wage-settlements. Wage legislation thrust a legal weapon into the hands of employers which some of them attempted to use. But higher wages granted by more open-handed employers were bound to have created insurmountable difficulties for those who tried to impose lower ones. Men voted with their feet; and eventually Parliament was compelled to enact a settlement law. Meanwhile high prices made high wages bearable; and the legislation, for all its panoply of enforcement, was virtually a dead letter.

Times changed when grain prices fell but money-wages did not. That is what happened in the 1370s. It was then that the effects of cumulative attacks of the Black Death first manifested themselves. That is the meaning of the contrary movements of grain prices and money-wages at that juncture. When grain prices slumped in the 1330s and 1340s, wages followed them down. And they did so because some exogenous influence had exerted impartial pressure upon grain prices and wages alike. Had it been otherwise, as it might have been if resources of land or labour had become relatively scarcer than before, we should have seen evidence of the differential movement of wages and prices, then as later. When grain prices fell in the 1370s, wages continued to rise; and they did so because labour, at that period, was actually becoming scarcer, so that the products of the soil, and hence the soil itself, were becoming relatively more abundant. In short, the fall of rent, of which the fall in grain prices was merely a symptom, was the immediate cause of the rise in wages.

This is a common enough phenomenon. When rents fall, working farms and parcels of land which can be turned into small-holdings, are easier to come by. Farm-workers who have been obliged to work for a wage because they had no option but to do so, seize the opportunity of being able to work for themselves on a farm they can run with the help of the family, and thereby reduce the numbers available for paid work. This forces wage-rates to rise. All the new countries of the nineteenth century, such as Canada and the USA, Australia and New Zealand, were high-wage economies for that reason. Even in the Carribean, after the emancipation of the slaves, employers well-understood the importance of restricting the access of emancipated slaves to the land if they were to safeguard their supplies of cheap labour. A comparable problem exercised white Kenyan farmers later in the century.[37]

The dramatic change in standards of living, which occurred in the 1370s, is dramatically reflected in the Phelps-Brown index. It is also plain for all to see in the fortunes of demesne farming. It was in this decade that demesne farmers found themselves in serious trouble. Those with ample resources of servile labour were no less badly affected than those without. The impact of rising costs on a farm which depended on wage-labour, in a period of rising wages, was more obvious and immediate than it was on a farm which looked to customary labour to supplement the work of its *famuli*. But servile tenants were quick to perceive that the rents they paid, in service as well as in farm produce and money, were becoming more and more extortionate as rents fell wherever they looked and money-wage rates went on rising. The trouble was that their rents reflected a scarcity of land that no longer prevailed and their contracts were contracts for life. They had no lawful remedy for their plight except for proof of freedom. And few enough had any hope of emancipating themselves by pursuing that tortuous, costly and uncertain path. Those that did were a minority. There were cheaper, quicker and perhaps surer, if more seditious, ways of accomplishing their purpose. But it was those who turned

---

[37] S. L. Engerman, 'Economic Change and Contract Labour in the British Caribbean', *Explorations in Economic History*, vol. 21 (1984), pp. 133–50. P. Mosley, *The Settler Economies* (Cambridge, 1983).

to litigation who finally tried their lords beyond all bearing and thus brought into the open what was really going on in the countryside.

A petition to Parliament of 1373 tells of servile tenants coming to London in groups so as to bring their case for freedom before the courts.[38] Another of 1377 is more explicit. It speaks of withdrawal of labour, confederacies, threatening behaviour, the collection of fighting funds to defray legal costs, and even of the purchase of exemplifications of Domesday Book to provide evidence of freedoms subsequently lost.[39] These petitions are ominous portents. They tell of lords of manors overwhelmed by feelings of impotence, perplexity, apprehension, dismay, and even panic. Breaches of manorial discipline by servile tenants were actionable only in manorial courts. Henry II had seen to that. These petitions, therefore, tell of troubles that manorial lords felt they could no longer cope with in recognised and traditional ways. Servile tenants were becoming so ungovernable that manorial lords felt that they had no alternative but to swallow their pride and appeal for help in carrying out their jealously-guarded manorial disciplinary processes. The king responded. He ordered special commissions of inquiry under the Great Seal and gave an undertaking that actions taken as a result of those commissions would not prejudice the immemorial rights of manorial lords.

Meanwhile wages presented employers with another and quite separate problem. As we turn the pages of the Rolls of Parliament we are made conscious of an altogether unusual flurry of concern about the administration of the Statutes of Labourers. It starts in 1368, when farmers with no servile labour to call upon petitioned the king for redress because high wages were putting them out of business.[40] In 1372 petitioners appealed for help because labourers in search of high wages stayed so briefly wherever they worked that the courts could not catch up with them.[41] In 1373 petitioners asked for more frequent sessions of the courts.[42] In 1376 they complained that labourers were hard to come by because so many were sturdy beggars who would not work.[43] They demanded heavier punishments for such malingerers and recommended that Justices be paid according to the amount of work they did.[44]

Petitioners who asked for the labour laws to be strengthened got a tart response from the king to the effect that they already had all the legislation they required. It was an implicit reproof: for it tells of years of neglect of the machinery of justice provided for just such a contingency. Those whom it

[38] *Rotuli Parliamentorum* (1783), II, p. 319
[39] RP, III, pp. 21–2 reprinted by R. B. Dobson, ed., *The Peasants' Revolt of 1381* (1970), pp. 76–8.
[40] RP, II, p. 296
[41] RP, II, p. 312
[42] RP, II, p. 319.
[43] RP, II, p. 332
[44] RP, II, p. 341. In 1363 a petition claimed that JPs were using deputies to do their work for them. RP, II, p. 277.

now suited to enforce the law made it transparently obvious in their petitions that they were totally ignorant of its provisions. Nevertheless the evidence of all these petitions is unequivocal. It shows that everyone concerned with the employment of farm-workers, whether as wage-earners or servile tenants, was turning ever more desperately to processes of law in order to check, if not reverse, a trend which threatened to make the customary and hitherto accepted organisation of agrarian society unworkable. It also shows something else. It shows that agitation, sometimes violent agitation, in the countryside was being provoked by attempts to stop the unstoppable several years before taxation could have become intolerably burdensome and before anyone had breathed a word about poll-taxes.

It is customary, in historical circles, to blame the Peasants' Revolt, not upon the systematic and remorseless pressure of a wage-freeze, but on royal taxation policy. And indeed there is a colourable excuse for doing so; for taxation was the immediate cause of the Revolt. It ignited an inflammable countryside. There were no less than eight separate Parliamentary grants of taxation between 1377 and 1381 when the Peasants' Revolt broke out.[45] The first irrupted upon taxpayers who had enjoyed a dozen years of respite from direct taxation, which made the experience disconcerting enough, and consisted of an experimental tax on the parish, which doubtless compounded the mortification they felt. The last was the final instalment of another experimental tax which proved to be, for many, more than they were willing to bear. But smouldering resentment followed by open revolt against having to pay certain taxes is not an infallible sign that the taxes in question have become an intolerable burden except in the sense that they have become a burden that a number of tax-payers will no longer tolerate.

There are several objections to the proposition that taxation was a principal cause of the Peasants' Revolt because it imposed crippling charges upon ordinary men and women. Out of £382,000 worth of taxation assessed upon the lay population in the decade 1371–81, some £247,000 worth was payable as a result of the imposition of moveables taxes. These long-established taxes had had their fangs drawn when the compromise assessments of 1334 became permanent thereafter. The tax on moveables had brought in astronomical sums when it was first imposed upon an unsuspecting population in 1290, and very substantially reduced sums once that population had been alerted to its devastating power. The 1334 compromise conceded a secure competence to the king in return for his surrendering his chance of being able to wield an immensely powerful tool of fiscal policy. However often Parliament gave the king permission to take his fiscal bite out of the body politic, the 1334 compromise guaranteed that he could never, on any occasion, bite deep. So far as the bulk of the taxation raised in the decade 1371–81 is concerned, the time for rebellion was surely in 1290 when the

---

[45] For the details of these grants, see Charles Oman, *The Great Revolt of 1381*, with a new introduction by E. B. Fryde (Oxford, 1969).

real value of what Edward I raised makes comparison whit what Edward III
and Richard II managed to raise ludicrous.

It could be argued, however, that by the 1370s times had changed. A
shrunken population was then being laid under contribution for sums of
money which exceeded anything demanded since Edward III had taxed and
borrowed in order to finance the introductory phase of his war with France.
The shrunken population was not, however, a poorer one. Aggregate wealth
may have diminished; but individual wealth had very substantially increased.
The compromise taxation of 1334 was not a greater burden than before: the
very worst possibility is that it was an equal burden. And what that burden
was we can roughly calculate.

We know how much the 4d poll-tax raised in 1377, and hence how many
tax-payers contributed to it. There were 1,320,000 contributors. If we assume
that similar numbers of tax-payers contributed to all the other taxes levied in
the decade 1371–81, then we can easily work out a very approximate average
charge per head for taxation in that period. The moveables taxes were always
worth about £38,000. The parish tax yielded about £50,000. And the poll-
taxes raised about £22,000, £20,000 and finally £45,000. Sometimes Parliament granted the king a double tax, as it did in 173 and 1377. And once, in
1380, it granted him one and a half. Thus in any particular year of the
decade the tax-paying population of 1377 would have been called upon to
make an average contribution of 9d to the parish tax, 7d to any single
moveables tax, and 8d to the most notorious of the poll-taxes: the poll-tax
collected in 1381.

These calculations exaggerate the weight of taxation that the average
tax-payer had to bear because they assume a tax-paying population of
1,320,000. But the poll-tax of 1377, from which this figure is derived, unquestionably minimises the size of the taxable population. Poll-tax assessors
merely charged wherever they found someone chargeable and collectors
then returned whatever sums of money they subsequently levied. Assessors
were not told, in 1377, how much money they could expect to raise. Nobody
knew. Nor did it lighten any tax-payer's burden to inform on a neighbour
who had managed to evade payment. Moreover poverty was accepted as
exempting those who were genuinely unable to pay, thus furnishing others
who had no right to exemption with plenty of scope for cheating. We are
bound to conclude, from all this, that the first poll-tax substantially under-
estimated the size of the taxable population. Taxes other than poll-taxes
caught a much larger taxable population in their toils for the simple reason
that they assessed the community, not the individual, and then left the
community with the responsibility of collecting contributions from its members. In practice this meant forcing contributions from as many members as
possible so as to lighten the burden of all. And for us it means that the
burden of taxation, in the 1370s, was rather lower than it appears to be in
the estimate of average liability calculated above.

These were extraordinarily small sums of money for tax-payers to find in
the 1370s and well within the means of most of them. We have only to

compare taxes of 7d or 9d, levied in the 1370s, with the fines and amercements of 3d, 6d, and even 12d, which were commonplace in the earliest
manorial courts whose records we possess, to appreciate how very much more
thirteenth-century manorial authorities were able to wring from ordinary
villagers than Parliament allowed the king to take from their descendants.[46]
In real terms, the manorial levies were incomparably more burdensome than
any Parliamentary tax granted to Edward III or his grandson, if only because
standards of living were very substantially lower, for the overwhelming majority of the population, in the thirteenth-century, than they were to be in
the decade 1371–81.

But there were other differences too. In the thirteenth-century manorial
fines and amercements were collected as well as imposed. Manorial courts
were practical institutions. They did not impose levies that nobody could
pay. Nor did they reckon to ruin those whom they dunned. When someone
was too poor to pay he was usually let off. Sometimes an amercement was
merely a tax on trade. There would have been no point in killing the trade
by taxing it out of existence. By charging what the market could bear
manorial courts themselves did a flourishing trade; for the fines and amercements were paid; and the courts made a worthwhile and often handsome
contribution to manorial revenues. And they did so without concentrating
their attention upon a minority of well-to-do servile tenants. By hook or by
crook manorial courts usually contrived to get something from nearly everyone and, often enough, several times a year.

In the 1370s, however, ordinary tenants were not only far better off than
they had been a century before: they were also harder to control and hence
less amenable to the fiscal discipline of the manorial courts. They not only
earned more; they kept more of what they had earned. The more recalcitrant
of them could no longer be beaten up or murdered without provoking more
antagonism locally than manorial authorities could afford, given the atmosphere and the economic realities of the time.[47] And there was another reason
why they kept more of what they earned. The real burden of taxation was
shifting. When land is scarce and rents are high, landlords will always be able
to pass taxation down the line because their tenants will have no option but
to pay a taxation-inflated rent or clear out. When land is abundant, however,
and rents are low, tenants have to be wooed and landlords are obliged to offer
inducements which will encourage and attract them to take up land whose
rents have been suitably moderated so as to relieve them of any financial
responsibility for tax bills. That was certainly what was happening in the
1370s when rising money-wages tell us of falling rents and when landlords
who might otherwise have found it difficult to let their tenancies were

[46] See, for example, F. W. Maitland, *Select Pleas in Manorial and Other Seigneurial Courts*,
Selden Society, vol. 2 (1889).
[47] Z. Razi, 'The Struggles between the Abbots of Halesowen and their Tenants' in T. H.
Aston *et al.*, eds, *Social Relations and Ideas* (Cambridge, 1983), pp. 162–3.

obliged to take royal taxation into account in deciding how much to ask potential tenants to pay rent.

How long it took for an ordinary labourer to earn the money the king demanded in tax we can fairly easily find out. The Statute of Labourers sets out maximum rates of pay for certain jobs. The Statute looks backwards in 1351. It wants everyone to be satisfied with the rates current in 1346. It cannot foresee that the pestilence so recently endured will return again and again until it manages to disrupt all traditional economic relationships. Nor can it foresee that inflation will presently drive all prices, including the price of labour, sky-high. It decrees, therefore, that reapers are to get 2d or 3d per day, threshers of wheat 2½d, carpenters 2d or 3d, and so forth. These rates had very little chance of being respected, except perhaps where special circumstances granted a brief respite from the realities of life to some big and locally powerful estate like the Abbey of Westminster.[48] We can see what was happening generally by examining the cases of infringement that got to court. But even if we stick to statutory prescription it is clear that the king's taxes took no more than two or three days' earnings from the ordinary farm-labourer. For a generation like ours which works for the Queen's government for four or five months in the year, this looks like paradise. For peasants who staged a revolt which went on for several weeks without inflicting lasting damage upon themselves it cannot have been more than a trifle.

Taxation obviously had its part to play in provoking the Peasants' Revolt. But the root cause of the Revolt is to be found elsewhere. It is to be found in the persistent attempts made by manorial lords and employers of all degrees to halt changes which no power on earth could check or halt, still less reverse. If there had been no attempt made to interfere with these changes there would have been no Revolt. Everyone would have been too busy to care. Royal taxation was undoubtedly a nuisance and an irritation, particularly when the king took it into his head to experiment with new forms of taxation. On its own, however, it was negligible as a provocation. But when everyone in authority, wherever one turned for work, seemed to be in a conspiracy to snatch back all the advantages and opportunities that surviving the pestilence afforded to even the humblest labourer, then the king's foreign gambles, his everlasting proddings and probings for money, and his newfangled taxes, proved to be more than ordinary men and women were prepared to put up with.

A new world was in the making as a result of the very effective population control imposed by the Black Death. It is impossible to exaggerate the importance of the Black Death as an agent of emancipation. The land surplus it created swung the whole community of small farmers and farm-labourers out of its previous orbit. Indeed only its continuing virulence maintained the surplus and hence the well-being of the greater part of the

48 Barbara Harvey, *Westminster Abbey and its Estates* (Oxford, 1977), pp. 245–6.

community. If England's prosperity depended upon family planning then the Black Death guaranteed that prosperity because mortality stood-in for family planning. But if the later medieval English farmer had a short life there is no reason to believe that, from a material point of view, it was anything but a gay one. There was no starvation, no fear of the winter's cold, no dragging illness caused by the deficiencies that commonly go with poverty. Paradoxically people were healthier and stronger at a period when mortality-rates were at their peak than they had been before or would be again. They were healthier and stronger because they were better fed and better housed; and because they worried less about the future. They could afford to carry-over crop surpluses instead of having to consume most of what they produced and, for want of storage, to lose a good deal of what they kept. Poverty in later medieval society meant something quite different from what it had meant before. In this new world if harvests failed or businesses collapsed unqualified disaster was moderated into misfortune. And if conditions deteriorated generally, so that economic activities sank to a low ebb, those deteriorating conditions must be related to the general level of well-being below which it was most unusual, in that period, to sink.

Every comparison, indeed, between economic conditions before and after the Black Death must take these profound changes into account. Failure to do so renders such comparisons nugatory. Every sort of statistical measurement must make allowance for the consequences of the Black Death. Figures for exports and imports, calculations of money supply and bullion movements, taxation returns and the like, which are widely used to contrast earlier fourteenth-century achievements with later ones without reference to the momentous happenings that, from certain points of view, interposed an unbridgeable gap between the two periods, merely serve to confirm the prejudices and justify the scepticism of the innumerate majority which is always deeply suspicious of any argument which depends upon statistical manipulations.

All these considerations apply with particular force to the interpretation of the urban evidence. As a group the towns of England enjoyed a fair measure of prosperity in the changed circumstances of the later Middle Ages, Some signally failed to do so; and not all of those that did prosper, prospered equally. Nor did they all prosper by doing exactly what they had done before. But towns, from an economic point of view, were processing plants. In an economic system in which nearly everyone lived in the countryside, towns functioned by responding to the market demands of those who lived beyond their limits. How they did so was simply and brilliantly explained by Defoe in the early pages of his Plan of the English Commerce. Subsequent writers have refined his observations and modified them to take account of the changes brought about by urban industrialisation. But the majority of the historians who concern themselves with the workings of medieval and early modern towns appear to have forgotten how to evaluate the role of the towns in societies which depend upon farming and handicraft industry for the production of the bulk of their wealth. They treat such towns as if they were separate commonwealths with a record of economic activities which can be assessed in isolation, without reference to the fortunes of everyone else in the community. In absurd and extreme cases, historians have been known to deliver comprehensive indictments against all the towns in the economy, chartered and unchartered alike, at times when every indication we possess strongly indicates that, in the countryside, people were doing tolerably well by the standards of less happy days.

It is hardly surprising to find that many attempts have been made in recent years to demonstrate how poor and decayed the provincial towns of England were in the later Middle Ages. At first glance the evidence is irresistible. The towns of England were less populous than they had been. Does his not mean that they were poorer? They complained bitterly to the king that they could no longer afford his levies. Are they not to be believed? Urban rents had fallen. Does this not reflect a corresponding fall in the attractions and rewards of urban life? Leading merchants actually paid to be excused from taking their turn in municipal office. Would they have done so if business had been good? Gilds were incapable of paying their dues. Does this not indicate dwindling membership and flagging fortunes? With such a weight of testimony to support the view that towns were doing badly in the later Middle Ages can we wonder that so many historians are predisposed to credit any assertion, however unsubstantiated, that tends to show how badly off provincial towns were, and to discredit any proposition, however circumstantial, to the contrary.

And yet the presumption is not that towns were doing badly in the later Middle Ages: the presumption is that they were doing well. The burden of proof lies not with those who say that towns were flourishing at that time, but with those who say they were not. Towns were certainly emptier then they had been before the Black Death. But when the tide of population ebbs it leaves all the inhabited places with fewer people. Fewer does not mean poorer. When land is scarce rent compels the vast majority of people to do without most of the things that make life easy or comfortable. But when land is scarce population, by definition, is in spate. Towns grow, in such circumstances, partly because aggregate income has risen to some sort of peak; and partly because they are swollen by the tide of unemployed men and women, boys and girls, which sweeps into them in search of work. When land is in surplus, the basic necessities are soon provided for and there are earnings to spare for other things. That is the true significance of low rents in the later medieval economy. And towns, which are undoubtedly much slimmed-down by loss of population, are nevertheless occupied by citizens who, on average, are doing very much better commercially than previous generations did.

If rents were low in later medieval towns because there was so much empty property in them, so was rateable value. Annual charges based upon full utilisation of the building-stock were obviously inappropriate for towns which were short of rate-payers; and the towns were quick to point that out and to put in for remission of charges. They could easily have raised their rates. The aggregate market for all the goods and services provided by towns undoubtedly shrank as the population fell; but not in proportion, because income had risen. The rate-payers of most towns could very well have afforded higher rates because they were, on average, better off than they had been before the Black Death. But the towns never dreamt of compensating for loss of rateable value by raising the rates, partly because anything that increased business costs made rival towns which refrained from raising their rates that much more attractive to business men; and partly because there was no earthly reason why a town which could reasonably expect to get away with paying less should incur all the contention and unpopularity inevitably associated with paying more. Some towns, indeed, allowed arrears of payment to accumulate for years and when dunned for money simply put in another woeful plea for remission.

If leading merchants shunned office and paid to be excused from serving the town as alderman or mayor, we may not take it for granted that they were too poor to serve, particularly when they paid handsomely for exemption. Cardinal Wolsey laughed the Bristol men out of court when they pleaded that Bristol could not recruit officers for that reason. And York's senior merchants had been using that excuse for centuries.[49] When merchants shun office, the reason is much more likely to be that they have got better things to do than that they cannot afford what Wolsey regarded as the perfectly ordinary expenses that leading citizens can perfectly easily take in their stride.

Poverty is also given as the excuse for the failure of gilds to pay their annual dues to the king. The implication here is that the membership was poor because the gild was, or claimed to be, poor. But the poverty of gilds, if it were not feigned, is no criterion of the financial circumstances of their members, or of those who were expected to be their members but were not, or were members but failed to pay their dues. York's clothmaking gilds, whose members were famous for their work in the thirteenth-century, never managed to pay their dues in the thirteenth-century; and Lincoln's, in the next century, according to an Exchequer inquiry, were incapable of forcing the city's clothmakers to join them.

Despite everything that can be said in favour of the vitality of later medieval towns, as a group, so deeply has entrenched bias entered into current historical thinking that it is no longer necessary to prove the decay of a particular town: it is enough to assert it; and the assertion will be widely accepted as tantamount to proof. Nevertheless every indication, including the taxation evidence,[50] seems to show that we should believe what commonsense would suggest: that a thriving countryside makes for thriving towns. The enemy of prosperity was not the Black Death but population growth; and once the Black Death had lost its power to determine the size of

---

[49] J. I. Kermode, 'Urban Decline? The Flight from Office in Late Medieval York', *Economic History Review*, 2nd ser., vol. xxxv (1982), pp. 179–98.
[50] A. R. Bridbury, *Economic Growth: England in the Later Middle Ages* (1962).

the population by killing in very large numbers, as it did in the sixteenth century, the population inexorably made up the ground it had lost and began to choke the countryside, and then the towns, with an unwanted surplus of impoverished people.

It is hardly possible,in the present climate of opinion, to exaggerate the achievements of the later Middle Ages in the sphere of social and economic affairs. A period which has always been treated as notorious for its rancorous politics and its fatal entanglements abroad, and misprized for its distressing history of pestilence and for the inevitable wasting of land and habitation that pestilence brought with it, turns out to have been one in which the well-being of the vast majority of people was never greater, the productivity of land never higher, and manufacturing industry never more prosperous. These are surely not insignificant gains to be thrown into the balance when we measure profit and loss in the later Middle Ages.

The war with France has always figured prominently in any assessment of the misfortunes of the age. Its costs have always impressed everyone who has concerned himself with such matters, though English Parliaments, as we have seen, never allowed the fiscal cost of the war with France to make more than a superficial impression upon the resources of the community. But in a deeper sense the war with France was not a cost at all. It was a consumer good, a sport like hunting. It was one of the ways in which those who reflected the leading characteristics of feudal society in their lives and personalities chose to disburse the wealth they had accumulated in other ways. Indeed it is hardly going too far to claim that engaging in warfare was one of the purposes for which feudal society existed. For a majority of the members of the military aristocracies that ruled the societies of western Europe, if not for all, war was what life was all about. How else were these armoured knights with their embattled residences to spend their time and money if not in exercising the skills which they had devoted so much thought and energy to developing and training? War did not interrupt their lives or hamper their careers: it fulfilled them. And it did as much for their numerous retinues of followers and dependents. If others were made to suffer who wanted no part in the operations of war, if there was murder and rape, arson and theft, if crops were destroyed and townships desolated, those who were responsible could claim with justice that what they did was done in accordance with strict doctrines and enforceable codes of conduct universally acknowledged and as scrupulously observed as any doctrines and codes ever were.[51]

Indeed they could have gone farther and claimed that medieval warfare was nothing like as costly in capital equipment as the organised religion to which society paid its respects and its dues; and immeasurably less costly in life. The material fabric of the medieval Church and its swollen communities of clerical members absorbed prodigious quantities of resources and did so, not intermittently, but constantly, year by year. There can be no question but

[51] M. H. Keen, *The Laws of War* (1965).

that medieval society would have been even better-off materially if the Church had never existed than it would have been if warfare had been abolished. Moreover since so many members of society survived at the very margins of existence, the Church must be held responsible for the death of uncounted numbers of its communicants who might have survived by the barest margin but for its incessant levies and insatiable demands. Like warfare, the Church terrified ordinary people. Its threats were not directly of the sword and the brand but of everlasting and unimaginably harrowing punishments. And when it came to questions of murder and torture, the Church was very far from being able to disassociate itself from the wars that were fought in its name. In this connection it is worth remembering that the Church exercised a much more refined discrimination than warfare did over whom it tortured or murdered. It racked, burnt, and otherwise disposed of a fair number of society's braver and more independent spirits as well as a sprinkling of its blabbering imbeciles; and by a master-stroke of hypocritical self-righteousness exculpated itself from blame for the shedding of blood by handing its victims over to the lay power for dispatch.

No doubt the Church gave tremendous satisfaction, sometimes spiritually and often in other ways, to those who made a career out of serving it and to others who found it useful, profitable or even a source of strength, consolation and peace. But it did so at a price; and once we start dismantling a social system in order to submit its components to an accountant's costings, as historians have done with medieval warfare, we must end up by asking impossible questions about how much a society's ideals and purposes are worth in terms of the resources they absorb. Warfare, as it was conducted in medieval times, the Church, the feudal monarchy, the world of scholarship and the universities that gave it shelter, are all vulnerable once we start submitting them to measurement with the implicit intention of calculating what else society could have done with the resources that were devoted to their support. But the questions are not only impossible: they are pointless because in asking them we are in fact querying everything that integrated society and gave it coherence. And what is worse, we are in effect judging medieval society by standards which would have been comprehensively repudiated by every thoughtful member of that society however radical or iconoclastic his views. For every attempt to put the past in the dock and the present on the bench must be compromised by the thought that, if the past had its way, the roles would be reversed.

The Dark Ages

Great scholars, like other great men, cast long shadows. We pay heavily for their insights. Their thoughts set in a mould which becomes a prison for lesser men; and subsequent work done on problems transfigured by their gifts looks more like exegesis than a voyaging through strange seas of thought alone. The economic history of Europe in the early Middle Ages is just such a mould. What a stroke of genius it was to juxtapose Mohammed, the prophet of Islam, the spiritual inspiration of an empire as extensive as the Roman Empire and in its way more complex, more sophisticated, and more mature, and Charlemagne, the Alexander of the bleak north European plains! With this dazzling perception of affinities where others had seen nothing but independent and autonomous happenings, careers moving in separate orbits driven by unrelated compulsions and opportunities, Pirenne held the world in thrall for half a century. He contended that Europe's essential characteristic, until the age of Islam, was its dependence upon the Mediterranean. In Germanic times, as in classical, the Mediterranean linked markets in the heart of the Continent with supplies fetched by professional merchants from regions far and near. Trade induced specialization; and specialization conferred all the benefits familiar to those who are acquainted with the mysteries of economics. The incursion of Islam changed everything. The Arabs who swarmed across the littoral of North Africa accomplished something that was apparently beyond the capacity, or perhaps foreign to the nature, of Vandal, Visigoth, and Ostrogoth: they ruptured the main artery of European communications and turned the Mediterranean thoroughfare into a waste of water untravelled by Europeans from the west. The result was to transform Europe into a beleaguered and land-locked fastness. The intricate network of economic relationships which had survived the fall of Rome, and continued in a diminished and eroded state to serve the Merovingians, collapsed. The empire of Charlemagne was an empire thrown back upon itself. Professional trading dwindled and then ceased. Estates became self-sufficient. Europe retrogressed. The classical age was over. The axis of the world, for so many centuries a Mediterranean one, was displaced northwards, and in a new landscape peopled by races with bizarre traditions and inscrutable potentialities, the Middle Ages began.

Such is the Pirenne cataclysm with its extraordinary paradoxes of a trading people like the Arabs refusing to trade, and a Europe starved of goods because its merchants were obstructed by a blockade which must rank amongst the supreme masterpieces of that monotonous and wearing form of warfare: for to be effective it had to be subscribed to, and if Pirenne is right

© The Economic History Review 1969

was in fact subscribed to, with unfaltering unanimity by all members of what was in effect a notoriously disruptive confederacy, and was enforced despite the distances, the administrative problems and the incredible practical difficulties inseparable from the maintenance of permanent patrols.

The inherent improbabilities of Pirenne's arguments are so great as to provoke the reflexion that the most astonishing tribute paid to Pirenne by his critics is that they have persistently conducted the controversy on his terms. He declared that regular trade between western Europe and the Orient ceased at a certain period and stated his evidence: the disappearance of papyrus, silks, spices, and gold. His critics have long demurred to the confident finality of this proposition and are now so impressed by the quality of the contrary evidence, some of it uncovered since Pirenne's death, that Prof. Lopez, surveying the problems for the *Cambridge Economic History* in 1952, felt justified in doing so without actually mentioning Pirenne by name. But the omission was not in effect a declaration of independence. Prof. Lopez has been no more successful than his predecessors in emancipating himself from the bondage of Pirenne's structure of ideas: for his survey is substantially a catalogue of objections to Pirenne's evidence, not a fresh look at the problems.

These problems are only incidentally Mediterranean ones; and intense pre-occupation with the *minutiae* of Pirenne's arguments has only served to obscure the fact that Pirenne's own interest in Mediterranean matters sprang from his attempt to explain the central phenomenon of the Middle Ages: the eclipse of the classical lands and the transference of Europe's centre of gravity from the south to the north. As things stand at present, problems of European development in the Dark Ages, to the extent that they are still formulated in terms of international trade, stress the accessibility, or otherwise, of supplies of various commodities, to the utter neglect of the virtual extinction of the European demand for these things brought about by the collapse of the Roman Empire. Yet it is this near extinction of the market that renders nugatory any attempt to account for aspects of the evolution of medieval Europe in terms of external forces acting upon international trade.

The writers who see crucial problems of European development in terms of international trade may spare a few perfunctory comments for the market situation; but their real concern is never with demand. That this is no accident is plain from the way in which they treat the resurgence of trade that brings the early medieval period to an end in the eleventh century. Accounts of that resurgence say little or nothing about changes in the structure of European demand, but dwell at length upon the merchants and shippers who brought customers and suppliers together. It would be an exaggeration to say that they depict the whole thing as a triumph of Italian commercial proficiency and naval power, because they never fail to make vague reference to population growth. But since these references show that those who make them have grotesquely misunderstood the economic consequences of population growth, seeing population growth as synonymous with the growth of effective demand, it remains true to say that market demand is much neglected in current thought about the rise of medieval Europe. Europe is treated as if it were a corked bottle, the cork being inserted, more or less effectually, by diverse disrupters of commerce at one period, and removed by Italian merchants at another.

Yet what makes the argument based upon interference with the smooth flow of trade otiose, if not hopelessly irrelevant, is the dissolution of the aristocratic and middle-class market for whole ranges of commodities once the Roman Empire had collapsed. Vast patronage ceased. A terrific super-structure of administration disintegrated. Fabulous wealth, derived from landed estates for which every province of an immense empire had been laid under contribution, capitulated to new kingdoms whose inhabitants no longer acknowledged any obligation of rent, or tribute of taxation, to persons or authorities beyond the realm. It was Vienna without the Austro-Hungarian Empire multiplied many times over.

Nor did the new kingdoms offer compensations to those who had been cashiered or dispossessed which were anything like commensurate with what they had lost. These new kingdoms were, perforce, infinitely simpler in structure than the Roman Empire had been and consequently afforded far less scope for lucrative employment. Moreover, being both smaller and self-contained, they necessarily restricted the possessions of the wealthy to what could be picked up through marriage, patronage, or expropriation, within narrowly circumscribed boundaries.

Profound changes such as these, with the staggering losses of income that went with them, spelt mortification and hardship for those who had once dominated the empire, and for the multitudes which had once lived by serving them, or at any rate at their charge. The European market for internationally traded commodities was ruined, as indeed was the market for a host of other things which never travelled spectacular distances, rarely, if ever, got into the surviving records, but nevertheless made up the stock-in-trade of the merchants, manufacturers, and professional men and women of all degrees, whose sunken fortunes and eventual disappearance are portrayed and lamented in every assessment of these centuries.

Naturally even the most catastrophic reversals of fortune take time to work their way through the social system; inflict greater harm in some places than in others; and damage certain occupations and the trade in certain commodities more than others. And only the most stupendous calamities are incapable of being alleviated by countervailing forces bringing transient relief to a district or to a group of people, or even perhaps in some instances bringing relief which endures. In this case, however, all attempts to chart phases and to chronicle vicissitudes are foredoomed, so tenuous is the evi-dence for any particular region, or period, or commodity. What complicates matters still more is the length of the time-span. Over the centuries tastes altered, needs varied, costs fluctuated: some items of consumption were dropped, others introduced, and others again were brought in as substitutes for things which had been in common use hitherto, the changes being made for reasons which could very well have been wholly unrelated to the larger movements that historians have striven to document.[1] Differences between Merovingian and Carolingian Europe there undoubtedly were; but our knowledge of what they were and of what they signified is so patently a function of the sheer blind chance survival of a handful of records that we must dismiss from mind all hope of retrieving anything of consequence from oblivion. Only the broad outlines are firm. And these show that the rich and varied Mediterranean commerce of Roman times did not come to an end when imperial markets collapsed. It got diverted; for the rise of Islam brought to the southern shores of the Mediterranean a civilization as brilliant and colourful, as complex and enduring, as any that the Mediterranean had ever known.

The Roman Empire had once been far more highly integrated and coherently organized than Islam was ever to be. But although the differences between them may have been very great, what are perhaps most striking are the parallels and similarities between the two. Both grew rapidly as a result of the irruption of an obscure and unlettered people into areas of mature but decadent civilization, both threw up remarkable leaders and organizers; both endured lacerating civil wars which were followed by golden ages; both were penetrated by superior but militarily weaker cultures, Greek in the one case, Persian in the other; both were disrupted by successor states – Germanic kingdoms and anti-Caliphates; both were sustained by an infusion of new blood – Byzantine and Turkish; and corrupted by a barbarization of military institutions when the Romans and the Bedouins ceased to be the dominant groups in their respective armies. Both faced the problem of colonial advance to commonwealth status; found the costs of empire mounting against them; endured blows from well-intentioned saviours which were worse than the troubles they were meant to cure – Justinian on the one hand, the Turks on the other; and both gave their worlds centuries of peace and civilization.

Above all, both empires enriched themselves at the expense of dependent peoples; enabled their leading notables to accumulate vast landed fortunes; created elaborate bureaucracies; and fostered the lush growth of patronage. Consequently the destruction of imperial markets was followed, after an interval, by the creation of Islamic ones. Commodities which had once flowed to Rome and Lyons and to countless other centres of extravagant consumption in the west now flowed to comparable centres in the east and the south such as Damascus, Cairo, and Qayrawān. Egyptian corn, once the staple supply for Rome, now went to Syria and north Arabia instead.

Economic developments such as these, which have been dimly perceived but never seriously investigated before, are at last attracting the interest of historians. Scholarly energies, for so long fruitlessly expended on elucidating the trivial details of the trade that was not, are at last being devoted to the trade that was. And the publication of the first volume of Prof. Goitein's

---

[1] See, for example, R. S. Lopez, 'Mohammed and Charlemagne: a Revision', *Speculum*, vol. xviii (1943).

trilogy is an event of momentous importance in setting aspects of the commercial life of medieval Europe into better perspective by focusing a powerful light upon what was happening in medieval Islam.[2]

Not that Prof. Goitein has singled out commerce for particular attention. His ambition is to provide the world with a preliminary survey of Islamic society in the Mediterranean as it is reflected in the still unmeasured riches of the hoard of Jewish documents found in the Cairo *geniza*.

Genizas were once very numerous. They were, in effect, gigantic waste-paper baskets, repositories where papers of every description ended up after they had lost all value to their owners but not the sanctity that all writings acquired, in Jewish eyes, by bearing the name of God, by being in Hebrew, which the Jews with complacent effrontery took to be God's native tongue, or even by using Hebrew characters for other languages. The contents of such repositories were, accordingly, infinitely miscellaneous. And from time to time, when the repositories could hold no more, they were emptied, their contents being reverently laid to rest in cemeteries. The Cairo *geniza*, an annex of the Old Cairo synagogue, somehow escaped this fate. In this respect it appears to be unique. Its earliest manuscripts are ninth- and tenth-century ones. After 1002 manuscripts are frequent. By the twenties they have turned into a flood which does not subside until 1266. Thereafter they dwindle inexplicably. There are fourteenth- and fifteenth-century manuscripts; but they are few. Then in the sixteenth century there is a resurgence. Language and script, however, are quite different: refugee Jews from Spain, now domiciled in Egypt, have started to throw away their waste paper. Eventually the *geniza* fell into disuse. Its contents slumbered undisturbed until 1890, or thereabouts, when the synagogue was renovated. The waste-paper basket, now a priceless archive, was dispersed by dealers and acquired by libraries and private collections in Europe, America, and Israel.

The diversity and abundance of the documents to be found in a collection whose unifying principle was the simple but comprehensive one that the documents should be written in a certain language, or should use the characters of that language, pass belief. The whole life of a society, insofar as it is written down, gets recorded. And Prof. Goitein disclaims any pretensions to having done anything more than convey 'an idea of the topics and types of information to be found in the geniza documents'. Moreover, he confines himself to the medieval collection. Since the Jews, however, played a conspicuous and resourceful part in the economic life of Islam at this period these medieval documents are a revelation of what the world looked like from the southern shores of the Mediterranean. Prof. Goitein, wherever possible letting the documents speak for themselves, conjures up for us something of the teeming life of Islam in all its idiosyncrasy and flamboyance and profusion. In this volume, which explores the economic foundations, glimpses of the social structure of Islam, and impressions of its industries and

[2] S. D. Goitein, *A Mediterranean Society*, vol. I (Univ. of California Press, 1967).

its agriculture, its craftsmen and its slaves, are set off by an absorbing exposition of its techniques of commerce and finance vividly illuminated by snatches of biography, vignettes of merchants, bankers, commission agents, and the like, which Prof. Goitein has winnowed from his ample harvest. It is a remarkable achievement and promises to be the perfect foil to what Dr Daniel and others have taught us about the stubborn bigotry of Western opinions of Islam that were crystallizing at exactly this time.[3]

From all this it would seem that luxury, ostentation, fashion, and a taste for bizarre and expensive trifles did not vanish from the Mediterranean world with the fall of Rome and the disintegration of the empire. They continued to impart their counterfeit lustre to the life of the Eastern empire; and they were presently restored to the towns and cities of the farther shores of the Mediterranean by Islam. Only the kingdoms of western Europe lost their resplendent imperial panoply, and seemingly gained nothing.

Historians are predisposed to a gloomy view of post-Roman Europe by the intensity of their admiration for the Roman Empire. They even extend a qualified admiration to that travesty of empire that Diocletian clapped in irons, and are persuaded that when the end finally came, Europe, given over to the rule of Franks, Burgundians, and Ostrogoths, had exchanged one form of oppression for a worse. In the age of violence and disaster that ensued, they contend that, as a rule, the frontiers of social, political, and economic life shrank to the boundaries of the innumerable estates where benighted communities sheltered from the environing chaos as the tools and the victims of local potentates.

Life in Merovingian Europe may very well have been more turbulent than it had been before. But the evidence adduced to prove that it was is literary; and literary evidence as to the general frightfulness of life either under an uncongenial regime, or as a result of molestation, or the fear or threat of it, is exceedingly suspect. Historians are more than usually tempted to manipulate such evidence to suit their predilections. They stress the anarchy of Stephen's reign because they see the twelfth century mainly as an age of decline in demesne farming. They justify their cheerless picture of the fifteenth century by reference to the Wars of the Roses. But they say nothing about the uproar and confusion of John's later years, and ignore the Barons' War, with its bloody interludes, because these things do not square with their genial assessment of thirteenth-century economic conditions.

Occasionally it is possible to show that the literary evidence cannot bear the construction put upon it. Fifteenth-century violence, for example, looks much less disquieting when it is set against the wheat prices of the period. Lawless times should mean trampled fields, burnt crops, and disordered markets. And in these circumstances wheat prices should fluctuate wildly. But fifteenth-century wheat prices did nothing of the kind. They remained incorrigibly low and stable throughout the century. Chaos should be made of

3 N. Daniel, *Islam and the West* (Edinburgh, 1960).

sterner stuff. Another example is Anglo-Saxon England. The modern history of England begins with a racial transfusion of monumental proportions followed in later centuries by invasions and settlements which shook the political life of the country and left their mark upon its economic affairs. At the same time the province that Rome had unified dissolved into a congeries of principalities and kingdoms which late Anglo-Saxon kings welded together again only with much difficulty and after prolonged struggle. It might seem that a more unpromising environment for economic development would be hard to find. And yet between the Settlements and Domesday, England was transformed by a social revolution which if it did not give the country a village every few miles, at least made it a rare community which was more than walking distance from its neighbour. The countryside lost its primeval look; forest and moor were subdued; the heavier soils, an intractable problem to the Romans, grew corn. It was a stupendous achievement, implying painful adjustments to new social responsibilities, to unwonted rhythms in farming, and to novel, and hence unproven, tools. Obviously life can appear to have been very turbulent in the early Middle Ages without anything in fact having occurred to jeopardize vast improvements in productivity and profound changes in social organization.

If it is imprudent to assume, therefore, that Merovingian Europe languished economically because its political life appears to have been in perpetual ferment, it follows that it is also imprudent to assume that villages and estates became more self-sufficient than before. Estates which had once exported wine and oil to distant markets had certainly, by then, long ceased to do so. But once the Roman Empire had been broken up and the international market for these things was gone, they had no incentive to produce them except for domestic and limited commercial needs. And these needs they continued to supply. Evidence which purports to show that estates were, in other respects, more self-sufficient than before runs up against our apparently invincible ignorance as to how much self-sufficiency was normal on European estates in the placid days of Rome's prime. The earliest estates whose workings we can examine in detail are thirteenth-century English ones, whose wool sales and wine purchases are famous. But these things apart, what is remarkable about such estates is how much of what they needed, in an age not notable for resolute autarky, was nevertheless home-made and home-grown. Exchange may be vital to economic growth, but a substantial degree of self-sufficiency is not, apparently, inimical to it. A social survey written in late Anglo-Saxon times, in the midst of what was perhaps the greatest farming revolution in English history, takes it for granted that the average estate will be provided with looms for weaving cloth and will be supplied with wine from its own vineyards.[4] Earlier evidence of self-sufficiency has to be set into the perspective of considerations such as these.

---

[4] 'The Gerefa', in W. Cunningham, *The Growth of English Industry and Commerce*, vol. I, Appendix B(I). See also E. M. Carus-Wilson, *Medieval Merchant Venturers* (1954), pp.

There is, however, one profoundly important sense in which the disintegration of the Roman Empire brought changes which were very much for the better. The catastrophe that obliterated so much that masquerades as civilization, and is therefore universally deplored, had one consequence which is never itemized by those who perpetuate the view that the early Middle Ages were a confused and distracted period haunted by phantasmagoria and tormented by dreams of an immortal past. It lifted an overwhelming burden from the shoulders of the ordinary inhabitants of the empire who no longer had to find, from their meagre earnings, the resources with which Rome had built and then maintained a network of towns and cities many of which were mere imperial ostentation, an army which grew by what it fed on, and civil and military installations whose massive grandeur and formidable strength flattered the pride and sustained the ambitions of Rome but cost incalculably more than they were worth if they are valued, as they so often are, simply in terms of the law and order they preserved.

Roman law and order may have laid the political foundations for economic growth; and building an empire round an inland sea may have given it an incomparable setting by providing it with the cheapest freights to be had until the transport revolution of the nineteenth century wrought its miracles. But economic growth beyond a certain point was balked by Roman imperialism and the Roman social structure. The vaunted trade of the empire was to a very great though incalculable extent a traffic in rent and tribute. Unlike trade it did not generate income: it simply impoverished those from whom it was extorted. Hence, perhaps, the technological sterility of the Roman world. The market for luxuries induced a measure of specialization and technical innovation in the making of certain industrial goods and in the growing of such farm produce as was amenable to plantation methods.[5] But progressive technological change requires the stimulus of something like a mass market for simple wares in common use. And a mass market, or anything approaching it, was incompatible with the pretentious ambitions that Roman society and Roman politics nourished upon tribute from the provinces.

Consequently, when the empire collapsed it released the tax-paying millions of western Europe from a paralysing oppression. The resources no longer sequestered by Rome were not seized upon by any other public authority. The barbarian kingdoms stripped the baroque from public life and banished the rodomontade from politics and the flatulent pretensions that went with it. They found work and provided sinecures for only a fraction of those whom the empire had enriched, or employed, or at any rate kept. And aristocratic landlords, their incomes diminished by loss of foreign assets and depleted by the compulsory surrender of huge segments of their European

267–8, for examples of later plantings of vines and the subsequent paying-off of vine servants as the Gascon trade developed.

5 C. A. Yeo, 'The Economics of Roman and American Slavery', *Finanzarchiv*, vol. xiii, pp. 445–85.

estates to invaders who settled with their dependants on the land they had overrun, were in no position to command the services or indulge themselves with the luxuries of another age. The stringencies of the political and aristo- cratic classes were after all the chief cause of the collapse of the market for internationally traded commodities.

What was loss to the empire and to those who served it was gain to everyone else. The resources now retained for personal consumption presum- ably enabled the ordinary peasants of western Europe to live better than they had done before, and by living better presumably enabled them to live longer. And the farming population, augmented by those whom starvation and disease did not so readily claim, was further increased by barbarian settlements, and by the soldiers and the administrators, the servants and the skilled workers, the labourers and the permanently unemployed, who had once been fed by the farmers of North Africa and now were not fed at all unless they made shift to feed themselves.

No doubt in the long span that separates the fall of Rome from the age of Charlemagne there was time for every kind of transitional disorder. But in the long run constructive political movements matured in early medieval Europe which presupposed a moving frontier, the substantial colonization of new settlements, and a demand for basic things powerful enough to quicken the search for techniques with which to unlock the fecundity of virgin soils. Behind the tiresome complexities and everlasting family dissensions of Merovingian history can be discerned the emergence of the great plains irrigated by Loire and Seine, by Rhine and Elbe, into the political life of Europe. Districts which had once been little more than military canton- ments and colonial outposts, regions where sparse communities had once led a gypsy life of subsistence husbandry by making temporary clearances in the encircling forest and scrub and moving on when the soil was spent, had evolved by the early Middle Ages into centres of political power and cultural ascendancy. By the end of the eighth century, if not before, these political organisms were being sustained by a new and formidable engine of war, the cavalry. The culminating moment of this early phase of development came when the crown of the Roman emperors was placed upon the head of Charlemagne.

It is, perhaps, tempting to see the growing economic significance of the plains of Europe as the natural and inevitable consequence of the massing of Germanic tribes in the west. Centuries before the final collapse of Rome the distance between Roman and non-Roman had shrunk to the point at which the imperial frontiers no longer divided two worlds. To a very great extent that was because the empire had been deeply penetrated by Germanic influ- ences from outside and infiltrated by pre-classical cultures reasserting them- selves from within.[6] But beyond the frontiers things were also changing.[7]

---

6 R. MacMullen, *Enemies of the Roman Order* (Cambridge, Mass., 1966), p. 233.
7 R. E. Mortimer Wheeler, *Rome Beyond the Imperial Frontiers* (1954).

Whilst the empire endured, however, an iron curb hampered larger developments. Is it altogether fanciful, therefore, to see the forces released by the fall of Rome as the spring of changes in demand, and hence in farming techniques, which made these plains fruitful enough to sustain the political and military structures of which the empire of Charlemagne was the fleeting symbol?

The chronology of these changes is hopelessly obscure: so much depends upon archaeological finds, which of all types of historical material are the most fortuitous. But two things are clear beyond peradventure. One is that by Charlemagne's time the heavy plough had been at work upon some of the more difficult but more productive soils of northern Europe, perhaps for a century, perhaps for longer.[8] The other is that the horse had by then entered into its own. It could at last pull heavy loads without choking itself, thanks to a sensible collar which fitted round its shoulders instead of round its neck[9]; and equipped with saddle and stirrups it turned its rider into a projectile in war.[10] Gone were the days when the horse was little better than a means of taking men into battle: the age of cavalry warfare had dawned; the bonds of the Knight's Fee were fastened upon the countryside; and fodder demands mounted, at once a measure of what medieval farmers had already achieved and an earnest of needs to come.

In short, widespread and fundamental changes in productivity and in settlement patterns were having political and military consequences of the utmost significance for the future of Europe at a period about which historians are disposed to shake their heads, regretting the dwindling of international trade to a trickle of luxuries, deploring the instabilities that hampered economic change, and dwelling upon the baffling inscrutability of the scraps and fragments of evidence with which they are obliged to work.

Part of the trouble may indeed be the poverty of the material. But what makes it worse is the apparently insurmountable reluctance that historians of early medieval Europe feel about making use of everything they have got. There is no intercommoning between the disciplines. Political, economic, military, and technical writers all seem to be content to ignore one another's findings. And they all ignore Domesday Book, or handle it with uncomprehending ineptitude. Yet it is the greatest single record to survive from this obscure period, and the one record capable of enlightening their perplexities, even though it cannot solve their problems.

Between the Anglo-Saxon invasions and the Norman Conquest, English settlement patterns were revolutionized. We know they were because Domesday Book shows that by the eleventh century, in the words of a distinguished Domesday scholar, 'Anglo-Saxon society had passed beyond the colonial stage.'[11] Without Domesday Book our views about the

---

8   Lynn White, Jnr, *Medieval Technology and Social Change* (Oxford, 1962), p. 54.
9   *Ibid.*, p. 61.
10 *Ibid.*, p. 24.
11 R. V. Lennard, *Rural England, 1086–1135* (Oxford, 1959), p. 3.

chronology of early English social and economic developments would be as groping and tentative as they are about the chronology of such developments in Europe. Domesday Book cannot tell us when these developments started, how they progressed, what struggles lie behind its impassive statistics: it is a summary of achievements, not a collection of annals. But all social change is slow; social change precipitated by fundamental alterations of established farming routines, infinitely so. Moreover, no such changes proceed uninterruptedly. There are pauses; even reversals of trend. The more one ponders over the implications of Domesday Book the more it is borne in upon one that England in the eleventh century was indeed, in R. V. Lennard's phrase, 'an old country'.

To hope for an eleventh-century Domesday Book of western Europe, miraculously preserved like the geniza documents in some forgotten vault, is to pursue a chimera. But it may be a salutary corrective to orthodox views about the sluggish pace of early European economic development to reflect upon how such a record, had it ever existed, might have compared with the Domesday Book that William the Conqueror actually commissioned and got his clerks to compile. Can we imagine that it would have revealed a world which had lagged behind England economically and socially? Is it not far more likely that it would have demonstrated that the world of which Henry III was the emperor and Gregory VII the Pope had got nothing to learn from England in matters concerned with the organization of its economic life? And if that is the likelier alternative, does that not strengthen the authority of the heterogeneous pieces of evidence which suggest that the Europe of Charlemagne was very much farther advanced economically than the current notions of his period would have us believe?

Many years ago Marc Bloch adjured his colleagues not to deny themselves the benefits of the comparative method because of its obvious risks. Is this not exactly the sort of case he had in mind? The plain lesson of Domesday Book, for historians of early medieval European development, is surely that changes of the greatest moment are to be looked for in periods from which familiar and unambiguous signs of change do not appear to have survived. If they take that lesson to heart, it may not perhaps be too much to hope that henceforth we shall be spared these accounts of the economic life of the early Middle Ages that reduce problems of farming to quibbles about the meaning of words, devote themselves ever more sedulously to scrutinizing the polyptyque of St Germain-des-Près, and generally manage to convey the feeling that it was from books about this period that Hobbes got his ideas about the state of nature. We may even hear the last of the miraculous revival of Europe in the eleventh century, which is, at present, the consistent and entirely reasonable corollary of the view that the early Middle Ages were a long night and not a tremendous probation.

The latest survey of these and later centuries was published by Prof. Duby in 1962. It was received with acclamation and is now fluently translated into English for the sake of readers whose schooling almost invariably includes a prolonged and painful grounding in French.[12] According to a note added by the author, the English text 'reproduces in its entirety that of the first French edition', there being as yet no second edition because it is still early days for second thoughts and substantial revision. That being so, it would be out of place to comment at length on a book which has already been reviewed in the pages of this journal,[13] except to say that in dealing with Charlemagne's Europe, the period with which he begins, Prof. Duby has not improved upon his predecessors. He puts the leading technological changes a century or so later than the historians of technology do;[14] and he so far misconstrues the import of Domesday Book as to claim that in ninth- and tenth-century England corn was grown only on the light alluvial soils in the valleys.[15] This means that he allows England no more than a century in which to achieve the social and technological revolution of which Domesday Book is the unequivocal memorial. It also means that his assessment of early European movements adds nothing but modern instances to a conventionally doleful theme.

The economic problems of early medieval growth are problems still. Essentially they are the problems Pirenne formulated when he drew the attention of the scholarly world to an unexplained swing of the axis of European development which brought the great plains from the periphery to somewhere much closer to the centre of affairs. The empire of Charlemagne may not have been Europe's response to the advent of Islam. But the economic expansion upon which its political, cultural, and military burgeoning depended, and the new farming technology that sustained and enhanced the vigour of that expansion, still have no place in current writing about the period. Impressed by the signs of decadence and confusion that they find all about them, historians still prefer to tell a story of isolation and misery on the farms and of stultification in commerce and industry. Similar signs are to be found in profusion in Anglo-Saxon England; and there is no reason whatever to suppose that English conditions, at that period, were very different from European ones. But England has Domesday Book; and Domesday Book stands like a beacon signalling across the centuries that these signs are not to be taken at face value.

The economic growth of medieval Europe cannot be thought of, therefore, as something that began in the eleventh century with the revival of Italian maritime activity and the renewal of the urban life that languished after the fall of Rome. What emerged at that period was a superstructure whose foundations struck deep into the Dark Ages. Behind the reappearance of familiar landmarks lay centuries of experiment and innovation, unexpected setbacks, and unprecedented changes. And by the eleventh century the

[12] Georges Duby, *Rural Economy and Country Life in the Medieval West* (translated by Cynthia Postan. Edward Arnold, 1968.
[13] *Economic History Review*, 2nd ser., vol. xxvi, no. i (1963), 196–8.
[14] Duby, *op. cit.*, p. 109.
[15] *Ibid.*, p. 15.

luxury trades had begun to reassert themselves. Soon they began to exert their dominating influence over commercial and industrial development and land use. The market they served, however, was minute: a clear indication that the wealth of the community was being concentrated more decisively than for many years into the hands of the landowning classes. In a world of peasant farmers what else but land shortage, working insidiously through the economic system by way of rising rents, could have brought that about? The colonial period was obviously running into difficulties, if not drawing to a close. In these circumstances, the resurgent towns, the thriving export industries, and the ebullient merchant classes, thrusting their way to a blameless and even to an honoured and respected place in the social hierarchy, were not for many people, perhaps not for most, the splendid auguries of economic progress that they are commonly taken to be.

A wit once remarked that the Dark Ages were not so dark for the barbarians. When the history of these obscure centuries comes to be written we may very well find that he was right.

Seventh-Century England in Bede and the Early Laws

Seventh-century England is poorly served by literary sources. Consequently historians are compelled to recover what they can from its material remains. The application of modern technology to these remains has yielded results so remarkable that its promise is even more brilliant than its achievement. But there is a severe limit to what can be revealed by studying the material remains of a past age. There are questions about the past that we can only answer, if at all, by turning to the literary evidence, however inadequate it may be. This article is an attempt to take the two most familiar and well-respected of the literary sources for seventh-century English history and to examine them without sidelong glances at what was going on abroad at the time, or upon the Celtic fringes, and without reference to what the anthropologists have taught us to expect as a result of their knowledge of societies whose development, so they assure us, was at very much the same stage.

When Augustine landed in Kent, in 597, the Romans had been gone for two centuries and the mass immigration of the English, which may have started a generation or so after the Roman withdrawal, was virtually over. If we are to have any success in re-creating something of the social and economic life of the England that Augustine entered, then it is to Bede and the earliest laws that we must turn.

Bede finished his ecclesiastical history in 731, which was well over a century after the death of Augustine. But Bede's England was still full of Roman relics. Cities and temples, bridges and paved roads, ruinous though they may have been, bore witness in Bede's day to the endurance of the symbols of Roman rule.[1] There was even an earthwork surmounted by a palisade of logs, attributed by Bede to the work of Severus, which in Bede's day still traversed the northern frontier of what had been Roman Britain. Certainly Bede's description of it suggests that he, or someone whose witness he trusted, had seen what was left of it.[2] But there was more than visible evidence for Bede to use. He himself has testified to his use of records and of what we should call oral evidence and he called 'traditio maiorum' or folk memory.[3]

In particular, he used statistics. We do not expect to look to Bede for

---

[1] Bede I, 11. All references are to *Baedae Opera Historica*, ed. C. Plummer (Oxford, 1896).
[2] *Ibid.*, I, 5.

statistics; and indeed statistics are not an integral part of his ecclesiastical history. But he does not shrink from using them. He tells us, on the basis of a cited authority, how long and wide the mainland is. The Anglo-Saxon Chronicle gives us the same well-rounded figures. He also tells us how long the coastline is. Here too he cites authority. But the Anglo-Saxon Chronicle does not follow suit. It omits this interesting and possibly significant item of information. These lengths are all calculated in terms of miles.[4] Bede then tells us, incidentally, how big certain districts are. He does not tell us about them all.[5] And no obvious system appears to govern his choice. These he calculates in terms of households. The southern kingdom of Mercia consists of 5,000 households. Sussex is a land of 7,000 households. The Isle of Wight has a measurement (*mensura*) of 1,200 households. Ely is a district of about 600 households: '*regio familiarum circiter sexcentarum*'.[6]

We are never sure whether the household is a real one, in the sense that we are being told by Bede that there are in fact about 600 families living in Ely; or a notional one, in the sense that we are being told that 600 families could live there. Furthermore, *mensura* in the Isle of Wight entry suggests assessment rather than census. Whatever the significance of these figures, and Bede never tells us how he came by them, we can be quite sure that Bede has access to statistics about people as well as to geographical data about distances. When he quotes such figures Bede is likely to add, in parenthesis, some reservation about them such as 'so they say', or 'according to English reckoning', which seems to imply a degree of confidence in them which is less than perfect. Nevertheless some of the figures Bede quotes we can find in the Tribal Hidage; and unless we can push the date for the Tribal Hidage well back in time, Bede's figures suggest that the compilation of statistical returns in terms of a uniformly acceptable formula was carried out very early indeed in English history.[7] Who agreed the household formula? Who calculated the household assessments? And what political pressure, transcending lesser boundaries, generated the sedulous interest that lies behind these investigations?

Bede calls England remote.[8] But his history is full of journeyings. Augustine comes over to convert the heathen English, then travels to Arles, where he is consecrated archbishop of England, returns to England, sends messengers to Rome to apprise the Pope of the success of his missionary work and

---

[3] *Ibid.*, V, 24.

[4] *Ibid.*, I, 1. See also the preface to the Anglo-Saxon Chronicle. *English Historical Documents*, ed. D. Whitelock (1968), vol. 1, no. i, p. 138.

[5] C. Hart, 'The Tribal Hidage' in *Transactions of the Royal Historical Society*, 5th ser., vol. 21 (1971), p. 146, sets out in detail Bede's curious choice of examples.

[6] Mercia: Bede III, 24; Sussex: *ibid.*, IV, 13; IOW: *ibid.*, IV, 14 (16); Ely: *ibid.*, IV, 17 (19).

[7] Hart, *ut supra*. The Isle of Wight is reckoned at 600 hides in 'The Tribal Hidage' and at 1,200 in Bede, which suggests that Bede's source was independent of 'The Tribal Hidage'. Hart, pp. 134, 146.

[8] Bede I, 8.

to seek the Pope's advice. The Pope responds: another journey by a messenger; and then writes to the bishop of Arles, adjuring him to welcome Augustine should he happen to drop in: '*ad vos venire contigerit*'.[9] The context and the language suggest a casual encounter and invite a colloquial rendering. The Pope was Gregory the Great, celebrated amongst other things for his facetious remarks about English slaves in Rome: not Angles but angels. The slaves had come from north of York; and the story reinforces the impression that Bede conveys, of easy and regular communications, by suggesting that merchants as well as messengers were familiar with the routes that linked the regions of England to one another and to the continent.[10] At this time, according to Bede, girls of noble birth were often packed off to France for their education;[11] and some French girls, as we know from Bede and other sources, found husbands over here.

Many of these journeys were not simply across the sea but round the coast. Perhaps that is why it was so easy for Bede to find out how long the coast-line was. When Northumbria was in turmoil after Edwin's murder, Pauline, who was Augustine's co-adjutor in evangelising England, returned from Northumbria to Kent by sea. In the circumstances it is possible that the sea journey was less risky than a journey overland. But when Edwin's daughter returned from Kent to marry Oswy, she too travelled by sea.[12] Nobody apparently thought it too risky a journey for Oswy's bride to undertake. London at that time, according to Bede, was a market for masses of people who were attracted to it by land and sea: '*multorum emporium populorum*' is his phrase.[13] Bede was a man to use words carefully. He uses the word *populus*, not the word *gens*, because he has in mind ordinary English people, not men of many races. He is not saying that London was a cosmopolitan centre of trade; merely that it was a big market to which Englishmen came by land and sea. When he wants to distinguish races, Bede uses the word *gens*, in this case members of the English race: '*nostram, id est Anglorum, gentem*' as he puts it in another place.[14]

These are all successful journeys. We must search Bede very carefully indeed for references to ambush and piracy, ransom, injury and death, in connection with all this travel. There is very little committing of souls to God before such journeys are undertaken and no reference to will-making or other material precautions commonly taken by those who are about to face notorious perils.

In telling the story of how the heathen English were converted to the true faith, Bede provides us with a great deal of information unintentionally

9 *Ibid.*, I, 28.
10 *Ibid.*, II, 1.
11 *Ibid.*, III, 8.
12 *Ibid.*, II, 20; III, 15.
13 *Ibid.*, II, 3.
14 *Ibid.*, II, 1.

conveyed, and with a number of impressions which darken the colours of his triumphal portrayal of the outcome of the Christian mission.

In Bede we can watch the common language of the people being transformed. When the Britons lapsed into heresy after the withdrawal of the Romans, Germanus of Auxerre was dispatched to win them back for Roman Christianity. He addressed great crowds of people, according to Bede, and had marked success in his work. Bede does not tell us of interpreters. Germanus evidently had no difficulty with the language of the people and seems to have gone about his business amongst them without experiencing any problems in making himself understood.[15] Nor should that surprise us. It is not very likely that someone who qualified for such work, a member of a deeply Romanised oecumenical movement, should find it difficult to make himself understood in a country in which Roman rule had prevailed for 400 years and in which the memory of that rule was still fresh in everybody's mind. After the English settlements, however, things were very different. The problem was no longer one of redeeming heretics in a population which was still familiar with things Roman but of converting an alien population of heathens. Indeed the world into which Gregory the Great proposed to pitchfork Augustine and his companions was so very different from the one that Germanus had encountered and Gildas had excoriated that Augustine's party took fright, shrinking from the ordeal of treating with a barbarous, savage and mistrustful people – 'barbaram, feram, incredulamque gentem', whose language, according to Bede, none of them could understand.[16] Possibly they exaggerated the linguistic difficulties in order to strengthen their case for being excused from undertaking their mission. But Gregory took them seriously enough. He did not tell them that they would find plenty of people where they were going who spoke or still understood the old language in which Germanus preached. Instead he provided them with interpreters.[17]

Gregory's letter to the members of Augustine's party is notable for what it does not say. It offers no reassurance to faint-hearted adventurers. It does not attempt to stiffen their resolve by encouraging them to believe that when they land in England they will find British communities to shelter them, British interpreters to speak for them and British Christians to understand and help them in their work. Gregory's letter speaks only of duty and the promise of everlasting rewards when their labours are done. It is the kind of letter that commanders write in war-time when they are sending subordinates upon dangerous missions from which they have very little hope of returning. If there had been subterranean cells of believers who had survived the holocaust of the English settlements, Gregory would certainly have heard of them or from them. England, as we have seen, was by no means cut off from the continent. The Frankish interpreters provided by Gregory knew

15 Ibid., I, 17, 21.
16 Ibid., I, 23.
17 Ibid., I, 25.

the language of the people of England presumably because they knew the country. Nor should we forget that Aethelberht of Kent was himself married to a daughter of the king of Paris. But Gregory's letter, and indeed his subsequent correspondence with Augustine, tell us by implication of the total destruction of the religious and linguistic heritage of the Roman and post-Roman past.[18]

Augustine's subsequent adventures, once he had steeled himself and fortified his companions to accept their fate, did nothing to mitigate the overwhelming sense of isolation that he felt in early English society. Augustine and his companions were well-received by Aethelberht. In Bede's narrative we can feel their relief at not being chopped up and boiled for dinner. When Augustine wrote to Gregory for further instructions, he dropped barbarous and savage in speaking of the English and called them uncouth instead. It is necessary, he tells Gregory, to provide guidance for this uncouth race of Englishmen – 'rudi Anglorum genti'.[19] But conversation with Aethelberht can only have deepened Augustine's sense of isolation. Bede tells us that Aethelberht knew all about the Christian religion because his wife was a Christian. Indeed he tells us that her parents had only agreed to the marriage on condition that she was allowed to practise her religion with the help of the chaplain they sent with her to England.[20] And yet he heightens the drama of Augustine's first meeting with Aethelberht by making out that Aethelberht treated Augustine to a pantomime performance in which he cast himself in the role of an ignorant and nervously suspicious country bumpkin with an hospitable nature but an uncertain disposition. Aethelberht welcomed Augustine, according to Bede, as a traveller in strange spiritual wares which he was at liberty to offer to anyone who showed an interest in them, and did so without revealing his own knowledge of what Augustine was offering and without reassuring Augustine by telling him that there were amongst his subjects those of British descent who still practised the rituals of the religion Augustine had come to propagate. Once settled in Canterbury, Augustine and his companions soon discovered the old church in which Aethelberht's queen worshipped. But elsewhere they found the churches in ruins; for Bede tells us that they had to be restored.[21] There can be no more eloquent comment upon the absence of interest in Christianity than that. Aethelberht was clearly no persecutor of heterodoxy. If any of his subjects had professed a faith in Christianity, Aethelberht with his Christian wife was scarcely in a position to place obstacles in the way of his doing so openly. Nor would the churches have been ruinous if there had been many wanting to use them for the purposes for which they had been built. Obviously few or none, apart from Aethelberht's wife and her entourage, cared in the least for

18 Ibid., I, 23.
19 Ibid., I, 27: section viii.
20 Ibid., I, 25.
21 Ibid., I, 26.

the consolations of what everyone else regarded as an obscure and arcane religion.[22]

The controversy over the dating of Easter confirms this impression of a society transformed by the English settlements, not merely in Kent but far more extensively. The British church differed from the church of Rome in its timing of Easter and Augustine made strenuous efforts to bring the British Christians into line with Rome. He therefore summoned the bishops of the nearest British province to a conference. And the nearest British province turned out to be so far away that the conference had to be held on the borders of the West Saxons and the Hwicci.[23] There was no coherent and articulate British ecclesiastical presence closer at hand than that.

In short, Bede's impression, from the evidence at his disposal, was that by the time that Augustine had been dispatched to convert the English, a comprehensive revolution had taken place throughout the most populous regions of the mainland. The language with which previous generations of papal emissaries had had no difficulty was now gone. The Christianity which had been a prominent feature, if not a leading characteristic, of British cultural life, had been stamped out. Can we believe that the indigenous population had survived when we find that faith, and even more significantly, language, had been destroyed?

Changes on such a scale presuppose a bloody and destructive phase of conquest and supersession. But Bede's England appears to show few signs of it. There were border clashes and palace revolutions. But pillaging and burning, wholesale devastation of parts of the land and its people by marauding bands or invading armies, appear to have been confined to a few exceptional cases.[24] When Bede speaks of those parts of the country under Edwin's jurisdiction as being places where a woman could carry her new-born baby across the land from sea to sea without fear of harm, he seems to be reflecting the essentially tranquil atmosphere in which the work of conversion went forward.[25] We seem to sense that tranquillity in Bede's description of how the missionaries were received by the various kings of England. Wherever they go, Augustine and his companions are received with civility and respect. The kings with whom they treat display none of the signs of stress that one might expect them to display if the land were under constant threat of invasion or disruption. Wherever they go, seeking permission to evangelise,

---

[22] James Campbell, *Essays in Anglo-Saxon History*, 1986, pp. 72–3, takes a different view.

[23] Bede II, 2.

[24] *Ibid.*, IV, 12, 24 (26); see also F. M. Stenton: *Anglo-Saxon England*, 3rd edn (1971), pp. 69–70, 80ff. Ine cap. 13 para. 1 speaks of groups of delinquents as thieves, if there are fewer than 7; as marauders, if there are fewer than 35; and as armies if there are more than that. When there were breaches of the peace in the Middle Ages these were the range of numbers commonly involved; and the Middle Ages, with lapses, were not notably unquiet. All references to Anglo-Saxon laws, unless otherwise stated, are to *The Laws of the Earliest English Kings*, ed. F. L. Attenborough (Cambridge, 1922).

[25] Bede II, 16.

Augustine and his companions receive the same response as they got from Aethelberht in Kent. They are invariably given permission to peddle their spiritual panaceas and to make such converts as they can. They are allowed to exert whatever powers of persuasion they possess. But they are always warned against going beyond persuasion. They are always told that they may not use threat or force. And if they meet with success then no limit is ever prescribed to the extent to which they are to be allowed to be successful. Nothing is ever said or implied which could be construed to mean that success beyond a certain point might jeopardise established practices of religion and might therefore constitute some sort of provocation. We hear nothing from Bede about an organised and entrenched pagan priesthood, bitterly resentful of threats to its professional and social standing. According to Bede, who was no friend to paganism, the rulers of England responded to the challenge of missionary endeavour in an imperturbably liberal and pragmatic spirit.[26]

Without in the least meaning to do so, Bede gives us the strong impression that the basic needs of English communities, so far as religious practices are concerned, were very satisfactorily met by the pagan rites they observed. Without an aggressively antagonistic pagan priesthood to contend with, however, it was not difficult for the Christians to achieve a measure of success in their missionary work. But in the absence of a well-organised parish and diocesan administration with which to consolidate their advances, the Christians found it equally difficult to hold any position they may have occupied. In such circumstances, conversion to Christianity, according to the testimony recorded by Bede, seems to have been very much a matter of *cujus regio, ejus religio*. And relapse from Christianity seems to have been natural and inevitable as soon as a dynasty changed.[27] When Augustine, and later Bede, report that whole peoples have been converted, we may take it, therefore, that what is really meant is that the king and some of the leading families have embraced Christianity and have done so without prejudice to what may happen should that king's successor prove to be a pagan, happy to restore customary and familiar practices.

In striking and discreditable contrast to the behaviour of the pagan kings with whom they came into contact, according to Bede's version of events, was the attitude and conduct of the missionaries. Augustine himself was an unpropitious choice as papal emissary. His faith may have been profound; but it certainly was not informed. The problems upon which he sought guidance from the Pope were problems about which no professional Christian of his standing and experience should have required instruction.[28] Moreover Bede shows him to have been tactless and boorish to a degree. He bragged egregiously about his missionary successes and had to be called to account by

26 *Ibid.*, II, 9; III, 19, 21.
27 *Ibid.*, II, 5, 15, 20; III, 1, 30.
28 *Ibid.*, I, 27. Thus Augustine asks about the relationships between bishops and clergy; about consanguinity; and about baptism.

the Pope for doing so.[29] When he met the British bishops he needlessly antagonised them by failing to get up and greet them when they arrived; and then antagonised them once more by threatening them with violence when they demurred to his demands.[30] The threats are very interesting in the context of our continuing doubts as to the nature and extent of the English settlements; for what Augustine did was to threaten to set the English upon the bishops and their followers: a clear indication that the English enjoyed a formidable reputation for massacre and devastation. But in fact Augustine set the tone for future treatment of everyone who got in the way of the Christian juggernaut once it had started to roll forward. In this he was stoutly supported by the Pope. Gregory recommended thrashing as a condign punishment for those who robbed churches, at a time when Aethelberht's laws show that English society had no place for corporal punishment;[31] and Gregory instructed Augustine to insist upon forbidden degrees of kinship in marriage which were, as he himself acknowledged, unknown in English practice.[32] These were portents, foreshadowing worse to come.

The laws of the earliest English kings do in fact seem to bear out the impression that Bede conveys of an England at once more peaceful and more receptive to ideas which were out of the ordinary than we might expect it to have been; and certainly more receptive than it would be once the Christian message had started to spread and Christian notables, by capturing the machinery of government, were able to exert repressive authority over the communities of England.

The earliest English laws to survive all survive from the seventh century. When that century ends we lose all evidence of law-making until Alfred's time, nearLy two centuries later. The seventh-century survivors represent the legislative achievements of four kings, Three of them were kings of Kent. The fourth was Ine of Wessex. The earliest of these laws are the laws of Aethelberht of Kent. They were issued during the lifetime of Augustine, as the century began, and reflect the pagan society that Augustine was sent to evangelise. The rest are clustered together in the last quarter of the century and appear to register the growing influence of the Christian church upon society.

All the Kentish laws we possess come down to us as a result of the survival of a twelfth-century collection of Anglo-Saxon laws known as the *Textus Roffensis*.[33] But Ine's laws survive because they were preserved by Alfred. When Alfred turned his attention to problems of law-making he drew up a code which was intended, so he tells us, to incorporate all that was best in the legislation of the kings of the past, suitably modified and revised so as to

29 *Ibid.*, I, 31.
30 *Ibid.*, II, 2.
31 *Ibid.*, I, 27, problem 3.
32 *Ibid.*, problem 5.
33 For a brief account. see the introduction to *English Historical Documents* Part II, *ut supra*.

take account of current needs and conditions.[34] He singled out for special mention the work of Aethelberht of Kent, to whom Bede also paid tribute, and the work of Ine and Offa. Ine's work survives because Alfred took what he saw fit to preserve of Ine's law-making and tacked it on as a supplement to the laws which he promulgated in his own name. The laws of Aethelberht and Offa were not given like treatment. But Aethelberht's laws were not neglected by Alfred. We can tell that they were not because we can compare an independent text of Aethelberht's laws with what we find in Alfred. And we can find so much of Aethelberht's substantive contribution to Alfred actually incorporated in the laws that Alfred issued in his own name that we can well understand why Alfred did not bother to preserve the text of Aethelberht's laws as he preserved the text of Ine's. To have done so would have been mere antiquarianism from Alfred's point of view. Offa does not survive in an independent text. We cannot tell, therefore, what if anything of Offa's law-making survives in Alfred's laws. But the example of Aethelberht suggests that Offa's work has not been lost even though we may be unable to recognise it.[35]

Aethelberht's world, as we perceive it in his laws, is a thoroughly pagan world. We may be forgiven for doubting that when we see that his first care is for the church, which he grants stiff terms of compensation for robbery. In particular, he grants to bishops who have been robbed even stiffer terms of compensation than he requires for himself.[36] But that tribute of recognition paid Aethelberht entirely ignores the church and its teachings thereafter. His decrees about matrimony, for example, are frankly non-Christian. Wives are bought and sold in Aethelberht's Kent without heed to the doctrines of the church. It is true that the financial aspects of matrimony are easily thrown into undue prominence by legislation because secular law deals with material and not with spiritual bonds. But Aethelberht is not concerned with bride-prices. A man who cuckolds another must get a replacement wife for the man he has wronged and pay for her with his own money. The wretched husband, having been wronged once, is thus possibly wronged a second time; for the law appears to give him no choice: he must presumably take what he is offered; and what he is offered can only be what the man who cuckolded him is minded to provide for him, or can get, or perhaps can afford.[37] The feelings of the women concerned may not appear to be considered; but divorce in certain circumstances is made easier for them than it will be for very many bitter Christian centuries to come. A bought wife may leave her husband, should she so desire, taking with her the children and

[34] For Alfred's preamble, see Attenborough, *ut supra*.
[35] It may be that Offa's laws consisted of endorsing the code of practice recommended in the report of the legates to Pope Hadrian upon their visit to England in 786. There are similarities between Alfred's laws and the capitulary incorporated into that report. See S. Keynes and M. Lapidge, *Alfred the Great* (1983), p. 305, note 5.
[36] Aethelberht caps. 1 and 4.
[37] *Ibid.*, cap. 31.

half her husband's goods;[38] and a childless wife may do likewise but without the material considerations that a wife and mother is entitled to claim.[39]

Essentially these laws consist of schedules of compensation payable by those who do wrong. And doing wrong in Aethelberht's world means doing material damage. Hence making amends is governed by the insurance principle of restitution. Nowhere are the laws disfigured and made vindictive by a sense of sin. There are only two sorts of crime. There are the crimes, like wounding, for which compensation is fixed and a tariff of rates can be set down. And there are the crimes, like robbery and murder, for which compensation depends upon the value of the property stolen or upon the status, and hence the value, of the person killed. For killing there is no refinement of definition and hence mitigation of responsibility. No allowance is made, except perhaps in one case,[40] for pleas of self-defence, manslaughter or inadvertence. Nor is there any need for mitigation of liability. If you kill you pay; and if you steal you pay. And what you pay is calculated to make full restitution for the damage done. Restitution is made in money and goods. Money circulates in Aethelberht's Kent. Aethelberht is quite clear about that. A murderer must pay the wergeld he is liable for in money and in property which is in a fit state to be used for the purpose.[41] And contemporary deeds appear to confirm the impression conveyed by Aethelberht's laws by testifying that money changes hands when property is sold.[42]

These laws are not arbitrary proclamations of will dictated by the king. They are the result of deliberations in which the leading members of the community are consulted, contribute their advice, and finally assent to what is proposed. Aethelberht did not need Romanist theory or Beaumanoir's speculations to appreciate that power must have a broad base to endure.[43] Aethelberht's laws mention no assembly. But the king has lieges whom he calls together: for those who molest them when they are in session are singled out for exceptional damages.[44] These lieges are unlikely to have included representatives of the church. Such was the tenor of the laws to which they assented that it is most improbable than any representative of the church would have had any part in approving them.

When we turn to the rest of the surviving laws of Kent, in particular to the laws of Wihtred, we enter a very different world. The preamble to Wihtred's laws tells us that they are the work of an assembly in which the archbishop, the bishop of Rochester and other representatives of the church who are not specified, unanimously assented, with the lay members, to the laws issued in

---

[38] *Ibid.*, cap. 79. If the husband wants the children, she gets much less. His wishes take priority: *ibid.*, cap. 80.

[39] *Ibid.*, cap. 81.

[40] *Ibid.*, cap. 86: a servant who has committed no offence.

[41] *Ibid.*, cap. 30.

[42] *English Historical Documents*, nos. 55 and 62.

[43] T. F. T. Plucknett, *Legislation of Edward I* (Oxford, 1949), p. 4 and note 2.

[44] Aethelberht cap. 2.

the king's name. The church is not merely an unmistakable presence in this legislative body: to judge by what follows it is a dominating influence. Henceforth, it seems, the laws of Kent are to supplement the insurance principle of restitution, in dealing with crime, with the spiritual principle of retribution. Excommunication, flogging, the death penalty and the threat of being sold into slavery oversea, all make their first appearance in Wihtred's laws. We can tell that this is probably their first appearance because the laws of Hlothhere and Eadric, which precede Wihtred's laws by a decade or so, continue to breathe the pagan spirit of Aethelberht's age.

With Wihtred's laws, Christianity ratifies its ascendancy. The church is offered extravagant privileges. Sunday observance becomes a matter for lay enforcement. Fast days are given legal sanction. Marriage is redefined. Unions are illicit if they are unconsecrated; or if they are bigamous; or if they are within the forbidden degrees. We are in a Christian world in which it is no longer enough to compensate victims for material damage; for sin requires savage expiation if it is not to prevail; and in a Christian world the occasions of sin multiply endlessly. By the end of the seventh century retribution had begun to supplant restitution as the leading principle of Kentish juris-prudence.

It would be wrong, however, to give the impression that in pre-Christian England men refrained from taking frightful revenge when they were pro-voked and even when they were not. The vendetta, of which we hear something in the laws, doubtless made violent antagonisms even more viol-ent and turned ordinary grievances into irreconcileable feuds. Nevertheless it is easy to exaggerate the insidiousness of the feud and the dedication with which it was pursued. Even in Beowulf, which depicts a swashbuckling society in an heroic age when giants strode the earth, money payments requited woundings and even death except when, as with Grendel, feelings ran too deep for material compensation.[45] And the laws were plainly an attempt to rationalise an existing system of compensation by putting the king's authority behind an agreed tariff of payments, thus perhaps making it easier for everyone to substitute restitution for revenge.

To some extent the tariffs appear to have succeeded. Perhaps they merely ratified prevailing opinions and sentiments. At any rate, the early laws seem to tell of family ties and family loyalties which are failing to respond to the demands they were normally expected to honour. People have to be told to do things that nobody would expect to be told to do if family responsibilities were being shouldered as willingly as they would have been if the vendetta system were flourishing rather than decaying. Aethelberht has to tell a murderer's family that it must pay half the compensation due if the murderer himself flees the country.[46] Hlothhere and Eadric have to tell the family of a fatherless minor that its mother must look after the child and its father's

45 Beowulf I, 469–71; 148–158.
46 Aethelberht cap. 23.

family must look after its property.[47] Ine has to remind the families of widows with children that they ought to maintain them. Moreover he feels under some obligation to spell out what that means: 6s per year for each child and a cow in summer and an ox in winter.[48] What the laws do not say is as interesting, in this connection, as what they do say. They do not condemn the damage done by those who pursue their vendettas with excessive exuberance. There is no tariff of surcharges payable by those who go beyond reasonable limits in exacting revenge for what their kinsmen may have suffered. In these early laws the kinship system appears to be made the subject of legislation because it is not working; not because it is working all too well. We hear about the failure of family concern, not about the excesses committed in its name.

Thus early English paganism, when we examine it through the partisan eyes of Bede, supplementing his testimony with that of the earliest laws, reveals an approach to social problems which is not so much in conflict with what we may perhaps call the Christian approach as utterly at variance with it. Between these two ideologies there could be no compromise because there were no points of contact. In religious matters, paganism seems to put the individual first, not the personal convictions of any particular king and his entourage. Consequently persecution in the name of truth or uniformity of opinion was unheard of, if we may take Bede at his word, until the Christian party managed to seize control of political power. Pagan jurisprudence also put the welfare of the individual first. Compensation attempts to put the victim back on his feet, or give his family a chance to recover from what might otherwise have been an overwhelming blow. Punishment of the wrong-doer, which progressively displaced compensation in legal thought and practice, revenges the victim by asserting the claims of society against those who break the rules. But it does nothing to help the victim or his family. We are bound to conclude, therefore, that as Christianity and retributive justice spread throughout the land, the individual, with his personal needs, was crowded out of consideration by the increasingly vociferous claims of church and state.

Compensation for injury, since it varied with the social standing of the victim, called for a tariff of rates which, in Aethelberht's laws, amounted to a survey of the social structure of early seventh-century Kent. There appear to have been three classes with property and status in Kentish society at that time: nobles, who were doubtless the leading men upon whom the king depended for advice and support; freemen; and ceorls. The distinction between nobles and freemen is unmistakable. But there is less to distinguish freemen from ceorls. In some contexts, ceorl is synonymous with husband or head of household. In matrimonial cases the husband is called a ceorl.[49] In

---

[47] Hlothhere and Eadric cap. 6.
[48] Ine cap. 38.
[49] Aethelberht cap. 85.

other contexts, the laws seem to be concerned, sometimes with freemen and sometimes with ceorls. Thus restraining a freeman, laying bonds upon him, as the laws have it, incurs a penalty of 20s, presumably because it is an outrageous violation of his *mundbyrd* or sanctity of person to impair his independence in that way.[50] But a ceorl's *mundbyrd* is 6s.[51] It is also the amount payable to a ceorl if one of his living-in servants is murdered.[52] The ordinary wergeld payable when one man kills another is 100s.[53] It is very probably a ceorl's wergeld. If anyone kills the king's smith he is to find such a wergeld.[54] The king's smith is a skilled man. But his skill is not a professional one. Moreover he is a household servant. But he is the king's servant; and the association must raise him socially. It is unlikely, however, to have raised him higher than the lowest level of the free classes. Thus it is very likely that early seventh-century Kentish society distinguished nobles or magnates from others whose landed possessions were not comparable with theirs; and from others again who possessed no more, on average, than a competence, and who doubtless made up the great majority of the peasant landholders of the kingdom: the Anglo-Saxon counterparts of the virgators and half-virgators of a later age.

Support for the view that the free classes were differentiated into three grades, comes from the clause listing the penalties payable for violating the *mund* of widows. There were four classes of widows. The most exalted class consisted of the widows of nobles. We can be sure of that because the laws tell us that it did. Widows of the second class were presumably the widows of freemen; and widows of the third class, the widows of ceorls. The laws do not actually say who qualifies for membership of these two classes. Aethelberht obviously assumes that everyone whom it concerns will know already whose widows belong to which class. And the same is true of widows of the fourth class. These widows, however, occupy places at the base of the social pyramid: for there are no widows in a lower class than they are.[55] We shall come across them in another connection. If they are correctly identified as the widows of men who stand socially below the level of the free, then they strengthen the presumption that the free classes are divisible into three.

The penalties incurred for breach of the *mund* of widows are all high. The nobleman's widow has to be compensated at the same rate as the king has to be when his *mund* is violated.[56] Evidently widows were considered to be a vulnerable class. Their protection has obviously been given much thought. When we find, therefore, that widows of the third class are to receive twice

---

50 *Ibid.*, cap. 24.
51 *Ibid.*, cap. 15.
52 *Ibid.*, cap. 25.
53 *Ibid.*, cap. 21.
54 *Ibid.*, cap. 7.
55 *Ibid.*, cap. 75.
56 *Ibid.*, cap. 8.

the compensation payable to ceorls for breach of *mund* we are not entitled to conclude that they could not possibly be the widows of ceorls.

Kentish society in Aethelberht's time was certainly complex; and the complexity of social grading to be found amongst its free members was more than matched by the baroque convolutions of grading to be found amongst its dependent classes.

Below the free classes come the *laets* and the slaves. There are three classes of *laets*; and killing a *laet* incurs liabilities ranging from 40s to 80s depending upon his value.[57] *Laets* of the highest class are thus clearly differentiated from ceorls without being hopelessly distanced from them. And below the *laets* come the slaves. There are no less than three categories of slaves. We are told about them in the clauses that deal with seduction. The king has female slaves: seducing a female slave of the top class incurs 50s worth of penalty; seducing a grinding slave incurs 25s worth of penalty; and seducing a third-class slave 12s worth.[58] Ceorls keep female slaves too. They may belong to any of the three classes; and their value, though naturally much lower than that of the king's slaves is also laid down.[59]

The laws also consider the dependent classes from other points of view. We have already been told that the king employs slaves to grind for him. No doubt all the laborious work in the king's household is done by slaves. But some work requires more delicacy and even refinement of touch, even in slaves; and some is more skilled than laborious. The only artisans to get separate mention in the laws are smiths; smiths need assistants; and the female grinder who is the king's slave is a second-class slave. Her work is presumably not wholly unskilled as it would be if her job were grinding corn. Hence she is probably a knife or sword grinder. Ceorls, according to the laws, sometimes employ loaf-eaters; for when one is killed there is a penalty to pay.[60] Loaf-eater suggests a living-in servant, a man who eats at his master's board: in short one of his *famuli*. In addition there are many servants in husbandry who do not live-in; for some of them marry, which is something that living-in servants never do. We hear about their matrimonial affairs because their wives attract other men; and Aethelberht has to decide upon the compensation to which their husbands are entitled when they yield to temptation.[61] Here, surely we have the men whose wives, when they have the misfortune to lose their husbands, become the fourth-class widows about whom we have already heard. No doubt many servants in husbandry were full-time employees. But the grading of the *laets* strongly suggests a range of occupations, from full-time employment at the lowest level to part-time paid work at the highest, the part-time work being undertaken by men who were

---

[57] *Ibid.*, cap. 26.
[58] *Ibid.*, caps 10, 11.
[59] *Ibid.*, cap. 16.
[60] *Ibid.*, cap. 25. See Attenborough, *op. cit.*, note p. 177.
[61] *Ibid.*, cap. 85.

compelled to supplement the yield of an inadequate small-holding with the remuneration of a wage-earner.

The *laets* may not have been the only dependent group whose members sometimes possessed sufficient means for a more or less independent existence. Even the slaves, or some members of one or other of the three categories of slave, appear to have possessed property; for slaves who steal are required by Aethelberht to pay back twice the value of what they stole.[62] Aethelberht does not suggest that their masters should pay on their behalf. He assumes that slaves will be able to meet their own liabilities; or perhaps it would be more exact to say that he does not assume, as a matter of course, that they will not be able to do so.

There are no Welshmen in these early Kentish laws. It is possible that the classes of dependent farm-labourers whom Aethelberht identifies as *laets* were, in fact, subjugated Britons. But if that is what they were, then we should expect to find, in laws as circumstantial as Aethelberht's, some reference, in another connection, to the subordinate status in the new order occupied by more exalted members of the British race who had managed to retain some remnants of former estates and some claim to rank and quality even though the invasions had swept away so many landmarks. But Aethelberht makes no provision for survivors with social pretensions; and his silence is surely ominous.

This mass of legislation called for, and indeed implied, courts of law in which evidence could be heard and judgements given. We hear nothing about courts of justice in Aethelberht's laws. But we hear about them indirectly. In several places, for example, Bede mentions the existence of royal country seats (*villa regia*), as if it were a perfectly normal practice for Anglo-Saxon kings to have retreats scattered about their realms;[63] and Aethelberht has to provide for those occasions when he feasts in the homes of his nobles, things get out of hand and offences are committed.[64] Aethelberht stipulates what are agreed to be suitable fines in such circumstances. Evidently the king goes on progress round the country; and when he does so, what could be more natural than that he should dispense justice? Indeed his interest in justice is far from abstract. Justice has immense political importance; and its fiscal benefits are not to be despised. Many compensation payments have to be accompanied by fines payable to the king. Murder normally costs 100s. But when murder is done, the king must have a fine of 50s.[65] The king has his own estates, as his nobles have theirs; but his revenues are supplemented by the profits of justice. It is very much in his interest to provide courts and judges so that the work of providing justice can go on when he himself is too busy to be in all the places where justice is needed. Three-quarters of a

62 *Ibid.*, cap. 90.
63 Bede II, 14; III, 22.
64 Aethelberht cap. 3.
65 *Ibid.*, cap. 6.

century later, in the laws of Hlothhere and Eadric, we shall hear of judges and arbitrators and of the processes of compurgation and vouching to warranty. But we are not entitled to assume that these innovations were introduced by them.

The laws of Hlothhere and Eadric do not follow on from those of Aethelberht. There has been a good deal of legislative activity since Aethelberht's time; for Hlothhere and Eadric claim that they are simply adding to the work of previous kings of Kent.[66] How they added to that work is suggestive; for Hlothhere and Eadric increased the number of occasions upon which the king collected a fine when his subjects collected compensatory payments for some wrong done to them. We may safely assume that the fines about which we know from the laws that survive are not the sum total of all the fines that were imposed. It is not likely that the kings who ruled in Kent from the death of Aethelberht to the accession of Hlothhere and Eadric were indifferent to a source of revenue that was undoubtedly lucrative and may well have been growing. Certainly by Hlothhere's time we see a great deal more evidence of trade, in the laws, than we saw in Aethelberht's reign; and trade generates disputes by multiplying contacts. Thus London features in the laws of Hlothhere and Eadric. It did not rate a single mention in Aethelberht's laws, despite the fact that Aethelberht built London's first English cathedral.[67] But there was enough London trade by the third quarter of the century to create problems for the king of Kent; and it was then that we find the king providing machinery of justice for Kentish men buying and selling in London.[68] Nor was trade, by then, merely with London. Traders were coming over the border into Kent to such effect that Hlothhere and Eadric were obliged to regulate the terms upon which such traders could be accepted as guests.[69]

Kent was not fundamentally changed by this increasing activity. Nor does it appear to have been essentially altered by the advent of Christianity. The laws of Hlothhere and Eadric, though brief and therefore easy to misinterpret, nevertheless seem to breathe the spirit that informed the laws of Aethelberht. When we turn to Wihtred's laws, however, despite the fact that they follow closely upon those of Hlothhere and Eadric, we can tell at once that something has transformed the ethos of Kentish society. It is now, insofar as we can judge of such things from a set of laws, a priest-ridden society. Paganism has been fatally subverted; henceforth it will survive only underground. Bede tells us of interregnum between the death of Eadric and the accession of Wihtred.[70] Possibly irreversible changes took place during that savage interlude.

Of the other facets of Kentish society to which earlier laws have intro-

66 Hlothhere and Eadric preamble.
67 Bede II, 3.
68 Hlothhere and Eadric cap. 16.
69 Ibid., cap. 15.
70 Bede IV, 24(26).

duced us, Wihtred's legislation tells us little more than we knew already. Slaves who do wrong can be offered a choice between a fine and a flogging; thus confirming the hint in Aethelberht that some slaves have access to the means with which to earn their own living.[71] Other dependent farm-workers, according to Wihtred, are certainly in a position to pay their own fines. Should they work on Sundays, contrary to the wishes of their lords, or should they ride about their own business on Sundays, they will be expected to be able to compensate their lords with a fine.[72]

Three features of this law deserve notice. One is the grant by the king to lords of men of a penalty which either the church or the state might reasonably have claimed for itself. Can we perhaps perceive in this grant an indication of the existence of private jurisdiction; that is to say of a system which is already capable of assessing and levying fines on behalf of lords of men? Another feature of this law is the evidence it affords of the survival into the late seventh century of Aethelberht's *laets* with their dependent status but respectable wergelds. And the third is the glimpse we are vouchesafed, in Wihtred's laws, of humble peasants, hovering in a twilight world between slavery and freedom, who ride about the countryside, presumably on horses, when they are not working on their own account on their own land or another's.

So far the earliest English laws have given us no more than meagre and tantalising glimpses of the rural scene. We see the king and his nobles in them; the lesser but still well-to-do landholders; and the ordinary peasant-farmers. Below these, in an astounding variety of conditions of dependence, we see the labouring classes: some of them living-in servants; others married, with cottages and allotments or small-holdings, working for the richer farmers when they lacked the means with which to live of their own; and everywhere slaves: often perhaps no more than a handful in a village; many no doubt indistinguishable, except at law, from dependent cottagers; some respected as skilled artisans or better; others again hard to tell apart from the animals with which they worked.

With Ine's laws, however, the rural scene suddenly lights up. We are no longer in Kent. We have switched to Wessex where, however, rural conditions may have been very different. Alfred preserved those clauses of Ine's laws that survive presumably because they incorporated rulings about farm discipline that he intended to enforce wherever his writ ran. But nearly two centuries and a world of turbulence separate Alfred from Ine. We cannot, therefore, assume that Ine's Kentish contemporaries would have been as familiar with the farming scene that Ine's laws depict as Alfred's codification might have led us to believe they were.

In Ine's laws the ordinary ceorl lives in a home which is fenced about to prevent the intrusion of cattle. Anyone who neglects his fences, according to

---

[71] Wihtred caps 13 and 15.
[72] *Ibid.*, caps 9 and 10.

Ine, must expect damage for which the owners of the cattle cannot be held responsible. He alone must suffer the consequences of his own negligence.[73] Presumably the damage suffered is mainly to kitchen gardens round the house. Nearly three centuries before Ine, in a very different world, Germanus of Auxerre, who was helping the British bishops fight Pelagianism, lay with a broken leg in just such a house as Ine may have had in mind in this passage. According to Bede, who tells the story and may have seen very similar houses, such houses were thatched with reed and very inflammable. When fire swept through the houses standing round about, Germanus was saved by a miracle which spared the house in which he lay.[74]

In Ine's world, fields were fenced as well as homes. Ceorls with land to fence, whether it be common meadow or other land which is divided up between them, often find, says Ine, that some of them neglect to fence their section.[75] Evidently the field boundaries are divided into lengths and everyone who occupies land is given responsibility for a length which is doubtless proportionate to the size of his holding. In later centuries town walls will be manned for defence on similar principles.[76] When someone fails to maintain his section, so that straying cattle can enter the field, the result is damage to grass or common crops. In such circumstances Ine decrees that those who neglect their fences must compensate the others who have suffered loss; and those who have suffered loss may also claim from the owners of the cattle. If a beast breaks through a hedge, however, then anyone who finds it on his cornland may take it and kill it, returning hide and flesh to its owner.[77]

This clause appears to make cattle-owners culpable for something which, when their cattle wander into closes, they are not held liable for. But its main interest lies in showing us how the fields are arranged. Meadow is used in common by all. The beasts that may lawfully graze, wander at will within the fenced area of the meadow. But the arable land is set out differently. The arable field is fenced, but the cornland lies open. It is cultivated in severalty by the peasants: for the ceorl who finds a beast on his cornland may kill it.

By the end of the seventh century, in the heartland of England, we seem to see the open-field system that will dominate English agriculture for many centuries to come. It may dominate English agriculture; it will not monopolise it. Aethelberht, for example, has several references to fencing: fencing round dwellings and fencing in other places. But Kent is not to be compared to Wessex without better grounds for doing so than Aethelberht's references afford us.[78]

Ine has other aspects of farming upon which to legislate; aspects of farming which will become very familiar and characteristic later. Thus land such as

---

[73] Ine cap. 40.
[74] Bede I, 19.
[75] Ine cap. 42.
[76] F. W. Maitland, *Domesday Book and Beyond* (Cambridge, 1897), pp. 188–9.
[77] Ine cap. 42, para. 1.
[78] Aethelberht caps 27, 28, 29, 32.

the cornland that Ine has discussed is not necessarily held by the farmer and his family by an indefeasible title. It is sometimes occupied by tenants. Ine speaks of those who take up parcels of land, measured in yardlands, for which they pay rent.[79] Already we seem to be in a familiar world. But we are not told what Ine means by yardlands. That is not his problem. The problem with which Ine deals arises when the lord wants service as well as rent from his tenants. Ine declares that the lord may have service as well as rent if he offers a dwelling as well as land to his tenants. Some farmers hire yokes of oxen.[80] Presumably the kind of farmer who has to hire oxen is also the kind of farmer who has to rent yardlands. Again we are not told. Ine's concern is that those who cannot pay for their hire of oxen in fodder should pay half in fodder and the rest in other goods.

Thus in late seventh-century Wessex we find lords hiring out land to tenants of two distinct classes: to those who need land and possibly oxen but not somewhere to live; and to those whose cirumstances are such that they are obliged to take a dwelling-place as well as land and oxen from their lord and to do so on terms which compel them to discharge some part of their rental liabilities in service and some part in kind. We are not told how the balance of the rent has to be discharged; but we are entitled to assume that it has to be discharged in money. Nor are we told how important these classes of tenant may be. But in another clause Ine legislates against brawling. He provides penalties for those who brawl in the king's house; for those who brawl in the houses of earldormen; and for those who brawl in the homes of rent-payers (gafolgelda) and geburs.[81] The list is far from complete. Nothing is said, for example, about penalties for those who brawl in the homes of farmers whose property is their own in the sense in which we should understand the meaning of that term in Ine's day.[82] But Ine goes to the trouble of legislating to protect tenant-farmers from those who brawl in their homes, and does so, we may assume, because tenant-farmers are numerous or significant enough as a group to warrant separate treatment.

In legislating to protect tenant-farmers Ine is concerned to distinguish the two categories of tenant-farmer from one another, finding them sufficiently different to merit separate identification and yet similar enough to justify their being classed together for certain purposes. Can we recognise any elements of the complex social structure of Aethelberht's laws in these

[79] Ine cap. 67.
[80] Ibid., cap. 60. Stenton believed that ceorls hired oxen from one another. The words used can certainly bear that meaning; and no doubt a good deal of hiring went on between ceorls. But the law takes note of persistent default, not merely routine breaches of contract. What is more likely, therefore, is that those who have to turn to a lord for land and a home will also have turned to him for the hire of oxen, only to find themselves constantly plagued by inability to discharge their obligations. F. M. Stenton, Preparatory to Anglo-Saxon England, ed. D. M. Stenton (Oxford, 1970), pp. 384–5.
[81] Ine cap. 6 and paras 2 and 3.
[82] T. F. T. Plucknett, Studies in Legal History (1983), chapter 1, reprinted from the Economic History Review, vol. vi (1935).

revisions of Ine by Alfred? We cannot look across from Wessex to Kent, or from the late seventh century to the early years of that century without anachronism. But would it be altogether fanciful to see the Kentish *laet* and the Kentish ceorl in the Wessex *gebur*? The *gebur* owes everything to his lord: land, home, oxen. He is even forbidden to quit without permission, according to another decree of Ine.[83] To that extent he is no better off than the Kentish *laet*. But Ine shows us that he is nevertheless free, severely compromised though his freedom may be. If a freeman works on Sundays, Ine decrees that he will be liable for punishment unless his lord has ordered him to work.[84] Who is this freeman whose lord may have given him an unlawful order to work if not the tenant who does service for his lord in return for a home in which to live? Ine's freeman is, or may be, in certain circumstances, a *gebur*. And as a freeman Ine's *gebur* has essential qualities in common with Aethelberht's ceorl. We are undoubtedly justified in claiming that the *gebur* of the eleventh-century *Rectitudines* is recognisable in Ine's laws.

It is much harder to pick other elements of the Wessex social structure out of Ine's laws. Lords who require service are farmers with land to cultivate. And farming is a daily grind that culminates in seasonal peaks of demand for labour. The daily work in Aethelberht's Kent was done by living-in servants, some of whom were slaves, with the help of other slaves who may not have had to live where they worked and of labourers who were married men living in cottages on the estate. When pressure increased, as it did seasonally, there were plenty of part-timers keen to supplement their earnings by working for the estate. Ine, however, gives us no hint of living-in servants apart from slaves. Apparently they set no legislative problem that called for special treatment either in Ine's day or perhaps later, when Alfred reviewed Ine's work. The daily labouring done by outdoor workers was the responsibility of the *gebur* in Ine's laws. And the evidence seems to indicate that lords of estates were applying pressure to ordinary villagers so as to increase the supply of such labour. The evidence may be slight; but when the king is called upon to define the circumstances which would justify a lord in requiring service from his tenants, we can sense the pressure being exerted by lords who were trying to get service out of tenants who may never have dreamt, when they rented their land, that part of the bargain to which they would be held might consist of performing labour services on the landlord's estate.

Below the level of contractual commitment, there were the slaves. Ine, like Wihtred, favoured a full range of savage punishments for wrong-doing; and this included enslavement. But slavery was not the same for all. As in Aethelberht's Kent, slavery in Wessex was graduated. Ine's laws, however, tell us only of a simple differentiation between Welsh slaves and English ones. Ine has a great deal to say about Welshmen. The proximity of Wessex

---

[83] Ine cap. 39. The law is more general than particular in its phrasing but must surely apply with special force to someone who is under such heavy obligations to the lord as the *gebur* is.

[84] *Ibid.*, cap. 3, para. 2.

to Wales, and to the unsubdued land to the west, explains that. But Welshmen are not all slaves. Some are rent-payers; some possess as many as 5 hides.
There are even Welshmen in the king's service.[85] They serve the king in
Wessex, but they are not assimilated. In Wessex society, according to Wessex
law, Welshmen are always deemed to be the inferiors of their English peers.
There is no question in Ine's Wessex of social absorption removing the
differences between invaders and natives. Nor is there, apparently, in Alfred's Wessex: for it was he who allowed these laws of Ine to stand. Wessex
law makes provision for Welshmen with land and social pretensions because
there are still Welshmen with property and status in Wessex society. The
contrast with the laws of Kent is striking. And there are certainly plenty of
Welsh slaves, if we may judge by the concern of the laws with their doings.
Centuries later, in Domesday Book, we find a concentration of slaves in the
western counties which, with startling exceptions, is not to be found elsewhere in England.[86] And Welsh slaves occupy the lowest position of all in
Wessex society. This fact Ine's laws make very plain; for there was, in Ine's
day, a slave trade in Wessex brisk enough to prompt Ine to forbid the export
of West-Saxon slaves abroad. The Welshmen, apparently, could go: they
were expendable.[87] Ine, or it may be Alfred, simply has nothing to say on
their behalf in this connection.

We may certainly assume that slaves did more of the work on Wessex
farms than they did on farms which lacked those opportunities for recruitment that Wessex enjoyed. But we may not assume that Wessex slaves did
only the most menial jobs. Ine's laws give us the most revealing indications
yet that slavery did not necessarily mean ignominious destitution and thral-
dom.

The Sunday observance laws laid it down that if a slave worked on
Sundays, at his lord's command, he was to be liberated; but that if he worked
without his lord's knowledge, he was to be fined or flogged.[88] A slave who
works without his lord's knowledge is surely working for himself: he would
hardly be likely to work for his lord when he was not obliged to do so. And
working for himself implies that he is either cultivating someone else's land
for pay, or cultivating land of his own. On Sundays it must be secluded land
that he cultivates. He could not hope to be able to work in the open fields
without being seen and reported; and informing has already made its earliest
known appearance in English law with Wihtred.[89] If he cultivates land on
Sundays, he must cultivate a close or garden enclosed by a hedge such as Ine

---

[85] Ibid., cap. 23, para. 3. Attenborough renders gafolgelda as tax-payer. But see English
Historical Documents, p. 367 and note 2. Ine cap. 24, para. 2; 33.
[86] H. C. Darby, Domesday England (Cambridge, 1977), p. 338. These are only the slaves
who work on manorial demesne lands. Slaves who work exclusively for other tenants
get no mention in Domesday.
[87] Ine cap. 11.
[88] Ibid., cap. 3 and para. 1.
[89] Wihtred cap. 11.

has already warned cottagers to keep in repair. Behind such a hedge a man could hope to be able to work on Sundays without fear of discovery. But cottagers with closes are not always ceorls with means sufficient to enable them to hire labour. There are many cottagers who cannot make do without themselves going out to work. There are some at least who are obliged to go out to work, as we have seen, simply in order to fulfil the terms upon which they occupy their cottages. Is it too fanciful to suppose that there are even a few slaves who have been rewarded with cottages on the estate so that when they are caught working on Sundays they are in fact being caught working for themselves? And if a few slaves have been settled in cottages in this way, may we not take the argument one stage further and surmise that they have been singled out for special treatment because they occupy positions of modest responsibility on the estate?

Village society is obviously complex. But lordship dominates it. No level of society is independent of it. We have only to examine the wergeld payments that Ine sets out, to see that every payment of wergeld, no matter how exalted the status of the person being compensated for, has to be accompanied by a fine payable to the victim's lord.[90] Even illegitimate children were deemed to have lords. Such a child, should its father repudiate it, did not, according to Ine, pass its wergeld to its father when it died, but to its lord and to the king.[91]

This payment of fines to an intermediary who is not the king is something of which we get only a passing hint in the laws of Wihtred of Kent.[92] But in Wessex we find lords of men actively collecting what are, in effect, judicial dues. Sometimes they are very obviously dues that the king might reasonably claim for himself. When, for example, members of the household of a *gesith*, who is a man of substance and social consequence, get into trouble, Ine rules that the *gesith* shall receive no share of the fines imposed upon them, on the grounds that he should have kept his men in order.[93] Ine is in fact legislating to frustrate what is apparently taken to be the normal expectation of a man of property that, when his men get into trouble with the law of the land, he should receive a share of the fines they must pay. Evidently fines are not always paid to the lords of victims in Ine's wessex. But what Ine makes very clear is that those who reckon to enjoy the profits of justice are expected to take responsibility for the good behaviour of their men, free and unfree. How can they do that without a court and the powers without which a court is impotent?

The laws seem to be telling us, by implication, of local courts held in conjunction with lordship and possessing powers of disciplining men. But common sense tells us that farming itself calls for judicial means with which

---

[90] Ine cap. 70.
[91] *Ibid.*, cap. 27.
[92] See above, note 72. Also, Wihtred cap. 5, and para. 1 for another possible case.
[93] Ine cap. 50. Cf. cap. 22 where responsibility for members of the household is again stressed.

to settle relatively trivial disputes about encroachments, breaches of routine and obligation, and the like. Such disputes could not have been taken before the king and his judges without absorbing more of their time and trouble than they would willingly spare them. Is it not possible that something like the Court Baron is in process of being created?

Lordship, however, is more than lordship over men. Those who are lords of men are also captains of infantry. They wear chain mail. They carry spears and swords. Their men are also armed; for military service is universal for everyone who is free. There are fines for those who fail to turn up for service.[94] One of the categories of men for whom service is obligatory is noblemen without land. Have we here some simulacrum of those royal household retainers in Beowulf who feast in the king's hall and sleep there when 'the benches were cleared away and pillows and bedding were spread upon the floor'?[95] Some, perhaps many, of these conscripted soldiers may even ride to war mounted on horseback. There are plenty of horses to be had. Ine, who allows wergeld to be paid in chain-mail and swords, tells us also that if anyone lends sword, spear or horse, to another man's servant, there will be penalties to pay. The anyone who does the lending could be from any social class: for none is specified. And the servant in question is very probably a slave: for that is what the rubric calls him.[96] Lending a horse to another man is a gesture or a business transaction that tells us nothing about the abundance or scarcity of horses. But when the lending is to another man's slave and is something that is being done often enough to attract the attention of the legislative authority, then we are surely justified in assuming that horses are not in desperately short supply. We are reminded of Wihtred's laets who break the rules about Sunday observance by riding through the Kentish countryside about their own affairs.

So many of the features of later manorial farming and estate management seem to be discernible in these early laws that we should not be surprised to find other routines, also familiar to later times, sufficiently characteristic of an earlier age to attract legislative attention. The lay magnate is peripatetic in medieval times. He moves round his manors so as to sustain his influence in the districts from which his power derives. He also moves round his manors because it is easier to move the household than the crops upon which it depends for sustenance. Such movements as these we can see in Ine; and we can do so because Ine and his advisors perceive difficulties for the king's revenues if such movements are uncontrolled. Ine decrees, therefore, that when he moves residence, an estate-owner may take with him only his reeve, his smith and his children's nurse.[97]

He may take his children's nurse, presumably, because he is taking his

---

94 *Ibid.*, cap. 51.
95 Beowulf II, 1239–40.
96 Ine caps 29 and 54 para. 1.
97 *Ibid.*, cap. 63.

children. He is not going to war. He is moving his family elsewhere. Nor is he leaving his own lands. He is permitted to take with him his reeve; and his reeve is doubtless a combination of major-domo and chief steward or land-agent. We are entitled to assume therefore that he is leaving one estate for another. He is also allowed to take with him his smith, as he will take with him his armourer in later times, because wherever he goes he will certainly hunt and may very well want to be accoutred to defend himself should the need arise. These removals are not necessarily permanent. Ine expects many of them to be seasonal; for he also decrees that church dues are payable upon the house and fields where mid-winter is spent.[98]

And that is not all. The migration of estate-owners, whether seasonal or permanent, may not be embarked upon without the fulfilment of certain very specific conditions. Estate-owners must leave most of their land under cultivation: 12 hides if they have 20; 6 hides if they have 10; 1½ if they have 3.[99] Why should the king concern himself with such matters? His fiscal interest in the land is indisputable. In addition to the profits of justice, about which the laws have already taught us something, the King, so Ine's laws inform us, collects a food-rent from every 10 hides; a blanket-tax from every hide; and a barley-rent from every labourer's employer.[100] It is not difficult to appreciate why Bede was able to calculate the size of kingdoms in terms of hides when we see how Ine exploits the hide as a unit of taxation.

All this revenue undoubtedly depends upon keeping the land productive. But then so does the income of the estate-owner. If he is moving away with every intention of moving back in due course, he cannot neglect the estate during his absence from it without jeopardising his own interests as well as the king's. If he is moving away because he has disposed of the estate, his successor can be expected to be every bit as keen as he was to make what he can out of it, and in so doing to safeguard the king's fiscal interest in it. If he strips the estate of its tenants when he disposes of it, as some commentators have supposed that he may be tempted to do, he will merely impair its marketability.[101] And if it is an estate which, for whatever reason, simply cannot be made to repay the effort that has gone into its maintenance, then the king cannot hope to do his fiscal interests any good by insisting upon the cultivation of land which those who know it best have thought fit to abandon.

Nevertheless it is obvious that the king is manifesting an interest in the management of land which its owners have every incentive to manage as

[98] Ibid., cap. 61. Winter means Martinmas, for that is when church dues must be paid: ibid., cap. 4. Stenton assumes that the ordinary ceorl does not necessarily spend winter where he spends other seasons of the year, but that must be wrong: Stenton, Preparatory, p. 385.
[99] Ine caps 64, 65, 66.
[100] Ibid., caps 70 para. 1; 44 para. 1; 59 para. 1.
[101] Notably by Aston in his 'Origins of the Manor', Transactions of the Royal Historical Society, 5th ser., vol. viii, 1958.

well as they know how. Nor is this the only law in which he manifests an interest in estate management. He decrees that a *gesith* who is evicted from his estate may be expelled from his house but not from his land.[102] The land in question is *setene* land. Some commentators have thought that *setene*, in Ine's law, meant settled or tenanted land; and Maitland has suggested that the law was intended to secure the titles of tenants when their landlord was being expelled.[103] But if Ine had meant to safeguard the tenants why did he not say so? What he says is that the *gesith* is not to be expelled from the *setene* land. He does not say that the tenants of the *gesith* are not to be expelled from their *setene* land.

If we take the view that, in these early laws, *setene* means cultivated and not tenanted, whatever it may mean centuries later,[104] then we are in fact brought much closer to an understanding of what lay behind Ine's legislation concerning the management of land. A *gesith* is being expelled. We are not told why. Evidently the reason for expulsion is not what matters. But the expulsion is lawful. And the law that Ine has declared says that a *gesith* who has been lawfully expelled may not be deprived of his cultivated land. More exactly, the cultivated land is unquestionably forfeit. If it were not then the word expulsion surely meant something very curious indeed to the Anglo-Saxon legal mind. But no term is given for the ending of what has been pronounced to be an unlawful occupancy. And none in fact is needed; for nature sets the term. It is harvest time. The land will be surrendered when the *gesith*'s crops have been gathered in and the king's taxes have been paid.

Something more follows from this. When a *gesith* was expelled from his estate, we must presume that his fallow land was seized at the same time as his house was taken from him. All land required fallowing; and that portion of a *gesith*'s estate which was not under crops at the time when his estate was declared forfeit, was not, strictly speaking, reserved to him by the terms of the law that allowed him to keep his *setene* land. If the law was strictly interpreted in this sense it suggests that the king taxed the cropping acreage of the land, not its total acreage. When he took his food-rents from every 10 hides he took them from every 10 hides of cropping land, not from every 10 hides of which some part was always in fallow.

We are now perhaps in a better position to understand the puzzling rules that Ine requires estate-owners to observe when they move away from their estates. The peripatetic estate-owner leaves his estate because he wants to go somewhere else. The evicted *gesith* leaves because he must. But from the king's point of view both removals set the same fiscal problem. It is the problem of safeguarding the king's interests when the estate-owner is, whether temporarily or permanently, non-resident. The king's solution, in cases of eviction, is to allow the estate-owner to reap where he has sown; and

102 Ine cap. 68.
103 Maitland, *op. cit.*, p. 238, note 1.
104 For later meanings, see Aston *ut supra*.

in cases of absenteeism, to insist upon a minimum cropping acreage, reinforcing his decree by restricting the number of management staff that a peripatetic estate-owner may take with him on his travels. The minimum cropping acreage stipulated by law is greater than the cropping acreage that the estate-owner would choose of his own volition. If it were not, there would be no point to the king's insistence upon it. Where the estate is large the king requires 60% cultivation; and this strongly suggests that the average Wessex farm, in Ine's time, practised a two-field course of husbandry, fallowing half the acreage every year, It also suggests that Ine was so anxious about his taxes that he was putting a great deal of pressure on his more affluent subjects to raise output, so as to make sure of paying his taxes, when their farming judgement told them to keep the soil in good heart by resting more of it than he will allow them to do.

In other respects, Ine's laws offer no surprises to anyone who has worked his way through the laws of the kings of Kent. The church dominates the legislative assembly in which Ine's laws are ratified, as it does perhaps the life of society. Punishments surpass even those of Wihtred's laws in the refinement of their savagery: mutilation and the ordeal join flogging, enslavement and the death penalty. But offences are the old ones itemised in the decalogue.

Ine's laws, however, come to us by courtesy of Alfred; and Alfred, as he himself tells us, submitted them to pruning and even revision before he passed them as fit for use. We may wonder, therefore, how much of his laws Ine would have recognised in Alfred's version of them; and consequently how much of late seventh-century Wessex we can actually discern in this late ninth-century recension. There is, for example, no reference to devil-worship in Ine as there is in Wihtred; or to sorcery, as there is in Alfred. It is unlikely that the church viewed with genial indifference the heathen cults practised in Ine's Wessex. And no doubt when Ine issued his laws he did his best to deal with them. But Alfred had his own laws upon the subject, presumably because, having examined Ine's, he decided that Ine's treatment was less appropriate to the needs of the time than his own.

We may be forgiven for wondering whether Alfred went even further than suppression and revision and actually interpolated passages into his authorised version of Ine simply in order to pass off changes of his own, or even declarations of current practice, as usages sanctified by their association with a name which was still remembered with respect. Farming, for example, is something that public laws rarely touch upon, so far as English experience goes, because arrangements about farming practice, and about the punishment of infringements of accepted farming practice, are usually settled locally by those whom they concern. Consequently, as a rule, the most important interests of the entire population are matters about which the highest authorities in the land have least to say. When the world seemed to be about to come to an end, in 1349, as a result of the Black Death, the king issued a hastily-drafted ordinance to check the rise of farm-wages: that is to say the wages paid as a result of contracts made in the open market. But he never presumed, either then or later, to intervene between manorial lords and their tenants by legislating to enforce the contracts that secured to manorial lords their rents, dues and other obligations, and to manorial tenants their farms. These contracts were adjudicated in the manorial courts. We speak of the labour legislation of post-Black Death England. But the labour in question was always the labour over which manorial lords had no manorial jurisdiction.

Thus when the law of the land tells us about farming practices, we must assume that there has been some grave and widespread dislocation of local control which has prompted the king to intervene in order to restore customary usages. We find such an intervention in Ine. But Wessex seems to have been remarkably free from anything that might have provoked a breakdown of ordinary life during Ine's reign. The course of events in Ine's reign may be obscure; but it is obscure because we cannot always know what Ine did: not because we cannot always find out what Wessex endured. There appears to be no problem of public order to justify a re-statement or clarification of farming regulations by Ine.[105] Alfred's position, however, was very different. His early years on the throne were wholly absorbed by the effort to contain the Viking attacks. His central years were given over to reconstructing the institutions of a country which had been over-run and badly mauled. It is at such times that law-making can make a resounding contribution to recovery. It is to this period, therefore, that we should assign the compilation and issue of Alfred's laws.[106]

We may never know why, if he did, Alfred should have thought it best to issue, in Ine's name, directives about liability for damage done by straying animals or about tenancy obligations which he himself obviously considered to be important enough to be given widespread currency at a crucial moment in the country's history. But these directives do more than give us a unique glimpse of the farming world: they suggest the workings of an intelligence to which wider considerations of jurisprudence were not unfamiliar. They do more than provide penalties for offences: they lay down principles upon which conduct may be judged. For all we know, Ine may indeed have been their author. But they suit Alfred's times better than they suit Ine's; and they certainly suit Alfred's temperament, intellect and political acumen.

And yet we must not be tempted to make too much of considerations which might lead us to conclude that the farming world of late seventh-century Wessex was not at all as Ine appears to depict it. After all, Alfred was concerned to restore not to innovate. If he did in fact attribute to Ine laws which he had himself devised, that in itself shows that he was anxious to put things back as they were before the Vikings. Moreover his laws were about liability. They took field-systems and tenancy relationships for granted and determined liabilities and assigned penalties so as to enable these systems

105 Stenton, *Anglo-Saxon England*, pp. 71–3.
106 S. Keynes and M. Lapidge, *ut supra*, introduction, *passim*.

and relationships to work as smoothly as possible. They made no attempt, so far as we can tell, to change or reform what it most interests us to see revealed.

But even if we may, with reservations, allow ourselves to see something of seventh-century English society in these early laws, we must never lose sight of the fact that the earliest laws can tell us nothing about life in the Thames Valley, or the Midlands, or even in East Anglia. Our seventh-century view of English society, from these laws, is strictly confined to what we can find out about two kingdoms, one to the south-east and the other to the south-west of the country. Nevertheless it is, from a medieval point of view, a society in which many features are very familiar.

The social structure plunges to the abject dependence of slavery at the bottom as it will never do again after Domesday. But dependence, even when it means slavery, has many facets in seventh-century society; and some forms of dependence imply a status and living standards which could easily be matched later. Moreover the freedom of the lowest classes of free peasants is already seriously compromised by Ine's insistence that many of them, perhaps very many of them, may only leave their holdings with permission. Ine is less than perfectly clear on this point. But he is unequivocally clear about the level of dependence to which free men can be degraded by their need to rent land, hire plough-teams and live in homes provided for them by their lords.

If the social structure is familiar, from the standpoint of the Middle Ages, so too are the field-systems of Wessex, with their two-field rotations, their yardlands in the open fields, their meadows filled with grazing animals and their woodland swine-pastures. A striking singularity of these early laws, however, is the all but complete absence of legislation on the subject of sheep.[107] The animal which will be the glory and boast of later generations of Englishmen and which will be accorded a special status at law, is almost entirely ignored by the laws and wholly ignored by Bede. The *Ecclesiastical History* opens with a brief survey of Britain in which Bede extols the natural riches of the country, commending its arable and pasture, its vines and fisheries, its minerals and hot springs. But not a word does Bede say about its sheep.

Everywhere in these laws values are expressed in terms of money even though payments were often made in kind. Sometimes payment in kind is stipulated; and sometimes part-payment in kind is allowed as if it were a concession. But it is impossible to scrutinise these early laws without coming to the conclusion that money circulated throughout the economy and at every level of society, so that rents, fines, compensation payments and dues specified on every page were rendered, to an unknowable extent, in coin rather than in kind.

Perhaps the most important payments prescribed by law were those that provided monetary substitutes for the vendetta. The vendetta was public

---

[107] See Ine caps 55 and 69 for incidental mentions.

order privatised. And the tariffs of compensation payments set out in the earliest laws should perhaps be seen as attempts by the early kings to win back for themselves some measure of that control over public-order issues that properly belonged to the function and dignity of kingship. Kings may have authorised monetary equivalents to the vendetta; but they could not provide their subjects with an enforceable code. The compensation payments were optional, though the fines that went with them, presumably were not. We cannot seriously doubt, however, the very substantial popularity of tariffs or commutation payments which reduced the fearful threat of death or mutilation to the proportions of an action for debt. Behind every wrong brooded the vendetta. Its threat was the best enforcement agency for a system of restitution that anyone could have hoped for in the circumstances of the time. Not everyone could pay, however willing his kinsfolk may have been to try. And not everyone who could pay was prepared to do so. The initiative was obviously left to the aggrieved party. There were no laws punishing those who preferred the avenging knife or prescribing limits to the vengeance they might take; though there were laws circumscribing the workings of the system. According to Ine, a thief killed as he ran away ought not to be compensated for or avenged; and an enslaved kinsman, whatever wrong he may have suffered, need not be.[108]

The sums of money involved in these schemes may appear to be exorbitant to anyone who makes the reasonable assumption, based upon the history of inflation over the centuries, that money has declined in value from some high point in the nebulous past. But such impressions need to be qualified by two reservations. One is that these charges were bound to be severe since they were calculated to make reparation for loss of earning power perhaps for very long periods, perhaps for life, as well as for other kinds of damage, social as well as material. The other is that these charges were intended to be shared. The early kings may have been obliged to intervene in order to remind kinsfolk of responsibilities which they were disposed to forget or neglect. Nevertheless the very severity of these compensation charges implies that those who have to make restitution for the harm they have done will have an extensive kin-group willing as well as able to bear a burden which nobody could be expected to shoulder on his own. Evidently in early English society it did not do to antagonise one's relations.

The circulation of money implied in so many ways in these early laws presupposes an economic system of considerably greater sophistication and complexity than we might otherwise be prepared to concede to it on other evidence. And when we consider the calls made upon the machinery of government we are bound to conclude that its development had to have been far more advanced than we might otherwise have supposed. The kings we meet in the earliest laws are not simple tribal leaders. The confer with counsellors. They issue laws. They impose fines. They levy taxes. They

---

[108] *Ibid.*, caps 35 and 74 para. 2.

administer estates. They treat with their peers at home and abroad. They muster armies. They required, and presumably employed, assessors and collectors, accountants and a secretariat of clerks who issued orders and digested information. But about such people we appear to know nothing at all.

Domesday Book: A Re-interpretation

When Stenton declared that Domesday Book[1] gave us an 'ordered description of a national economy', he expressed a belief about its nature and purpose which is widely, if not universally, shared not only by those who have devoted themselves to the study of DB, but also by those who invoke its authority for statements about the social and economic life of the towns and villages of eleventh-century England.[2] But this belief that the Domesday survey can provide us with a view of English society which combines some of the elements of a census of production with those of a study of the social structure, is not as well-founded as it is generally thought to be. The evidence examined in the following pages shows, on the contrary, that the Domesday survey was commissioned because the King wanted to find out what the manors of England were worth to his tenants-in-chief, not in aggregate as estates, but individually, manor by manor. And he wanted this information because the current system of taxation, upon which he relied for part of his revenue, imposed an income-tax on his tenants-in-chief on the basis of an assessment of the annual value to them of the manors of their estates. Accordingly the King sent commissioners round to find out not only how much his tenants-in-chief received from their manors, but also how that income was made up. The commissioners set down, for every manor investigated, details of demesne stock and labour supply, of arable capacity calculated in terms of the number of ploughteams that were commensurate with the income of that particular manor, and a list of manorial appurtenances whose benefit was enjoyed by the tenant-in-chief in question, including mills, meadows and woodland.

DB was an income-tax inquiry in the fullest sense possible at the time. And since the income in question was the income of the tenant-in-chief, DB fastens upon the interests of tenants-in-chief to the exclusion of everyone else's interests. When it tells us about other classes of tenants, apart from mesne tenants, DB tells us about them only to the extent that they contrib-

---

[1] Throughout this article DB will be used as an abbreviation for Domesday Book. References to the Record Commission text will only be made where it is unavoidable. The severely contracted Latin acts as a barrier to everyone but the specialist and limits intelligent discussion of Domesday problems to those who have made a professional career out of studying them. The *Victoria County History* (henceforth VCH) translations are all the work of outstanding scholars and leading students of DB. They are accurate, readable and accessible, and are used, as a rule, here.
[2] F. M. Stenton, *Anglo-Saxon England*, 3rd edn (Oxford, 1971), p. 656.

ute to the manorial income of the tenants-in-chief. Villeins and bordars feature in abundance in the folios of DB; as do the freer classes and even the slaves. But we learn nothing at all about these interesting people apart from how they contribute to the incomes of their illustrious manorial lords. Much, perhaps most, of the agrarian life of England inevitably escapes the attention of the Domesday commissioners because the agrarian life of England, except in the restricted sense in which they were required to investigate it, lies beyond their terms of reference.

These are the themes that will be pursued in the following pages. There are, no doubt, many ways in which they could be tackled; but the simplest way is probably the best. It is to take an ordinary Domesday manor and explain the account of it given by the Domesday commissioners in terms which will justify a revision of that traditional interpretation of its meaning to which Stenton lent the authority of his tremendous reputation.

Entries in DB, generally speaking, conform to a pattern whose essential features are adequately displayed in the following extract from the Buckinghamshire survey:

> Archbishop Lanfranc holds Monks Risborough. It is assessed at 30 hides. There is land for 14 ploughs. In demesne are 16 hides and on it are 2 ploughs. There 32 villeins with 8 bordars have 12 ploughs. There are 4 slaves, meadow for 6 ploughteams, woodland for 300 swine. In all it is worth £16; when received 100s; TRE [Tempore Regis Edwardi] £16.[3]

In Kent these hides are called sulungs; and in Danelaw counties like Leicestershire they are called carucates. But these are differences of nomenclature, not of substance. In every county, the first question asked by the Domesday commissioners, once they were satisfied about a manor's tenancy, concerned its hidage. Their preoccupation with hidage was unremitting. When they came upon a manor whose hidage could not be expressed in whole numbers, the commissioners made use of fractions or, where they found it more convenient to do so, expressed these fractional quantities in terms of virgates and acres. Their doing so, however, does not mean that the Domesday hide was a measurement of land. At other times, and in other contexts, it had been. And when it measured land it very often consisted of 120 acres divided into virgates of 30 acres. Consequently the Domesday commissioners, without any sense of incongruity, adopted these virgates and acres for their own purposes as a ready-made way of representing fractional quantities.

In DB, however, hides are fiscal hides. They measure liability to taxation. They do not measure land. And the liability they measure is liability to the payment of geld. 'The King holds Calne . . .', says DB, 'it never paid geld;

---

[3] *VCH Bucks.*, i. 233.

hence it is unknown how many hides are there'.[4] 'The King holds Crewkerne
. . .', says DB, 'it did not pay geld, nor is it known how many hides are there'.[5]

The link between hidage and geld which we can observe in DB, we can
corroborate from the geld records. The archive of geld records was once,
doubtless, immense. The administration of a national taxation system could
hardly fail to have generated a formidable accumulation of returns. Of that
accumulation very little now remains. We have an abbreviated return for
Northamptonshire for a levy in the 1070s;[6] and a more revealing series of
returns for the south-western counties compiled in response to a levy in the
1080s.[7] These returns show that geld was collected hundred by hundred and
county by county throughout the kingdom. If we examine particular entries
in the records of the levy of the 1080s, in conjunction with DB, we shall find
the Domesday hides in the geld returns. Thus DB tells us that the Bishop of
Salisbury held the manor of Salisbury in Wiltshire.[8] In King Edward's time it
paid geld for 50 hides. Of these hides, DB tells us that 10 were in demesne.
When we turn to the geld records, there, in Underditch hundred, we find
the Bishop's hides: 50 in the manor and 10 of these in demesne.[9]

The geld records invariably distinguish demesne hides from the rest of the
hides. DB does not. Indeed many Domesday counties make no mention of
demesne hides. Some, like Buckinghamshire, appear to follow no rule in the
matter. This seems to point to a serious deficiency in DB; for the geld returns
tell us why demesne hides are so punctiliously separated out. We hear so
much about them because demesne hides are exempt from geld. The geld
return for each hundred sets out that hundred's gross liability in terms of
hides and then itemizes the demesne exemptions. At the end of the entry for
any particular hundred, there is sometimes a statement of that hundred's net
liability for geld, again expressed in terms of hides, though often there is not.
Thus the gross liability of the Bishop of Salisbury's manor of Salisbury, which
was for 50 hides, became a net liability of 40 hides as a result of the
exemption of the Bishop's demesne, which was rated at 10 hides. At 6s per
hide, which was the current rate at which geld was levied when these returns
were made, this meant that the liability of Salisbury manor for geld, which
was £15 gross (6 x 50 = 300 shillings), was reduced by the exemption of the
demesne to £12 net (6 x 40 = 240 shillings).

In DB we seem to have a big report which unfailingly notes the gross
liability of manors for geld but which either says nothing about demesne
exemptions or, if it does say something about them, does so, to all appear-

---

4 VCH Wilts., ii. 115.
5 VCH Somerset, i. 439.
6 D. C. Douglas and G. W. Greenaway, eds, English Historical Documents 1042–1189
(hereafter EHD) (London, 1968), no. 61, pp. 483–6.
7 See, for example, Victoria County History: Dorset, iii, and Darlington's masterly work
on the Wiltshire accounts in VCH Wilts., ii.
8 VCH Wilts., ii. 121.
9 Ibid., ii. 180.

ances, without pursuing a consistent policy in the matter. Exemption is the bane of any taxation system because exemption slips easily into tax avoidance; and tax avoidance has brought many a promising taxation system low. Has DB really failed to provide the King with important information on this vital matter?

In fact DB appears to provide its own solution to this problem and in doing so suggests that DB was actually intended for use in conjunction with the geld records. Where DB names the hundreds within which particular manors are to be found it thereby provides a reference enabling a busy administrator to retrieve the information he is looking for from the geld returns. When it does that it scarcely matters whether it mentions demesne exemptions in its manorial surveys or not. Where, however, it omits the hundreds, then DB makes a rule of stating demesne exemptions because finding a manor in the geld returns without knowing the hundred in which it was to be found was a task calculated to raise the blood-pressure and lower the life-expectancy of anyone told off to carry out such a task. This need for constant reference to the geld returns seems to be implicit in the structure of DB and emphasizes the close connection there was in the minds of those who compiled DB between DB and the fiscal records of the time, and hence between DB hides and geld hides.

Once it has determined a manor's taxable capacity and ascertained its exemption allowances DB then, apparently, turns to matters of wider import. In every Domesday entry we find that the gross hidage figure is followed, in all but a minority of counties, by something that seems to betoken a broadening of the perspective of those who are investigating the manors of England. We seem to be turning to general questions of farming. 'There is land for 14 ploughs', says the Monks Risborough survey; and this phrase, or one very like it, is to be found nearly everywhere in DB.

When DB says there is land for so many ploughs on a particular manor, it seems to be saying something comprehensive about the arable capacity of the manor by transcending fiscal questions and ignoring property boundaries within the manor, thus taking into account the land held not only by the manorial lord in demesne but also the land held by all his tenants. We seem to be embarked upon that comprehensive survey of English agrarian life which so many commentators have told us to expect from DB. Appearances, however, can be deceptive; and the survival of earlier drafts of DB, containing fuller details of the information actually collected, reveals to us what DB in its edited Winchester version conceals from us, in the sense that it takes for granted commonplaces of thought which are no longer commonplace.

Thus: the Abbey of St Peter of Cerne holds Cerne Abbas in Dorset.[10] In King Edward's time it paid geld on 22 hides. DB then tells us that there is land for 20 ploughs and that there are 3 hides and 3 ploughs in demesne and

---

[10] VCH Dorset, iii. 74–5, where the Winchester and Exon Domesday versions are printed one after the other.

5 slaves and 26 villeins and 32 bordars with 14 ploughs. In this cryptic entry, very familiar in form to anyone who turns the pages of DB, wherever he may care to look, the phrase 'land for 20 ploughs' conveys the strong impression that we have here an assessment of the total capacity of the manor for arable production. But we possess also the Exon Domesday account for Cerne Abbas. It is more explicit, at this crucial point, as it is in many cases, wherever its coverage extends. It tells us, as DB did, that in King Edward's time Cerne Abbas paid geld for 22 hides. It then tells us that 'these hides 20 ploughs can plough': 'Has possunt arare xx carucae'.[11] Elsewhere the story is the same. For the entire county of Wiltshire, only one example survives of the Exon Domesday version of a manorial survey. It is the survey for Little Sutton, in Sutton Veny, held in chief by William de Mohun. But when we examine it we find the same form of words as we do wherever the Exon Domesday enlarges upon DB. 'Terra est iiii carucis', says DB. 'Has possunt arare iiii carucae', says the Exon Domesday, referring here to the hides of the previous sentence: 'These (hides) 4 ploughs can plough'.[12]

This use of the demonstrative pronoun by the draftsmen of the Exon Domesday utterly changes the significance of the ploughteam entry throughout DB. It must be the most portentous use of a pronoun, so far as we are concerned, in the whole corpus of Domesday records. There is no question here of a scribal slip of the pen. The reference to the gross hidage figure in the ploughteam estimate is common form throughout the Exon Domesday. Nor can we construe the Exon Domesday phrase to mean what we have for so long taken to be the meaning of the words of the Winchester Domesday, but here expressed in a careless variation of language which could be misunderstood only by someone who read it in a spirit of perversity. There is no ambiguity about the words of the Exon Domesday. They tell us that we are not dealing with the arable capacity of the manor, in any comprehensive sense, when we come across that familiar phrase 'there is land for so many ploughs'. We are instead dealing with hidage capacity. We are being told about the hides. Land for so many ploughs is evidently Winchester shorthand for hidage land for that number of ploughs. The DB commissioners were very familiar with this concept of hidage land. Newport Pagnell, in Buckinghamshire, for example, is assessed at 5 hides. There is a manor and there are burgesses. The burgesses have ploughs working 'outside the 5 hides'; that is to say, beyond Newport Pagnell's taxation complex. These

---

11 *Domesday Book, Record Commission* (hereafter DBRC), vol. iv (London, 1816), fo. 36. The Exon Domesday uses 'has' where there are several hides and 'hanc' where there is one.

12 *VCH Wilts.*, ii. 44. A variation of this phrase occurs at the end of the Exon Domesday where we find that Robert, son of Giraldus, has manors in Wilts. and Dorset of whose hides it is said: 'haec terra sufficit liiii carucis et dim.'; and manors in Somerset of whose hides it is said: 'quas possunt arare xx et ii carucae'. DBRC, iv. fo. 530b.

ploughs were not necessarily working in another place. They were simply working where geld was payable on another manor's hidage-rating.[13]

Hidage, as we have seen, tells us about taxable capacity: it is a fiscal concept. Domesday ploughteams tell us about productive capacity; for, in DB, they are real enough. Thus in Claxby by Normanby, in Lincolnshire, Ivo Taillebois' man has 2 villeins who 'do not plough'.[14] In West Wykeham, also in Lincolnshire, Rainer de Brimou has 10 men who 'do not plough'.[15] And in Addlethorpe, in the same county, Chetelbern has 3 villeins who 'do not plough'.[16] In Essex, at Witham, in King Edward's time, 'the men had 18 ploughs; now 7; and this loss took place . . . through the death of the beasts'.[17] At Hatfield Broadoak, also in Essex, Little Domesday notes another loss of ploughteams and attributes it to the same cause.[18] The same point is put another way when DB notes that manorial tenants plough for their lord but not with their own ploughs. Hugh de Grentemaisnil has a small piece of land in Barton in the Beans, Leicestershire. It is held by another Hugh. 'There is land for half a plough. This he has there, with 1 villein and 2 bordars'.[19] Clearly the villein ploughs and it may be that the bordars do too. But they bring nothing but their labour to the plough. Elsewhere DB is even more explicit. In Bottesford, also in Leicestershire, there is land for 12 ploughs: 9 in demesne 'and 7 sokemen with 2 villeins and 13 bordars have 2 ploughs between (them) all. Some have nothing'.[20] Nothing, that is to say, but the obligation to supply labour which, of course, the lord may use or commute according to his needs.

What DB has done is to take hidage capacity and link it with productive capacity as expressed in ploughteams. In Monks Risborough there are 30 hides. These hides 14 ploughs can work. The productive capacity of these ploughs is the productive capacity required by a manor which has been rated, for taxation purposes, at 30 hides. But ploughteams earn their keep by working an annual cycle. We are being told about the annual production of wealth, not about capital value. Hidage in DB is thus linked to income, not to asset value.

And in fact DB leaves us in no doubt that this was so. Whether they did so by scrutinizing written submissions or by interrogating witnesses, the DB investigators in fact procured a statement of value from the tenant of every manor they surveyed. This statement of value is not a statement of capital

13 VCH Bucks., i. 255. Compare the Ely Inquest's 'outside the geld': EHD, no. 215, p. 884.
14 The Lincolnshire Domesday, trans. C. W. Foster and T. Longley (Lincolnshire Record Society, xix, 1924), p. 80.
15 Ibid., p. 161.
16 Ibid., p. 201.
17 VCH Essex, i. 428.
18 Ibid., p. 429.
19 VCH Leics., i. 319.
20 Ibid., p. 322.

value: it is a statement of annual value. There are clear indications that this was so scattered throughout DB. Laindon, in Essex, was worth £9 in King Edward's day. Now it is worth £10. But the Bishop, says DB, receives £14.[21] Royal farms are noted. Sometimes their commuted value is given, as it is for Chippenham, in Wiltshire.[22] A royal farm is an annual obligation, laid upon a particular royal manor, to supply the royal household with its sustenance for a stipulated period. Even mills are sometimes given a value which is expressed in words which tell us that value means annual value. At High Wycombe, in Buckinghamshire, 6 mills are worth 75s per year.[23] But the clearest evidence comes from the Exon Domesday, where it is frequently stated that particular manors are worth so much per year. Thus Puddletown, in Dorset, with all its appurtenances, rendered £73 per year when Harold held it and does so now.[24]

Whatever we may find in DB, in the way of ancillary information, we can always depend upon it that the Domesday investigators will provide us with an estimate of every manor's annual value and an assessment of its liability to taxation expressed in terms of hides. Nor can it be merely fortuitous that this should be so. There is an indissoluble bond between value and assessment. We must, therefore, suppose that those who planned DB expected to be able to work out, as a result of its findings, a more equitable, or at any rate, a politically more plausible relationship, between these two magnitudes. But, we must ask, whose income is being considered when the Domesday commissioners probe into questions of manorial value? Every manorial survey culminates with an estimate of value. Many surveys of sub-manors do likewise. What does it mean?

A manor was, in effect, a cluster of farms bound together by common services such as mills, meadows, woodland and the like, and by obligations of rent to a common landlord. In valuing the annual returns of a manor did DB attempt to estimate the aggregate value of the annual turn-over of all these farms? Or did DB confine itself to an assessment of the value of the manor to its lord? Generally speaking, manors consisted of demesne and tenant land. The demesne produced an income for the manorial lord; and the tenant land, so far as he was concerned, produced rents in money, kind and service, as well as a miscellany of dues. Obviously there could be a very substantial difference between the aggregate value of a manor, taking into account the annual yield of all its farms to those who farmed its land, and the value of that manor to its lord. The lord's share of that aggregate annual value was bound to be a minority share, partly because the demands he could make from even his most heavily burdened tenants had to leave them with an adequate margin for survival, and partly because so many tenants were

21 VCH Essex, i. 437.
22 VCH Wilts., ii. 116.
23 VCH Bucks., i. 258.
24 VCH Dorset, iii. 66.

attached to their manors by ties which were often slender and, not infrequently, tenuous or even nominal.

In fact DB did indeed value manors in terms of what lords of manors got out of them and not in terms of the aggregate yield of all the farms that acknowledged some connection with particular manors to everyone who had some claim upon their annual product. But this conclusion is not always made transparently clear by the evidence. The Domesday commissioners very naturally took for granted habits of thought which time and change have now rendered unfamiliar and even obscure. When they stated the worth of particular manors they knew that everyone who was authorized to consult DB would recognize that worth meant worth to the manorial lord. Occasionally they state the worth of a manor in a way which leaves no doubt about who benefits as a result of that worth. Sometimes the tenant-in-chief gets more from his manor than the surveyors thought it was worth and the higher income draws an illuminating comment from them. This is what happened at Laindon, in Essex. Sometimes there is a royal farm to provide us with a clue as to who receives the foodstuffs and other provisions. Sometimes the farm, in this sense, was an ecclesiastical one, as it was at Farningham, in Kent, where £4 of the manor's income was appropriated to the clothing needs of the monks of Canterbury.[25] Sometimes there is a sub-manor as well as a manor and, particularly in the Exon Domesday, the surveyors go to some trouble to establish who receives the manorial income and who gets what the sub-manor yields. Cerne Abbey, to take one example from many, holds Long Bredy, in Dorset. 'This manor', says the Exon Domesday, 'renders £16 for the use of the Abbot and £3 for the use of the thegns.'[26]

All these examples could be multiplied endlessly; but there is no need to stress what is, after all, an uncontroversial finding. In DB the value of the manor is the annual value of that manor to its manorial lord.[27] And by its manorial lord DB means the King, or the tenant-in-chief, or those mesne tenants upon whom the tenants-in-chief have devolved some of their manors or some parts of some of their manors. DB stops there. It does not look farther down the ladder of sub-infeudation. When it describes mesne tenants it treats them as lords of the manor in every respect. It imputes to them a share of the gross hidage and may very well note their demesne exemptions. At Cerne Abbas, in Dorset, for example, there is a discrepancy between the total geldable hidage (22 hides) and the number of hides for which the demesne and the villeins are responsible (18 hides). There is also

25 VCH Kent, iii. 214.
26 VCH Dorset, iii. 76.
27 It is possible that these Domesday returns of manorial value were computed, not on the basis of income actually received, but on the basis of an agreed valuation. Under Schedule A arrangements, as they were for many years until sharper probes were devised, the Inland Revenue assessed landlords on the basis of an agreed value which was only revised after a term of years. The practice of allowing old and possibly unrealistic assessments to stand is itself perhaps old.

a discrepancy between the total number of ploughs (21) and the number working on the demesne and with the villeins (17). The liabilities of the manor and its resources are greater than the sum of the liabilities and resources of its major parts because there is a sub-manor which discharges the balance of the liabilities with the balance of the resources. The sub-manor has an annual value to its tenant, which is noted in DB, and the tenant pays a rent to his superior lord, which is noted in the Exon Domesday. From the mesne tenant's point of view, his income, his gross hidage liability, and the ploughteams imputed to the hidage of his manor, give him a status as a tax-payer comparable with that of the greatest tax-payer in the land.[28]

Even quite small tenants turn out to be mesne tenants, and hence lords of manors, in DB. In Cambridgeshire, for example, innumerable mesne tenants hold '1 hide and 22 acres', or '1½ virgates', or '40 acres'. These are not land measurements. They are hidage codings: for the tenants in question hold all the appurtenances of a manor in the shape of men and ploughs and even perhaps a mill.[29] In Norfolk we find the same thing. At Ormesby, for example, 80 sokemen have 4 carucates and 46 acres; in Mileham and Bittering 'a certain widow' holds 1 carucate and 12 acres; in Freethorpe 9 freemen hold 60 acres.[30] In Acre, the villeins actually hold ½ carucate and hold it as principals, not as servants of the manor.[31]

Not all tenants, however, are lords of manors. DB may not pursue manorial lordship beyond a certain point. But it tells us about a great many tenants who are not lords of manors; and in doing so reveals something about its approach to such tenants which is of the utmost significance to any attempt to dispel the mystery that still shrouds its purpose. We are, in fact, approaching the central problem of Domesday studies. So far we have a coding system expressed in hides which tells us how much geld a manor must pay, given the current rate of taxation; and an income assessment which tells us what the manor yields to its lord. The assessment of income is subject to allowances; and allowances must surely mean that income which is not exempt is liable for taxation. We may reasonably deduce from this that there is some connection between manorial hidage and the lord's income. But we cannot yet say what that connection is. We must investigate what DB has to say about the ordinary tenants of manors. Presumably if these tenants make some contribution to the tax paid by the manor, on the basis of what they earn, then their contribution will be, in some measure, reflected in the hidage codings, and the Domesday commissioners will be found to have made strenuous efforts to reveal the true nature of the resources out of which these contributions are being made.

In fact, DB tells us very little about such tenants. And that is a very significant omission; for, with the exception of the humblest members of this

28 VCH Dorset, iii. 131.
29 VCH Cambs., i. 374, 376, 378.
30 VCH Norfolk, ii. 45, 49, 51.
31 Ibid., p. 49.

very extensive class of tenants of lords of manors, they all ran farms; they all managed assets such as buildings, equipment and animals; and they all showed some sort of return on these assets as well as on their own skill and labour. Between them these tenants may have accounted for the greater part of what we are accustomed to calling the gross domestic product of the country. Any survey of England which neglected to investigate their activities and assess their worth would have neglected some of the chief assets of the kingdom. And yet that is what DB does. It says nothing whatsoever about the incomes of such tenants. When it counts their ploughs, or notes their lack of them, it does so in a way which makes the information it compiles virtually useless for taxation purposes. It fails to distinguish between the ploughs with which tenants fulfil their manorial obligations by working their lord's demesne arable, and hence maintaining his income, and those with which they work their own lands. No doubt, in many cases, the same ploughs performed both functions. But if DB is appraising assets with their taxable potential in mind, then a tool which one man owns but which is committed to the maintenance of another man's income, cannot be said to be making a contribution to the owner's taxable income. It is, in this context, merely paying his rent; and to count it as his without indicating how it is being used must, if that is what DB is actually doing, provide the King with grossly misleading, and indeed mischievously distorted information.

But asset appraisal with a view to reassessment of taxable capacity was far from being the purpose of the Domesday commissioners' scrutiny of the tenants of lords of manors. We can tell that this was so by studying what DB has to say about tenant livestock. DB has nothing whatsoever to say about tenant livestock, though livestock was every bit as important to the manorial tenant as it was to the manorial lord. Indeed nothing in DB conveys more strikingly the quite extraordinary failure of the Domesday inquiry to make those comprehensive investigations of the English countryside with which it is so frequently credited than its treatment of livestock statistics.

The Winchester abridgement explicitly excludes all reference to livestock numbers except for plough oxen and the occasional horse. When it tells us about swine it does so simply in order to indicate woodland capacity. It says nothing about who, if anyone, owns the swine. But Domesday investigators did a great deal of work on the subject of livestock, as we can see by consulting the profusion of preliminary reports and early drafts that lie behind the Winchester version of the survey. From these records we can pick up a great deal of valuable information which was rigorously excluded from the final revisions. The *Inquisitio Comitatus Cantabrigiensis*, for example, which is a twelfth-century transcript of an early Domesday record, tells us that 'the cattle on the demesne' of Snailwell manor, in Staploe hundred, amounted to '111 sheep, 16 pigs and 1 horse'. It says nothing about anyone else's livestock.[32] Nor does it do so elsewhere. If Little Domesday, which was

32 VCH Cambs., i. 400.

another draft report, often leaves room for doubt as to whose livestock is being listed, the Exon Domesday does not. It banishes doubt from our minds. 'The King has a manor which is called Pimperne and Charlton Marshall . . . There the King has 18 villeins and 68 bordars and i colibert and 5 slaves and 2 packhorses and 16 beasts and 25 pigs and 400 sheep and 36 goats and 2 mills which render 40s. 6d . . .'.[33] The Abbey of Abbotsbury has a manor called Hilton. 'There the Abbot has 17 villeins and 12 bordars and 8 slaves and 3 packhorses and 8 beasts and 20 pigs and 406 sheep and 25 goats and a mill which renders 20d . . .'.[34] And so on.

When these very full reports tell us about livestock, they tell us only about demesne livestock; though if they had been concerned with searching out the truth about the wealth of the whole community, as we are so often told they were, they would surely have told us about the livestock held by the tenants of manorial lords who, possessing very little individually, as many of them did, nevertheless probably held between them the greater part of the country's resources of cattle and sheep. In later periods that is what they unquestionably did.[35] This omission from the Domesday drafts is significant enough. But what is perhaps even more significant is the way in which those who compiled these inventories unhesitatingly catalogued the manor's stock of villeins along with its supply of goats and pigs. This may be something which is profoundly abhorrent to modern feelings. But nothing could be more devastatingly revealing. In these draft records we seem to catch a glimpse of how Domesday investigators appraised the agrarian status and purpose of the ordinary dependent tenant on the ordinary manorial estate. The tenants, like the ploughs and the pigs, were manorial assets; and in conjunction with the ploughs and the pigs were enumerated and valued for what they could do for the manorial lord.

We come across the same intense preoccupation with the interests of the manorial lord when we turn to the Domesday accounts of mills. Domesday mills are valued when they earn an income for the manorial lord; and they earn him an income when his tenants use them. When they serve the lord himself they may earn their keep, but they cannot return their value in cash because the lord does not charge himself for the use of his own resources. When that happens DB records the fact that the mill in question has no value because it works exclusively for the demesne.[36]

If the tenants of lords of manors are not being assessed for taxation on the basis of what they are worth or what they earn, they are certainly required to pay the taxes with which the manor is charged. The Domesday survey, which evidently collects none of the information upon which the King could base a rational taxation policy for the tenantry, nevertheless makes it abundantly

33 VCH Dorset, iii. 65.
34 Ibid., p. 80.
35 A. R. Bridbury, 'Before the Black Death'. Economic History Review, 2nd ser., xxx (1977), 398–9, reprinted below, pp. 180–99.
36 VCH Cambs., i. 378; also EHD, p. 880.

clear that the tenantry foots the tax bill. Thus: the King has a manor called
Little Puddle, in Piddlehinton, Dorset. It is assessed at 5 hides. 'There', says
the Exon Domesday, 'the King has in demesne 2½ hides and the villeins
have as many'.[37] The demesne is exempt; and the Dorset geld accounts
record its exemption in Puddletown hundred. If the villeins are held responsible for 2½ hides of geld liability, as Domesday says they were, that means
they pay Little Puddle's tax debt to the full extent of Little Puddle's assessment net of exemptions. On other manors the incidence of geld taxation can
be seen to have fallen differentially upon the tenants. Robert de Olgi held
Iver, in Buckinghamshire. It was assessed at 17 hides, of which 2 were in
demesne. There was land for 30 ploughs, 4 of which were in demesne. The
rest of the ploughs were held by 32 villeins, of whom 5 held 6 hides. This
means, presumably, that 9 hides of tax liability were variously assigned to 27
villeins. But we are not told how.[38]

The plainest indications to be found anywhere in DB, however, that
manorial tax liabilities were laid upon the tenantry as a matter of formal
responsibility, are to be found in Middlesex, where, for reasons that nobody
has yet fathomed, the hidage responsibilities of the villein and bordar tenantry are set out in full. The representative Middlesex entry runs as follows:
Westminster Abbey holds Staines for 19 hides. There are 11 hides in demesne; and 3 villeins each with ½ hide, 4 villeins with i hide, 8 villeins each
with ½ virgate, 36 bordars with 3 hides, 1 villein with 1 virgate, 4 bordars
with 40 acres, 10 bordars each with 5 acres, 5 cottars each with 4 acres, 8
bordars with 1 virgate and 3 cottars with 9 acres.[39]

These measurements look uncommonly like measurements of area. And
indeed measurement by area is far from being unusual in DB. Meadow and
pasture, and even at times woodland, are all measured, generally in terms of
length and breadth, sometimes in terms of acres. In Norfolk and Suffolk, the
whole manor, or to put the matter more exactly, the whole of the manorial
area that concerned the Domesday surveyors, was measured in terms of
length and breadth. The villeins and bordars of Staines are not holding their
land as principals. Their hidage responsibilities have not been set out by the
Domesday surveyors of Middlesex because these surveyors had been deluded
into thinking that each one of the villeins or bordars was a mesne tenant in
his own right. The Staines tenants are very obviously the servile tenants of
the Abbot of Westminster and work the land of the Abbot as everyone did
who held land on servile terms at that time. Does that mean that DB has, by
a stroke of exceptional good fortune, left us precious testimony as to the size
of Middlesex farms held by peasants who stood at, or near, the bottom of the
social structure? It certainly looks like it; and many Domesday commentators
have assumed that it does. But when we do our sums we find that DB has not

---

[37] VCH Dorset, iii. 67.
[38] VCH Bucks., i. 257-8.
[39] VCH Middlesex, i. 123.

departed from its standard practices. The hide remains immutably the fiscal hide. Middlesex differs from the other counties only to the extent that in Middlesex liability to the geld is imputed to individual peasants, or to groups of peasants, instead of being stated as a general burden on the peasantry whose detailed incidence did not need to be made explicit in the survey.

Thus at Staines, the net liability of the manor for geld amounts to 8 hides. This is the gross liability (19 hides) less demesne exemption (11 hides). When we add together the peasant hides, virgates and acres, we find that they add up to virtually 8 hides. There are 16 villeins who are responsible for 3¾ hides; 58 bordars who answer for 4 hides; and 8 cottars who find geld for 3/10 of a virgate. But this is the manor's net liability for geld.

Nor is Staines unusual in Middlesex. DB surveys 98 Middlesex manors. But we cannot check our calculations by working through them all. Many of them, unfortunately, as set out in the Winchester Domesday, lack some vital figure or other. But there are 38 cases for which we have everything we need: gross and net liability to taxation; and full details of the hidages attributed to the villein and bordar peasantry. In 27 out of these 38 cases there is an exact or a reasonably close correspondence between net manorial liability for geld, as expressed in hides, and the sum of all the hides attributed to the villeins and bordars. The rest of the cases in this restricted sample are more or less random, with wide disparities, on occasion, between net manorial hidage and the sum of all the peasants hides.

In assessing the value of these figures we must beware of emphasizing the erratic results to the detriment of what seems to be the general rule. We must not be surprised to find anomalies in DB. The Domesday commissioners undoubtedly expected them. Had there been none, their work would have lost a good deal of its purpose. And what the Middlesex statistics show is that, in two-thirds of the cases we have been able to examine, the net manorial liability for geld, once demesne allowances have been deducted, equals the hidage attributed to the peasantry. For all the shortcomings of the sample, the Middlesex evidence tells us, as plainly as it can, that DB has recorded the tax liabilities of the manorial tenantry, not the size of their holdings. It tells us that the settled intention of the tax system was to charge the tenantry of England with the tax assessed on the manors of England. What we see in these Middlesex examples is how that tax liability was distributed in detail.

What then are we to make of the Domesday survey as a result of this investigation of the principal elements of a fairly average Domesday entry?

Every entry starts with a tax-coding. Some entries mention demesne allowances. The fact that many do not is not evidence that demesne allowances are unusual. A glance at the surviving geld accounts will quickly dispel any such suspicions. The tax in question is the geld. It is paid by manorial tenants, the majority of whom are villeins and bordars. Liability to tax cannot wholly ignore capacity to pay. But the Domesday commissioners make no attempt to find out whether those who pay the taxes can bear the weight of taxation with which they are burdened. Instead they tell us about the incomes of manorial lords. They also tell us about productive capacity. But the index of productive power with which they deal does not resolve our problem. Productive capacity, expressed in terms of ploughteams, is related in DB to tax-codings; and this still leaves us with the problem of deciding how tax-codes are related to capacity to pay.

Can we perhaps resolve the problem of relating all these magnitudes to one another by approaching DB from another direction altogether? Unfortunately we lack direct evidence of the instructions with which the Domesday commissioners were issued or of any explanatory gloss that may have accompanied those instructions. The Ely Inquest, which appears to give the closest approximation to a schedule of instructions, is not contemporary with Domesday. It is a twelfth-century survey of the property of the Abbey of Ely.[40] Nor is it altogether satisfactory even as a simulacrum of the Domesday terms of reference. Its introductory preamble purports to set out a schedule of questions to be asked. But in fact this schedule asks questions which are not answered in the body of the inquest and fails to ask questions which are punctiliously answered in the inquest. The schedule requires answers to questions about how much has been added or taken away and whether more could be had. But the inquest says nothing about such matters. The schedule does not ask how many ploughs can work the land. Nor does it ask about livestock. But answers to these apparently unasked questions are abundantly forthcoming in the inquest.

Contemporary comment seems to bring us closer to an understanding of what was required of the commissioners. The Anglo-Saxon Chronicle declared that the primary object of the investigation was to find out how many hides of land there were in each county and how much land and livestock the King himself possessed throughout the kingdom. That done, the investigation was then instructed, according to the Anglo-Saxon Chronicle, to find out how much land or livestock the other landholders had. By landholder the Anglo-Saxon Chronicle specified whom it meant without specifying all whom it meant. It specified archbishops, bishops, abbots, earls and then referred, more generally, to all other landholders.[41]

It calls for very little deductive skill, however, to work out, from the clues supplied by the Anglo-Saxon Chronicle, the likely status of landholders who could be included in a class of men of property whose membership was dominated by the leaders of society. Landholder, in this instance, surely meant magnate. And the Anglo-Saxon Chronicle, in a sense, confirms this interpretation of its words. It says nothing about anyone else's land. It says nothing about the land of ordinary sokemen or villeins, for example. But it does say something about the thoroughness with which the commissioners did their work; and in doing so tells us more than it says. Nothing escaped

[40] For extracts, see *EHD*, no. 215, pp. 881–5. The preamble is printed in W. Stubbs, ed., *Select Charters*, 9th edn (Oxford, 1913), p. 101.
[41] *The Anglo-Saxon Chronicle,*. trans. G. N. Garmonsway (Everyman Library, London, 1953), p. 216.

the scrutiny of the King's commissioners, according to the Anglo-Saxon Chronicle: not even an ox or a cow or a pig. But in DB the pig in question was always the demesne pig. It was never the pig belonging to the ordinary villein or bordar; nor even the pig belonging to sokeman or freeman. Domesday livestock was always demesne livestock; and demesne livestock meant the livestock of the manorial lord who, in DB, was either a tenant-in-chief or his mesne tenant and as such usually, but not invariably, a man of wealth and influence.

The clear impression conveyed by the Anglo-Saxon Chronicle, that DB was a survey of the landed possessions of the tenants-in-chief, is strengthened by the testimony of the only other contemporary commentator whose words survive. Robert of Hereford, who may very well have been at the Gloucester meeting at which the Domesday project was put in hand, wrote of DB that it was a description of the property of the magnates, of their fields, manors and men, of their ploughs, horses and other animals, and of the services and dues accruing to them. 'Descriptio . . . in possessionibus singularum procerum, in agris eorum, in mansionibus, in hominibus . . . in carucis, in equis et ceteris animalibus, in servitio et censu . . . omnium.' Here, as before, the commentator removes all possible ambiguity as to whom he means by specifying the animals. Only demesne animals make any of the running in the Domesday survey.[42]

Thus contemporaries leave us in no doubt as to whose landed property DB was commissioned to investigate. Indeed they tell us as plainly as they can what DB is not. They warn us against supposing that DB can provide us with anything as comprehensive as a social survey or a census of production. Instead they tell us to expect something far more circumscribed in scope. They tell us to expect an investigation into values, property rights and so forth, restricted to those who belong, for the most part, to the most exalted class in society.

That the Domesday survey is very much less ambitious in scope than many writers have taken it to be is something that its structure certainly suggests. To a cursory inspection, DB looks like a land register. Closer examination reveals, however, that it is not one register but many. It is a collection of county registers. But each register is entirely independent of all the others. Nowhere are the registers collated. There is not even a general index. If DB is a register of the land held by the greatest magnates in England then it is a register of the land held by men who were bound to have held land in many of the counties of England. But DB does nothing to help in the compilation of a comprehensive tally of any magnate's estates. This must be done laboriously from the county evidence; and it must be done with prior knowledge of where to look: a curious deficiency in a record for which so much has so often been claimed.

---

[42] Stubbs, *Select Charters*, p. 95. The translation in *EHD*, no. 198, p. 851, is somewhat misleading.

At the county level DB is more helpful. Before the first landed entry in each county there comes a list of the names of those who held land in that county. Evidently it was thought to be more important to be able to find someone's possessions in particular counties than it was to be able to find out, at a glance, where all his possessions lay. The list is, as the Anglo-Saxon Chronicle and the Bishop of Hereford would lead one to expect, a very exclusive one. The King's name comes first whether he holds much land or little in the county; and the King's name is followed by the names of all those who hold land as tenants-in-chief in that county down to the humblest person to do so. The names are set down in order of feudal precedence. Those who hold more land may very well appear lower down the list than those who hold less; and those who do not hold land as tenants-in-chief do not appear on the list at all, though it is possible that one or two of those who hold land as tenants of tenants-in-chief may count for more as property holders in particular counties than some of those who appear high on that list.

Once the tenant-in-chief whose possessions are being searched for has been spotted in a county list, turning up his possessions takes no more than a moment to do; for his possessions are grouped together under his name. But again DB seems to be dedicated to frustrating the busy administrator; for each manor within such a group is surveyed in DB as if it stood uniquely alone as that tenant-in-chief's sole possession in the county. No attempt is made, even at county level, to summarize the information for quick reference. There is no figure for total ploughteams, or total value, or total liability for taxation. Indeed where DB locates a magnate's manors by interposing the name of the hundred within which each of his manors lay, into the listing of his possessions, such interpositions must have distracted the attention of anyone who tried to aggregate figures for ploughteams, values and the like.

As a land register DB seems to have made the information collected within its pages as irretrievable as it possibly could. Moreover as a land register DB suffers from the further disability that it made no provision for erasure or emendation. The nature of property is that it is escheated, inherited, exchanged, donated, bought and sold. A land register is obsolescent as soon as it is completed. Within a generation it is of no more use than last year's hotel guide. But DB was close-written as if there were to be no tomorrow.

In short we are wrong to think of DB as a directory of landed estates. It is quite hopeless from that point of view. It will not tell us about estates when they cut across county boundaries; and it will not tell us about estates when they do not. In DB nothing is aggregated. When the Anglo-Saxon Chronicle declared that finding out 'how many hundreds of hides of land there were in each shire' was the King's highest priority in having his survey made, it showed how thoroughly misinformed it could be. In DB the county hidage can only be calculated by adding together the individual assessments of all the individual manors in any particular county. Anyone who required county totals of hidage would have done better to send for the latest set of geld returns than to toil over the involutions of DB. And yet DB works well for anyone who wants to turn up details of a particular manor and knows the name of the magnate who is its tenant-in-chief. What it does well must surely tell us what it was designed to do. And what it was designed to do is plain enough. It was designed to provide a quick reference system for all the relevant information compiled by the Domesday commissioners concerning the basic unit of any magnate's estate: the manor, where income was generated and tax liabilities were incurred.

Thus wherever we turn in studying the Domesday evidence we are constantly being compelled to recognize the transcendent importance to the Domesday survey of the tenant-in-chief, his income and his manorial rights and possessions; and to acknowledge the fact that, apart from an indication of their social standing, we are told no more about the other tenants who feature in DB than that they plough with a stated number of teams. How can we avoid the conclusion that all these Domesday statistics are locked together by a survey which tells the King, for every manor, the name of its lord; his income; the hidage-coding that reflects his income in tax liabilities; possibly his allowances; the number of ploughteams required by the land that answers for that income and hidage-coding; the demesne appurtenances and perhaps the demesne stock associated with that level of activity; and the labour supply upon which the lord was authorized to call as a result of obligations of tenure?

There is nothing in DB to demonstrate beyond peradventure that the hidage-coding system was linked to the manorial lord's income as there is to show that hidage-coding was linked to ploughteam capacity. Consequently there is nothing in the evidence to preclude us from contending that the statistics of income and the hidage-codings relate to different aspects of the manorial economy, the income to the lord's interests and the hidage-codings to the aggregate interests of everyone whose earnings can be said to have contributed to the annual value of the manor. But if we argue in this way we make nonsense of the Domesday inquiry. If the ordinary tenants were to be charged on their earnings their circumstances required investigation. None is attempted. The manorial demesne is investigated in depth. The demesne, however, is exempt from taxation. The lord's income is assiduously recorded; but to what purpose if the greater part of the aggregate income of the manor is not? Even the ploughteam figures are useless for taxation purposes. How could the fiscal authorities hope to be able to tell how many ploughs the ordinary tenants employed on their farms when the figures fail to distinguish the tenant ploughs which maintained the lord's income from those that maintained their own incomes?

Everything falls into place, however, if we take the view that tax is paid on the income of the lord of the manor. This means that the hidage-coding tells the lord of the manor about his gross liability to taxation and his allowances, though these are not always recorded in the Winchester edition of DB. It also means that the ploughteam figures express the income of the manorial lord in real terms. They tell the King how many ploughs the manor needs in order to be able to produce the income that corresponds with the hidage-coding assigned to it. We are at last dealing with a survey of English manorial life that seems to make sense within the limitations of purpose implied by its structure and attributed to it by contemporaries.

For one thing, the allowance system becomes immediately intelligible once we assume that geld is an income-tax levied upon the net yield of the manor to its lord. It becomes intelligible in terms of what we know about subsequent principles of taxation. The manorial lord drew his income from his demesne lands and from other properties and perquisites within the manor. The manorial demesne lent itself readily to the operation of a famil-iar medieval fiscal concept reaffirmed in Magna Carta: the idea that a man should not be taxed in respect of the tools of his trade or the means whereby he maintains his status in society.[43] Demesne exemption from geld seems to provide us with an early example of this principle in action. A proportion of the total value of the manor to its lord is exempt; the rest is not. And the coding system tells the manorial lord all he needs to know about his tax assessment, gross and net.

In this connection, the Domesday material seems to provide us with curious confirmation of this analysis. If it is a correct analysis then the manorial lord was compelled by the exigencies of the taxation system to find out how his income was divided between demesne land and the rest. He could scarcely be expected to understand what was going on if he did not. And by an administrative accident we appear to possess a small sample of the kind of summary general surveys that some of the bigger magnates kept. They appear to show how taxation systems influenced accountancy practices in the eleventh century.

At the back of the Exon Domesday we find summaries of the total pos-sessions of a small number of tenants-in-chief with holdings throughout the south-western counties. Thus Robert of Mortain, with manors in Wiltshire, Dorset, Devon and Cornwall, is said to have 623 manors in these counties, rated at 832 hides and 1½ virgates, worked by 2,480 ploughteams and worth £1,408 13s 2d. In demesne he has 198 hides. His tenants have 654 hides and 3½ virgates.[44] The arithmetic of this summary leaves something to be desired. There are more hides in demesne and amongst the tenants than the total allows for. But the summary itself is readily intelligible in terms of the familiar Domesday pattern. The ordinary DB entry tells us about the individ-ual manor. These summaries take the particulars of individual manors and aggregate them. Robert of Mortain's gross tax liability is for 832 hides. But he has 198 in demesne. That means his net liability is for 634 hides; a liability which is correctly imputed to his tenants.

What makes this summary so particularly interesting and important, how-

---

[43] Clause 20: a freeman to be amerced 'salvo contenemento suo'; a villein 'salvo waynagio suo'. Stubbs, *Select Charters*, pp. 295–6.
[44] *DBRC*, iv. fo. 531.

ever, is not so much its collating of material that DB scatters in any number of separate entries, as its use of material that is not to be found in any of the ordinary Domesday entries: for the Mortain summary tells us what the demesne and tenant lands are separately worth. We are told that Robert's demesne lands yield him an income of £400 plus one silver mark; and that the lands of his tenants yield an income of £999 13s 2d. We are not told to whom this income is yielded. The Exon draftsmen take it for granted that those who consult their work will know. That the income imputed to the tenants of Robert of Mortain is, in fact, his income from the land his tenants hold from him we have no reason to doubt. We are told his income from his 623 manors. It is a shade over £1,408. If we add his declared income from his demesne lands, which was slightly more than £400, to the tenancy income, which was just under £1,000, we find that the sum total falls very little short of what we know his income from those 623 manors was said to be. From these particulars we can see that demesne land on the Mortain estates was deemed to be worth, on average, £2 per hide and tenant land subject to hidage, about £1 10s.

The intrusion of these extraordinary summaries into the Domesday record points to an origin for them which lies beyond the investigations organized or instigated by the Domesday commissioners. No one could have found out how demesne land differed from tenant land in respect of hidage valuation on the Mortain estates without having access to more information than DB reckoned to provide. And no one could have put together a summary account of the aggregate value, size and hidage liability of the entire Mortain interest in these south-western counties, without doing a great deal more work than the Domesday commissioners and their coadjutors reckoned to do. When we come across a statistical digest that tells us things that we are not told elsewhere in the Domesday record, and collates information in a way in which it is not collated elsewhere in that record, then we are entitled to suspect that the Domesday commissioners are far less likely to have collected more material than they needed than they are to have been offered more material than they asked for and could handle. And when we find that this statistical digest has not been incorporated into the body of the Domesday report but has been tacked on to the end of it, then we can reasonably assume that the Domesday commissioners, finding themselves at a loss to know what to do with all the material contained in the digest, but recognizing its interest and possible value, simply decided to attach it, possibly with the intention of sending it on in case it should prove to be something they could use at Winchester.[45]

If we may trace the intrusion of these digests into the Domesday record to

---

[45] That this is not an entirely fanciful account of how these valors got into the Exon Domesday we may conclude with some confidence when we recall that the Exon Domesday also harbours the only extant records of the geld levied at that period. Someone in the south-western circuit headquarters was evidently an inverterate hoarder.

some sort of misunderstanding of what was required of them, then we are perhaps justified in thinking that what the Domesday commissioners appear to have been offered, by the estate managers of a handful of tenants-in-chief in the south-western counties, was the eleventh-century equivalent of the summary financial statements known to fifteenth-century estate management as valors. These eleventh-century valors, if we may call them such, had evidently been prepared by estate managers to provide the kind of classification of income and hidage-rating that we seem to find everywhere in DB without the compelling plausibility of evidence for a connection between the two that we find in these summary accounts. We do not come across valuations drawn up in quite this way later, because the taxation of hidage came to an end in the twelfth century; and the disappearance of hidage taxation inevitably brought about significant changes in the way in which manorial lords looked at their income and, particularly, in the way in which they had their surveys of total income prepared.

If we interpret DB along the lines that suggest themselves when we take the view that manorial income, manorial hidage-codings and manorial ploughteams are linked together, then we are bound to come to the conclusion that everything in the manorial surveys compiled by the Domesday commissioners was subordinated to the purpose of giving a clear account of the lord of the manor's interest in his manor to the exclusion of everyone else's. Some stubborn Domesday problems resolve themselves easily if we decide to look at the Domesday manor in this way. There is, for example, the problem that arises whenever the figure for total manorial ploughteam capacity differs from the combined figure that results from adding together the separate figures for demesne and tenant teams.

In DB the ploughteam surveys take one of three forms. DB may say that there is land for so many ploughs on a particular manor and find that these ploughs are actually there, some on the demesne and the rest in the hands of some or all of the tenants. It may find, however, that there is a deficiency of ploughs available compared with the number that the land could employ, either because the demesne could carry more or because the tenants could. And DB could find, as it does so often in Nottinghamshire or Lincolnshire, that there are more ploughs available on the demesne and amongst the tenants than there is land for these ploughs to work.

This disparity between capacity and supply, where supply exceeds capacity, has puzzled Domesday commentators. But it has puzzled them only because they have assumed that, when DB says there is land for a given number of ploughs, what it means by that phrase is that the land of the manor, taking both demesne and tenant land into account, has an aggregate arable capacity which, the climate, soil and lie of the land being what they are, require the services of that particular number of teams. If, however, we drop the assumption that Domesday is committed to a survey of the manor as an aggregation of demesne and tenant farms and change the point of view from which we consider these disparities, then the puzzle will vanish. If we bear in mind that DB is an investigation exclusively concerned with the income of the manorial lord and its constituents, that is to say with the land and obligations from which the manorial lord derives the income with which he is credited in DB, then the paradoxes will resolve themselves.

When DB says, for example, that the villeins on some particular manor could run another plough or so, it does not mean by this remark that these villeins, for reasons wholly dissociated from their liabilities to the manorial economy, really could, if they buckled to and set their minds to it, manage one or two more ploughs on their holdings. Such an interpretation reduces DB to the status of an agricultural advisory service admonishing dilatory small-holders for neglecting their opportunities. And whatever else DB may have been, it was emphatically never that. When DB says the villeins could supply more ploughs, it means that they are, like the geburs in the *Recti-tudines*, set up with land and oxen in return for services which, in that particular instance, they are not doing, whatever the reason may be. It does not mean that these villeins have not got the ploughs in question. DB does not tell us about their personal circumstances. It is concerned with their obligations to the lord of the manor. For all we know, these villeins may possess much more than they need in order to discharge their obligations. The Domesday juries, with their local knowledge, presumably have a very shrewd idea as to whether the villeins in question can or cannot easily do what has to be done. But that is not the matter at issue. A manorial obligation exists and is undischarged. DB notes the fact because an undischarged obligation detracts from the income of the lord of the manor and hence from the taxable capacity of his manor.

Similarly, when DB says that the demesne could run an extra plough or so, what it means is that the services available from the tenantry are such that, when the tenants have done everything they are obliged to do, the demesne will still require more services than it has hitherto provided for itself and will require the number specified in order to bring the total up to capacity and hence bring the income of the demesne up to scratch. It may strike us as curious that the Domesday commissioners should express such interest in the income that manorial lords drew from their demesne lands. Demesne was, after all, exempt from taxation. But their task was to convey to the King the most exact account they could compile of the truth about manorial income and its sources, leaving it to him to settle problems connected with future revisions of codings and allowances.

And when DB says that there are more services available than there is land for them to cultivate, what it means is that the demesne, not the manor with its tenanted virgates and acres, is over-supplied. The over-supply is as natural and inevitable as the under-supply; for the notion that there is some providential symmetry to be found in the structure of the manor, balancing demesne needs with service obligations, is one that was laid to rest many years ago as a result of much brilliant work on regional manorial structures. Some manors were adequately endowed with service obligations in relation to their needs. Many were deficient in such obligations; and there were others again which found themselves excessively provided for and quite unable to use all the obligations that their tenants were required to afford them. These were the manors, plainly visible in later records, that we find in DB, with land for many fewer ploughs than there are ploughing obligations available for use on such land. These surplus obligations are no problem to the manorial economy. When obligations to plough are surplus to requirements they can always be commuted for a fee. The lord's income does not suffer because the lord cannot employ all the services he is entitled to receive, even though in DB such unfulfilled obligations appear to be recorded as unrequited debts.

When we discard the notion that DB is some sort of census of production, surveying the productive capacity of the manor as an aggregation of many farms, we can readily appreciate why it says so little about the tenantry and so much about the lord of the manor. With its concern strictly bounded by the interests of the lord of the manor, DB tells us about his tenants only because they contribute to those interests and only to the extent that they contribute to them. When we are told that some tenants bring two oxen to the demesne plough, we are being told about service obligations; we are not being given an inventory of possessions. In DB only demesne possessions are ever made the subject of an inventory. Consequently the oxen do not give us a glimpse of how the other half lived. Those who do little for the manorial lord are not necessarily poor because their obligations are few. They may be, on the contrary, very well-to-do. Much dedicated work on Domesday statistics reflects, unfortunately, an entirely false reading of the significance of these Domesday figures.

When we turn, therefore, to the villeins and bordars with whom DB is constantly preoccupied, and to the sokemen and other free tenants who figure, from time to time, even in the counties in which they are least conspicuous, we find that when the focus of attention appears to change, the focus of concern does not. Whatever we examine in DB matters only because it matters to the tenant-in-chief or his tenant. In Barton-on-Humber, in Lincolnshire, for example, where there is land for 27 teams, Gilbert de Gand 'has 7 teams there in demesne and 63 villeins and 16 bordars with 9 teams and 42 sokemen and 67 bordars with 10 teams.'[46] In this manor, the sokemen work with the villeins and bordars and they all work for the lord; for it is his demesne income that their labours help to determine. And slaves make their contributions alongside those of the other villagers. Slave participation in ploughing, when both ploughs and slaves are said to belong to the demesne, is familiar enough to Domesday studies. But what are we to think when we are told about Avening, in Gloucestershire, where, in addition to the demesne ploughs, there are 24 villeins, 5 bordars and 30 slaves with 16 ploughs;[47] or about Tickford, in Buckinghamshire, where 6 villeins with 4

46 *The Lincolnshire Domesday*. p. 106.
47 DBRC, i (1783), fo. 163b.

slaves have 6 ploughs?[48] These slaves may very well belong to the villeins and even, perhaps, to the bordars. But they do not work exclusively for their owners; for DB has earmarked some share of their time for the benefit of the manorial lord. They must work, as their owners do, to swell the demesne income of the lord of the manor.

As tenants, these sokemen and villeins work directly for the lord of the manor by providing him with services on his demesne. But they also work for him indirectly by paying rent and other charges according to the terms upon which they have tenure of their holdings. The land that pays rent to the lord of the manor also pays geld to the King; for rent is income so far as the lord of the manor is concerned; and income is rated for hidage when it is the income of the lord of the manor.

All the tenanted land pays rent, though some rents may be so light that they scarcely merit the name. Hence all the tenanted land of the manor lies within the hidage. But rent does not absorb the whole product of the tenant-farm. If it did the tenant would be left with nothing to live on. Even the most pessimistic estimates of what the harshest landlords demanded of the most oppressively-treated tenants concede that such landlords were bound to have taken no more than half the product of their tenants' farms in the form of rent, dues, tallages, amercements, fines and the like.[49] And very many tenants, in some regions perhaps the greater number of tenants, were far better treated than that. This means that the ploughteams listed by the Domesday survey may not give us anything like an adequate account of the number at work on the average manor. DB lists the ploughteams required by the manor so as to maintain the lord of the manor's income and hence his tax-rating. These are the ploughteams required in order to make productive the demesne arable of the manor and that portion of the land of the tenantry that represents rent, and hence income, to the lord of the manor. In a sense much, perhaps in many cases most, of the land of the manor lies outside the hidage because its yield, net of rent, is beyond the control of the manorial lord. That is the land whose profits, if any, accrue to the tenantry. It does nothing to increase the income of the lord. Consequently it lies beyond the cognizance of the Domesday inquiry.

If it is true that the King raised taxes by imposing a geld upon the manorial incomes of tenants-in-chief or their mesne tenants, having allowed them to deduct their demesne earnings from their liabilities; and that this geld was actually paid by the ordinary freemen, sokemen, villeins and bordars, who lived and worked on their manors; then the consequences for Domesday studies are serious. If the Domesday commissioners investigated the manorial tenant only to the extent that he contributed to the cultivation of his lord's demesne and to his lord's income from rents and other charges, then it is no

---

[48] VCH Bucks., i. 257.
[49] E. A. Kosminsky, Studies in the Agrarian History of England (Oxford, 1956), pp. 230–42.

exaggeration to say that DB, far from providing us with a unique and compendious insight into the agrarian life of Norman England, in fact excludes most of that life from its purview.

There is one final consideration, which may carry weight with those who are disposed to take a sympathetic view of the interpretation of the Domesday evidence outlined above. It is concerned with the statistical work done by Maitland and recently confirmed and reinforced by two scholars who have employed the resources of modern statistical techniques in order to test his conclusions. Maitland found a close correlation in DB between manorial income and hidage-ratings. By comparing the gross hidage totals for twenty counties with the total income estimates for those counties, he got a result which drew from him the comment that: 'No one can look along these lines of figures without fancying that some force, conscious or unconscious, has made for one pound one hide.' He then excluded certain dubious items from his calculations and did the sums again; and again concluded that: 'one pound one hide seems to be the central point of this series, the point of rest through which the pendulum swings'.[50]

Maitland did not pursue the implications of his discovery further because Round persuaded him to believe that hidage-ratings, far from being commensurate with manorial income, had in fact been imposed upon the land in 5-hide units without any regard for capacity to pay.

The statisticians are now happily embroiled in these Domesday figures; for Maitland's champions are now under attack by other statisticians who find merit in what Round had to say.[51] It is not for an innumerate spectator to intervene between these formidable antagonists. But if Maitland was right about his correlations then, whatever Round's figures may mean, they cannot mean that, by the time the Domesday commissioners were sent on their errands, hidage ratings were still independent of capacity to pay. If Maitland was right then, somehow or other, a tax system whose original purpose and incidence may have been very different from what they appear to be in DB, was rough-hewn over time so as to enable the King to levy an income-tax from his chief men on the basis of a simple coding device, and to have that coding device checked by sending his agents round the shires to find out whether the men and resources on the ground corresponded with what the records told him.

Nobody, least of all Maitland, has claimed that these correlations are

50 F. W. Maitland, *Domesday Book and Beyond* (Cambridge, 1897), p. 465. J. McDonald and G. D. Snooks published three articles in 1985 confirming and extending Maitland's analysis. These articles are: 'Were the tax assessments of Domesday England artificial?', *Economic History Review*, 2nd ser., vol. xxxviii (1985), pp. 352–72; 'The determinants of manorial income in Domesday England', *Journal of Economic History*, vol. xlv (1985), pp. 541–55; and 'Statistical analyses of Domesday Book', *Journal of the Royal Statistical Society*, ser. A, vol. cxlviii (1985), pp. 147–60.

51 Thus, for example, R. A. Leaver, 'Five Hides in Ten Counties', *Economic History Review*, 2nd ser., vol. xli (1988), pp. 525–42.

perfect. Exceptions and aberrations abound; patronage and fraud create anomalies in every county list. Domesday scholars, eager to demonstrate the fundamental indeterminancy of the relationship between income and hidage, have made the most of these. And indeed they vexed and exasperated the King as much as they have bemused us; for behind the probings and siftings of the commissioners and their provisional attempts at correction in detail, for which there is evidence, here and there, throughout DB, we can sense the restless suspicion of the King that there were reserves of wealth, in the hands of his tenants-in-chief, awaiting his exploitation, that ingenuity and subterfuge had rendered inaccessible to him hitherto. Nevertheless, such anomalies, as Maitland pointed out, and recent studies have confirmed, remain anomalous. The correlations are too close and numerous for coincidence. They suggest that there is a statistically verifiable link between manorial income, which was the income of the tenant-in-chief, and hidage, which bears all the signs of being the tax-coding corresponding to that income; and by doing so, these correlations appear to strengthen the conclusions worked out above, on the basis of other Domesday evidence, as to the true purpose and limited usefulness of DB as a guide to the social life of England in Norman times.

The Domesday Valuation of
Manorial Income

Wherever we turn in Domesday Book we find the commissioners making assessments of the value of the manors they have been instructed to investigate. 'The Bishop of Lincoln holds Stoke Mandeville' say the Buckinghamshire commissioners. 'In all it is worth £20.' 'The Bishop of Salisbury holds Potterne' say the Wiltshire commissioners. 'The demesne of the bishop is and was worth £60.' 'The Bishop of Rochester holds Bromley' say the commissioners for Kent. 'Now (it is worth) £18.' The form and substance of these phrases are familiar to every student of Domesday. And their meaning is not in doubt. Worth in Domesday Book means income; and income, in Domesday Book as elsewhere, is reckoned annually.

With assessments such as these it takes no more than patience and application to work out, as Corbett did, approximate figures for the annual income from property enjoyed by the king and his tenants-in-chief.[1] Income alone cannot possibly tell us all we should like to know about the relationships with one another of those at the top of the social pyramid; but it does give us a structure for our thoughts, however many allowances we have to make for error, evasion and collusion in the collection of the facts.

Nor is the use of such assessments confined to elucidating problems of social structure. Domesday statistics of income seem to offer us our first intimations of orders of magnitude when it comes to questions of taxable capacity or patterns of aristocratic expenditure. And they provide us, or apparently promise to provide us, with a bench-mark against which to measure subsequent changes in manorial profitability. The manorial records of the following centuries set before us statistics of income which bear every appearance of being strictly comparable with those of Domesday. Indeed it is widely believed that one of the main reasons why the Domesday report could be so rapidly completed was that manorial records were readily available for submission to the scrutiny of local investigators. But such comparisons over time are, in fact, always hard to make. They have to allow for the effects of inflation, which raises money values without necessarily raising real values. And income itself is a difficult concept to handle. We cannot, for example, tell whether Domesday income was assessed net or gross, and if net, whether the expenses allowed for were simply costs of production and maintenance,

---

[1]   W. J. Corbett in *Cambridge Medieval History*, vol. V (Cambridge, 1926), chapter xv.

or included elements, all too common in later manorial accounts, which could not possibly be construed as essential to the farming of the land.

Nevertheless such comparisons are regularly made and generally yield most encouraging results. As a rule they show how very much more success-fully manorial husbandry was managed in the century or so following the Conquest than it had been either in the Conqueror's day or on the day when Edward the Confessor was alive and dead. For the most part manorial in-come has been shown to have been so very much higher in the twelfth and particularly in the thirteenth century than it had been at the time of Domes-day that we seem to be left with no option but to endorse unhesitatingly the all but universal judgement of historians of medieval estates as to the exube-rance of the growth of prosperity over these years however generous the allowances we feel obliged to make for inflation and the idiosyncracies of medieval book-keeping.

Unfortunately such uses of Domesday income statistics may not yield us the results we are so anxious to derive from them. We may find that value in Domesday means annual income in our terms without necessarily meaning that what was commonly accepted by the general run of Domesday jurors as to the value of particular manors reflected anything like the full annual income accruing from those manors to their seigneurial lords. In short we may find that there was something like a convention governing the defini-tion of what constituted value in the eleventh century which the great majority of Domesday jurors fully understood and accepted and which the Domesday commissioners were content or obliged to recognise and confirm.

The clue to what may have been common form in eleventh-century England was provided in 1858 when the Camden Society published a selec-tion of the early records of the cathedral of St Paul's. The selection was edited by W. H. Hale, the incumbent archdeacon of London.[2] Amongst the records he published was an inquisition of 1181 which set out, for each manor in the cathedral's possession, its hidage rating, its income by way of farm and other rents, and its cash revenues, aggregated but not individually itemised, under the heading of 'Summa Denariorum'. What this 'Summa' consisted of was not immediately apparent. Hale also published the contents of a torn fragment which is all that survives of what appears to have been a comprehensive survey of the holdings and obligations of the tenantry of St Paul's carried out manor by manor in that same year. Being fragmentary this record tells us very little except for the fact that it was part of a cartulary. Fortunately St Paul's possessed, and Hale published, the magnificent cartu-lary of 1222. This cartulary appears to have been drawn up in exactly the same way as the fragment of 1181 and survives intact. What is more it explains the 1181 'Summa'.

The 1222 cartulary, amongst other things, gives details, manor by manor, of the cash payments for which the St Paul's tenants were liable. Hale added

<hr />

[2]   W. H. Hale, *The Domesday of St Paul's*, Camden Society o.s., vol. lxix (1858).

these sums together for each manor and found that each total corresponded very closely with the 'Summa Denariorum' to be found at the end of each respective manorial entry in the 1181 inquisition. Hale very reasonably concluded that each 'Summa' in the 1181 inquisition was made up of cash payments; that the 1181 cartulary would have supplied details of individual tenant liability had it survived; and that the 1222 cartulary supplies the deficiencies of the earlier cartulary.

These cash payments, according to the testimony of the 1222 cartulary, consisted simply and solely of those rents that tenants paid in cash. They did not take into account the money value of the labour services that most tenants provided in some sort and many provided in substantial measure. Nor did they monetise rents in kind. Moreover there is no hint, in the 1222 cartulary, of any contribution to the 'Summa' being made by court dues or seigneurial levies. The cash payments in question were itemised accounts of the rents paid in cash. Other important sources of manorial income were equally excluded from the purview of the 'Summa'. There is, nowhere, in any of them, any reference to proceeds from the sale of animals or produce. Indeed it is not too much to say that excluded from the 'Summa Denariorum' were most of the income-generating activities of the various manors of St Paul's.

These are vitally important considerations because Hale then went one stage farther; and his doing so brings us to the point of this somewhat discursive account of his editorial work. Hale got out the Domesday figures for the manors of St Paul's and found that the Domesday valuations of these manors bore an astonishingly close relationship to the cash totals of 1181 and 1222.[3]

At this point Hale lost interest and turned to other problems of editorial concern. But what he appears to have discovered may prove to be of first-rate importance. His evidence shows that, taking one manor with another, the Domesday commissioners had accepted valuations for the various manors of St Paul's which reflected, not the aggregate income that the manorial lord derived from produce and sale of produce, from court dues and rents in kind and in service and from seigneurial perquisites and levies, but merely the cash yielded by those rents that were paid in money. Can we really believe that the manors of St Paul's were assessed to geld and other taxes on the basis of a valuation which comprehensively ignored the greater part of their wealth-generating capacity? If they were, and the St Paul's evidence looks hard to fault, then we must ask ourselves whether St Paul's was unique or even unusual in this respect. Should we find that it was neither, the consequences for our views about the wealth of Norman England may be that we shall have to submit them to serious revision.

There are two obvious objections to the view that the St Paul's evidence

---

[3] See Table I. Hale uses the 1066 as well as the 1086 Domesday figures. But the 1086 figures are the ones used throughout this study.

reveals a widespread practice of grossly undervaluing manors when they were submitted to assessment for taxation and perhaps other purposes, as they were at the time of Domesday. One is the objection that St Paul's was the singular beneficiary of preferential treatment either regionally or as a result of intercession on its behalf at or near the top. Regional preference, however, is unlikely. St Paul's had a great deal of property in Essex; but the balance of its possessions lay in Hertfordshire, Middlesex and Surrey. Its possessions thus straddled the boundaries of two of the putative circuits of Domesday administration. But Domesday assessments for St Paul's do not vary topographically as they should have done if the administration of one of these circuits had been more favourably disposed towards St Paul's than the other. Equality of treatment regionally suggests that any influence brought to bear on behalf of St Paul's originated from somewhere higher than that. And if St Paul's benefited comprehensively and uniquely from such influence that will undoubtedly show if we find that few or none of the other estates with surviving records for us to examine were similarly treated.

The other obvious objection is that the comparison of the Domesday statistics with the summary totals of 1181 is inadmissable because of the length of the period between the two sets of figures. A whole century of change and development separates them. Hence it is arguable that St Paul's had become so very much more prosperous by 1181 than it had been in Domesday times that by 1181 its tenants were paying in cash alone as much as whole manors were worth a century before. Cash rents, even rents which were established by custom, certainly did change in the course of time. But they do not seem to have done so everywhere. There could hardly be a more spectacular case to the contrary than that of Tavistock Abbey where fourteenth-century rents of assize at Leigh, Burrington and Plymstock, correlate almost perfectly with the Domesday valuations of those manors.[4] On the manors of St Paul's, as Hale was at pains to point out, cash rents hardly changed at all between 1181 and 1222, though we now know, as Hale did not, that there was a bout of very severe inflation between these two dates.[5] We must be encouraged to presume, therefore, that cash rents at St Paul's did not rise from some level about which we know nothing until by 1181, by the most fortuitous concatenation of circumstances imaginable, each manor's cash rents contrived to correspond with the Domesday assessment of what we have always taken to be its income from all sources.

The St Paul's evidence seems to clear the more obvious hurdles. We must now turn to the corroborative evidence such as it is. The dearth of twelfth-century cartularies and rentals is notorious. Those that survive are all ecclesiastical in provenance. And none can tell us about possessions which lay farther north than Derbyshire. But within these limitations our twelfth-

---

[4]   H. P. R. Finberg, *Tavistock Abbey* (Cambridge, 1957), pp. 241, 256.
[5]   P. D. A. Harvey, 'The English Inflation of 1180–1220', *Past and Present*, vol. 61 (1973); D. L. Farmer, chapter 7 of *The Agricultural History of England and Wales*, vol. ii (Cambridge, 1988) takes a slightly different view of the chronology of this inflation.

century records do not serve us badly. Geographically they range from Somerset and Dorset in the west to Cambridgeshire and Norfolk in the east; and from Staffordshire and Derbyshire in the north Midlands to Hampshire in the south. They cross several Domesday circuit boundaries. And some were compiled within a generation of Domesday Book.

Taking them chronologically brings us first to Burton Abbey. There are two early surveys of Burton. The earlier was compiled in 1114 or 1115, the later about twelve years after that. An editorial whimsicality has decreed that the earlier survey should be known as Survey B. This survey clearly separates villeins and villein services from *censarii* and other cash-paying tenants whose services, though varied, were always comparatively light. And setting the cash payments of Survey B against the Domesday valuations of the manors of Burton Abbey shows clearly that, so far as the Domesday commissioners were concerned, Burton Abbey's income from each of its manors amounted to a sum of money which correlated very closely with the aggregate of cash payments made by the tenants of each of those manors.[6]

As a matter of fact much more income accrued to Burton Abbey than its tenants paid in cash rents. A glance at Survey B reveals a succession of scenes of busy demesne husbandry. Such scenes, however, those who ratified the Domesday returns for Staffordshire and Derbyshire were as content to ignore as were those who ratified the St Paul's returns for Essex, Huntingdonshire and the other counties in which St Paul's property was to be found. So far as the Domesday commissioners were concerned the aggregate income of each of these two ecclesiastical institutions was deemed to be whatever the cash rents of their tenants made it.

After Burton Abbey comes Peterborough Abbey which found itself in the king's hands as a result of the vacancy of 1125/8. The survey upon which we depend for our knowledge of the Abbey's financial affairs survives from this resumption.[7] The manors of the Peterborough estate were all let out to *firmarii* during this interlude so that, in addition to the rents paid in cash, we have a record of how much the various manors were thought to be worth net of expenses. One or two of the manors were let for no more, or for very little more, than their Domesday assessments reckoned they were worth. But that was very far from being the rule. In most cases *firmarii* were required to return annual rents for the manors in their charge which were twice and sometimes three or four times as much as the Domesday assessors of these manors had deemed them to be worth only thirty-nine years before.

The cash payments themselves do not always make as good a fit with the Domesday assessments as they might have done. But when we compare Peterborough's cash payments and the Domesday assessments with the renders for which the *firmarii* were made responsible, we can readily appreciate that the payments and assessments belong to one order of magnitude and the

6   See Table II.
7   See Table III.

renders to an altogether different one. If we cannot always say with confidence that the Domesday commissioners accepted assessments for the value of the manors of Peterborough Abbey which simply reflected the value of the cash payments made by the tenants of those manors, we can at least say with every confidence that the Domesday assessments rarely did better than reflect a moiety of the total annual value of those manors and often enough did much less well than that.

Chronologically the next records for examination are probably those for Shaftesbury Abbey. Shaftesbury has two, possibly three, cartularies for this period. The earliest was compiled some time during the reign of Henry I. The later one, or ones, appear to belong to a period not later than the reign of Henry II. The Shaftesbury records are somewhat disorganised and confusing. They have never been edited. But there appear to be nine manors in the earliest cartulary whose rent payments in cash we can more or less retrieve for scrutiny.[8] Of these perhaps four or five can be said to display the by now familiar pattern of correspondence with their respective Domesday assessments. Donhead is included in this quintet because, despite the evident loss of its principal account, it has a supplementary account, displaced to the end of the cartulary, which makes such a substantial contribution to its cash account as to suggest that the total cash yield of the manor, could we but know it, would very likely bring Donhead's cash rents into something approaching parity with the Domesday assessment. And Bradford is included because its cash rents amount to a sum which is over two-thirds of its Domesday assessment. The other four manors of the Shaftesbury group apparently yield very little in the way of cash rents for the Abbey. Labour services are sedulously recorded; payments in kind are diligently noted. But there were, it seems, very few cash rents to be had from these particular Shaftesbury manors.

A manor from which the seigneurial lord received few, if any, cash rents is, on the face of it, an oddity. By passing on to the next estate in this chronological review of the evidence we may be able to find out whether such manors were exceptional in fact or only in seeming. The next estate to be examined is Ramsey Abbey's.[9] Its earliest cartulary was drawn up after the death of Henry I but not so long after as to exclude from its purview tenants who had held Abbey land during Henry I's reign and continued to hold their land after his death. There are thirty villages and hamlets formed into twenty-three complete and identifiable manorial complexes in this cartulary. This includes the manors of Brington, Weston and Bythorn, which were grouped together by the Domesday commissioners and have got to be treated as one for that reason. Other manors or manorial complexes are either incomplete or unidentifiable. And in fact the Ramsey list of manors is considerably shorter than it appears to be. There are eight manors or

8   See Table IV.
9   See Table V.

manorial complexes for which there is no entry in Domesday under the
Ramsey rubric and, including these eight, twelve manors for which labour
services and renders in kind are set out in scrupulous detail but whose money
rents are accounted for in a most perfunctory way, if at all.

This was the problem at Shaftesbury. And it is this problem that the
Ramsey cartulary's evidence may help to elucidate. At Barnwell there were
fourteen bond-holdings consisting of a half-virgate of land and a messuage.
Each Barnwell tenant, according to the cartulary did service for his holding.
The service itself was set out in detail. But nothing was said about rents
payable in cash. If the Barnwell survey had left matters there we should know
as little about the half-virgators of Barnwell as we know about the tenants of
so many manors whose cartulary surveys are bafflingly uninformative at that
point. But at the end of the section in which the names of the half-virgators
are listed there is a summary item which states that the bondsmen are
together liable for a payment amounting to £10. At Barnwell there are two
other lists of tenants, one of free tenants, the other of small-holders. Each list
is set out in the way in which the list of half-virgators was set out. And each
list is followed by a summary account of money rents payable by the tenants
in question. We can only wonder as to how many surveys at Ramsey, and
indeed elsewhere, would yield a very different tally of cash rents if accountants who had omitted such rents from their detailed surveys of tenancy
obligations had made amends, as the Barnwell accountant did, by appending
a figure for total cash liability at the end of each section of their surveys.

The remaining eleven manors of the Ramsey estate consist of manors and
manorial complexes for which we have both Domesday assessments and an
adequate or at least a plausible showing of cartulary cash rents. Seven or
eight of these eleven sets of figures correlate well or very well; and with the
Barnwell evidence in mind we are bound to wonder about the rest.

At Ramsey there are twelve manors or groups of manors for which we are
told what is paid by *firmarii* for custody. Sometimes *firmarii* pay for their rights
of custody in kind. Fortunately, at Brington and Weston we are given the
cash value of a full render in kind. And with this information we can tell
that, at Ramsey as elsewhere, one or two exceptions notwithstanding,
manors were usually worth two or three times as much to their seigneurial
lords as they were reckoned to be worth by the Domesday commissioners.

Thus the Ramsey statistics, so unpromising in prospect, nevertheless, in
the event, provide firm support for the view that Domesday Book seriously
undervalued manorial income and did so, in particular, by accepting valuations for the majority of manors which equated value with the income that
accrued to manorial lords from the cash payments made by tenants for land
and, in some cases, for other real resources such as mills.

With Glastonbury and Winchester we approach the end of this survey of
evidence and pass the centenary of the completion of Domesday Book.
Glastonbury Abbey's rental was drawn up in 1189; and the Bishop of
Winchester's earliest Pipe Rolls are all thirteenth-century ones.

At Glastonbury tenants were required to make a compulsory gift (*donum*) in addition to paying rent (*gabulum*), and did so everywhere except, apparently, at Idmiston and at Western Zoyland and Middlezoy. The gift was very likely a custom old enough to have been known to the Domesday jurors; for at Christian Malford the accountants recorded the proceeds '*de dono assiso*'. Altogether, intact returns survive for twenty manors in this rental.[10] Ten correlate closely or at any rate adequately with their respective Domesday assessments. Ten do not. The Domesday assessments show that these ten manors were worth twice or three times as much to the Abbey in 1086 as the cash payments they rendered were worth over a century later. Some of the cash payments due were perhaps under-recorded in the Glastonbury rental as we have seen they could be elsewhere. Others, at Glastonbury as perhaps elsewhere, were reduced or altogether excused for the sake of a retired servant, for the sake of a family in distressed circumstances, or as a plain matter of patronage. Where the sums in question are often small, minor considerations such as these play havoc with nice calculations of less or more.

If Glastonbury's testimony is less than wholly satisfactory from the point of view of the argument being put forward here, Winchester's makes up for it. The Pipe Roll of 1210/11 gives full details of twenty-two of the Bishop's manors.[11] It records assize rents as a separate item, entered gross and without reference to other sources of cash income such as mills. Each mill is accounted for in its own right and elsewhere in the record. Domesday always itemises mills when they earn an income for the manorial lord. In the Winchester table below, therefore, mill values have been deducted from Domesday assessments so as to make these assessments more nearly comparable with Pipe Roll rents of assize. The result shows that, in fourteen cases out of twenty-two, assize rents are more or less in line with Domesday assessments; in five cases assize rents are lower than Domesday assessments; and in three cases assize rents are high above them.

These results call for closer examination. Apart from the five manors whose Domesday assessments are greater than their Pipe Roll assize-rent values, there are eight manors whose Domesday assessments correlate very closely with their Pipe Roll values and nine manors which show reverse gaps. In every instance of a reverse gap income from assize rents in the year 1210/11 is greater, and sometimes much greater than Domesday income as returned in 1086. Taking into account the size of the gross receipts of these manors in 1210/11, the length of the period separating Domesday assessment from Pipe Roll returns, and the serious bout of inflation with which the period ends, we can scarcely wonder that some estate managers had the wit, or the determination, to make necessary adjustments even to receipts which were conventionally fixed. The surprising thing is that such adjustments were not made universally, though we know from examples already cited how obstinately static assize rents often proved to be.

10 See Table VI.
11 See Table VII.

The conclusion to which these Winchester figures point is surely the conclusion we are justified in drawing from the majority of the examples set out in this brief review of some of the more important collections of twelfth and very early thirteenth-century evidence. It is that when income was laid under contribution for what we should now call public purposes, the unspoken but widespread and possibly universal understanding was that income should be narrowly defined so as to exclude from liability what was, as a rule, the greater part of the value of the annual returns of the landed property of the kingdom. The cartularies examined here are not unanimous on this point. Indeed they show quite clearly that Domesday juries sometimes returned assessments of manorial income which reflected to the full the annual value of particular manors to their seigneurial lords. But such true bills are rare in the sample examined here. The general practice, approximating in many places to a rule, seems to have been to accept assessments which might amount to more, or less, than the cash rents paid by manorial tenants, but which rarely departed far or often from the order of magnitude within which such rents were to be found.

If the evidence suggests that cash rents set a limit, however roughly defined, to the level at which manorial assessments were pitched, then we have to accept the fact that the Domesday commissioners agreed to assessments of manorial income which, in many instances, represented no more than one-half, and in some instances no more than one-third, or even one-quarter, of the true annual value of the manors in question. How many manors were assessed in this way we shall never know. The evidence is far too meagre for a comprehensive investigation. But it has certain merits. It is random; it is scattered geographically; and some of it was compiled within a generation or so of Domesday Book itself. There seems to be no reason why we should doubt the meaning it suggests. Moreover it makes sense from another point of view.

Royal taxation, Danegeld in particular, exempted tenants-in-chief as a matter of general practice, possibly as a class. Accordingly, the burden of royal taxation fell upon those who were the tenants of tenants-in-chief. Some of these tenants were redoubtable figures socially and politically. But overwhelmingly they were not. And if ordinary tenants were to support the burden of royal taxation their tax liabilities would have to suit their means. If the king had attempted to find out what his ordinary subjects could afford in the way of tax he would have had to ask for a Domesday Book infinitely more complex and difficult to compile than the one he got. The administrative sophistication of late Anglo-Saxon government was amazing enough. But demands on this scale would have overwhelmed it. If, however, taxation could take account of the means of those who had to pay without the necessity of having to examine the circumstances of each tax-payer, the problem would be solved. And solved it was, apparently, by adopting the broad principle that rents paid constituted adequate evidence of means available. The rents were known because they were matters of manorial record; and the rents appear as manorial income in so many Domesday entries because taxation of the tenantry, not the true income of the tenant-in-chief was what immediately concerned the king.

If we are now bound to see so much of what passes for manorial income in Domesday Book in an altogether different light from the one to which we have been accustomed, we must be prepared, as a result, to revise some of our most cherished notions about the wealth of Domesday England. The landed classes certainly had much more more money to spend than we thought they had. But the implications of their having more money to spend are not, perhaps, quite as simple as they may appear to be. If they had more money than we thought they had that was because they were getting more money, one man's income being another man's expenditure. How then did they come by the income that Domesday Book so signally failed to register? Nearly all the income of a medieval estate came from rents, from sales of farm produce, and from a miscellany of levies, dues, fines and the like. We know about the rents. These were either paid in service on the land, in which case they helped to sustain the household and contributed towards sales; or they were paid in cash, in which case they appeared in Domesday Book in the guise of manorial income. And we know enough about manorial courts and manorial levies from later records to be sure that money appropriated from the tenantry by such means, though often substantial enough in amount, made only a subsidiary contribution to seigneurial income as a general rule.

Only sales remain to be accounted for. If we are to double or treble many of these Domesday assessments in order to arrive at a more likely estimate of manorial income than we have had hitherto, then we have no choice but to explain that income in terms of sales of farm produce made either directly by demesne lords and their bailiffs or indirectly by *firmarii* and lessees of demesne land who themselves disposed of that produce and discharged their rental obligations from the proceeds. But explaining income in terms of sales means looking beyond the demesne farm to the economic system of which it was merely one constituent part. It means asking about buyers and therefore speculating about the size and purchasing power of the population at large.

It is arguable that, at current prices, demesne produce in fact cleared the market because the Domesday population, as Domesday scholars now estimate it, was fully capable of absorbing whatever the manorial demesne lands of the bigger estates may have offered for sale. According to the numismatists, Domesday England was rich in currency. These were not hoarded riches. The manorial records examined above are surely evidence enough of the extent to which the economy of Domesday England depended upon exchanges in which currency played a major rôle. Nor were they inflationary riches. No modern survey of the evidence, such as it is, has ever contended that Domesday England was afflicted by that particular malady. It is not implausible, therefore, to claim that ordinary villagers and townsfolk disposed of enough cash to account for the sales that earned the demesne income missing from so many Domesday manorial surveys. Theirs may have been an aggregate demand made up of a multiplicity of penny packets. But a demand that was big enough to account for the demesne surpluses did not have to be big enough to exercise a profound influence upon the economy as a whole.

There are, however, other considerations to be taken into account which make it difficult to accept this conclusion. The sample of manorial accounts examined above is a purely random one. Its testimony is all the more cogent for that. It tells us, as we have seen, that if we are to arrive at a sensible notion of how much income accrued to lords of manors in eleventh-century England, we must double or perhaps treble many, if not most, of the assessments of income to be found in Domesday Book. But if we do that we shall be compelled to take a very different view of subsequent economic developments in England and, in particular, of the evidence that historians now appeal to in order to justify their belief that the economy grew very substantially in the century or so between the compilation of Domesday Book and the accession of Edward I. And the implications of a revision of current beliefs about the growth of the economy in those centuries cannot fail to reflect back upon our assumptions about the size and wealth of the economy of Domesday England.

At present everyone is agreed that the economy grew tremendously in the twelfth and thirteenth centuries. Most historians believe that the population had doubled by the end of that period. Some bold spirits contend that it had trebled. Towns sprawled into the countryside and multiplied in number; farming reached into marginal regions and encroached upon forbidden areas; industries expanded. If the evidence for all this development is largely circumstantial, depending upon an accumulation of impressions, the same cannot be said about the income statistics of the bigger landed estates. These seem to provide incontrovertible witness to what was taking place by enabling historians to introduce measurement and calculation into their otherwise purely narrative accounts. By comparing Domesday assessments of income with later records of the income that accrued to those estates, making every allowance for acquisitions by gift or purchase which may have enlarged the capacity of such estates in the meantime, historians have been able to demonstrate that enormous improvements took place in the financial performance of the great majority of estates in the intervening period, thus vindicating their conviction that these improvements, which occurred in an environment that favoured change and development, nevertheless owed a great deal to the drive for management reform and progressive husbandry that those who ran the bigger estates often pioneered.

This very familiar account of the course of events owes its majestic sweep and thrilling climax to assumptions whose validity must now be called in question. One assumption is that Domesday assessments, whatever their incidental shortcomings, were based upon manorial returns which purported to disclose all sources of manorial income. And the other is that, having acknowledged the fact that the economy was subjected to what is thought to have been a severe bout of inflation at the end of the twelfth century, we have then done all we can to pay tribute to the whimsicalities of behaviour exhibited by monetary phenomena, and may thankfully ignore them hence-forth. But what are we to make of the consummate achievements of manorial policy in post-Domesday England once we have doubled or trebled the Domesday assessments of particular estates whose later achievements have been so much admired by their historians? And what are we to make of these achievements once we have increased the augmented Domesday figures so as to allow for the fact that post-inflation money values are com-parable with earlier ones only if we raise the Domesday figures or lower the later ones?

In the overwhelming majority of cases we lack the evidence with which to compensate for Domesday's limitations as a record of manorial income; and, given the poverty of the sources for price history at the time, we are no better able to assess the effect of inflation upon the early thirteenth-century economy. In these matters we are driven to weighing the imponderable and putting a figure upon the incalculable. But it is clear from the handful of examples analysed above that Domesday assessments must be substantially added to, as a general rule, if we are to use them comparatively, as they have been used in the past. And if we heed what we are told by those who have studied the price history of the period then we must be prepared to make significant allowance for changes in the value of money. The practical diffi-culties of compensating for the limitations of the evidence are probably insurmountable. But difficulties which are so great that they exonerate us from tackling such problems as these cannot excuse us for ignoring them. And this discussion will have served its purpose if it has succeeded in demon-strating that the case for believing in the vastly improved financial perfor-mance of so many thirteenty-century estates, to the extent that these improvements depend upon ignoring the limitations of Domesday and changes in the value of money, is now profoundly suspect.

But what can we say about wealthy medieval corporations whose financial record, once it has been revised and corrected, tells of a performance which is more likely to have been sluggish and indifferent than confident and successful? And this at a time when the population is said to have been in process of doubling or more than doubling and when we know that the national flock of sheep was increasing by millions. By the mid-thirteenth century, at latest, the wool of five to seven million sheep was being sent abroad every year to feed the looms of Flanders and North Italy. This was a trade which was virtually unknown to Domesday England because the cloth-making centres whose demand for wool the English farmer so abundantly supplied later were then too few and too small to need much of it. The productivity of medieval sheep-farming was so incredibly low that an export trade of such magnitude called for the diversion of a great deal of land from other uses in addition to the congestion of districts already devoted to grazing. The opportunites for profit afforded to the big medieval corporations by an immense increase in the scarcity of land ought to have been as various as they were unprecedented; for land was the resource with which they were richly endowed. Even if the economy had been able, by some miracle of adaptability, to achieve the necessary expansion at constant costs, partly because additional land for corn and wool could be made available more or less freely, and partly because labour productivity could be quickly, easily and dramatically improved, the results, so far as the bigger corporations were concerned, ought to have yielded sharply rising receipts as an increased volume of marketable crops was sold at prices which did not have to defray the extra cost of producing more. But the evidence does not tell us of irrepressible buoyancy. It suggests that, for the most part, these corporations were no more successful financially in the thirteenth century than they had been at the time of Domesday. Had some extraordinary collective paralysis of will overcome them all? Or is there perhaps another explanation?

The grain prices of the period certainly suggest that there may be. Grain prices are the most important as well as the most reliable of the price series to which we can appeal. But they can provide no evidence of massive pressure upon resources caused by the simultaneous impact upon the economy of a population explosion and a prodigious investment in sheep. There were no booming grain markets for medieval farmers to serve or exploit. Grain prices did not rise in the thirteenth century as they did in the sixteenth century. Except for brief interludes of inflation, at the beginning and in the middle of the century, they remained more or less stable. If there was a population explosion it took place without causing that cumulative rise in grain prices which increasing pressure upon limited resources ought to have brought about. The wool trade undoubtedly grew spectacularly; but wool-growing evidently managed to insinuate itself into the economy without reacting upon grain prices, despite its appetite for land. In short, the course of grain prices accounts for the prosaic financial record of the bigger corporations and, in doing so, absolves them from the reproach of excessive torpor. And it does something more. It enormously strengthens the case for believing that what we have accepted hitherto as evidence of the striking growth of manorial income between Domesday and the thirteenth century owes more to our misinterpretation of the significance of the Domesday assessment than to any substantive improvement in manorial returns.

But if the economic system distributed to those who controlled the largest aggregations of landed resources, returns which, allowing for misconceptions about the meaning of income in Domesday Book and for inflation, were not very different at the end of Henry III's reign from what they had been at the end of William the Conqueror's, then we are surely obliged to set a very severe limit to what we conceive to have been the economic expansion that took place in that period. It is impossible to envisage circumstances in which dramatic changes in population and foreign trade could have taken place at that period without profoundly affecting the fortunes of those whose stake in the economy was more substantial than anyone else's. And in the absence of such changes of fortune we are left with no choice but to accept the implications of concluding that changes in the economy as a whole are likely to have been similarly muted.

In particular, this means that we can no longer countenance the assumption that there was a population explosion in the century or so after Domesday. Neither the course of prices nor the behaviour of manorial income is intelligible if we make such an assumption. Whatever we take to have been the size of the population at the time of Domesday must henceforth circumscribe our expectations as to the possible size of the population later. If it grew at all after Domesday the population grew without making an insoluble problem out of the task of explaining how millions of extra sheep came to be accommodated upon English farms, without apparent difficulty, and how everyone continued to be fed, after a fashion, without the effort made provoking a sharp rise in grain prices and hence in rents and manorial profits. It may well be that we should postulate a Domesday population which was very much bigger than everyone has yet thought possible. But there is no point in attempting to assign numbers to our guesses. The numbers game is played out. Counting tenants in Domesday Book and adding something to compensate for Domesday's omissions cannot possible tell us how many people occupied the land as sub-tenants or as tenants of sub-tenants or even as squatters with no legal standing of any sort. Nor can we approach the problem obliquely by asking how many the land could actually support. A good deal of the productivity of the soil depended upon the care and attention with which it was treated and its adequacy in supporting human life upon the expectations of those whom it sustained.

We seem to be driven to the conclusion that the population of England, in the age of Domesday, far from preparing itself for a mighty surge forward, had in fact by then more or less stablised its numbers. If there was a limit to the numbers that the country could sustain, given the other calls upon land-use and the technological constraits of the age, then that limit had been more or less reached by the time of Domesday. Massive population growth was a phenomenon that belonged to an altogether earlier period. The racial transfusion that turned a land of Romanised Britons into a land of barbarian Angles, Saxons and Jutes, inevitably depopulated the countryside in the process. The invaders sustained their antagonism until all vestiges of the former natives had virtually disappeared from the historical record and the linguistic map. When invaders cannot swarm across land frontiers but have to cross dangerous seas in open boats clearance is more easily accomplished than re-occupation. Once victorious, however, the invaders settled contentedly enough into a regimen of farming and tribal warfare and, no doubt, soon began to re-colonise the regions and districts that the Britons and perhaps their forebears had once tamed. We know least about the period when the rate of expansion was presumably at its maximum and most about the period when expansion had virtually ceased. The temptation, therefore, is to make much of the changes we can see and to say very little about changes which we can neither date nor measure. And yet the statistical material reviewed above ought to warn us against exaggerating the importance of the changes we can see even though it leaves us without guidance as to when and where the changes in which we are interested actually took place.

If, however, we can accept the possibility that the Domesday population of England ran to a good deal more than the million or so that conjuring with the Domesday figures has given us hitherto, then other things become easier to understand. When Professor Sawyer marshalled his reasons for believing that England was a wealthy country in the eleventh century he had to stifle our doubts by overwhelming us with facts we could not deny.[12] But doubt remained. If England was as sparsely populated as everyone believed it to have been when Sawyer wrote; and if its wool export trade was as limited as we must accept that it was at the time; then how could such a country attract and employ as much currency as Sawyer, and indeed numismatists writing on later occasions, confidently asserted that it possessed? How are we to explain the low prices we find in an economy which was, according to Sawyer, so full of silver that it offered an irresistible temptation to all the scavenging marauders of the northern world? These prices were not simply low in a comparative sense. They were absolutely low in the sense that, in terms of the currency's chosen denominations, they could hardly go much lower without sliding off the scale altogether. Indeed when we review the numismatic evidence from the point of view that assumes a much bigger population of Domesday England than Domesday Book seems to sanction, then we can see that the evidence assembled by the numismatists appears to support the belief that late Anglo-Saxon England was not so much 'awash with silver' as awash with people, and that the currency was very far from being remarkable for its abundance when we take that fact into account. Danegeld could be collected, not because there was so much loose change in Anglo-Saxon pockets, but because there were so many Anglo-Saxon pockets from which some contribution, however modest, could be extracted.

It is surely clear from this discussion that if we are compelled to revise our views about the meaning of the manorial assessments we find in Domesday Book then the consequences for established interpretations of important historical trends will be profound. And yet a lightning tour of the most prominent features of the historical landscape, such as this review of the evidence has conducted, is likely to leave us more breathless than convinced. No doubt there is much more to be said. But whatever may transpire as a result of keener and more perceptive searching of the evidence it will be hard to explain away what Hale found at St Paul's and what the records of the other ecclesiastical institutions reviewed here have to tell us in corroboration of his findings.

[12] P. H. Sawyer, 'The Wealth of England in the Eleventh Century', *Transactions of the Royal Historical Society*, 5th ser., vol. 15 (1965); D. M. Metcalf, 'Continuity and Change in English Monetary History', *British Numismatic Journal*, vol. 50 (1980), pp. 20–49; vol. 51 (1981), pp. 52–90. In the absence of a big wool export trade it is hard to see how England could have made up for Danegeld losses of silver if we assume that the currency levied for Danegeld was usually exported. The obvious presumption is that Danegeld, on the whole, was not exported but spent in England and thus restored to circulation.

TABLE I
St Paul's

All values are given in £ s d

	Domesday Book			1181 Inquisition		
Drayton	6	0	0	6	8	11
Sutton	8	0	0	7	8	11
Barnes	7	0	0	3	7	10
Kensworth	3	10	0	10	7	0½
Caddington	5	10	0	7	6	11½
Ardleigh	7	0	0	5	13	10
Luffenhale	1	0	0	2	0	0
Sandon	16	0	0	12	2	10
Chingford	5	0	0	4	6	11
Beauchamp	16	0	0	13	8	2½
Wickham	4	0	0	1	18	5
Tillingham	15	0	0	6	10	3½
Norton	1	0	0	1	4	5
Navestock	10	0	0	7	7	1
Runwell	8	0	0	2	12	5½
Heybridge	8	0	0	4	4	0½
The Sokens	30	13	4	14	2	1½
Barling	6	0	0	3	10	6

Notes. The inquisition figures are all taken from *The Domesday of St Paul's*, ed. W. H. Hale, Camden Society, o.s., vol. lxix (1858), pp. 140–152, except for the figure for Norton which has had to be taken from the 1222 cartulary because the 1181 inquisition has not recorded a total of cash payments for Norton. *Ibid.*, pp. 73–4.

The Domesday counties are: Hertfordshire, Essex, Middlesex and Surrey. All Domesday valuations, throughout the tables, are those of 1086.

TABLE II

Burton Abbey   (Survey B 1114/1115)

All values are given in £ s d

	Domesday Book			Censarii			Farm		
Burton	3	10	0	4	3	8			
Branston	2	0	0	0	14	0	5	0	0
Stretton	2	0	0	4	6	4			
Wetmore	2	10	0	2	4	4			
Abbot's Bromley	1	0	0	0	18	0	3	10	0
Okeover	1	0	0	1	11	9			
Ilam									
Leigh	2	0	0	1	16	0	5	0	0
Darlaston	1	7	2	1	8	0	2	0	0
Mickleover	10	0	0	3	14	6			
Littleover									
Stapenhill	3	0	0	1	6	3			
Winshill	3	0	0	3	10	8½	4	0	0
Appleby	3	0	0	1	8	0			

Notes. The Burton Abbey Twelfth-Century Surveys, ed. C. G. O. Bridgeman (The William Salt Archaeological Society, 1916, publ. 1918), pp. 212–245. For Branston both rental and farm accounts are incomplete; for Abbot's Bromley, the farm account is incomplete. The Appleby account is muddled.

The Domesday counties are: Staffordshire and Derbyshire.

TABLE III
Peterborough Abbey

All values are given in £ s d

| | Domesday Book | | | 1125/8 Vacancy | | |
				Assize Rents			Farm		
Kettering	11	0	0	6	8	0	26	0	0
Tinwell	7	0	0	4	1	0	15	0	0
Oundle	11	0	0	8	19	6	11	0	0 +
Pilsgate	4	0	0	4	8	0	14	0	0
Longthorpe	2	10	0	0	17	0	1	5	0 +
Collingham	9	0	0	16	0	0	20	0	0
Cottingham	3	0	0	2	9	10	12	0	0
Great Easton	5	0	0	2	13	10	12	0	0
Warmington	11	0	0	7	11	4	10	0	0 +
Thurlby	3	0	0	1	13	0	3	0	0
Alwalton	7	0	0	4	17	0	4	0	0 +
Werrington	7	0	0	1	4	0	2	0	0 +
Peterborough	9	15	0	9	8	8	30	0	0
Glinton	3	0	0	2	1	7	5	0	0 +
Castor	2	10	0	4	11	4	6	0	0 +
Fiskerton	17	0	0	5	2	4	20	0	0
Scotter	10	0	0	17	1	8	22	0	0
Fletton	5	0	0	1	2	0	Render only		
Irthlingborough	6	0	0	2	3	0	—		
Stanwick	5	0	0	2	19	0	—		

Notes. Chronicon Petroburgense, ed. T. Stapleton (Camden Society, o.s., vol. xlvii, 1849), pp. 157–166. The Peterborough rents have had to be estimated. The plus signs mean that certain farms include renders. No attempt has been made to assign a monetary value to such renders.

The Domesday counties are: Lincolnshire, Nottinghamshire, Huntingdonshire, Northamptonshire and Leicestershire.

TABLE IV
Shaftesbury Abbey

All values are given in £ s d

	Domesday Book			Henry I		
Cheselbourne	16	0	0	6	11	9
Sixpenny Handley	12	0	0	11	14	4
Iwerne	14	0	0	13	18	0½
Fontmell	15	0	0	5	6	8
Tisbury	30	0	0	31	5	1
Bradford	60	0	0	43	2	10½
Melbury	13	0	0	6	10	10½
Compton	10	0	0	5	0	5
Donhead	22	0	0	14	10	0 +

Notes. British Library, Harley MS 61 fo. 37 *et seq*. The Domesday counties are: Dorset and Wilts.

TABLE V
Ramsey Abbey

All values are given in £ s d

	Domesday Book			Post Henry I					
				Rents			Render		
Elton	16	0	0	13	18	11¾	31	0	0
Brancaster, Depedale and Burnham	10	0	0	9	1	9½	25	0	0
Ringstead and Holm	5	10	0	4	17	0½	15	0	0
Stukeley	4	10	0	—			7	0	0
Hemingford	10	0	0	4	0	6	15	0	0
Houghton and Witton	15	0	0	10	19	6	31	0	0
Lawshall	12	0	0	10	18	0	—		
Hilgay	3	10	0	3	14	7¼	10	0	0
Elsworth	16	0	0	6	12	9½	—		
Cranfield	9	0	0	8	14	6½	36	0	0
Ellington	9	0	0	—			10	0	0
Shillington and Pekesdene	22	0	0	6	18	7	29	0	0
Brington, Weston and Bythorn	18	0	0	—			21	0	0
Girton	4	0	0	—			10	0	0
Barnwell	4	0	0	15	19	6	—		

Notes. The cartulary is to be found in W. H. Hart and P. A. Lyons, eds, *Cartularium Monasterii de Rameseia*, vol. 3 (Rolls Series, 1893), pp. 241–318.

The Domesday counties are: Norfolk, Suffolk, Bedfordshire, Huntingdonshire, Northamptonshire, Cambridgeshire.

TABLE VI
Glastonbury Abbey

All values are given in £ s d

	Domesday Book			Rents (1189)		
Winscombe	8	0	0	5	15	9
Shapwick	12	0	0	5	9	7
Weston Zoyland, Othery and Middlezoy	24	0	0	16	4	3
Walton	15	0	0	5	9	2
High Ham	10	0	0	5	2	1
Butleigh	10	0	0	4	15	7½
Batcombe	7	0	0	6	8	0
Wrington	30	0	0	13	2	3
Ditcheat	12	0	0	6	14	8
Ashcott	2	0	0	1	19	6
Brent	50	0	0	12	9	9
Pucklechurch	30	0	0	25	7	0½
Christian Malford	10	10	0	13	14	5
Damerham (incl. Martin)	45	0	0	37	18	8
Winterbourne Monkton	20	0	0	8	1	9½
Idmiston	6 0 0/10 0 0			7	0	10
Grittleton	12	0	0	5	17	0
Badbury	10	0	0	6	18	6
Nettleton	13	0	0	8	19	8
Sturminster Newton	25	0	0	9	7	0

Notes. Rents taken from *Liber Henrici de Soliaco*, ed. J. E. Jackson (Roxburghe Club, 1882).

The Domesday counties are: Dorset, Wiltshire, Somerset and Gloucester. The Weston Zoyland group is under-estimated because a donum is only recorded for Othery. In Domesday, High Ham includes Low Ham. In the rental it does not. The Domesday assessment for Brent rose from £15 when the manor was received to £50 in 1086. The jurors thought Damerham worth £45 and a farm of £61, which was asked for in 1086, unsustainable. Idmiston's Domesday assessment is confusing; and its rental lacks an entry for donum.

TABLE VII
Bishopric of Winchester

All values are given in £ s d

	Domesday Book	Assize Rents	Gross Receipts
Alresford	30 17 6	27 0 0	51 6 4½
Twyford	28 0 0	41 3 5	88 16 9
Bishopstoke	7 10 0	12 4 0½	24 15 5
Crawley	35 0 0	10 1 0	30 5 4
Bishop's Waltham	29 2 6	46 11 4½	98 9 8½
Overton	46 17 6	19 2 0	39 7 2½*
West Meon	29 10 0	74 11 11½	115 1 9
East Meon	4 17 6	4 17 4	62 7 2½*
Fareham	14 15 0	23 8 6½	72 10 4½
Wield	10 0 0	5 14 10	20 7 1½
Bentley	11 10 0	10 7 3	confused
Highclere	10 17 6	18 7 6½	65 10 10
Itchingswell	7 11 8	8 8 6	23 17 6½
Taunton	144 6 1	133 0 5½	418 14 11½*
Rimpton	7 0 0	4 9 10	18 5 10*
Witney	23 7 6	30 14 0	114 3 4 (less borough)
Adderbury	18 10 0	24 3 2	86 5 0*
Wycombe	15 0 0	48 2 7¾	107 2 3¾
Farnham	35 13 8	81 19 10	111 0 2½
Harwell	15 17 6	15 12 7	30 14 6½
Brightwell	22 15 0	13 11 8	37 3 11½
Downton	77 0 0	35 5 8	139 19 7½

Notes. Rents and receipts from: N. R. Holt, ed., *The Pipe Roll of the Bishopric of Winchester, 1210–11* (Manchester, 1964).

The Domesday counties are: Hampshire, Surrey, Berkshire, Wiltshire, Somerset, Oxfordshire and Buckinghamshire. Asterisks mean that the totals given by the accountants have been corrected for arithmetical errors.

The Farming Out of Manors

The twelfth century is important in manorial history because it is the first age in which we can study the workings of the manor from records of its management. It is also important because of the universal belief that it witnessed the disintegration of the manorial demesne and the commutation of its services. That belief we owe to Prof. Postan. When he delivered his paper on 'The Chronology of Labour Services' to the Royal Historical Society in 1937 he transformed manorial studies.[1] Who would have believed, before that memorable paper had been given, that the manor was capable of responding to changes in economic conditions by undergoing radical alterations of structure which were nevertheless reversible? When economic conditions did not favour direct management, as Prof. Postan argued they did not in the twelfth century, landlords allowed their manors to be crumbled into pieces of a size to suit the limited means of the villeins and small-holders who took them over. When conditions improved, as they did towards the end of the twelfth century, manors were resumed and reconstituted, and manorial management achieved thereafter those miracles of profitable enterprise that no textbook of medieval economic history fails to commemorate and glorify.

'The Chronology of Labour Services' has taken its place in the ranks of those writings which have been generally acknowledged to be classic expositions of their subjects. It has commanded unhesitating assent from the moment of its appearance in print – even in the face of contrary evidence. For there is, scattered throughout the records, a good deal of evidence to show that assarting was widespread in the twelfth century, even indeed during what we are always taught to believe were its most inauspicious years.[2] And there is evidence enough to show that competitive bidding for land was not simply another Norman barbarity authorized by William the Conqueror when he was trying to find tenants for his estates. It went on, so far as we can tell, in the twelfth century, and in much less exalted circles than his.[3] But the

---

[1] M. M. Postan, 'The Chronology of Labour Services', *Transactions of the Royal Historical Society*, 4th ser., vol. xx (1937), reprinted with very minor changes in W. E. Minchinton, ed., *Essays in Agrarian History*, 1 (Newton Abbot, 1968) and with these changes, in M. M. Postan, *Essays on Medieval Agriculture and General Problems of the Medieval Economy* (Cambridge, 1973). All references are to this latest reprint.

[2] E. Miller, 'England in the Twelfth and Thirteenth Centuries: An Economic Contrast?' *Economic History Review*, 2nd ser., vol. xxiv (1971), p. 6.

[3] R. V. Lennard, *Rural England, 1086–1135* (Oxford, 1959), p. 157; J. A. Raftis, *The*

indications that land was being colonized and that rents were buoyant, if not rising, at a period when Prof. Postan had declared that manorial lords were surrendering their manors in despair to their villeins, has proved to be more of an embarrassment than a worry even to those who have worked upon the records and found that things were so.[4]

The legal historians have been no less profoundly impressed by Prof. Postan's arguments than the economic historians. In his important and influential survey of the *Obligations of Society in the Twelfth and Thirteenth Centuries*, Austin Lane Poole showed that the lawyers were hard at work in the twelfth century trying to decide who might seek the protection of the king's court for their rights and property and who might not.[5] The king could protect freemen. But villeins were another matter. When they turned their attention to problems involving villeinage, the lawyers were soon preoccupied with the *minutiae* of status. The earliest surviving records of cases thrashed out in the courts reveal that their preoccupation was very far from being mere antiquarianism. But how are we to explain the punctilious zeal with which the lawyers were attempting to define the servility of villeins at a time when, according to 'The Chronology of Labour Services', manors were disappearing, as working organizations, from the face of the countryside, and when villeins were no longer doing those burdensome and degrading services which, to the lawyers, constituted the most telling evidence of servile status? Lane Poole could not do so; and the dilemma vitiates the chapter of his survey in which he turns from Prof. Postan's account of the improving circumstances of the twelfth-century villein, to his own account of the way in which the lawyers were inexorably degrading the villein in the sight of the law.

But the argument of 'The Chronology of Labour Services' confirmed so much that everyone believed to be true about twelfth-century conditions that it was difficult to concede more to those who found evidence which was not easily reconcilable with its arguments than a reluctant acknowledgement that there are exceptions to every rule. The belief that the twelfth century was a tumultuous and distracted one dies hard.[6] Stephen's reign casts a long shadow over it; rancorous discords tarnish the brilliance of Henry II's reign; and the quarrels of his sons mar its close. What Prof. Postan did was to offer a circumstantial demonstration of how the ramifications of misgovernment in

---

Estates of Ramsey Abbey (Toronto, 1957), p. 82; B. A. Lees, ed., *Records of the Templars in England in the Twelfth Century* (Oxford, 1935), p. 41. Barbara Harvey, *Westminster Abbey and its Estates in the Middle Ages* (Oxford, 1977), shows income rising by over 40 per cent between Domesday Book and 1173 (p. 69) despite the fact that the abbey added very little to its possessions in that period (p. 28).

[4] Miller, *loc. cit.*, p. 8. See also his reply to critics: 'Farming of Manors and Direct Management', *Economic History Review*, 2nd ser., vol. xxvi (1973), pp. 138–40.

[5] Austin Lane Poole, *Obligations of Society in the Twelfth and Thirteenth Centuries* (Oxford, 1946), ch. II *passim*.

[6] See, for example, the comments offered by Prof. Warren Hollister to a conference on Stephen's anarchy in *Albion*, vol. vi (Autumn, 1974).

the twelfth century ran right down into the economic foundations of society. At such a time who could seriously doubt, once it had been pointed out to him, that manors would disintegrate, much as they did in a later period of universal distress, after famine, plague, and revolt had shaken fourteenth-century society to its depths, and manorial demesnes were parcelled out to villagers in penny packets at rents which they could afford or were willing to pay? 'Manorial documents of the twelfth century show,' claimed Prof. Postan, 'on the bulk of the manors which they cover, labour services declining and the cultivation of the demesne receding'; 'a movement towards the commutation of services and the dissolution of the demesne' as a result of which we find, as he said on a later occasion, 'numbers of peasant holdings . . . carved out of the demesne'.[7]

When he published his further thoughts about this movement he sought to strengthen the case for believing that the central years of the twelfth century were 'specially unfavourable to the direct management of the demesne' by supplementing his evidence that manors disintegrated in the twelfth century with evidence that manors were often farmed out whole in the twelfth century.[8] But this was a mistake. For one thing the farming out of manors was no twelfth-century innovation. Prof. Postan himself conceded that it was 'widespread on royal land as well as on lands of other landlords at the time of the Domesday survey'. If farming out is to be used as evidence of hard times then we must be prepared to spread a pall over Anglo-Saxon and Norman England as well as over the twelfth century. For another thing, if landlords found conditions perplexing and prospects cheerless how could they expect farmers who had merely stepped into their shoes to do better than they had been able to do, or indeed to be willing to endure all the anxieties and frustrations of making the attempt when they were not obliged to do so? No doubt farmers sometimes let the manors in their charge run down. Safeguards against their doing so are a familiar feature of twelfth-century leases. They were also known to drive their labourers too hard; for they were warned not to do that also.[9] But if ruining an estate were the only way in which to get it managed as a whole why could not the landlord ruin his own estate without going to the trouble of getting a tenant to do it for him?

If we are to be convinced, despite the evidence to the contrary, that the twelfth century was a difficult period when the greater landlords were at a loss to make ends meet, not because they were unduly extravagant, but

---

[7] M. M. Postan, ed., *Cambridge Economic History of Europe*, 1, 2nd edn (Cambridge, 1966), p. 585.

[8] *Ibid*. Farming out is a confusing phrase. In this context it simply means leasing out. A farm of a manor is a lease; the farmer a lessee. Even when the manor is not leased out whole the lessee is still called the farmer, the lease a farm. In the following pages, however, *firmarii* are farmers of whole manors, except in the discussion of the Boldon Book.

[9] Lennard, *op. cit.*, p. 199; Raftis, *op. cit.*, pp. 82–3.

because they could not earn a living from the land, then we must expect to be shown a representative selection of twelfth-century estates which were no longer being cultivated, sometimes by landlords through their agents and sometimes by tenants of rank and consequence through theirs, but which were breaking up because in such conditions only small tenants with family holdings carved out of the larger estates could hope to thrive.

In his original essay Prof. Postan analysed the estates of ten ecclesiastical institutions in some detail in order to show how the demesnes of the larger estates were faring in the unpropitious circumstances of the twelfth century. In recent years three of these estates have been studied in much greater detail than he was able to study them in a brief survey. One of these three he himself granted to be an exception to his rule. The records of Peterborough Abbey exhibited, he said, 'manorial economy at its most robust'; and Dr King has demonstrated just how successful Peterborough's estate-management policy had proved to be.[10] The second is Glastonbury Abbey about which Prof. Postan wrote at greater length some years after 'The Chronology of Labour Services' had appeared. He did so as a result of his having been introduced by Dom Aelred Watkin to a collection of Glastonbury surveys at Cambridge of whose existence he had been unaware when he published his original results. His article on Glastonbury, written in the light of fresh evidence, drew a sharp attack from the late R. V. Lennard and a controversy ensued which was both complex and inconclusive.[11]

Fortunately, Glastonbury Abbey has attracted the interest of a scholar who comes fresh to its problems. Dr Stacy, who has written a remarkable monograph on Glastonbury Abbey, supports Lennard's objections, and finds that 'the available evidence does not warrant a conclusion that demesnes were diminished and severely run down while the Glastonbury estate was in the hands of *firmarii*: if it allows any conclusion at all, it suggests that the scope of their agriculture probably did not alter much in the century or so following Domesday Book.'[12] Dr Stacy's results are interesting enough in view of the controversy that preceded them. But what makes them particularly notable is that, as a consequence of all the work done on Glastonbury, we now have yet another example of the failure of the Civil War to create havoc in the countryside; for many of Glastonbury's manors lay where the war was fought and the land plundered almost incessantly for nine or ten years.

The third estate to be studied more closely than Prof. Postan was able to

---

[10] E. King, *Peterborough Abbey* (Cambridge, 1973).

[11] M. M. Postan,'Glastonbury Estates in the Twelfth Century', *Economic History Review*, 2nd ser., vol. v (1953); R. Lennard, 'The Demesnes of Glastonbury Abbey in the Eleventh and Twelfth Centuries', *ibid.*, viii (1956); M. M. Postan,'Glastonbury Estates in the Twelfth Century: A Reply', *ibid.*, ix (1956); R. Lennard, 'The Glastonbury Estates: A Rejoinder', *ibid.*, xxviii (1975).

[12] N. E. Stacy, 'The Estates of Glastonbury Abbey, c.1050–1200' (unpublished D.Phil. thesis, Oxford University, 1971), p. 112. It is much to be hoped that this valuable work will not remain unpublished.

do, is Ramsey Abbey. Ramsey is quite exceptionally important for his case because Geoffrey de Mandeville made it his headquarters during the Civil War. If any institution were brought low by its enforced complicity in the ambitions and violence of one or other of the contestants that institution was Ramsey Abbey. And this time closer scrutiny of the evidence seems to have produced harmony of views between Prof. Postan and the scholar who followed him in examining the records he had used. For Prof. Raftis has only sombre things to say about Ramsey's fortunes. 'From the early years of Abbot Walter's term of office (1133–61),' he declares, 'until the last decade of the century . . . [the] . . . story of property alienation, purprestures, and loss is cumulative. Needless to say the farming of manors would become stagnant and contribute to this deterioration, so that 'farming' must have become synonymous with decay.'[13]

But if Prof. Raftis appears to corroborate everything that Prof. Postan had to say about Ramsey, his conclusions nevertheless consort ill with the story of twelfth-century Ramsey Abbey that he himself tells on other pages. He has a long list of losses of land *ad opus* suffered by the Abbey at Holywell, Elton, Upwood, Lawshall, Shillington and Pegsdon, Burwell, Brington, Weston, Bythorn, Brancaster, Burnham, and Depedale, which it is difficult to reconcile with the increases of rent and the colonization of land whose appearance in the Ramsey records of the period is all the more remarkable because, as Prof. Raftis reminds us, they appear in these records only incidentally.[14]

And, indeed, upon closer inspection, the Ramsey surveys that Prof. Raftis uses seem to tell a different story from the one that he tells. These surveys were drawn up fairly late in the twelfth century and compare conditions then with those of Henry I's reign.[15] They are neither complete nor without fault. And they do indeed speak of losses. There are places where the number of service tenancies declines. There are mills that earn less than they did; and there are tenants whose rents have gone down. There are even places, like Hemingford, where the church lands return nothing, apparently, because the *firmarii* will not pay up: 'nihil volunt dare,' says the jury. But unless one comes to this remarkable collection with eyes only for decadence and loss it is impossible to read it through without getting an overwhelming impression of an organization which is active and prosperous and successfully making everything it can out of everything it has got.

Nor are the losses listed by Prof. Raftis always what they seem to be. Prof. Postan noted that the service tenancies at Holywell had declined from 23 virgates *ad opus* to 15.[16] He was not the first modern writer with a case to

---

[13] Raftis, *op. cit.*, p. 89.

[14] *Ibid.*, p. 71.

[15] W. H. Hart and P. A. Lyons, eds, *Cartularium Monasterii de Rameseia*, III (Rolls Series, 1893) (hereafter Ramsey *Cart.*).

[16] Postan, 'Chronology', 95; Raftis, *op. cit.*, p. 88. Postan censures scholars for their neglect of the Ramsey records and then dismisses them in a brief paragraph.

make against the twelfth century to have fastened upon this unfortunate manor as a characteristic example of what was going on at the time. And yet it is a most unsatisfactory example to choose. There is nothing else quite like it on the Ramsey estates; and thanks to the vigilance of the late R. V. Lennard we now know why.[17] As it stands the twelfth-century survey of Holywell is merely a fragment. Where it breaks off the Lawshall entry begins. It begins without warning. The Rolls Series' editors had no suspicion that something was amiss and printed the Lawshall survey as part of the survey of Holywell. Once the two surveys have been separated, however, it is clear that we need to know much more than we are told before we can be sure that Holywell was in a sad state at the time when the jurors reported on it. We are told what services are to be done by those who continue to do services. We are also told the names of those who hold the 8 virgates which are said to be at rent. Of these virgates most are still burdened with ploughing services. Evidently a good deal of the demesne is still functioning as a working entity; and it is, after all, what happens on the demesne that matters most so far as Prof. Postan's argument is concerned. But we cannot know anything more about circumstances at Holywell because the Lawshall entry starts just where we might have expected some enlightenment.

In this context, however, the Lawshall survey is very instructive. On the face of it the Holywell story seems to be repeated at Lawshall. Only 12½ virgates are *ad opus*; 5½ pay rent instead of service; one is excused. A separate block of demesne is being farmed out whole. Does this not mean that Lawshall is an example of what Prof. Postan would have us believe to be the general experience of the age? If the Lawshall entry had broken off at this point, as the Holywell one did, we might have been tempted to think so. But what follows in the survey does not square with this view of the manorial fortunes of Lawshall. There are 11 oxen and three horses on the manor. This does not suggest a seriously diminished demesne. Time and again, moreover, the tenants of service virgates can be seen taking possession of their holdings in association with others. *Alanus et socii ejus* runs a typical entry. Clearly the virgates are crowded. When we look farther we see a possible explanation. Lawshall has got at its disposal the services of a host of small men whose contributions are subsumed under the rubric *de minimis hominibus*, many of whom are, perhaps, the colonists remarked upon by Prof. Raftis elsewhere in his book.[18] If they are, then it is very probable that their contributions to the servicing of the manorial demesne have been added since the days when the demesne was heavily dependent upon what could be got out of the virgators. That there is colonization on the manor is perhaps suggested by the some-what bizarre name given to the virgator who is excused his services, as colonists often were. He is *Walterus Novus Homo*. At any rate it is not

[17] R. V. Lennard, 'An Unidentified Twelfth-Century Custumal of Lawshall', *English Historical Review*, vol. li (1936), pp. 104–7.
[18] Ramsey *Cart.*, p. 284; Raftis, *op. cit.* pp. 71–3

obvious from the survey, first impressions notwithstanding, that Lawshall's resources have been grievously depleted since Henry I's time.

At Elton, which is next on Prof. Raftis's list, the case for extreme caution in taking the evidence of decline at face value is even stronger.[19] At Elton, where there were once 35 virgates *ad opus*, there are only 28½ at the time of the survey. But Elton continues to return the same farm as it did. Its mill which used to be worth 40s when valued together with the income from 1 virgate and 6½ acres of land now returns 100s. Nothing is said about the land that was once valued with it. A glance at the plough-team figures, however, reveals what in any other century than the twelfth would qualify, *prima facie*, as resounding evidence of the successful application of progressive management techniques. Where there were five ploughs, each pulled by eight oxen, there are now four, each pulled by six oxen and two horses. Upwood, which is next on the list, has lost a half-virgate *ad opus* and hardly deserves a mention. Shillington and Pegsdon which have lost 2½ virgates *ad opus* since Henry I's time have lost them to no less a personage than Walter, the brother of the Prior of St Ives.[20] That the manor is nevertheless thriving we see by looking at the mills which used to be worth 20s and are now worth 30s. Burwell's losses are equally freakish. Of 3½ virgates *ad opus* lost, 1½ went to someone whilst he was the farmer and have not been returned, 1 to a tenant called Michael *Clericus*, and 1 to Hugo *Decanus*.[21] Brington, which Prof. Raftis mistakenly set down as having lost 5 cotlands, possessed 4 service cotlands in Henry I's time of which only one is not *ad opus* when needed.[22] With the help of Weston and Bythorn, Brington rendered a whole farm in Henry's time.[23] Nothing is said about the present position, but since Henry I's time the group has lost 1½ virgates *ad opus* out of 46. It is not likely, therefore, that the group would have sought relief from its burden of render on the ground that its resources were no longer equal to the paying of its former render in full. Brancaster, Burnham, and Depedale were in the fens.[24] A good deal of their land was in *landsetagio* and subject to somewhat different service requirements than other places.[25] Altogether there were well over 800 acres in this special category. Prof. Raftis calculated that 156 acres had been freed from it since the reign of Henry I. The printed survey has more like 72 acres released, half of these being liable still for ploughing services. Demesne is also let out. But of 133 acres released to tenants since Henry I's reign 14 remain subject to full works, 84 continue to plough, and 11 are still in *land-setagio*.

Elsewhere on the Ramsey estates the story is very much the same. Farms

---

[19] Ramsey *Cart.*, pp. 257–60: Aethelingtuna.
[20] *Ibid.*, pp. 307–8.
[21] *Ibid.*, pp. 308–10.
[22] *Ibid.*, pp. 310–11.
[23] *Ibid.*, pp. 311–13.
[24] *Ibid.*, pp. 261–6.
[25] *Ibid.*, pp. 268–9.

are paid as they should be. Sometimes, even, they have gone up, partly because of the colonization of land, partly because rents have risen since Henry I's reign. Mills are worth more. And if someone has been to Elton making sensible changes to raise productivity, either he or a like-minded colleague has also visited Stukeley where two ploughs now do the work of three, and Houghton and Witton where the eight-oxen plough-teams have been strengthened by substituting two horses for two oxen on each plough.[26] In both places the farm has been raised since Henry I's time. If demesne disintegration is to be the general rule in a war-torn twelfth-century England it had better be made of sterner stuff than this.

Having dealt with Peterborough, Glastonbury, and Ramsey, Prof. Postan turned next to the Boldon Book which surveyed the estates of the Bishop of Durham in 1183.[27] Here Prof. Postan found three groups of manors – one in which 'manorial institutions function with undiminished vigour'; one in which 'manorial organisation is not so complete'; and a third in which 'the very name of villein has disappeared and the bulk of the population consists of money-paying molmen, or more commonly *firmarii*.' In this group the manors 'do not contain any functioning demesnes, though they must have possessed them at some time.' When we look at this division more closely, however, we shall see that it springs from what proves to be, at times, a most curious handling of the evidence.

The Boldon Book does not always survey the demesne. When the demesne is at farm the Boldon Book generally makes a note of it. But when it is not it may very well pass it over in silence. At Newton next Durham half the demesne is said to be at farm. We hear nothing of the other half. At Sedgefield the villeins do the same services as villeins do at Boldon. But no demesne is mentioned. The same goes for Norton, Preston, and other manors throughout the inquiry. At Darlington the villeins do much lighter services than villeins do at Boldon. No demesne is mentioned, but at Oxenhall which is said to be part of Darlington the farmer ploughs for the bishop and sows with the bishop's seed. Other places where the villeins work, but do lighter services than the villeins of Boldon, are Blackwell, Cockerton, Wilton and Fulforth. No demesne is mentioned at Blackwell or Cockerton. But before we conclude that the demesne has been lost with the result that villeins have been let off their traditional services we had better turn to the entry for Wilton and Fulforth, which states that the demesne is in hand. Elsewhere the demesne is equally elusive. At Lanchester all we hear of the demesne is that 18 acres of it are waste. At Great Ussworth we are told of the

---

26 *Ibid.*, pp. 274–5, 278–80.
27 W. Greenwell, ed., *Boldon Buke* (Surtees Society, xxv, 1852). In *VCH Durham*, i (1905), G. T. Lapsley collated all the surviving medieval copies of the book including one that Greenwell was not allowed to use. Where his translation differs from Greenwell's text I have therefore preferred it. Lapsley also explains in terms of local conditions some of the idiosyncrasies of manorial structure for which Prof. Postan finds economic causes. Postan makes no reference to Lapsley's work.

demesne plough but not of the demesne. At Carlton we are told that 2 bovates are to return to the bishop's demesne on the death of the tenant but nothing more about the rest of the demesne. So much for the disappearing demesne.

Even when the demesne is at farm the bishop's villeins and *firmarii* nevertheless do a variety of services for him. Sometimes these services are reserved because the bishop does not always farm out the sheep and pasture when he farms out the demesne. This was the state of affairs at Cleadon and Whitburn and at Easington and Thorp. At Tursdale the bishop still holds mill, copse, wood, and meadows. The *firmarii* do services for him, some presumably on the land that he has not farmed out. Thus at South Biddick, where the villeins hold the village at farm, they nevertheless find 160 men to reap for the bishop. No doubt he has retained the meadows and needs their services. This is plain at Norham where there is a borough and a manor. The manorial demesne is at farm. The meadows and pasture are not, and with them go the 'operationes villanorum de Grendona, quantum opus fuerit ad prata falcanda de Norham, et foenum levandum et quadrigandum.'

The mention of works done by neighbouring tenants illustrates the further point that not all the many services that are reserved when so much was at farm were necessarily done on the spot. The services due from men of Newton next Boldon were done at Boldon. South Biddick villeins had to carry at Houghton. Morton *firmarii* had to plough there. Tursdale tenants were obliged to perform services at Quarrington. Villeins of Great Ussworth are told that for the future they will do at Gateshead the work they used to do at Washington. Hutton men plough at Shotton, Binchester villeins at Coundon. And cutting across all this work on the land come the requirements of the hunt which takes all the villeins and all the *firmarii* of Auklandshire away from their work, makes inroads into the time of innumerable tenants who feed dogs and horses, provide ropes, do forest service unspecified or, as in the case of the villeins of Auklandshire, services which include the making of the bishop's hunting lodge in the forest, which is to be 60 ft long and 16 ft wide with a buttery, a chamber and a privy, and a chapel no less than 40 ft long and 15 ft wide.

It should be abundantly clear from all this that the Bishop of Durham's manors display none of the characteristics of disintegration or decadence that Prof. Postan imputed to them. The estate is manifestly in full vigour. Much is cultivated by the bishop's agents on his behalf. Much is at farm. There can be no question but that the demesne is being maintained intact and that villein service upon it is being preserved in its full integrity. Naturally, the manors are not uniform. Customs varied on the Durham estates in accordance with traditions and local circumstances of which Lapsley has given us a masterly exposition. But of the erosion of the traditional structure there is no hint in the Boldon Book. When the villeins hold South Biddick they do so as a syndicate in a way which is very different from the way in which they would have to hold it if they were to justify Prof. Postan's claim that they were dissolving the bonds of the manor. Indeed, while arguing that villeins of the Bishop of Durham were actually to be seen embarked upon that very purpose, Prof. Postan omits the evidence that demonstrates beyond peradventure that they were in fact doing nothing of the kind.

Of the Ryton group of manors Prof. Postan says: 'we are told in the 1183 document that the men of Ryton, Crawcrook, Winlaton, and Westow hold their manors, demesnes and works at farm . . . The process is described best . . . in the 1183 survey of the village of Whickham. The entry in the Boldon Book tells us that the 'dominium . . . erat tunc in manu episcopi, nunc autem predictum manerium est ad firmam cum dominico' and then, as in Ryton, we find the later survey showing the demesne held in parcels attached to the customary holdings.'[28] The later survey is Bishop Hadfield's. It was made in the late fourteenth century and adds nothing to the unmistakeable clarity of the words of the Boldon Book. The Boldon Book certainly tells us that the men of Ryton hold Ryton. But it does not tell us that the men of Crawcrook, Winlaton, and Westow do likewise. It tells us something far more important and not in the least what Prof. Postan says that it tells us. It tells us that Crawcrook is 'ad firmam cum villanis et dominio et molendino et cum instauramento.' It tells us that Winlaton is 'ad firmam cum dominio et villanis sine instauramento.' And it tells us that Westow is 'ad firmam cum dominio et molendino et villanis et operationibus et cum instauramento.'[29] When it turns to survey the village of Whickham the Boldon Book certainly says, as Prof. Postan tells us it does, that 'praedictum manerium de Quykham est ad firmam cum dominio'. But the sentence in which it does so does not stop at the word 'dominio'. It goes on, as it does in describing what was happening at Crawcrook, Winlaton, and Westow, adding the words 'et villanis et molendino et cum instauramento.'[30] The demesne is not disintegrating in these places: whole manors are at farm.

When we turn to the Domesday of St Paul's what we learn, as Prof. Postan says truly but without irony 'does not differ much from what we have observed in the surveys already mentioned'. Prof. Postan claims that 'rent-paying tenants of every sort and description' predominated on the cathedral estates of St Paul's 'at the time of the principal survey of 1222'. What we find, however, is that the manors of St Paul's are held by *firmarii* in 1222 who supply the Chapter with food and cash, and control the overwhelming bulk of the demesne arable of the estate. Rent-paying tenants, in Prof. Postan's sense of multitudes of lesser tenants dividing up the demesnes between them, predominate only at Caddington and Thorpe, which are small manors by St Paul's standards, and possibly at Luffenhall which is tiny.[31] Chapter policy is

---

[28] Postan, 'Chronology', p. 96. By mistake Postan transcribed 'dominio' as 'dominico'.
[29] *Boldon Buke*, p. 35. Winlaton is actually Wynlaktona et Berleia in the record.
[30] *Ibid.*, p. 34.
[31] W. H. Hale, ed., *The Domesday of St Paul's* (Camden Society, 1857, publ. 1858), pp. 1–7, 38–43, 19–20.

not difficult to make out. On the big manors of Sandon, Ardleigh, Walton, Heybridge, Navestock, Barnes, Wickham, and Barley, comparatively few tenancies of this nature are permitted to encroach upon the integrity of the demesne arable. Tillingham and Runwell are exceptions to this rule: on these manors about one-quarter of the demesne arable is in the hands of small rent-paying tenants;[32] and on Beauchamp manor, the biggest of all, with 676 acres of demesne arable, such tenants occupy about one-fifth of the demesne.[33] But on the smaller manors, such as Kensworth, Drayton, and Norton, as much as one-third or even one-half of the demesne is tenanted in this way. In this group too there are exceptions: Chingford with 180 demesne acres has no such tenants, and Sutton with 210 acres has 10 of them occupied by small rent-payers.

The lettings, such as they are, Prof. Postan then tries to link with twelfth-century movements in two ways. He refers to the survey of 1181 as providing clear evidence that the disintegration of the manor that he finds virtually accomplished by 1222 had in fact taken place at a much earlier date. In the manor of Beauchamp, Prof. Postan says, we find in 1181 'roughly the same proportion of land held for rent in the demesne, land let out and land assarted as we find in the survey of 1222'. Prof. Postan is perfectly right about the proportions. But if we read on we find that, at the end of the list of tenants who hold parcels of demesne, the jury says: 'Remanent in dominio de terra arabilis circiter 500 acras.'[34]

In short, according to the surveys made at the time, four-fifths of the demesne arable of Beauchamp manor were at the disposal of the Chapter or its farmer, both in the late twelfth century and in the early thirteenth century.

Prof. Postan then tries to link the thirteenth-century evidence of lettings with the names of some twelfth-century farmers who are mentioned in the course of the 1222 survey. But this does not answer to his purpose because so few of the few lettings that are associated with the names of farmers can be safely attributed to such men.[35]

---

[32] Ibid., pp. 58–64, 69–74.

[33] Ibid., pp. 28–33.

[34] Hale, ed., op. cit., p. 116.

[35] Postan, 'Chronology', p. 97. Thus Richard Rufus released 5½ acres of demesne to tenants at Thorp; 20 acres at Runwell, and some at Navestock. At Navestock, however, he is only one of four responsible at various times for the lettings that were made. The fourth is Agnes, the present farmer. Postan writes with such bold assurance about the new demesne being 'largely let out' at Navestock and of 'a large number of men holding portions of the 'old demesne' there that it takes an effort of mind to recollect that in 1222 we are concerned with a demesne of 340 acres and total lettings of about 50 acres.

At Runwell there is another entry which concerns Richard Rufus. It states that the entire demesne as well as other land was let 'a tempore Ricardi Ruffi'. According to a further entry, lower down the page, Rufus was then archdeacon. Postan wants us to believe that Rufus let the entire demesne in small parcels. If Postan's case for believing that such policies were quite the usual thing in the twelfth century had proved to be a

Having disposed of the estates of St Paul's, Prof. Postan turns next to the Bishop of Worcester's manors, to the Templars' estates, to the Burton Abbey surveys,[36] and so on. But wherever we look, whether we look at the Templars' estates,[37] or the Bishop of Worcester's,[38] or with Prof. Du Boulay at the

strong one it would have been reasonable to give him the benefit of the doubt in this instance. But as things have turned out Runwell is his best evidence so far for a case which seems to have very little to be said for it. We cannot therefore assume anything about the fate of Runwell's demesne in the twelfth century except that Postan's presumption is unlikely.

Hugh de Runwell let 20 acres of land in Walton (Hale, ed., *op. cit.*, p. 49) but this was not demesne land. It was land said to be 'tam ad censum quam ad operationem'. Its work-load was set out later (*ibid.*, pp. 51–2). All the other examples cited by Postan are concerned with places where very little demesne land was let out in 1222.

36 The Burton Abbey surveys that Postan reserved for special treatment at the end of his essay consist of two surveys. Postan states that the earlier one was drawn up in 'the first quarter of the century' and the later one 'a few decades, perhaps a generation later' ('Chronology', p. 104). According to Round, however, and also according to the editor of the surveys, the later one was drawn up c.1126, and the earlier one, perhaps a dozen years before (C. G. O. Bridgeman, ed., *The Burton Abbey Twelfth-Century Surveys* (The William Salt Archaeological Society, 1916, publ. 1918), p. 300; J. H. Round, 'The Burton Abbey Surveys', *English Historical Review*, vol. xx (1905), p. 278 and n. 9. Postan gives no hint of his reason for rejecting these conclusions. But if they are right, and we must assume that they are, then the Burton surveys are useless from the point of view of his argument, which depends on the time of troubles starting about 1130. Cf. Postan, 'Glastonbury Estates: A Reply', p. 118.

A similar problem of dating occurs with the Shaftesbury MS (British Library, Harley MS 61). Postan says the two Shaftesbury surveys belong respectively to decades early and late in the twelfth century and acknowledges Stenton's help in dating them. No one would lightly question anything that carries Stenton's authority. But the whole collection consists of copies. The surveys are transcribed with other thirteenth-century material rather than with earlier material and contain no obvious hints of twelfth-century provenance. The collection requires and deserves editing.

37 The Templars' estates, sometimes compact, often were not. Hence they had to be grouped together for fiscal purposes, as was the Bristol group, and let out for ease of handling. This makes Templar property an exiguous basis upon which to build a case. Nevertheless the Templars worked a surprising number of properties. The Essex manor of Witham and Temple Cressing is in hand; in Kent, Ewell manor; in Oxfordshire, Cowley and Merton; in Gloucestershire, Temple Guiting; in Hertfordshire, Weston; in Bedfordshire, Sharnbrook; in Wiltshire, Temple Rockley; in Shropshire, Lydley. Even in Lincolnshire and Yorkshire manors are in hand and services are done. Moreover when at farm manors are very often farmed whole. It is obviously a thriving group, making a new park at Balsall, imposing unconvenanted customs at Lockeridge, offering small-holdings to the highest bidder at Cardington. It is hard to know how to answer Postan when he says that with a few exceptions 'for which the evidence of the document is not clear, the Survey has very little beyond rents and very light services to record' (Postan, 'Chronology', p. 98, citing B. A. Lees, ed., *Records of the Templars in England in the Twelfth Century* (Oxford, 1935)).

38 About the Worcester estates Postan says that 'many of the rents were undoubtedly a result of recent commutation' (Postan, 'Chronology', p. 98). He gives Hartlebury as an example, where the tenants 'deberent esse operarii' – 'that is,' he says, 'should be, but are not'. The entry reads as follows: 'Isti deberent esse operarii ita ut de unaquaque

estates of the Archbishop of Canterbury, which show no signs of 'dramatic demesne dissolution' in the twelfth century, but simply 'the traditional farming system' working 'on the whole to the advantage of everybody',[39] nowhere can we find wholesale dissolution of demesne, grievous loss of service, widespread commutation. When demesne leasing and commutation occurred in the twelfth century, the records show with unmistakable clarity that they occurred then, as they did in the thirteenth century, for a variety of reasons which explain individual cases, without amounting, when taken together, to evidence of a widespread movement induced by general economic causes.

In short the overwhelming testimony of the records is that 'The Chronology of Labour Services' was the invention and not the discovery of its author. It has stood for too long as an obstacle to our understanding of twelfth-century economic life. It has contradicted everything else we have learnt about economic developments between Domesday Book and Magna Carta. It has made nonsense of the legal degradation of the peasantry that took place at that period. If we can, as we should, dismiss it without qualification from our thoughts, as being contrary even to the evidence adduced in its support, then we shall be able, at last, to see what the records so plainly show. We shall be able to see that twelfth-century manors functioned very much as we might have expected them to do in an environment of which the distinguishing economic feature was steady expansion rather than confusion, paralysis, and headlong decline. We shall be able to see that there was never any question of a recovery in the thirteenth century from the dissolution of the manor's most important relationships in the twelfth, because there was never any question of the dissolution of those relationships in the twelfth century. The view, accepted by a whole generation of medieval scholars, that the manor was some sort of factory subject to temporary shut-down in periods of bad trade, has nothing whatsoever to be said for it; for the manor was never called upon, in the twelfth century, to survive in a shorn and emasculated form the wholesale fragmentation of its demesne and the wholesale abandonment of the services that went with it.

Henceforth, therefore, our views concerning the development of the manor must take more account of what other scholars from Seebohm to Lennard have tried to teach us than they have been free to do for many years. The early history of the manor may be lost for ever in the obscurity of inscrutable texts and contentious issues. But when we first see it clearly, as we do in late Anglo-Saxon times, the manor is already in full panoply, familiar in structure and detail. It is often at farm. But this must not deceive

virgata operari debent iiii dies in ebdomada et in i istorum dierum arare cum quot animalibus habent de singulis aratris singulas acras et eas herciare die Veneris et Sabbati summagia facere et nuncia.' (M. Hollings, ed., *The Red Book of Worcester* (Worcestershire Historical Society, 1934), p. 206). In short, in Postan's idiom, 'should be and are'.
[39] F. R. H. Du Boulay, *The Lordship of Canterbury* (1966), p. 204. Manors on the highly successful estates of Westminster Abbey were also leased out whole in the twelfth century. Barbara Harvey, *op. cit.*, p. 79.

us. Farming out was bound to generate records because it called for safeguards which had no meaning for the man who simply ran his own estate. And when the king's records begin to accumulate we must not conclude too readily that farming out was prevalent because we find so many of the estates that get back into the king's hands put to farm. The sheriff's office was not equipped for estate management. It knew how to manage money not men. A temporary farm suited it admirably, therefore, without in the least inconveniencing the king.[40]

Historians are strongly disposed to deprecate the farming out of manors. They see it at best as a mark of want of enterprise on the part of landlords and their estate managers; at worst as a confession of failure or defeat. In this they do the system a profound injustice. Farming out was an extremely flexible device which achieved the maximum benefit to all concerned with the minimum of effort. It enabled a landlord, before the strenuous days of the 'High Middle Ages', to solve the problem of getting his estates looked after and his income from them guaranteed, by finding tenants for them who would shoulder some of the responsibilities of management in return for a lease. Sometimes the landlord handed over the whole of a particular estate; sometimes he reserved parcels of land or particular rights. Sometimes he stipulated a term of years for the duration of the farm; sometimes he authorized his farmers to hold his lands for as long as it suited him to let them do so. Often enough he went so far as to concede to his farmers tenancies for life or lives. But a lease for life could very well mean, in the end, the disinheritance of the landlord and many landlords learnt the hard way that nothing clings like land, whatever assurances their lawyers may have given them to the contrary.

The best kind of lease, from this point of view, was the lease that went with the job and terminated naturally when the job did. Property tied in this way was usually safe. And many ecclesiastical institutions, at some time or other in these early centuries, found the money they required for the purchases they wanted to make, and procured the food and drink they consumed, by attaching rents and renders from various estates to particular offices in the administration and then making the officer concerned responsible for seeing that the institution got its money and renders when and where it needed them. In such cases the lessee was, in fact, in his other capacity, one of the lessors. When we first see the farming system clearly at work, however, farming out often meant finding tenants who had no other connexion with the landlord than that of the lease.

It does not follow from this, however, that the prospective farmer always

---

[40] P. D. A. Harvey, 'The Pipe Rolls and the Adoption of Demesne Farming in England', *Economic History Review*, 2nd ser., vol. xxvii (1974), p. 353. Harvey notes 'the evident prevalence of leases on a very short-term even annual basis: in such cases an estate's system of management may have been changed rapidly and radically when it came into the King's hands'. Such rapid change was surely even more likely when what came in made the sheriff's office responsible for doing an estate steward's work.

had to be offered an exceptionally generous inducement before he could be prevailed upon to undertake the responsibilities of estate management, particularly in the twelfth century, when land was in demand. Nor can it be said that the farmer was generally an abject and timorous fellow who had been driven by an importunate neighbour or cajoled by a masterful patron into accepting a responsibility for which he really had no stomach. All the early evidence we possess goes to show that the farmer was usually a man of substance and often a man of standing.[41] Even when the farmer was a syndicate, as sometimes happened, the syndicate was made up of men who were not lightly to be treated without respect.[42]

In such circumstances, at any rate in the twelfth century, with landlords who were not disposed as a general rule to give their farmers a free hand with their estates in return for ridiculously modest demands in the way of rent and render, and with farmers who were very much in a position to stand out for reasonable terms, the leases that were taken up are very likely to have been the result of hard bargaining. And behind the bargaining lay much administrative thought and action.

The lease that granted a farm usually conveyed stock as well as land; and the land conveyed, as the records make abundantly clear, normally carried with it the labour services with which the farmer expected to work it. This made a valuable and complex property. On big estates with many such properties the landlord could not possibly decide upon a rent or a series of renders which would give him a reasonable return unless he had a clear idea of what he possessed. He might be a man of simple needs which were easily satisfied without his having to institute inquiries with a view to getting more out of his estates. He might have friends or relations, servants to reward, or creatures to patronize, whose farms he would not dream of questioning. Generally speaking, however, the development of the consumption habits of the medieval well-to-do is more than anything else a story of people unremittingly asking for more. It would be utterly wrong to pretend that estate management contributed substantially to providing them with the means with which to gratify their wants. When they got what they asked for it was usually because patronage, inheritance, or marriage had supplied them with the means with which to do so. Medieval estate management, struggling with embezzlement and theft, rarely achieved anything better, on the whole, than a regular income which was not an outrageously meagre share of what was produced. But if even this modest objective were to be achieved farming out had to be preceded by inquiry.

Moreover there was another incentive. Without taking the elementary precaution of drawing up an inventory of what had been handed over to his

41 Lennard, op. cit., ch. vi, passim; Du Boulay, op. cit., p. 203.
42 R. S. Hoyt, 'Farm of the Manor and Community of the Vill in Domesday Book', Speculum, vol. xxx (1955), pp. 147–69.

farmers, no landlord could have the least confidence that they had restored everything intact to him when their tenure came to an end.

We have records of landlords farming out their property almost as soon as we have records of their doing anything at all.[43] But our records of the inventories they compiled, the valuations they made and the leases they then granted, are mostly very late. And yet behind the simple statement that this or that estate was at farm for so much money or such and such renders there will surely lie an investigation into what that estate comprised, what it was worth, and an agreement between lessor and lessee as to terms. No doubt these things were not always written down, or if written down preserved beyond the term of their usefulness. But without them estate management was lost.

Enough evidence survives to show that immense trouble was taken, on many of the estates for which we have early records, to compile inventories of property and property rights which, by plunging into the most minute particularity, strove to safeguard the interests of the landlord and maintain his capital intact. And from what we now know, and even more from what we now suspect, as to the sophistication of early administrative methods,[44] it would be wrong to conclude that the methods of investigation that these records reveal are not older, perhaps much older, than the records themselves.[45]

We have not now got all the various types of document, the extent, valuation and lease, that were drawn up in connexion with the farming out of any particular twelfth-century estate, though in the various collections extant we have certainly got examples of every kind of document that the farming out of manors could give rise to in the twelfth century. The St Paul's survey is a good example of the standard of investigation that could be achieved and, for all we know, was commonly achieved by manorial administrators other than those whose work has survived.[46] It is late: it was drawn up in 1222. But the fragment of the 1181 survey that survives contains the terms of reference by which those who carried it out were to be guided. Since the fragment conforms to the pattern of the 1222 survey, and the inquiries ordered in 1181 were every bit as searching as those carried out in 1222, it is hard to believe that the finished product of 1181 could have differed greatly in range or depth from what has actually come down to us from 1222.

Sworn juries testified as to the facts on the St Paul's manors as they did elsewhere. And they reported comprehensively. They said how big each manor was, how much demesne arable it had, how much meadow and wood,

[43] A. J. Robertson, ed., *Anglo-Saxon Charters* (Cambridge, 1939), p. 38; F. M. Stenton, *Anglo-Saxon England* (Oxford, 1943), p. 285.

[44] J. Campbell, 'Observations on English Government from the Tenth to the Twelfth Century', *Transactions of the Royal Historical Society*, 5th ser., vol. xxv (1975).

[45] F. Seebohm, *The English Village Community* (Cambridge, 1890), ch. v.

[46] Hale, ed., *op. cit.* See also L. J. Downer, ed., *Leges Henrici Primi* (Oxford, 1972), pp. 174–5.

how many ploughs the demesne needed, how many animals the ploughs required, how much stock the manor could carry, what mills and other appurtenances there were, what condition everything was in. When the demesne had been marled they made a note of it. They found out what repairs and improvements had been made. Often they reported who had been responsible for carrying them out. They declared what needed to be done or what was worth less because what ought to have been done had not been done. They then listed demesne lettings and all the other tenancies, according to their various types, together with their yields in money rent, service, and render.

Work comparable with this was done by many estate managers in the twelfth century as we can see by looking at such records as those discussed above. The scope of the information collected was no less remarkable than the scrupulous detail in which that information was sought. With such information to hand, estate management lost half its terrors. With such information to hand, an estate could be kept in demesne without fear of loss due to ignorance or helplessness in the face of the depredations of the tenantry, or it could be farmed out without risk of scandalous under-valuation. To judge by these documents, Walter of Henley had nothing to teach that those who worked in twelfth-century estate management had not already learned: his precepts were their daily practice.

Farming out did not in the least mean that landlords were necessarily or usually committed for long periods to whatever terms they may have nego-tiated. The *Dialogus de Scaccario* called farms of manors firm and unchange-able.[47] But whatever the *Dialogus* may have meant by this phrase it cannot possibly have meant that farms could not change or had not changed in the past. Many had periodic increases written into the terms of their agree-ments.[48] At Peterborough where the estate had been halved by subinfeuda-tion by 1086 the abbey had made up its losses of income within two generations by dint of increasing its remaining demesne farms. It was, said Dr King, 'perhaps the most remarkable of the Abbey's managerial triumphs in the period studied'.[49] The Archbishop of Canterbury's estates, at farm in the eleventh and early twelfth centuries, were 'leased out at prices which were liable to fluctuate, usually in an upward direction'.[50] At Ramsey farms rose as small-holdings in wood, waste, and fen were added to the manors.[51]

Naturally, when farming out meant making contracts for life, this enor-mously diminished the scope of management. Even the formidable Abbot Sampson of Bury St Edmunds was obliged to tread deferentially in the presence of the formal lease. Manors at farm on less ceremonious terms he resumed more or less unceremoniously. But some farmers had life tenancies,

---

[47] C. Johnson, ed., *Dialogus de Scaccario* (1950), p. 30.

[48] Lennard, *op. cit.*, pp. 182–5.

[49] King, *op. cit.*, p. 144.

[50] Du Boulay, *op. cit.*, p. 199.

[51] Raftis, *op. cit.*, pp. 83–4.

and charters to show for them. When the wife of Herlewin of Runcton, who was one of them, died suddenly, Sampson's reaction was to exclaim: 'Yesterday I would have given 60 marks to free that manor: to-day the Lord has freed it.'[52] Such tenures assumed that economic conditions, if not the personal circumstances of the various landlords, would remain stable for a long time. They were hostages to fortune with a vengeance. When prices rose only those farms that had been granted for payments in kind kept pace. Consequently, when the farming out system persisted into later centuries it seems to have done so mainly when the farms consisted of renders rather than money rents.[53] But very many twelfth-century farms were for money rent, or had a substantial element of money rent in their composition. When this was so the twelfth-century landlord who discovered that he was in a position to improve the terms upon which he had granted farms for life or lives, if only he could revoke them, found himself trapped in the same way as Abbot Sampson was.

The trap could be sprung. Farms for lives were, after all, no worse for twelfth-century landlords than copyhold tenures were for sixteenth-century landlords. And they were a good deal less common. Accordingly, twelfth-century landlords who found themselves trapped, and, no doubt, landlords who were not trapped but preferred a capital sum to an increased flow of income, resorted to an expedient which was not new then and had a long and chequered future ahead of it: they imposed entry fines.[54] Stable farms no more meant static incomes in the twelfth century than stable rents necessarily meant static incomes in the sixteenth. The farming-out system in the twelfth century was apparently equal to what was, perhaps, its most intractable hazard: fixity of terms of tenure in an age of improvement.

At the end of the twelfth century, estate management had to cope with inflation. Whilst prices rose, the terms upon which estate managers could get labour much improved: for population was beginning to press upon resources. The problem, especially when land was farmed out, was one of adjusting obligations to exceptionally rapidly changing circumstances and unparalleled opportunities. This did not call for revolutionary changes in the structure of the manor or of its administration. And indeed none occurred. A new type of report appears: the annual account. But it hardly represents new thoughts about the land or its supervision. The sales and purchases, the collection of rents, the imposition of increments, the payment of wages, the employment or commutation of labour, the repairs and improvements, all these things, as our twelfth-century records plainly show, were part of the common round of life on the manor in earlier days. The annual account writes down what used to be done without benefit of clerical assistance,

---

[52] H. E. Butler, ed., *The Chronicle of Jocelin of Brakelond* (1949), pp. 32–3.

[53] Lennard, *op. cit.*, p. 185.

[54] Raftis calls the entry fine 'the touchstone of a hereditary lease' (*op. cit.*, pp. 41, 50). The *gersuma*, which was a fine paid as a condition of taking up tenure, did not create hereditary right (Lennard, *op. cit.*, pp. 180–2).

systematizes it, and consequently makes it easier for everyone concerned to see at a glance what has been done and what is still outstanding. But it most emphatically is not the reason for the immensely increased profits that are earned in the thirteenth century. It is very tempting to attribute to management techniques the credit that properly belongs to the impersonal forces that inflated prices and kept labour costs down, and in doing so to forget that in a world of fallow fields and starved animal husbandry there was in fact very little that management could do to contribute to such profits.

Nevertheless, historians make large claims for thirteenth-century estate management. Whether farming out was normal practice in the twelfth century or not we may never know. It was certainly unusual in the thirteenth century. Historians always assume that this was a change for the better. But are we entitled to assume that estate management was more active because manorial operations were directed with a lord's authority, exercised through his stewards and bailiffs, rather than with a farmer's? A commercially minded farmer presumably did his utmost to get what he could from the land and yield as little of it as may be to his landlord. The twelfth-century evidence, such as it is, certainly suggests as much.[55]

The manor itself, therefore, was not necessarily rendered more productive as a result of the switch from farming out to direct management. Run by the reeve, it merely answered to a different master.

Moreover, a thirteenth-century landlord had none of a twelfth-century farmer's interest in management. Under the farming-out system he got fixed returns and the farmer, usually, the benefits that accrued from such items as market sales, profits of court, and the like. Some of these more fluctuating items of income the landlord might reserve for himself when he farmed out his manors. In twelfth-century conditions, however, landlords, as a general rule, probably saw no need to reserve such items rather than compound for them in the farm: not till well into the final quarter of the century is it likely that prices rose so quickly that farms could not keep pace with them. And the farmer, when conditions were more or less stable, was bound to stir himself if he were to do as well as he might. When his manors were restored to him much of the landlord's income continued to be fixed, in the sense that much came from items such as rent which, as the extents and accounts clearly show, were revised only occasionally. But much was not fixed. Consequently, it was from such fluctuating items of manorial income that automatic and immediate gains were made by landlords once the inflation had begun. It may very well be that the vast majority of landlords derived the chief benefits of direct management from this source. With market forces making it progressively easier for them to do so, their incomes rose without their having to introduce any reform of methods of work or control on their estates. Hence the thirteenth-century landlord had very little incentive to manage his estates directly for the sake of the greater control that direct

[55] Above, p. 133, n. 3.

management enabled keen administrators to exercise on his behalf over organization or husbandry.

Reforms and improvements there undoubtedly were.[56] But we cannot possibly assume that estate management was more active in this respect in the thirteenth century than it had been in the twelfth. Twelfth-century evidence is slight because so few records survive, perhaps because so few were made. It is, after all, early days for the white-collar worker. The educational effort that will staff all the bureaucracies comes in the thirteenth century and brings with it a spate of records. Are we not, perhaps, excessively impressed by the evidence of thirteenth-century improvement because we have so many records from which to study it? If anything, indeed, the twelfth-century evidence constitutes a far more impressive tribute to the managerial proficiency of the age than the later evidence does, because in a small and random sample of records we seem to see so much being done on the estates.

In the end the farming-out system prevailed. Further bouts of inflation, starting in the middle of Henry III's reign, delayed its advent by making direct management essential if estate income were to keep pace. And when the farming-out system came into its own it did so in the sixteenth century when, according to this analysis, no landlord with an eye for the easy gains to be won at a time of inflation should have farmed his manors out.

By the sixteenth century, however, the medieval manor had dwindled irretrievably, although the medieval system of husbandry had not yet greatly changed because, in matters of costs and prices, the sixteenth century displayed the closest possible affinity with the thirteenth. The manor had dwindled by then because it had proved to be utterly incapable of withstanding the kind of strains that Prof. Postan had claimed that it was perfectly capable of taking in its stride. The lesson of the sixteenth-century fate of the manor is that wholesale fragmentation of demesne and commutation of services were not proof of manorial adaptability: they were portents of dissolution. When landlords were compelled by later medieval movements of costs and prices to surrender their manors to the peasantry, as Prof. Postan has always urged us to believe they did in the twelfth century, their surrender marked the end of the manor as a unit of estate management organized in accordance with medieval usages. In the sixteenth century, when conditions again favoured the rigorous exploitation of manorial rights and privileges, the powers that landlords could exercise, though often substantial, were nevertheless confined to those that proved to be compatible with the dissolution of the manorial labour force and the irrevocable alienation of some, perhaps much, of the manorial demesne.[57] The social structure that the

---

[56] The administrative reforms have been admirably surveyed recently by P. D. A. Harvey in his *Manorial Records of Cuxham, Oxfordshire, c.1200–1359* (Oxfordshire Record Society, vol. 1, 1976).

[57] For an illuminating discussion of these matters, see E. Kerridge, *Agrarian Problems in the Sixteenth Century and After* (1969).

Middle Ages had built upon its system of husbandry was, apparently, incapable of surviving, without irreparable damage, a cycle of changes comparable with the one that Prof. Postan had once conjured from the records of the twelfth and thirteenth centuries. The manor never performed the vertiginous gyrations he had attributed to it in those centuries. The sixteenth-century evidence suggests that it could not perform them, even when those who stood to gain by its being able to do so had every incentive to restore it to what it had been in its prime.

Thirteenth-Century Prices and
the Money Supply

The thirteenth century has always been a favourite with historians. It commends itself to scholars of diverse interests as the culminating age of medieval achievement. Not least in this company are to be found the agrarian historians. For them, until recently, the thirteenth century was quite simply the classic age of demesne farming; and demesne farming was, for them, the classic expression of buoyant market forces working in a feudal context to promote the interests and advance the prosperity of the baronial and knightly classes upon whose welfare the achievements of the age depended.

In recent years a bleaker interpretation of the evidence has darkened the prospect that agrarian historians once viewed with such unqualified satisfaction. As so often in historical questions, the facts are not in dispute. No one denies the rising trend of thirteenth-century prices and rents. But historians whose concern is with the 'condition of the people' now stress the misery to which thirteenth-century market forces reduced everyone who was unable to take advantage of them. Rising markets undoubtedly favoured the lucky, the enterprising and the well-born; but according to recent investigators, for people in general, thirteenth-century conditions spelt want and degradation and even ruin.[1]

Can we be sure, however, that the underlying assumption made by everyone concerned with the issues, is justified by the evidence? Is it in fact true to say that demesne farming flourished in the thirteenth century as a result of market conditions in which it was very hard for demesne farming to fail? The evidence for this universal belief in the buoyancy of thirteenth-century conditions is partly circumstantial. Expansion is to be found practically everywhere that one looks for it in the thirteenth-century records. Clearances, the reclamation of marsh and fen, changes in land use and new settlements, all seem to tell of thrust and growth. The direct evidence of rents is, apparently, no less telling. By the end of the century, rents were altogether more onerous for the tenantry than they had ever been before; and if entry fines, though sometimes spectacularly high by then, did not always rise in proportion to the rise in rents, we are assured that commercial considerations were not the only ones that governed what was demanded.[2]

---

[1] For a recent survey, see J. R. Maddicott, 'The English Peasantry and the Demands of the Crown 1294–1341', *Past and Present*, Supplement no. 1 (1975), esp. pp. 70–2.

[2] J. Z. Titow, *English Rural Society 1200–1350* (1969), pp. 76–7; B F. Harvey, 'The

Fines, however, like rents, are not the easiest of payments to interpret. Moreover, if we are to believe what we are told about thirteenth-century market conditions, we ought to look closely at the evidence of prices. Fortunately there are price series for a variety of farm products. And some of these do indeed show that the prices paid, or obtained, for certain products, rose throughout the thirteenth century. But not all these series are equally reliable or indeed significant. Farm products were anything but homogeneous. Livestock quality varied infinitely; so did the quality of manufactured foods like cheese; and the range of quality to be found in wool is notorious.[3] Furthermore the volume of usable evidence for product prices varies enormously. Grains varied in quality as other farm products did. But grains provide us with what is easily the best attested evidence; and grains were easily the most important products so far as farm profits were concerned. Livestock prices or dairy-produce prices meant very little to thirteenth-century demesne farmers because few of them depended upon sales of such things for more than a fraction of their incomes. Even wool was no more than a subsidiary source of income even for the biggest wool farmers.[4] The medieval demesne farmer was essentially an arable farmer. In Postan's felicitous phrase, the big estates were little more than 'federated grain factories'. Much of the income they received consisted of cash earned by selling grains; and a good deal of it consisted of cash paid by tenants who sold grain in order to be able to pay their rents. Accordingly, if we want to know how demesne farmers fared in the thirteenth century it is to the grain markets that we must address ourselves in the first instance; and we must count ourselves fortunate that the most important price series are, in this case, also the most reliable.

I

As a result of Dr Farmer's exhaustive labours in the archives, we can be reasonably confident of knowing as much as we are ever likely to know about the trends of grain prices in the thirteenth century.[5] But what we can know about these trends is somewhat less than we should like to know because there are seemingly irreparable deficiencies of material in the mid-century decades. Dr Farmer has warned us about these deficiencies; but his warnings

Population Trend in England between 1300 and 1348', *Transactions of the Royal Historical Society*, 5th ser., vol. xvi (1966), pp. 25–7.

[3]   T. H. Lloyd, 'The Movement of Wool Prices in Medieval England', *Economic History Society Supplement* 6 (1973).

[4]   A. R. Bridbury, 'Before the Black Death', *Economic History Review*, 2nd ser., vol. xxx (1977), p. 398, also reprinted below, see pp. 185–6.

[5]   The cereal prices used throughout this article and in the accompanying graphs are taken from D. L. Farmer, 'Some Grain Price Movements in Thirteenth-Century England', *Economic History Review*, 2nd ser., vol. x (1957). Dr Farmer's years are those in which the harvests were gathered.

have not always been heeded. Nevertheless, between 1226 and 1244 there are at present prices for the principal grains for only four years out of eighteen; and between 1255 and 1262 there are grain prices for only two years out of seven.

We can perhaps supply these deficiencies in a sense. If we take 4s 6d per quarter as the middle-market price, when wheat was neither cheap nor dear, then we find that there were roughly twice as many years between 1210 and 1270 when wheat was less than 4s 6d per quarter than when it was more. Taking middle-market prices for the other grains produces comparable results. We may perhaps make the tentative assumption, therefore, that if we had quotations for the missing years we should find that they confirmed rather than upset the evidence that Dr Farmer has examined and collated.

But even if we make a much more modest assumption and assume merely that prices fluctuated in the missing years as they did in other years, the grain prices nevertheless force us to conclude that between 1210 and 1270 we can perceive no long-term trend. Grain prices rose and fell, as good years succeeded bad, and bad good, without displaying any long-term tendency either up or down.

Contemporary farmers had very little idea of how the cereal market had developed, and of course, none of how it would develop. Historians all too easily forget that farmers coped with market prices as they formed and looked back with imperfect knowledge and failing memory on a comparatively short span and narrow compass of experience. So far as contemporary farmers were concerned, grain prices, as they rose and fell in the course of the thirteenth century, did so without offering them any hope that high prices had come to stay or any confidence that high prices would not be followed by years of prices which could easily cancel the gains previously made. The only lesson that market conditions could teach the more perceptive farmers was that if good prices did not last, neither did bad ones.

After 1270 a decisive change takes place. Henceforth, so far as wheat prices are concerned, 4s 6d per quarter no longer serves as the middle-market price dividing cheap years from dear ones. Between 1270 and 1325 we find that wheat only falls below 4s 6d per quarter when harvests are quite exceptionally abundant. The line that divides years of cheap wheat from years when wheat is dear must be drawn, henceforth, at 5s 6d per quarter or even perhaps at 6s. Once again, moreover, there is no easily recognizable trend either up or down. There is not even an increase in the violence of fluctuations as we approach what were, for most people, the terrible years that followed 1315. The most violent fluctuations of price recorded in this period occurred between 1287, when wheat stood at 2s 10½d, and 1295 when it rose to 9s 2¾d. This was worse than the worst fluctuation previously recorded, which occurred between 1254, when wheat fell to 2s 11¼d, and 1257 when it touched 8s 0¾d. And both these fluctuations in fact exceeded in violence the worst fourteenth-century fluctuation before 1315. This occurred between 1306, when wheat stood at 4s 6d, and 1309, when it rose to 7s 11¾d.

Wheat was always the dearest of the grains as oats were the cheapest; but wheat prices differed in behaviour from that of the prices of other grains only in the violence of their fluctuations. In other respects what was true of wheat after 1270 was true also of barley, rye and oats.

In retrospect we can see a pattern in the price history of the thirteenth century that no one living at the time could possibly have perceived. We can see that the history of grain prices in the thirteenth century was dominated by two periods of significant change, the first of which began in the final quarter of the twelfth century, and the second in the final quarter of the thirteenth century.[6] As a result of the changes that took place at those periods grain prices were established at new and higher levels which persisted for several generations. These changes irrupted suddenly and without warning; and only now can we see that what, at other times, proved to be nothing more than a violent aberration, at these junctures inaugurated a new era.

Once the shock of change had worn off, experience offered no clear guidance to those who managed the big estates and determined manorial policy as to how they should proceed. If those in charge had assumed that a period of high prices would inevitably bring low prices in their wake, as they always had done before, then prudent management required no more of them than that they should put by the profits of the fat years against the long haul of lean years to come, using some of the profits perhaps to attend to some of those thousand and one repairs and renewals that get postponed when times are bad or endlessly delayed when the weather makes it impossible to carry them out at the only season of the year during which they can be done. No doubt many demesne farmers took this view of farming prospects in the 1270s; and even those who came to the conclusion, for whatever reason, that this time high prices had come to stay, would have had no warrant for the further assumption that the future would break so completely with the past that the high prices they were enjoying would prove to be merely the prelude to still higher prices later on. And in fact anyone sanguine enough or rash enough to look forward to such a double break with the past and to act upon his expectations would soon enough have found his manors encumbered with more debt than they could bear; for once the new price levels had been established they stabilized in the sense in which they had stabilized between 1210 and 1270.

II

Modern discussions of investment policy in thirteenth-century farming have generally assumed that demesne farmers made decisions about investment in the confident expectation that prices would continue to rise in the future as

---

[6] P. D. A. Harvey, 'The English Inflation of 1180–1220', Past and Present, vol. 61 (1973).

they had done in the past. On this assumption historians have often expressed surprise at how little investment, by modern standards, demesne
farmers appear to have undertaken.[7] But it is clear from the evidence that if
demesne farmers had judged by experience they would have had no such
confident expectations about the future. They could not have made investment decisions on the basis of optimism about the future course of prices
founded upon grateful recollections of the past because there was no such
past, at least no such past in the recollection of anyone living, to which they
could have appealed.

In the short run, once grain prices had jumped to higher levels in the
1270s, experience may not have been a sure guide for demesne farmers, who
could have been forgiven for allowing optimism about the future course of
grain prices to colour their vision. But once it became clear that grain prices
would henceforth fluctuate about stable levels, as they always had done in
the recollections of those with the longest memories, it also became clear, as
it had done after the previous jump in grain prices, that grain prices cannot
change sharply and permanently without having profoundly important ramifications for many other relationships.

At first demesne farmers found themselves sharing with their tenants the
welcome experience of uncovenanted benefits in the form of higher prices
and hence higher profits than ever before. This sharing was inevitable until
contracts were revised, because manorial tenants with crops of grain to sell
were bound to gain, in proportion to their sales, as much as their landlords
did. Demesne farmers even found themselves sharing these benefits with
some, perhaps with many, of their non-servile labourers. Such labourers were
often paid partly in kind. Some were paid mainly in kind.[8] And no one can
fail to be impressed by their importance in thirteenth-century rural society.
Consequently when grain prices rose as they did in the 1270s, payment in
kind spread the benefits even to them. But these were purely temporary
gains. There could be no permanent rise in general well-being on the land
without some profound change improving the availability of land for farming. And there is no reason whatsoever why we should suspect that any such
improvement had taken place at that time.

On the contrary, historians who have taken rising thirteenth-century
grain prices for granted, have argued that rising prices reflected an increasing
scarcity of land caused by a growing pressure of population which was, in its
turn, aggravated by a contraction of the arable acreage as a result of loss of
productivity due to over-exploitation. But grain prices did not rise in the last
quarter of the thirteenth century. Nor did they do so earlier in the century.
On each occasion when they changed a jump took grain prices to a plateau.
This is not in the least how an intensification of population pressure exerts

---

[7] See, for example, R. H. Hilton, *The English Peasantry in the Later Middle Ages*
(Oxford, 1975), chapter x.
[8] For an interesting discussion of these matters, see N. R. Goose, 'Wage Labour on a
Kentish Manor', *Archaeologia Cantiana*, vol. xcii (1976).

its influence upon grain prices. Population pressure is a force of cumulative power, not of sudden onset and subsequent surcease. If we want to see how population pressure reacts on grain prices, in the absence of widespread improvements in the organization and techniques of farming, we cannot do better than follow the relentlessly progressive trend of grain prices in the sixteenth century.[9] Whatever allowance we ought to make for accessory monetary influences upon it we surely cannot fail to see that the steadiness of the trend is not the least notable of its features. The contrast with twelfth- and thirteenth-century changes could scarcely be more striking. Where grain prices rose steadily in the sixteenth century, they rose suddenly in the twelfth and thirteenth centuries. And where they pursued a rising trend in the sixteenth century, they pursued level, if not at times, falling trends, in the thirteenth century. Whatever may have been happening to population size in the thirteenth century, we cannot use grain prices as evidence that the pressure of population was actually increasing at the time.

Stable grain prices may be incompatible with increasing population press- ure. But they are not necessarily incompatible with an increase of the size of the population. It is not inconceivable that the pressure of population was contained at this period because land lost to arable cultivation, whatever the cause, was more than compensated for by land newly added to the arable acreage as a result of colonization. The mass of evidence of colonization is, in its way, as impressive as the mass of evidence of land lost to arable cultiva- tion. But it is evidence of a different kind. The evidence of land lost to arable is usually evidence given to excuse a bailiff who was required to account for rents which were not forthcoming, or to exonerate a taxpayer from a liability. The evidence of colonization is, for the most part, evidence of grants made upon payment of a fee. The evidence of land lost by arable cultivation may not mean what it says. Indeed there is a strong presumption that it does not.[10] But the evidence of colonization is unmistakable. And what it seems to tell us is how difficult colonization was becoming. If colonization had still been easy it would not have made such a stir in the records. And when we recall the stability of thirteenth-century grain prices we cannot readily be- lieve that the quantities of land involved were anything like as extensive as they needed to be if they were to do more than compensate for any losses there may have been, still less if they were to improve the food supply.

If thirteenth-century grain prices give the impression that colonization, at best, could do no more than keep the arable acreage constant in relation to needs expressed in terms of market demand, so does the evidence provided

[9] W. G. Hoskins, 'Harvest Fluctuations and English Economic History 1480–1619', Agricultural History Review, vol. ii (1953–4), reprinted in W. E. Minchinton, ed., Essays in Agrarian History (1968). This study has been subjected to keen criticism, but not so as to invalidate its use here. See C. J. Harrison, 'Grain Price Analysis and Harvest Qualities 1465–1634', Agricultural History Review, vol. xix (1971).

[10] Thus for example, A. R. H. Baker, 'Evidence in the Nonarum Inquisitiones of Contracting Arable Lands', Economic History Review, 2nd ser., vol. xix (1966).

by the catastrophic famines of the years 1315–17. The consequences of severe famine were comparable with those of a notable colonizing movement. Famine was as capable of adding to the supply of land as colonization was. When it did so, it worked by diminishing the population instead of by increasing the arable acreage; but the effect upon the relationship between land and population was the same.

Opinion about the effects of the early fourteenth-century famines has moved away from Postan's view of them as a cataclysmic disaster which signalized the onset of debilitating problems that dominated economic life until the end of the Middle Ages. Miss Harvey's survey suggests that very little changed in agrarian England between 1300 and 1348.[11] Even Dr Kershaw, who has tried so hard to curdle our blood with his account of an early fourteenth-century crisis, of which the famines were the centrepiece, was obliged to conclude his survey by conceding that 'in many of the wealthier and more densely populated parts of the country there is no indication that the agrarian crisis initiated a lasting decline in production and occupation of the land'; and to confess that his evidence to the contrary was drawn very largely from estates situated in 'the poorer and less populous regions'.[12] Studies of replacement rates, though few and not altogether satisfactory, are at any rate scattered geographically and seem to indicate, in the words with which Dr Razi concluded his remarkable study of the Halesowen evidence, that English villagers in this period 'were able not only to replace themselves from generation to generation, but also to produce a surplus of offspring to maintain population growth'.[13] If Dr Farmer dissents from these views it is only to the extent that he perceives some shift in the economic balance between the period immediately before the famines, when grain prices 'had a hair-trigger sensitivity' to harvest yields, and the period of the 1330s and 1340s when they seem to have lost that degree of sensitivity.[14]

Dr Farmer's extensive studies of crop yields, wages and prices, have added a new depth to the discussion. His conclusion that yields did not change in the period 1271–1410 except when farmers kept more livestock, will not please those who contend that the famines inaugurated an era of impaired productivity on the land. But there are difficulties about the behaviour of prices in the 1330s and 1340s that Dr Farmer's researches may not have settled. Good harvests in that period seem to have had the effect of driving prices to lower levels than any known since the general enhancement of prices in the 1270s. Was this the result of the easing of population pressure after the famines? The accumulation of surpluses, which takes the sharpness out of harvest failure, also has the effect of forcing producers to lower prices more than they

11 See note 2 above.

12 I. Kershaw, 'The Great Famine and Agrarian Crisis in England 1315–22', *Past and Present*, vol. 59 (1973), pp. 49, 46.

13 Z. Razi, *Life, Marriage and Death in a Medieval Parish* (Cambridge, 1980), p. 33.

14 D. L. Farmer, 'Crop Yields, Prices and Wages in Medieval England', *Studies in Medieval and Renaissance History*, 6 (1983), p. 137.

would have done in more stringent circumstances in order to dispose of stocks which supply less urgent needs than they once did. It would be tempting to see the workings of this mechanism in the grain price movements of that period but for the behaviour of money-wage rates. An easing of population pressure at that time might reasonably be expected to have induced some increase in money-wage rates, or if not something as positive as an increase, then at least it should have imported an element of firmness into the labour market. But it did not. Money-wage rates, after a long history of gentle advance, seem to have chosen just this period of the 1330s and 1340s for an equally gentle retreat.[15]

The advance of wage rates in the thirteenth century is perfectly intelligible if we accept that the jump in grain prices that took place in the 1270s was part of a wider movement that caught up the remuneration of labour in its wake. The advance of wage rates at that period suggests indeed that this wider movement was one that it would not be unreasonable to call inflationary. That is to say, in the final quarter of the thirteenth century, as upon an earlier occasion, prices expressed in money rose generally without reflecting a change in the relative scarcity of resources. Is this perhaps what we can see happening in reverse during the 1330s when a series of abnormally low grain prices seems to have dragged money-wage rates down to lower levels? The retreat of money-wage rates makes it difficult for us to interpret the fall in prices as a sign that the post-famine decades bore witness to a substantive improvement in the ratio of land to labour. And if the abnormally low grain prices of the time do in fact indicate that the country was, however briefly, in the grip of deflation, then what could be more likely than that money wages should fall into line with a change in monetary relationships which did not reflect any change in the relative scarcity of resources?

III

What sort of world was it then in which neither the colonizing achievements of the thirteenth century nor the clearances executed by the sharp famines of the early fourteenth century were capable of restoring a measure of slack to the economic system? The land market was evidently saturated. If we may judge by the behaviour of grain prices, the land market had been saturated for a century or more. What it required was a more rigorous exorcism than any it had yet received. And when the time for exorcism came, as it did with the Black Death, it took recurrent visitations of that dreadful pestilence before land could be had on easier terms; and before that decisive clearance

---

15 Farmer, ibid., p. 144. Cf. E. H. Phelps-Brown and Sheila V. Hopkins, 'Seven Centuries of Building Wages' in E. M. Carus-Wilson, ed., Essays in Economic History, II (1962), p. 174.

there was patently no scope for any general and abiding improvement in standards of living in the English countryside.[16]

The inflation of the 1270s, like the previous inflation that began in the late twelfth century, was not progressive: it ended in stability. A new structure of prices supplanted the old one; but contracts fixed before inflation naturally took no account of the fall in the purchasing power of money brought about by inflation. Consequently the new levels of prices, once they had worked their way through the economic system, left demesne farmers with higher profits as producers but with lower real incomes from monetary sources. The higher profits earned by so many estates at this period are not, as they are so often taken to be, indisputable proof of the energetic efforts made by the more active and able demesne farmers to realize the potentialities of hitherto neglected or imperfectly developed resources. They are very largely the results of inflation; and they may very well have helped to conceal from less vigilant demesne farmers the fact that monetary income was actually diminishing in real value at the same time.

The fall in the purchasing power of money doubtless suited many demesne farmers; for they were, as a class, inveterate borrowers. But many of them received half their incomes in cash;[17] and the insidious effects of the declining purchasing power of money were bound to have had their impact upon the most torpid and ineffectual of them in the end. We can perhaps see something of the alacrity of some and the lethargy of others in the differences of opinion expressed by Dr Titow and Miss Harvey on the subject of whether the general level of rents and fines rose by much or little in this period.[18]

Once they had grasped the fact that higher prices had come to stay, demesne farmers were compelled to start revising as many of their rents and other charges as they could. But they did not embark upon any fundamental reorganization of the manorial system. Nor did they lose confidence in the system by surrendering the manorial demesne lands they had managed to a series of tenants. It would be difficult to imagine how such a move could possibly have improved estate solvency or profitability in conditions such as those of the late thirteenth century.

Some demesne farmers certainly did lease out fractions of demesne to tenants at this time. But there was nothing abnormal about that. Fractions of demesne were always being leased out in this way. When Postan saw this being done in the twelfth century he converted what he saw into a trend;[19] and historians of thirteenth-century farming are equally disposed to see the beginning of the end of demesne farming in any evidence of demesne leasing

---

16 A. R. Bridbury, 'The Black Death', *Economic History Review*, 2nd ser., vol. xxvi (1973). Reprinted below, pp. 200–17.

17 E. Miller, *The Abbey and Bishopric of Ely* (Cambridge, 1951), p. 93.

18 See note 2 above.

19 A. R. Bridbury, 'The Farming Out of Manors', *Economic History Review*, 2nd ser., vol. xxxi (1978), also reprinted above, pp. 133–53.

then. But when the Bishop of Ely's managers let small parcels of demesne land to tenants at this period, we should be quite wrong to interpret their action as a fearful omen, since 'high farming' on the Ely estates, according to their historian, 'may have reached its highest pitch of intensity and profitability in the reign of Edward II'.[20] And when the Bishop of Winchester's estate managers seriously diminished the demesne farming of the estate they were, apparently, pursuing a policy whose logic was not in the least determined by despondency about market prospects for grains.[21] We can see from the evidence that Dr Titow has used in his study of population pressure on the Bishop of Winchester's manor of Taunton that demesne leasing, though pursued vigorously there, was dictated neither by shortage of labour nor indeed by poor market prospects. The manor was evidently choked with labour; and entry fines of as much as £40 were paid or pledged for virgates on the estate.[22] Entry fines capitalized expected income flows. A farmer with £40 to pledge was not a starving peasant desperately giving hostages to fortune. He was a man who could choose where to farm and presumably someone who could take a rational and informed view of farming prospects on Taunton manor. Whatever may have been behind the leasing policy carried out on the Winchester estates, the Taunton evidence makes it extremely difficult for us to believe that the policy was prompted by prophetic insight into the bleak future that lay ahead for demesne farming in the late fourteenth century.

We cannot hope to see how estate management reacted to the sudden change of price level that occurred in the late twelfth century with anything like the same clarity as we can see how it reacted to the later one. But we can at any rate see how the twelfth-century price change left its mark. Assized rents, that is to say the customary rents that were once the full rents for tenancies, continued to be entered separately on many manorial account rolls before the increments were recorded, that is to say the additional rents that turned assized rents into the closest approximation to rack rents obtainable. And the price change also left its legacy of immutable dues. Commutation payments, as Denton remarked a century ago, originally intended perhaps to be the cash equivalent at current wage-rates of the services performed by tenants, were never revised, so that once inflation had raised wage-rates above their twelfth-century levels, such payments no longer provided thirteenth-century demesne farmers with the cash they required in order to be able to hire an equivalent force of wage-labourers if they needed one, or with the equivalent purchasing power over other things if they did not.[23]

[20] Miller, op. cit., p. 98.
[21] Titow, English Rural Society, pp. 52–3. See above, pp. 26–7.
[22] J. Z. Titow, 'Some Evidence of the Thirteenth-Century Population Increase', Economic History Review, 2nd ser., vol. xiv (1961).
[23] W. Denton, England in the Fifteenth Century (1888), p. 107, note i; Harvey, 'The English Inflation', p. 18. See note 6 above.

Demesne farmers were often marvellously fertile in expedients with which to overcome the problems created by immutable dues and tenures whose terms could not be changed except after a more or less prolonged lapse of time. Nominal profits undoubtedly rose as a result of the adjustments that were made after the twelfth- and thirteenth-century price changes; but it would be taking much for granted if we were to assume that these increased profits always provided demesne farmers with as much purchasing power as lower profits had done in earlier days.

IV

The sudden inflation that set such problems for contemporaries has not lost its power to baffle; for it sets its problems also for us. How are we to explain these extraordinary irruptions? The late twelfth-century inflation is more obscure than the later one because it occurred during the infancy of the public records. There are no mint output figures for the late twelfth century; no records to tell us how big the export trade was; no accounts of the money sent abroad to finance Angevin foreign policy. We cannot even be sure that the price change was as sharp as it looks, so meagre is the price material upon which we are compelled to depend. The sharp rise of late thirteenth-century grain prices, however, is not so much obscure as inscrutable. There is by then no shortage of public records; but the records. only deepen our perplexity instead of dispelling it; for prices rose in the late thirteenth century at a period of tranquillity for the country. The king may have been bankrupt; but the civil war was over and done with; and if the Lord Edward's response to Flemish seizures of men and goods in 1270 had any immediate effect upon the wool trade it was surely in the direction of reducing bullion flows to England rather than increasing them. Mint output figures survive from 1234, and mint output in the early 1270s was in fact lower than at any time since extant figures began.[24]

When grain prices rise sharply and permanently and then stabilize at a higher level without displaying any pronounced tendency to rise or fall subsequently, and do this twice, with an interval of a century between each rise, we are irresistibly drawn towards a monetary explanation of what has happened. But the relative inactivity of the mint in the 1270s, when grain prices had just made their thirteenth-century jump, is surely a warning that we must not expect a monetary explanation of these phenomena to be easy to justify.

---

[24] The mint output figures used in this article are taken from J. Craig, *The Mint* (Cambridge, 1953), and Mavis Mate, 'Monetary Policies in England 1272–1307', *British Numismatic Journal*, vol. xli (1972). The figures are rendered graphically in terms of average monthly output over twelve-month periods in N. J. Mayhew, 'Numismatic Evidence and Falling Prices in the Fourteenth Century', *Economic History Review*, 2nd ser., vol. xxvii (1974), p. 11.

One potential source of doubt we can eliminate from the start. For most of the Middle Ages, and for most purposes throughout the Middle Ages, the currency issued by the mint consisted of silver pennies. These pennies scarcely varied at all, in the thirteenth century, either in fineness or in issued weight. They were made of silver mixed with copper in ratios which were generally within a few points of 925 parts of silver to 75 of copper; and the weight of metal used, measured in terms of the number of coins cut from a mint pound, varied only from 240 to 245. If we are looking for a monetary explanation of the price history of this period we shall not find one in mint manipulation of the fineness or weight of the coins issued.

Once they had started to circulate, however, these coins soon began to deteriorate in quality and diminish in number. All of them lost weight in use because silver is a soft metal which soon rubs away; some were clipped; others were sliced into halves and quarters to provide small change; and others again simply disappeared into hoards, or were lost or exported. Anything that reduced the number of coins circulating ought to have raised the value of those that survived, with the effect of depressing prices. And anything that caused a growing disparity between the face value and the silver content of the surviving coins, if it had any effect whatsoever on relative values, ought presumably to have had the effect of diminishing coin value and hence of raising prices.

The mint could only keep the currency supplied and thus maintain the king's monopoly of the right to coin all the money circulating in the country if it could attract enough silver with which to do so. The mint was kept fairly busy at all times because there were always people who had to have their bullion turned into coin however unfavourable the terms they were offered, just as there are always people today who are forced by personal or business needs to sell assets which, if the profitability of their investments were their sole consideration, they would certainly not sell at that particular moment. But the terms upon which the mint accepted old coins did nothing to encourage the population to have its poor coin restored to mint condition. For the mint, in buying coins for renewal, was interested in buying silver, not in acquiring currency. Consequently the mint weighed rather than counted the coins it was offered, and charged a fee for its services which defrayed its costs and left a residue which provided a welcome seignorage for the king.[25]

The terms upon which coins were renewed in thirteenth-century England in fact severely discouraged everyone from offering deteriorating or damaged coins to the mint. Recoinage without the incentive of debasement was the rule; and since coins did not, as a general rule, lose purchasing power as their

25 C. Johnson, ed., *Dialogus de Scaccario* (1950), p. 36 *et seq*. See also, C. Johnson, ed., *The De Moneta of Nicholas Oresme* (1956), p. 54. Salisbury Municipal Records, Ledger A, fols 82–82d (1421), recites a royal writ which states that the subsidy shall be paid in gold half-nobles and nobles worth 5s 8d by due weight of the noble; that anyone who pays with coins worth more will have the excess returned to him; and that coins worth less will not be accepted.

silver content rubbed away as a result of constant handling, it follows that those who surrendered poor coin to the mint surrendered purchasing power with their poor coin and thus paid dear for their bright new pennies. And the poorer their coin the greater the forfeit they paid, so that those who held coins whose condition gave rise to expressions of the gravest public concern were least likely of all to have submitted them for renewal without offering the most strenuous resistance to the king's charge.

Had coins lost purchasing power as they lost silver, so that many poor coins bought neither more nor less than the smaller number of new coins by which the mint was prepared to replace them, then currency standards would have been much easier to enforce. To some extent, indeed, they would have been self-regulating. As the currency deteriorated so prices would have had to rise in terms of nominal coin values in order to reflect the changes in real values that had taken place. This rise in prices would have made monetized silver more valuable than before in terms of bullion or ornamental silver because coins in mint condition command a premium in markets in which coin values vary with silver content. As more silver was monetized so prices would have fallen because coins of mint condition were restoring higher real values to the unchanged nominal values in which the currency was expressed. But thirteenth-century grain prices did not rise and fall as we might reasonably expect them to have done if the periodic deterioration of the currency had caused widespread changes in the purchasing power of coins.

Where thirteenth-century English kings wielded the stick in their efforts to force silver into their mints, elsewhere in Europe monetary authorities proferred a carrot. Recoinage campaigns abroad were sweetened by doses of debasement.[26] Indeed in many countries monetary authorities had got precociously addicted to the use of various forms of debasement as a way of attracting silver to their mints long before English kings had resorted to any but the mildest interference with accepted standards of fineness and weight; and had plunged ever more deeply into addiction at a period when English kings, who had come late to the true practice of debasement, were indulging an acquired taste for it, sparingly and at decent intervals. Debasement had the effect of raising prices by increasing the volume of currency. It forced everyone with better coins than the debased ones to exchange their better ones for a larger number of poorer ones. Anyone who failed to do that soon enough found himself paying out more silver than necessary for any particu-

[26] Debasement does not necessarily mean reducing the silver content without changing the face value. It can equally mean raising the face value without altering the silver content. But medieval English kings never resorted to this particular device. Sometimes the seignorage was reduced in an attempt to attract more silver to the mint. But this could hardly make enough difference to be worth doing. A lowering of the rate by, say, 3d in the pound, meant that, on an investment of £100, a currency speculator saved 25s. But this was, roughly speaking, the clear profit he could usually make out of an £8 investment in a sack of wool. If he were in any doubt, he could always risk less by going into wool.

lar purchase; and anyone quick enough to spend his debased coins before prices rose found himself satisfactorily in pocket as a result of debasement.

But debasement and the inevitable inflation that followed did not play havoc with established patterns of trade between countries. There was no question of goods and services from countries whose price levels were comparatively low, because their currencies had not been debased, sweeping the board in countries whose debasements had caused an inflation of costs and prices. The active arbitrament of silver in exchanges between currencies meant that medieval debasements had few of the international repercussions that we associate with modern devaluations. Such devaluations, which alter otherwise fixed parities so as to cheapen a particular domestic currency in foreign exchange markets, invariably stimulate exports, at least in the short run, and discourage imports, by enabling exporters to translate their prices, upon favourable terms, into the prices they will actually obtain in markets abroad, and by making things correspondingly harder for importers, who find that they can translate their prices into those of the devaluing country only by doing so at rates of exchange which render their goods less saleable than before.

Such feats of monetary prestidigitation were utterly beyond the powers of thirteenth-century monetary authorities, because monetary exchanges between medieval countries consisted of exchanges of silver embodied in coins of diverse provenance and a variety of denominations whose value was determined fundamentally by the quantity and quality of the silver they contained. Foreign coins were, everywhere, weighed and even assayed, not counted; and exchange rates expressed the appropriate silver parities suitably discounted for transaction costs.[27] If the mechanism of international exchange had worked without friction, the effects of debasement and inflation would have been stopped at the frontier, or at any rate at the Channel. When silver's relative scarcity has not changed, a pound's weight of silver of a given fineness will undoubtedly buy more coins in one country than in another if the monetary authorities of the former country have taken it into their heads to raise revenue by debauching the currency whilst the monetary authorities of the latter have not; but a pound's weight of silver ought not to be able to buy more goods and services than before in either country. The purchasing power of coins may have been altered as a result of debasement, but not the purchasing power of silver. Exchanges may have had to fluctuate in the Middle Ages as the silver content of coins was changed; but prices expressed in terms of silver ought surely to have stayed the same.

In practice debasement took time to work its way through the system. The lag between debasement and inflation that enabled ordinary members of a community in which the currency was being debased to make a profit out of debasement, before prices rose, by being quick off the mark in having their heavier coins exchanged for the new lighter ones, also enabled international

[27] On these costs, see J. D. Gould, The Great Debasement (Oxford, 1970), chapter 5.

operators to do the same. Exchange rates responded at once to debasement. Domestic prices, by failing to do so, gave exporters a margin between these lower prices and the prices that would have prevailed if the volume of domestic currency had increased to the point at which it monetized, on debased terms, the entire stock of silver that the currency had previously employed, given an unchanged velocity of circulation. This margin made exports cheaper; and by the same token made imports dearer. When we turn to English grain prices, neither their long-term stability in the thirteenth century nor their sudden changes of level, is easily explicable in monetary terms. The paradox of medieval debasement is that a country which was inflating as a result of debasement could actually improve its terms of trade with countries which had not resorted to debasement. England, which did not debase its currency in the thirteenth century, was bound to have found that international terms of trade, if they moved at all, had to get worse as other countries made their markets harder to enter and their own products more saleable abroad. Balance of payments problems, in such circumstances, had to manifest themselves in bullion movements. A modern disequilibrium under a system of fixed exchange rates produces a foreign exchange crisis: a dollar shortage or the like. A medieval disequilibrium did not, because there could not be an excess supply of any currency upon the foreign exchange markets when mints everywhere stood ready to turn silver in any shape or form into coin of the realm, whichever realm it happened to be, and indeed welcomed the chance to do so for the sake of the fees they earned.

Nevertheless the evidence of grain prices does not suggest a persistent loss of silver gradually eroding the foundations of the currency and deflating the economy. Indeed if we were to judge silver supplies by the behaviour of grain prices we should be compelled to conclude that England had received a sudden bounty of silver in the late twelfth century and again in the late thirteenth century as a result of which prices had jumped to higher levels which were then maintained for long periods during which flows of silver into the country were balanced by flows out of it. Grain prices suggest, in fact, that debasement did not confer much benefit upon debasing countries which traded with England in the thirteenth century.

V

But grain prices, significant though they may be for a general analysis of most aspects of many medieval economies, may not tell us what we want to know. After all, the advantage that a debasing country could derive from changes in its terms of trade depended not so much upon how long it took debasement to inflate domestic prices in general as it did upon the responsiveness of the particular domestic prices whose sluggishness made the terms of trade more favourable. Such prices might respond to changes in the terms of trade very much more rapidly than the general level of prices did; and this was particularly likely if changes in the terms of trade brought a rush of foreign business to producers who, for one reason or another, could not readily increase output. Moreover the advantages of debasement in the special case of trade with England might very well have been nullified for debasing countries as a result of an entirely different factor: the inflexible demand for English wool. If the volume of English wool sold in the markets of debasing countries were no more dependent upon price in the thirteenth century than it proved to be in the fourteenth,[28] then exports from England would have been able to match exports from such countries, with the result that there would have had to be no movement of bullion from England to pay for imports which could no longer be requited in any other way.

The strength and indeed the independence of the English economy derived mainly from such forces as these. And yet English kings get the credit for having accomplished far more in the field of monetary management than they could possibly have achieved. It is fortunate, in this connection, that one of the most famous attempts to manage the currency occurs in this period, so that we can turn Dr Farmer's grain prices to account in gauging its efficacy. It was carried out by one of the most celebrated of English kings. As a test of the power of the kings of England in monetary affairs it would be hard to find a more significant case-study than that of Edward I's recoinage campaign of 1279. Coercion not debasement was the spur; and no king used coercion as an instrument of monetary policy with more resolution than did Edward I.

Mint figures show that recoinage began in London in April 1279, and in Canterbury in January 1280. Recoinage was then taken up at many provincial mints, some of which had been opened for the purpose, in the course of the year 1280. The provincial mints were then shut down in the early summer of 1281, so that although we have got no accounts for their output, they are not likely to have had time to make a substantial contribution to the total output of new coin. Recoinage continued at London and Canterbury. By September 1281 these two mints had turned out over £420,000-worth of new coin. But this was by no means the end of the matter. It is perfectly obvious from the figures that the London mint continued to turn out unusually large quantities of coin from native bullion until August 1286, and from imported bullion until April 1290. Canterbury meanwhile coined more imported silver between September 1281 and July 1290 than it had coined from silver whatever its provenance between January 1280 and September 1281.

If we take it, therefore, that Edward I's recoinage began in London in April 1279 and ended at Canterbury in July 1290, then we shall find that London and Canterbury, between them, issued about £400,000-worth of coin manufactured from native bullion and about £470,000-worth of coin manufactured from imported bullion. We must make certain reservations about these figures. They exclude the work of the provincial mints. They include the

28 A. R. Bridbury, Medieval English Clothmaking (1982), pp. 89–90.

normal work of the mints that proceeded year by year in periods of recoinage as in periods when the king left the mints to do what work came their way. And they tell us of coin issues, not of coin circulation.

It is impossible to do justice to the contribution of the provincial mints or to calculate how much of the foreign bullion minted in England went straight back whence it came to provide mercantile communities abroad with the kind of monetary stability that Maria Theresa dollars provided them with later.[29] But we can perhaps make some attempt to estimate how much difference Edward's recoinage made by deducting from the gross figures of mint output an allowance for the reconditioning process that went on normally, as bullion was exchanged for coin and old coin was exchanged for new, in periods when a comprehensive recoinage was not the order of the day.

How much we should deduct from the gross figures it is not easy to say. The mint records, which begin in 1234, include an earlier period of recoinage in their run. This recoinage began in 1247 and came to an end in 1250. If we ignore it, the mint figures seem to tell of an output between 1234 and 1270 which averages out at something like £30,000-worth of coin per year. If we may assume that Edward's recoinage went on for about a decade, this means that we ought to deduct somewhere in the region of £300,000 from the gross output of nearly £900,000 in order to get anywhere near an estimate of how much difference Edward made to the currency. When we probe farther by asking how much difference it made to the currency to be renewed, for the period of a decade, at a rate which, even when we have made reasonable allowance for coinage export, must have been at least twice the normal rate and, on occasion, may have been three times the normal rate, we ask the most difficult question of all, because no one can say how much coin circulated, as a general rule, at times when there was neither an exceptional influx of silver from abroad nor an abnormal outflow, such as there was whenever English kings succumbed to the temptation of assuming the rôle of pay-master to a succession of European allies.

But we need not know how much of the currency Edward recoined in order to be able to measure the success of his efforts. We can instead trace the impact of his reforms on grain prices. And grain prices do nothing to commend to us the enthusiastic approbation that Edward I's monetary policies generally receive. For the early years of recoinage, particularly the years 1280–83, when we might have expected cereal prices to fall as a result of Edward's efforts, were in fact marked by a sharp rise in grain prices. Such a

---

[29] If English coins circulated abroad, this stands Gresham's Law on its head, and does so because bad coin only drives out good when the bad coin buys as much as the good, so that the good can be melted down with advantage in order to provide more coins of equal purchasing power. When good coins continue to circulate they do so because they buy more than other coins do. If English coins were held in such esteem abroad it was clearly in the interests of currency speculators to bring silver to the English mints and then smuggle abroad the coins that they issued.

rise in prices occurred whenever harvests were deficient. Consequently if we looked neither back nor forward we might reasonably conclude that the rise that took place in these years reflected great credit upon Edward's campaign to renew the currency because it kept within bounds what might otherwise have been a sensational surge of prices. But when we look back we find that grains have been fluctuating in cycles of high and low prices, similar in amplitude and level, since 1268 or 1269. And when we look forward we find these cycles of highs and lows continuing without diminution.

When grain prices do indeed plunge, as they do in 1287 and 1288, they fall even farther than they fell in 1267. Had it lasted, this fall would have been hailed as a triumphant vindication of Edward's currency reform, despite the fact that a response in 1287 to a strenuous programme of reform which began in 1279 was surely unaccountably belated. In the event, however, the fall proved to be a mere aberration. Cereal prices quickly returned to the loftier regions whence they had strayed. And in a longer perspective we can see that the prices of 1267, and of the scatter of years immediately before 1267 for which grain prices survive, were memorable because prices as low as these recurred thereafter only when something wholly exceptional drove prices down below their normal range for a year or so.

This fact is, in itself, a curious reflection upon Edward's reforms: for in 1267 we are within a decade of the complaints that apparently convinced Edward that he had to act in order to remedy an accumulation of defects in the currency. Numismatic historians who insist that Edward acted in good faith tell us that these defects were the culmination of many years of wear and tear of the currency, of abuse of the currency, and of adulteration of the currency as a result of the importation of foreign coins as well as of the circulation of counterfeit native coins. Are we to conclude, as a result of our knowing how low grain prices were in the 1260s, that these defects were, in fact, of very recent accumulation and revealed themselves in the sudden rise in grain prices that began at the very end of the decade?

Is it likely that so much deterioration had taken place so quickly? Sharp rises in grain prices had been known before, one of them at least, in 1255 and 1256, a mere five or six years after the last recoinage had ended, sharper than any recorded in extant documents until 1295. But these rises had always been followed by equally sharp falls. What made the rise from 1267 to 1271 so remarkable was that it broke with usage in this respect and established much higher prices as normal. Consequently if Edward had been disposed to listen sympathetically to those who argued for currency reform, we need not assume that he did so for the somewhat discreditable reason that he badly needed an excuse to replenish his coffers from a source which had proved to be disappointingly unproductive for many years.

In the event, however, as we can plainly see from the subsequent course of grain prices, filling his coffers was about the only tangible result that Edward achieved with his currency reform. Nor was this reform the only major monetary upheaval to produce little or no effect upon grain prices at this period. Between 1294 and 1298 Dr Prestwich estimates that Edward shipped about £350,000-worth of coins abroad.[30] Between 1300 and 1302 over £262,000-worth of coins were minted in order to replace the foreign pollards and crockards which had circulated so freely hitherto. And between September 1303 and the end of Edward's reign the London and Canterbury mints were inundated with foreign silver: they coined over £361,000-worth.

These were, to all appearances, huge transfers of coin. But the only noticeable feature of grain prices during the period of Edward's export of coin to pay for his Flemish and Gascon expeditions was the soaring peak of 1295, followed by the plunging fall so characteristic of grains after dear years, and succeeded by recovery, in 1297, to levels normal for the late thirteenth century. Can it be that we perceive no evidence of deflation in these figures because, denuded of its native coin, England was being invaded at this period by floods of counterfeit and foreign coin? The crisis caused by the widespread currency of pollards and crockards undoubtedly overlapped with the period of coin export. But if pollards and crockards had reversed what might otherwise have been a deflationary trend, how are we to account for the fact that between 1297 and 1303 wheat prices fell in every year, and that other grains fell almost in unison?

Edward did not move against the pollards and crockards until Christmas 1299, and did not demonetize them until Easter 1300. These were years of good harvests, as we shall see. It is not impossible that good harvests, comparable with those of 1287 and 1288, offset the pernicious effects of these alien coins, so that prices which ought to have risen against a corrupt currency fell instead as a result of a series of bumper crops, and then fell still more because it took time before the mint could replace the demonetized coin with its own issues. But if we are not very careful we shall find ourselves invoking harvest abnormalities in order to explain every failure by a monetary factor to exert the influence we had attributed to it. The influx of foreign silver with which Edward's reign ended, provides a case in point. As it began, prices rose. As it continued, prices fell. Then, in 1306, prices started a rise which continued until 1309 and took wheat to a higher peak than any yet recorded in extant accounts, except for 1256 and 1295. The peak was then followed by a plunging fall such as we have so often seen in grain prices, and a recovery whose subsequent course was interrupted by the phenomenal experiences of 1315.

VI

How are we to interpret this sequence of prices? Can we really blame the harvest for rising prices whenever monetary policy decreed that prices should fall, or whenever monetary factors ought to have depressed them? And can

[30] M. Prestwich, 'Edward I's Monetary Policies and their Consequences', *Economic History Review*, 2nd ser., vol. xxii (1969), p. 411.

we really attribute falling grain prices to bumper harvests whenever every-thing we know about the contemporary monetary scene leads us to expect such prices to have risen?

The evidence of crop yields that Dr Farmer has recently published discour-ages any such interpretation of the evidence.[31] Dr Farmer's yields, however, do not tell a plain story. For one thing they are drawn exclusively from Winchester and Westminster material, not from the wider selection of ma-terial upon which Dr Farmer based his price and wage series. The exigencies of the material available make it somewhat harder to match harvest success with price changes than it might seem to be. For another, crop yields, in Dr Farmer's series, do not seem to move together as grain prices do. To take the most important crops, wheat and barley, there were between 1271 and 1346 many occasions when wheat crops were good, according to Dr Farmer's index, and barley crops bad. In 1278 and 1279, when wheat yielded very nearly the best crops Dr Farmer has ever found, barley returned miserable results: in 1279 worse results than in 1316, at the height of the famines. In 1293 when wheat plunged, barley soared. In 1296 the roles were reversed. After the famines correlations were, on the whole, better though there were glaring exceptions such as in 1340 when wheat rose and barley dipped.

Obviously it is not easy to interpret the fluctuations of grain prices in terms of Dr Farmer s index of harvest success. According to that index wheat was clearly the more reliable of the two most important crops. Thus between 1271 and 1346, out of seventy-six years there were thirty-four bad or at any rate disappointing wheat crops and forty-two bad or disappointing barley crops. The rest more or less lived up to expectation or exceeded it. Had good and bad crops been equally good or bad, and had they been evenly dis-tributed throughout the period, the task of interpreting Dr Farmer's find-ings in terms of currency factors would have been made much easier. But good or bad crops tended to cluster together in runs. Again wheat had a more even record than barley.

Thus barley crops were generally bad or more or less inadequate before 1308 and better thereafter. Between 1271 and 1307 there were twenty-seven poor crops out of thirty-eight: between 1308 and 1346 only fifteen poor crops out of thirty-nine. So far as wheat is concerned there were runs of bad crops between 1281 and 1295; and runs of good or very good ones between 1296 and 1314, that is to say right up to the eve of the famines. In these nineteen years before the famines there were only five bad crops, whereas in the previous fifteen years there had been only two good ones. After the famines, in the years between 1325 and 1346, when farming had perhaps got over the immediate effects of those disastrous years, there were only six bad wheat crops out of twenty-two.

Not only was wheat's crop record more reliable than barley's, but wheat crops were, on the whole, better than barley crops. When barley crops were

[31] See note 14 above.

bad they were worse than bad wheat crops except when wheat was really bad, as it was in 1315, 1316, 1321 and 1339. When they were good they were seldom as good as good wheat crops, with rare exceptions such as 1323, 1325, 1333 and 1338. Wheat was obviously a better crop as well as a more valuable one than barley. It was, not unreasonably, much favoured by medieval farmers. Consequently it is likely to have responded more sensitively to the impact of currency factors upon prices than barley did.

When we turn back to the currency history of Edward I's reign, we can now see that Edward's recoinage of 1279 coincided with a run of bad harvests. These bad harvests, however, cannot account for the astonishingly contrary response of wheat prices to Edward's monetary reforms. The bad harvests of 1281 to 1286, with the exception of the harvest of 1283, were no worse than those of the 1270s. But wheat prices rose as sharply and very nearly as far, as a result of bad harvests during the recoinage years, as they had done before. No doubt we should make some allowance, in interpreting these figures, for the fact that Dr Farmer's price material derives from a wider range of sources than his crop yields do. Nevertheless this is not how prices should have responded to what looks like a fairly normal run of poor harvests at a time when the volume of currency circulating ought to have been seriously diminished as a result of the terms upon which Edward I had authorized his recoinage. We cannot expect a recoinage to eliminate fluctuations caused by real factors; but we have every right to expect a successful recoinage to lower the levels at which prices fluctuate and perhaps to diminish the amplitude of such fluctuations. Evidently the grain prices of these years had not been damped down as they should have been if the recoinage had had the success so often claimed for it.

If these price fluctuations suggest that Edward's recoinage was not a conspicuous success, there is another factor, with no connection with monetary policy, which reinforces their testimony. And that is the harvest record of the years immediately preceding the recoinage. The wheat harvests of 1275 and 1278 were not merely successful: they exceeded by an enormous margin the yields achieved by every other successful harvest in Dr Farmer's series. This was in fact a period of good harvests; for between 1275 and 1280 only the harvest of 1276 was disappointing; and the third-best harvest of the period, that of 1279, would have held the yield record but for the unparalleled achievements of 1275 and 1278. These harvests certainly brought prices down. But when we consider how good three of them were, what is most surprising is how little effect upon prices these harvests had.

In an economy as stretched as England's was, in the later decades of the thirteenth century, exceptionally abundant harvests ought to have produced a very much sharper response than the harvests of those years actually did, if only because there were, comparatively speaking, so few buyers with enough cash to be able to clear such copious stocks of wheat without a bigger adjustment of prices than we find. Wheat prices fell farther in 1287, 1296 and 1303, when harvests, though good, were nothing like as good as the best ones had been between 1275 and 1280. When prices fail to adjust to changes in supply as they should we are bound to suspect that those who can afford to do so are storing rather than selling their surpluses. If that is what these wheat prices mean, then presumably the stocks accumulated during the good years were released subsequently when harvests failed and better prices prevailed. What then are we to think of the high wheat prices that we find on the morrow of Edward's 1279 currency reform? Are we not entitled to conclude that Edward achieved very little with his recoinage because wheat prices rose far more in those years of reform than they should have done when we recollect that the bad harvests of those years were likely to have been offset to some extent by sales of stocks of grain held in reserve as a result of the exceptionally abundant harvests of the years immediately preceding them?

These disparities between what we expect and what we find are not confined to the years following upon the inauguration of a period of currency reform in 1279. As we have seen, they occur later. Currency history with its theme of comprehensive cleansing and renewal is evidently irreconcilable with the results of price history. Nor do these results offer any comfort to those who attempt to show that mint issues and coin movements between England and the Continent regularly and as a matter of course exercised either an important independent influence or a powerful contributory influence upon thirteenth-century price levels. Whether we search early or late in the thirteenth century, we can correlate grain-price fluctuations with monetary changes only by straining the credulity of those we are trying to persuade and by conveniently ignoring similar fluctuations which occurred at other times and in quite different monetary conditions.

If, however, the king's issue of coins and the king's transfer abroad of subventions of coin in pursuit of his foreign ambitions had no readily perceptible effect upon grain prices, then we must surely conclude that however impressive the king's monetary activities may look they were, nevertheless, upon too small a scale to impress themselves upon the money supply. And if the volume of money in circulation were so great that it was beyond the king's powers of control, then we must expect to find that there was a great deal more foreign money or unauthorized English money in the form of counterfeit or token money circulating than we had thought possible; and we must also expect to find that the stock of money accumulated in the economic system as a result of previous mint issues was very much larger than we have been given to understand that it could have been.[32]

We know that foreign coins circulated freely in England, and we know that these coins were popular because the king was forever exercised by the need to eradicate them from the system. We also know that token and

---

[32] Tallies were universally employed for the registration of debt. They were therefore available as a form of currency, and doubtless passed from hand to hand suitably discounted. Debts, however, were usually repaid; so that tallies which swelled the money supply during their span of life then diminished it on being retired at redemption.

counterfeit coins circulated; and we know what the king did to counterfeiters when he caught them. But we cannot take his word for it that these intrusions into his money supply were as pernicious as he said they were, because we know what vital interests of prestige and profit impelled him to take measures to rid his mint of the competition of rivals. Ordinary currency users did not share the king's repugnance because they did not share his interests and evidently trusted a whole range of unauthorized coins well enough to be content to pass such coins from hand to hand whenever they could do so with impunity. How they did so we do not know. Obviously people got used to handling many different sorts and conditions of coin. We come across so little comment upon the quality or provenance of the coin in which debts were paid or obligations discharged that we are surely justified in assuming that, for most purposes, coins circulated at face value unless they were outstandingly fine or obviously inadequate. Presumably in making payments, particularly tax payments, you paid with the worst coins that would pass muster; and in saving you picked out the best you could find. Cautious creditors did sometimes specify the quality of the coin in which they required payment to be made; and the Exchequer had its own ways of compensating itself for the deficiencies of the poor coin it was offered. Coins certainly deteriorated in use; but if there were many more of them in circulation than we had suspected they presumably deteriorated more slowly than we have been told they did.[33] Moreover the worst ones were probably demoted, so that effectively they were turned into the small change for which there was always such insistent demand and which the mint was always reluctant to supply because small change was so expensive to produce.

But if the spectacular intervention of the king in monetary affairs, whether as the guardian of the purity of the coinage or as the paymaster of Europe, shipping abroad thousands upon thousands of the coins whose integrity he had so scrupulously preserved, cannot explain the lesser fluctuations of thirteenth-century grain prices, how can we hope to explain in political terms the far more profound changes that took place in the late twelfth and again in the late thirteenth century as a result of which prices jumped to new levels which they then maintained for decades together?

We are surely entitled, in such circumstances, to look for an explanation of this recurrent phenomenon in terms of changes affecting the entire region which depended upon the import of silver for the maintenance of its stocks. For none of the countries of western Europe possessed indigenous resources of silver. Consequently each of them depended upon a favourable balance of trade in order to attract silver to itself. But a favourable balance of trade is not something that all countries can enjoy at the same time; and measures taken by any one of them with the object of putting the rest at a disadvantage could always be met by retaliatory measures taken by those which were

[33] C. C. Patterson, 'Silver Stocks and Losses in Ancient and Medieval Times', *Economic History Review*, 2nd ser., vol. xxv (1972).

losing silver with the object of reversing the flow. In normal circumstances, therefore, the countries of western Europe found themselves by turns gaining currency and then losing it. These were, however, strictly temporary gains and losses; and the English evidence strongly suggests that even when international flows of silver were as big as political authorities could make them, they were never big enough to make serious inroads upon domestic currency supply. It is of course true to say that western Europe as a whole somehow maintained a favourable trade balance with the mining communities that supplied it with its silver. But to say that does not help to explain why the terms upon which silver was supplied suddenly changed for England in the twelfth and thirteenth centuries, and changed so decisively that we may confidently assume that they changed for all the other countries of western Europe which lay within the same silver-deficient region.

These, however, are not problems which can be pursued here. So far as English estate management was concerned, sudden changes in the level about which grain prices fluctuated made for trouble rather than for easy profits. Generally speaking, as we have seen, the market for grains, particularly for wheat, was extraordinarily volatile in the thirteenth century without ever compensating the farmer with a rising trend. In this far from auspicious environment it was much harder for estate management to increase the profits of farming by investing in the land than by reducing the remuneration of labour, and where possible increasing the usage of labour or employing more suitable or more skilled labour than hitherto; for the labour market was the only important market that may have improved in the course of the thirteenth century from the point of view of the demesne farmer. Population pressure which, to judge by grain prices, was no longer capable of raising the effective demand for arable products, may not yet have reached the point at which it was no longer capable of lowering the real wages of labour. At any rate that is what the evidence of peasant hardship seems to tell us.

In such circumstances, with high profits being constantly offset by low ones, the inflation of prices that occurred twice in this period, by reducing the real burden of the fixed charges paid by tenants, threatened to turn real profits into paper profits. Demesne farmers could only restore real incomes by revising every charge and obligation within reach, with the result that money incomes rose on many big estates by the end of the thirteenth century. Painter's sample of 272 baronial estates whose manorial revenues rose prodigiously between Domesday and 1250 and significantly but not spectacularly thereafter, whatever its shortcomings, does seem to reflect the greater severity of the earlier inflation as we see it in the grain prices and the comparative mildness of the later one.[34] It also, perhaps, reflects the sense of urgency with which demesne farmers responded to inflation; for these higher incomes are not the evidence of farming prosperity, or the vindication of

[34] S. Painter, *Studies in the History of the English Feudal Barony* (Johns Hopkins, 1943), p. 160. But see above, pp. 111–32.

improved management techniques, that they are often taken to be. Essentially they reflected the efforts made by demesne farmers to compensate themselves for the losses they had incurred when inflation miraculously and fleetingly improved the terms upon which whole sections of the peasantry could hold their land.

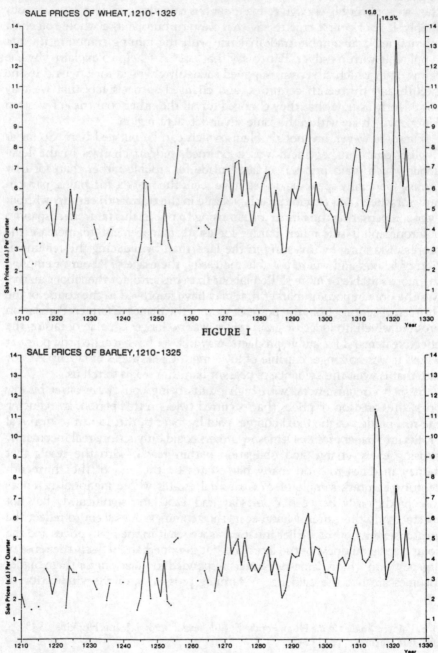

FIGURE I

FIGURE 2

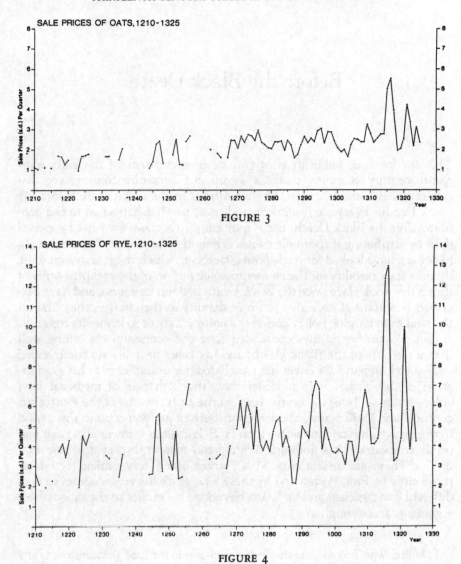

FIGURE 3

FIGURE 4

Before the Black Death

I

The simultaneous publication of two fresh assessments of the early four-teenth-century economy marks a significant departure from recent dis-cussions of the problems raised by conditions in the countryside before the Black Death.[1] Everyone has his own ideas as to what happened to the eco-nomy after the Black Death. But any attempt to account for what happened then by attributing it to simple causes is bound to be suspect. Consequently, historians have looked for predisposing factors to which they can assign some share of responsibility for the momentous subversion of the accepted order of things that took place once the Black Death had run its course, and have per-ceived symptoms of excessive strain or debility in the changes they find on the land or in farming policy during the half-century or so before its coming.

Prof. Postan has always contended that the economy was failing well before the days of the Black Death; and his views have always commanded widespread support.[2] Dr Baker has concluded, for example, from his examin-ation of the *Nonarum Inquisitiones* that 'the high tide of medieval land colonisation . . . [was] . . . on the turn' in the early decades of the fourteenth century;[3] and Dr Kershaw, who has contributed a pastoral crisis in this period to the saga of crop failures with which H. S. Lucas has made us all so familiar, firmly corroborates his findings.[4] Widespread support, however, is not una-nimity. There are dissentients. Miss Harvey, using very similar records to those cited by Prof. Postan and by those who share his views, comes to very different conclusions;[5] and Dr Watts has added his proffer to the range of her arguments and examples.[6]

[1] E. Miller, 'War, Taxation and the English Economy in the Late Thirteenth and Early Fourteenth Centuries', in J. M. Winter, ed., *War and Economic Development* (Cam-bridge, 1975); J. R. Maddicott, 'The English Peasantry and the Demands of the Crown, 1294–1341', *Past and Present*, Supplement no. 1 (1975).
[2] M. M. Postan, *Essays on Medieval Agriculture and General Problems of the Medieval Economy* (Cambridge, 1973), pp. 14, 201ff.
[3] A. R. H. Baker, 'Evidence in the Nonarum Inquisitiones of Contracting Arable Lands', *Economic History Review*, 2nd ser., vol. xix (1966), p. 518.
[4] I. Kershaw, 'The Great Famine and Agrarian Crisis in England, 1315–22', *Past and Present*, vol. lix (1973).
[5] B. Harvey, 'The Population Trend in England between 1300 and 1348', *Transactions of the Royal Historical Society*, 5th ser., vol. xvi (1966).
[6] D. G. Watts, 'A Model for the Early Fourteenth Century', *Economic History Review*, 2nd ser., vol. xx (1967).

To a controversy conducted in these terms there can be no foreseeable end. Given the haphazard inheritance of records upon which historical inquiry depends, a plausible case can always be made out to support the contention that colonization went on in the early fourteenth century, and to strengthen the claim that land went out of cultivation because no tenant could be found to take it up.[7] The latest attempts to deal with the problem of the early fourteenth century, therefore, have very sensibly shifted the angle of attack upon it. Prof. Miller's article lightly sketches the outlines of an argument which Dr Maddicott investigates in much greater depth. Indeed, Dr Maddicott has added immeasurably to our understanding by taking us into the countryside, with the aid of the kind of records that Prof. Fryde once recommended for this purpose,[8] and showing us what the grand designs of great kings meant to the peasants whose goods were taxed, purveyed, and fraudulently converted, and to those who managed to turn other men's troubles to their own advantage.

Though they differ substantially in approach from other writers on the subject, they differ very little from one another. Using roughly the same range of records, they arrive at very similar conclusions. They take the view that the quarrel between England and France imposed so great a strain upon the economy, at a period which was in any case one of exceptional stress for the mass of the population, that it could not have failed to cause irreparable damage to the fabric of society. 'If the population was checked during this period,' says Dr Maddicott, 'and if the area under cultivation shrank, it was not solely because a countryside full of land-starved smallholders had become especially vulnerable to the impact of poor harvests and grain short-ages, but rather because dearth, seigneurial exploitation and the King's taxes all worked together to place the peasant's resources in a new and more precarious position.' 'Turning points and watersheds are part of the his-torian's stock-in-trade,' he adds, 'but it may be that in the history of rural England such terms are used less justly of the famine of 1315–17 than of the wars with France and Scotland which had begun twenty years before.'[9] Prof. Miller echoes Dr Maddicott's words. 'The precise part played by government financial measures in generating economic change,' he comments, cannot be accurately measured; but it may well be that those measures were as signifi-cant in the economic field as they were in instigating those constitutional developments which made the reigns of the first three Edwards a watershed in English history.'[10]

Does this mean that we have now got, particularly as a result of Dr Maddicott's very learned work, an interpretation of early fourteenth-century economic movements which is not only plausible and coherent but also one

[7] Kershaw, loc. cit., 43–4.

[8] E. B. Fryde, 'Parliament and the French War, 1336–40', in E. B. Fryde and E. Miller, eds, Historical Studies of the English Parliament (Cambridge, 1970), p. 250, n. 44.

[9] Maddicott, loc. cit., 75.

[10] Miller, loc. cit., p. 27.

which is unlikely to be compromised by the disclosures that will follow the next set of estate records or Exchequer returns to be examined? Did government policy, acting upon population pressure, drive the early fourteenth-century peasant to the brink of catastrophe, as it was once contended that the terms of emancipation coupled with the orthodox financial policy of the Russian government drove the masses of the Russian peasantry to the brink of catastrophe before the terrible famine of 1891–2?[11]

Whether it did so or not this interpretation of the course of events lays claim to our serious attention for two reasons. It links the political ambitions that provoked successive financial and constitutional crises in this period and culminated in resounding victories on the field of battle, with the more obscure movements of the economic system that so frequently ignored the reigns of kings and the machinations of politicians. And it has the signal merit of forcing us to think seriously about the repercussions of war, particularly its repercussions upon those who bore its burdens at home in England. Hitherto these repercussions have been given as little serious attention by historians of social and economic affairs as the cognate problem of what the church actually meant to the ordinary medieval villager has been given by historians of ecclesiastical institutions. Dr Hewitt's pioneering study of the impact of the early decades of the Hundred Years War upon those who actually fought in the war or endured its consequences makes him the Coulton of war studies in this sense.[12] Dr Maddicott and Prof. Miller are to be congratulated upon following where he led.

Anyone who tells us, however, that the poor and the politically weak suffered more than those who were neither poor nor weak, when kings decided to settle their differences by war, can hardly expect to arouse a storm of controversy by doing so. What he can tell us about the tribulations of the vulnerable classes is bound, therefore, to add more to our knowledge than to our understanding. But Prof. Miller and Dr Maddicott handle their twin themes with sufficient skill to make them inseparable. The period of conflict and manoeuvre that began in 1294 with the formal confiscation of Gascony by Philip the Fair, and ended in 1360 with the signing of the preliminaries of peace at Brétigny, has for many years claimed a share of the attention of historians which is disproportionate to its length but not to its importance in constitutional, military, and financial history. Are we now justified in seeing it as no less important in its consequences for the economy?

Unfortunately, a multitude of difficulties stands in the way of our doing so. Perhaps the most intractable of these is posed by the problem of determining the cost of waging the wars of the later Middle Ages. When historians speak of the costs of medieval war they generally have monetary costs in mind. These costs were unquestionably much heavier in the later Middle Ages

---

[11] Apparently, as with its medieval parallel, there is more than one view of this famine: R. G. Robbins, *Famine in Russia, 1891–2* (New York, 1975).

[12] H. J. Hewitt, *The Organisation of War under Edward III* (Manchester, 1966).

than they had been in earlier times. One important reason for this was the greater power of certain weapons. The mounted knight, who was little more than a light cavalryman at the time of the Conquest, had been transformed into the medieval equivalent of a tank by the beginning of the Hundred Years War. And the castle which had so often been no more than a stock-aded and perhaps moated pile of earth in the eleventh century had become, by then, a thing of intricate and massive strength.

But costs had risen not solely because warfare had become more sophisti-cated. They had risen also because the price level had risen, apparently, with devastating rapidity between the late twelfth and mid-thirteenth centuries.[13] This period of price history is still so obscure that it is difficult to assign an exact meaning to what is said about it. But if prices had indeed risen as they are said to have done, then any comparison of military cost incurred early and late in the thirteenth century must make large allowances for monetary changes, before we can be sure that more was bought by Edward I with the money he spent than Henry II or even John could have obtained by spend-ing less. When everything costs more than it did we have to do some complicated sums before we can be quite sure that war has become more expensive than it was.

The problem of value for money raises the allied question of paid and unpaid service. Norman feudalism has always had the reputation of having provided the king with an army which served in order to discharge obliga-tions for land rather than because it was paid to do so. In fact, one of the lessons of Norman feudalism is that services, once territorialized, were very soon diminished, if not lost. This meant that the king was presently obliged, perhaps even eager, to pay for military services instead of taking what he was offered, or standing on his rights. Consequently the 'whole history of the development of Anglo-Norman administration,' in the words of one of its most acute students, 'is intelligible only in terms of the scale and the pressing needs of war finance: the expenditure on the wages of troops, the construc-tion and repair of castles, the pensions to allies, the bribes which eased the course of campaigns and diplomacy, and the upkeep of the bureaucracy itself.'[14] Paid service, however, did not altogether supersede unpaid until Edward III's time. Powicke's impression was that 'in broad terms Henry III's armies until 1257 were based upon the feudal levy.'[15] And even when the infantry was mainly a paid force, as it was later, under Edward I, the most recent opinion is that the cavalry on all the major campaigns was provided mainly by 'magnates who refused to accept pay for themselves or their men'.[16]

13 P. D. A. Harvey, 'The English Inflation of 1180–1220', Past and Present, vol. lxi (1973).
14 J. O. Prestwich, 'War and Finance in the Anglo-Norman State', Transactions of the Royal Historical Society, 5th ser., vol. iv (1954), p. 36.
15 F. M. Powicke, The Thirteenth Century (Oxford, 1953), p. 554.
16 M. Prestwich, War, Politics and Finance under Edward I (1972), p. 91.

This substitution of paid for unpaid services has had the unfortunate incidental result of fortifying the belief that war was becoming more expensive in the later Middle Ages. The belief may well be justified. But the monetization of military services that occurred when the king bought the services he required, instead of depending upon his tenants to fulfil their military obligations whenever he reasonably required them to do so, does not itself prove that war was becoming more expensive to wage. The financial evidence of taxes paid and money spent cannot be handled safely, therefore, without making reservations about its use which may be fatal to its value.

There is no denying, however, that very much more was spent on war after 1294 than for many years past. Wars are not evenly distributed throughout the centuries. They come in clusters. The series that began in 1294 brought to an end one of the most protracted periods of military inaction yet known in English history. It was by no means an unbroken period of peace. But it was in such striking contrast with what followed that we are liable to forget that it was also very different from what went before. This does not mean that when Edward I gratified his more mettlesome aristocratic subjects by restoring the profession of arms to its glamorous rôle in society, he henceforth devoted to unproductive uses resources which had been better employed hitherto. It is difficult to give our phrases a meaning which would convey anything to the men of the Middle Ages, or to say which of other possible uses of resources they might have preferred. But money which was not spent on waging war never found what we should call a more productive outlet in times of peace. All the evidence we possess goes to show that the landed classes invariably squandered every penny of income they received, and as much more as they could persuade or cajole others to lend them. Frugality and solvency, care for the land and thought for the morrow were no more characteristic of ecclesiastical landowners than of lay ones. Everywhere we look we find the fruits of the earth being consumed by swelling staffs of retainers and servants, by lawyers and builders, and by all who were lucky enough to be permitted to eat, drink, and amuse themselves at the expense of the landowners and their creditors.

War did not change all that. Indeed in the households of the military classes it would be surprising to find that war did much more than quicken the pace of life during periods of active campaigning. Even when war did change routines of life and patterns of expenditure it made much less of an impact upon the economy than it appears to have made upon historians. That was so not simply because monetary costs had risen without necessarily reflecting increased real costs. It was so mainly because the economy itself had got so much bigger since war was last a principal preoccupation of foreign affairs. Accordingly, we cannot hope to make sense of the costs of waging war in the reigns of Edward I and Edward III without first taking the precaution of setting those costs against the vastly increased capacity of the economy to sustain them.

II

The size of the fourteenth-century economy is not something that we can easily visualize. When McFarlane tells us that 'armies of more than 10,000 were very rarely put into the field';[17] when we learn that battles were occasionally fought in which over twice that number of men took part;[18] what are we to make of such numbers? An army of 10,000 men had more grown and active men in it than there were males of all ages in some of the very biggest English provincial towns at the time. Behind the soldiers stood those who organized and supplied them. After the campaigns were over there was garrison duty to be done. What sort of burden did all this impose? A few statistics may put the problem in perspective. By the end of the thirteenth century the economy supported a population of over 17,000 men and women living under rule in religious houses, and possibly twice that number of ordained priests in the parishes.[19] Very few of these priests, whether regular or secular, were not socially superior to the average infantryman. Fewer still were too poor to employ servants. Some employed many. And these servants no more formed a uniformly depressed class than ordinary infantrymen did. They numbered many thousands. So did those who administered the assessment and collection of taxes on movables in Edward I's reign. It has been calculated that in Lincolnshire alone nearly 4,000 men were required to assist the chief commissioners when Parliament authorized a levy.[20] Taxation was a notoriously sensitive and laborious preoccupation of local government. But how many men were called upon in the country as a whole for these and other less demanding administrative duties, when so many were required in a single county to cope with one Parliamentary levy?

These are impressive numbers. They seem to tell of a countryside crowded with farms. And that is, in fact, what the statistics of wool exports also suggest. In this period between 30,000 and 40,000 sacks of wool were exported in an average year. Each sack contained 364 lb of wool. The average fleece yielded between 1 lb and 1½ lb of wool. Consequently, every sack contained the wool of some 243 sheep.[21] It may be, as Eileen Power remarked, that when thinking about wool production 'it is the large land-

---

17 K. B. McFarlane, 'War, the Economy and Social Change', *Past and Present*, vol. xxii (1962), p. 4.
18 Prestwich, *War, Politics and Finance*, ch. iv, *passim*.
19 D. Knowles and R. N. Hadcock, *Medieval Religious Houses*, 2nd edn (1971), p. 494; J. R. H. Moorman, *Church Life in England in the Thirteenth Century* (Cambridge, 1945), pp. 52–3.
20 W. S. Thomson, ed., *A Lincolnshire Assize Roll for 1298* (Lincolnshire Record Society, vol. xxxvi, 1944), p. xlv. Some were poor men, or at any rate procured exemption as if they were: p. xlvi.
21 E. M. Carus-Wilson and O. Coleman, *England's Export Trade, 1275–1547* (Oxford, 1963), p. 13 and tables. See also S. F. Hockey, *Quarr Abbey* (Leicester, 1970), p. 57.

owners who particularly attract one's attention.'[22] But at such low rates of productivity what sort of contribution to the export trade could such producers have made? The Priory of St Swithun's, Winchester, kept 20,000 sheep in its early fourteenth-century flocks.[23] We know of no estates with more sheep at that period. Even under Henry of Eastry's management Canterbury Cathedral Priory kept fewer than 14,000.[24] With such numbers, however, these immensely wealthy institutions could have contributed no more than 77 and 54 sacks respectively to the total exported.

Even if we allow for the firmly held belief, common amongst historians, that the big farmers were more productive than the small, these figures nevertheless show that it would have taken the entire clip of roughly 400 estates the size of St Swithun's, or perhaps 550 the size of Canterbury Cathedral Priory, to supply the demands of the export trade. In fact very few estates were anything like as big as that. We must conclude, therefore, that when Eileen Power said she had 'a suspicion that even in the heyday of demesne farming peasant sheep flocks exceeded those of demesne,' she expressed herself with altogether excessive caution.[25] If we assume, for example, that the average sheep-farmer kept a flock of 260 sheep, at a period when, according to Prof. Postan's investigation of village livestock in a sheep-farming region, a man was wealthy who had half that number,[26] and that the big landowners supplied one-third of the volume of wool exported, which is unlikely even on the most favourable view of their productivity, then we are at once in a world in which no less than 20,000 very substantial and affluent sheepfarmers, each with his 260 sheep, devoted themselves exclusively to the export market.

How many farmers actually looked to the export market for wool sales we shall never know. Nor shall we ever know how many supplied the home market. But if it is no less fanciful to postulate an economy in which 20,000 sheep-farmers each had 260 sheep, than it is to envisage one in which there were over 500 estates of the size of Canterbury Cathedral Priory, does this not point to the likelihood that the number of those who kept sheep to supply the export market alone could easily have run into hundreds of thousands?

A further indication of the size of the early fourteenth-century economy, and of its aggregate wealth, is perhaps furnished by the evidence of the resources devoted to the building and rebuilding of the national stock of towns, cathedrals, parish churches, fortifications, religious houses, and private homes of all types. As the economy grew so did its stock of buildings; and as the stock increased, the volume, though not necessarily the proportion, of resources devoted to its renovation and renewal had to be

---

[22] E. Power, *The Wool Trade* (Oxford, 1941), p. 24.
[23] *Ibid.*, p. 34.
[24] R. A. L. Smith, *Canterbury Cathedral Priory* (Cambridge, 1943), p. 153.
[25] Power, *op. cit.*, p. 29.
[26] Postan, *op. cit.*, p. 243.

increased also. At some period an inheritance of mainly wooden structures was turned into a bequest whose larger buildings were chiefly made of stone. This was a colossal and unparalleled achievement. It was plainly not the work of any one period, however defined, even though we cannot look back with the aid of surviving evidence and watch the architectural landscape slowly transforming over the centuries. Would it be carrying speculation beyond the bounds of credibility to suggest, however, that this tremendous revolution was carried farther forward during the thirteenth and early fourteenth centuries, when the aggregate economic strength of the country was at its medieval peak, than it had been perhaps in all the previous centuries put together?

III

It was upon an economy as various and opulent as this that the martial Edwards imposed the burden of their wars. What sort of wars were they that their burden could have weighed as heavily in real terms, as we are asked to believe they did, upon an economy so massively expanded? We can tell more or less how much money was spent on war because so much of the financial history of the period has been thoroughly investigated. And we can be all too easily tempted to believe that war costs rose more rapidly than the resources of the economy could possibly have increased, simply because we can calculate the costs but, in the absence of anything remotely comparable with modern facilities for the estimation of gross national product, not the rate of expansion of the economy. Ignorance on this score might have tempted us to exaggerate that rate of expansion but for the storms of outraged propriety that lashed any medieval king whose spending on war exceeded what the political classes were willing to tolerate. These storms are exceedingly well documented. They are profoundly impressive. But do they really mean that royal spending on war sometimes exceeded the capacity of the economy to sustain it? With this question in mind we cannot turn to the financial historians for help because, with eyes only for deficits and surpluses, they see nothing but grave financial problems and the expedients whereby successive kings endeavoured to mitigate their consequences. And yet it would be utterly wrong to take the view that the economy was embarrassed financially simply because the king was, or to assume, without much better corroborative evidence than that of the passionate outbursts of the Commons, that the economy was necessarily stretched to the limit because those who were asked to sanction the king's policies by paying his bills made so much fuss about doing so, particularly when they took exception to what he was doing or how he was doing it. The king was not organized financially for waging war. He had means enough for an extravagant life-style. But even a small war was more than he could manage without getting himself into financial trouble. Consequently the crisis of finance and politics that ensued when the king ran out of money and credit was not necessarily a crisis for anyone else but the king.

Naturally the bigger the king's debts the graver, on the whole, the subsequent crisis. And some of the debts look formidable enough. Yet it is difficult to believe that they were as disastrous for the country as they were so loudly proclaimed to be, if only because the wars that caused them were not the devastating experiences, at least for the English, that they were sometimes made out to be. They were got up to be portentously splendid melodramas, impeccably stylized and masterfully stage-managed. But they were, in fact, little better than caricature: petty gang-warfare flamboyantly decked out and caparisoned, but for the most part, mere swagger and bluster, clamour and rodomontade. Campaigns were few and brief. Armies were small, so small indeed that the biggest of them, such as those investigated recently by Dr Prestwich, did little more than provide an outing for the unemployed.[27] Weapons were simple, so simple that the damage they were able to do so was strictly confined to the neighbourhood in which they did it. In a world in which most people depended for absolute necessities upon what they and their neighbours could produce, this meant that it was exceedingly difficult to inflict losses which had really serious repercussions beyond the district within which they occurred.

Strategy and tactics were rudimentary. Professional knowledge and discipline, in such matters,were erratic. To the knightly classes war offered scope not so much for the exercise of leadership skills as for characteristic displays of military prowess in the shape of bouts of single combat rendered infinitely more exhilarating in wartime by the prospect of ransom. Consequently, a resolute crowd of virtually untrained peasants or townsmen could, at times, defeat formidable armies, not only when it caught one at a disadvantage but also when it had to deal with one in the pride of its power. A wealthy and highly organized kingdom like England was, at times, quite incapable of coping with its small and threadbare neighbours. Time and again the Welsh and the Scots matched the forces and surpassed the military thinking of the English. The English king often enough spent to the limit to contain or avenge attacks from Wales or Scotland. But he could rarely sustain his riposte because he never had the means at his disposal with which to do so, even when he was not diverted from his purpose by other enemies or other problems.

Does this not suggest, despite appearances, that the military efforts made by the English were never, or at any rate not often, very great? Does it not suggest, in fact, that war had a very different significance for medieval English society from the one that we are tempted to attribute to it? Does it not look as if the political community of the realm, which furnished the means and was never averse to sharing the thrills or the spoils of war, took a favourable view of war, not only because it enjoyed war but also because it

27 Prestwich, *War, Politics and Finance*, pp. 94–5.

never allowed war, for any length of time, to cost more than it could easily afford, or to absorb energies which it preferred to devote to other interests? And do we, perhaps, invest the martial efforts of those who took part in war with greater economic significance than they deserve, because we fail to grasp the fact that the fuss made when things went wrong was utterly disproportionate to the damage done or the costs incurred?

IV

This was undoubtedly a period of unprecedented strain for the mass of the peasantry. The expansion of the economy, to which so much historical evidence testifies, had been accompanied by the progressive impoverishment of increasing numbers of ordinary people. Did their impoverishment render the community less capable than before, despite its expansion, of providing for armies which were in some respects better equipped, and for campaigns which were sometimes more arduous than they had been? Was the community incapable, despite its expansion, of providing for the material requirements of medieval warfare without calling upon its poorer members to make a proportionate contribution to the costs of war, or even perhaps a contribution which was more burdensome in proportion to their means than it may have been in earlier times?

Every effort was certainly made to impose upon them as many of the burdens as could be effectually transferred. The great value of Dr Maddicott's work is to show in detail how that was done. And the effect upon individual families, even perhaps upon whole villages, was often disastrous. But when war consists of intermittent raids, armies are small and weapons simple, can this really mean, in the context of early fourteenth-century England, the transfer of burdens which, whatever they might do to the individual, could overtax the aggregate resources of the economy and subvert its structure? It is the gravamen of the case made out by Prof. Miller and Dr Maddicott that it can, because the peasantry was at, or even beyond, the limits of endurance before the demands of war imposed their additional strains.

Indeed when Prof. Miller writes of 'a retreat of demesne' which 'was not balanced by a comparable advance of peasant economic activity',[28] he exactly expresses the views of very many historians who see the decades before the Black Death as a period when the countryside began to wear a derelict air because population loss had taken the vitality out of rents, and there were beginning to be more farms to let than farmers to occupy them. Everything apparently conspires to confirm their views – the sensational famines that carried off, no doubt, many thousands of the poorest in the land; the epidemic diseases that decimated flocks and herds; and the signs that Prof. Postan and others have interpreted to mean that nature was at last

[28] Miller, loc. cit., p. 25.

exacting retribution for the improvident exploitation of the soil by medieval man.

But the statistical evidence, such as it is, does not offer the least support for the belief, more often implicit in the arguments of those who take this somewhat cheerless view of the early fourteenth-century prospects for de-mesne farming than expressed in their writings, that rents were lower at that time than they had been formerly, and that cereal prices were less satisfactory than those that farmers had grown accustomed to expect.[29]

The fourteenth century, until it was three-quarters over, was not, so far as those who have worked with the evidence can tell, a century of low rents and unsatisfactory prices for the principal grains. On the contrary, until the 1370s, the fourteenth century was remarkable for the persistence of what were, by thirteenth-century standards, unusually high cereal prices. The price level, which had been buoyant enough until 1309, rose decisively thereafter and remained high until 1333. Then it dropped, and stayed low until 1351. But that fall was not prophetic of things to come. A depressed market for cereals was certainly one of the characteristic features of the later Middle Ages. But this was not when the market started to be depressed. By 1351 cereal prices had recovered, and for twenty years or more the evidence shows that they ruled at a level which was higher than ever before. In a longer perspective this means that the boom in cereal prices that began sometime in the late twelfth century lasted, despite fluctuations and inter-ruptions, until the late fourteenth century. More than a century was to pass before farmers were to see its like again.

There is nothing incompatible, in the evidence of prices, with the conten-tion that land was actually going out of cultivation, in the early fourteenth century, because it had been so grievously misused. The effect of soil exhaus-tion upon land prices, in the absence of countervailing factors, is not to depress but to raise them. Withdrawing land from cultivation, or getting less from the land as fertility diminishes, makes what is left more valuable, not less so. It is, so to speak, a negative assart. It may be a symptom of bad farming, and its economic consequences may be bad for everyone who is obliged subsequently to pay rents which reflect the rising value of the land he farms. But it is not bad for those who receive such rents and, if Prof. Postan is right about soil exhaustion, helps perhaps to account for some of those excellent results that so many large estates returned during the three decades of high prices with which the fourteenth century began.

Rent, however, was not the only substantial charge that ordinary farmers were obliged to set against gross receipts. There were many others. Of these labour was often one. In the later Middle Ages it was to be the decisive one. Did rising labour costs make farming risky even when prices were as high as they were in the early fourteenth century? According to Prof. Miller and Dr Maddicott labour bore the brunt of the consequences of famine and war.

[29] For references see A. R. Bridbury, 'The Black Death', below pp. 200–17.

Were these consequences reflected in wage rates which rose more quickly than prices, and thus made it impossible for farmers to pay their wage bills as easily as they had done hitherto?

V

Much work still needs to be done before we can be satisfied that the wage-rate material now being used by historians gives an altogether reliable indication of the movements that actually took place. But, so far as we can tell, wage rates merely conformed to movements of prices during the first three decades of the century, as they did later, immediately after the Black Death. What can this mean if not that the early fourteenth-century population surplus was big enough to enable landlords to dispose of all the vacancies that occurred, and to do so without having to offer anyone an exceptional inducement to take them up? Whatever war and famine may have done, if we may credit what the statistics of wages and prices suggest, they did not make life difficult for landlords. If one or two estates foundered, if a farm here or a village there was reputedly distressed or abandoned, we cannot invest such phenomena with the significance of a portent without having first disposed of the statistical evidence altogether.

Then in 1333 prices fell. Are we to assume that demographic forces had begun to exert their influence at last? If so, then wage rates should have continued to rise, as they did in the 1370s. But they did not. This had nothing to do with the war. Edward III's war and the preparations for it had not started when prices fell in 1333. And when the war did start it utterly failed to raise either prices or wages, though if Edward's war is to rank as the formative influence upon the economy that Prof. Miller and Dr Maddicott want it to be, then we are surely entitled to expect it to have made for shortages.

If the population had been depleted as a result of the succession of adversities to which it was exposed in these decades, then wage rates should have risen as prices fell, as they did later, so as to reflect the relative scarcity of labour. Those who received higher rates than before for the work they did might not have been allowed to keep the money and perquisites they earned. If Edward III's wars had told upon the economy as we are asked to believe they did, then taxation of one sort or another might very well have left the peasantry as destitute as it had been when its remuneration was smaller. But taxation, whatever form it took, could not have prevented a relative scarcity of labour from being reflected in its price.

Before the phase of low prices ended the Black Death arrived. Did the Black Death ravage a depleted population? If it did, then how are we to explain the readiness with which vacancies were, nevertheless, filled as soon as they had been created by the dying, not simply for a year or so after 1348, but in many places, for more than a generation after that? Did it ravage a population which had recovered from its supposed losses despite the fact that the wars from which it is said to have suffered in every sense had been at their most demanding only a few years before the Black Death paid its first visit? If we assume that the population had recovered by then, we can explain more reasonably than it would otherwise be possible to do why the Black Death took so long to work its way through the surplus population to the core. But if we make so damaging an assumption where are we to look for the losses that recovery has so miraculously made good? Have we not been pursuing a chimera which should be dismissed from our minds henceforth?

If we must replenish the countryside of fourteenth-century England in the decades before the Black Death because any attempt to deplete it seriously runs into difficulties to which it is not easy to find an answer, then we are at once back in a world, familiar enough in the thirteenth century, in which nothing but misfortune or wanton and invincible mismanagement could stand between the bigger landowners and a prosperity which was uninterrupted for five decades of the century out of the first seven.[30]

In these fortunate decades, the bigger landowners found that prices were high enough to offset any possible encroachment by rising wages upon profits. If they faltered then, they had only themselves to blame.[31] If they leased out their land they were not surrendering in the face of impossible market conditions: they were merely pursuing some purpose of their own that we have not managed to penetrate. Prof. Miller and Dr Maddicott have both argued that landowners had an incentive to lease their land before 1334 which was not simply a private one, because they avoided liability to movables taxes by having no movable farm property to tax.[32] But leasing out did not exempt landowners from paying movables taxes. We know they paid on the rents they received in kind because particular attention was paid to the

[30] Dr Kershaw's murrain losses were presumably soon made good. Dr Farmer's livestock prices continue until 1325 and do not seem to reflect any exceptional shortages by then: D. L. Farmer, 'Some Livestock Price Movements in Thirteenth-Century England', *Economic History Review*, 2nd ser., vol. xxii (1969). And Dr Kershaw has himself noted that the tripling of Bolton Priory's sheep flock in the fourteen years between 1296/7 and 1310/11 was 'mainly brought about by reproduction within the flock': *Bolton Priory, 1286–1325* (Oxford, 1973), pp. 80–1. Once the infection had gone, many wasted flocks and herds were, no doubt, replaced in the same way later.

[31] Dr Mavis Mate has recently contended that early fourteenth-century estate-owners did much less well than we might think they did when prices were high because they lost when they bought farm produce what they gained when they sold farm produce. She cites Canterbury Cathedral Priory as an example of costs rising with prices: M. Mate, 'High Prices in Early Fourteenth-Century England', *Economic History Review*, 2nd ser., vol. xxviii (1975), pp. 15–16. But did estate-owners spend on farm produce anything like as much as they earned by selling farm produce? If they did then they must always have been hardpressed: for the argument is equally cogent at all price levels. Obviously they did not. Moreover Dr Mate's example of Canterbury Cathedral Priory's costs rising does not help her argument because Canterbury's monastic population more than doubled between the beginning and the end of the period of which she writes: Smith, *op. cit.*, p. 3.

[32] Miller, *loc. cit.*, pp. 15–16; Maddicott, *loc. cit.*, p. 7.

possibility of double-counting in 1307, when it was stated that villeins were not to be charged on such goods since they formed part of the property for which their lords were liable. And we know they paid on treasure, which presumably meant money hoards, since treasure, unlike jewels and vessels of gold, silver, and brass, was never explicitly exempted from taxation, as they were, except in 1294 and 1295.[33]

Nor was there any reason why landlords, in the early fourteenth century, should have been obliged to incur the trouble and expense of finding tenants for their estates and of foregoing whatever benefits they thought that managing their estates for themselves might otherwise have brought them, simply in order to avoid a tax to which their own representatives in Parliament had given their consent. At that period landlords were very substantially insulated from the real burden of parliamentary taxation by their immense economic power. Prof. Miller and Dr Maddicott both testify to the reality of that power. They contend that the poor invariably paid more than they should have done because the rich bought and bullied their way out of making an appropriate contribution to the king's demands. They claim that goods and money taken in the king's name never reached the king. And they take very seriously contemporary allegations that whole sections of the population were stripped of their means of livelihood by ruthless assessors and collectors.[34]

In arguing this aspect of their case Prof. Miller and Dr Maddicott are surely justified in coming to some very depressing conclusions as to the

---

[33] J. F. Willard, *Parliamentary Taxes on Personal Property* (Cambridge, Mass., 1934), pp. 77–8. Prof. Miller (*ut supra*) has done some interesting work to show that one or two extremely influential landlords, who paid little enough in any case, nevertheless managed to pay less on manors which yielded rent rather than produce, than they paid on manors which yielded produce rather than rent. Even if these cases are not merely anomalous, and on this score Prof. Miller appears to have some misgivings, it is difficult to see how less-exalted landlords could have been confident of avoiding tax by leasing out their demesnes when the law was perfectly clear as to their liability. Recent work on this problem shows that we cannot hope to solve it by appealing to the records. Only a tiny fraction of the local rolls, containing detailed inventories upon which the assessments were made, has survived. The rural rolls frequently make no reference to money. But they sometimes do; and sometimes they conceal what we should like to know in phrases such as '*in omnibus*' or '*aliis bonis*'. Urban rolls are also rare. They show that citizens were assessed on money as well as goods. If this meagre evidence shows anything, does it not show that landlords took a greater risk and presumably put themselves to greater trouble by leasing in order to avoid tax than they incurred by bribing in order to evade tax? On all this see the admirable survey by J. F. Hadwin, 'Evidence on the Possession of "Treasure" from the Lay Subsidy Rolls', in N. J. Mayhew, ed., *Edwardian Monetary Affairs, 1279–1344*, British Archaeological Reports, no. 36 (1977).

[34] Miller, *loc. cit.*, pp. 18–19; Maddicott, *loc. cit.*, *passim*. Dr Maddicott states that 'when it came to bribing royal officials, villeins could hardly compete with their social superiors' (p. 20). This was undoubtedly so; but what strikes one as very curious in the extremely interesting evidence Dr Maddicott has put together is how little was apparently required, at least on some occasions, in order to buy the complaisance of those who were willing to take bribes (e.g. p. 19).

vulnerability of ordinary villagers, at a period when population pressure was intense, and landlords were as prosperous as they appear to have been in the early decades of the fourteenth century. The ordinary villager did not have to be liable for payment of taxes before he felt their weight. He knew very well that rents and taxes were linked. Prof. Hilton has recently drawn our attention to a complaint made in 1437 by tenants of the earl of Warwick who declared that they could not pay their rents because the king's subsidies were levied on them so often.[35] Such were the exigencies of estate management in 1437 that the earl's steward was presumably forced to bestow the most sympathetic attention upon such representations by the tenantry. But in the early fourteenth century any deputation of tenants which pleaded the importunities of the royal tax-commissioners as an excuse for its failure to pay rent would have got short shrift indeed. And any landlord of that period who felt that his own liability to taxation had been harshly assessed could then, if ever, have had rents raised or tallages imposed with impunity so as to compensate himself for the mischance that brought a stubborn or unappeasable assessor to his door.

If he had reason to fear that the purveyor might follow in the tax-collector's footsteps, the ordinary villager's plight, at times, was indeed parlous. Prof. Miller and Dr Maddicott have, perhaps, made more of the evidence that he lost to the purveyor much of the little he had, than they are entitled to do, if they are not to provoke their readers into asking how the king could possibly have made do with what he got from villagers who, as they have been at pains to show, possessed little that was even worth the bother of taking. Moreover, the fuss made by members of the landed classes when purveyances were being made was undoubtedly greater than it would have been if they had merely been protesting on behalf of others. Purveyance was so intensely abhorrent to members of parliament, indeed, that there were times when their protests, constantly and bitterly reiterated, recurring in every session, probably held up the business they had been summoned to transact, and made it difficult for those who managed the Commons to control proceedings.[36] But their loudly trumpeted denunciation of royal measures taken to provide for what were, in effect, very modest forces, must not be allowed to prevent our seeing what was done, in some sort of reasonable proportion, whether they provided some part of the means for such forces or not.

Dr Prestwich has itemized some of the quantities required from the counties when prises were called for as a result of Edward I's campaign needs.[37] From a much later record, the Black Book of the Household of Edward IV, we have estimates of the cost of running smaller households than that of the king, drawn up so as to give him some idea of what it might cost him to run a

35 R. H. Hilton, *The English Peasantry in the Later Middle Ages* (Oxford, 1975), p. 67.
36 *Rotuli Parliamentorum*, *passim*.
37 Prestwich, *War, Politics and Finance*, ch. v, *passim*.

more modest establishment in the interests of economy.[38] They show how lavish was normal expenditure on food and drink in the households of dukes, earls, barons, knights, and the like, and hence how rapidly the purveyances of Edward I's later campaigns could have been consumed by relatively modest forces on the march – with correspondingly modest effects, presumably, on aggregate supplies of food and drink for the community at large. The household estimates are not strictly speaking comparable with the prises, because the estimates budget for a year and the prises for very much shorter periods. But they are suggestive notwithstanding because the estimates reckon on ordinary household demand, and the prises were ordered for armies which were sometimes huge by the standards of the time, as they were in 1296 and 1297.

The purveyances made, and levies imposed, by those who took what the king required and sent it where it was meant to go, were supplemented by the depredations of those who merely helped themselves to whatever they could get. Presumably such depredations were always at the expense of those who could be impoverished or even expropriated with impunity because their fate was of no consequence politically. Prof. Miller and Dr Maddicott are inclined to speak of what was extorted in this way as if it vanished into space once it had been stolen. But wealth was not destroyed once it had been misappropriated. What was not consumed had to be circulated. As a medium of exchange animals, raw materials, and foodstuffs answer tolerably well. As a store of value they are subject to disconcertingly rapid rates of depreciation. Is it not likely, therefore, that a good deal of what was wrongfully taken from the farms found its way back into farming or went to market, as it might have done in other circumstances anyway, and that misappropriated taxes were spent? Naturally all this was not accomplished without dislocation and loss. The taxes that never reached the king were not necessarily spent where they had been levied, and the stolen farm equipment and farm produce were not necessarily sold where they had been seized. Nor were those who had been dispossessed much comforted when they found themselves obliged to buy back what they had lost, even when they were able to do so. But the urgent need to dispose of what could not be used or consumed, and the universal predisposition to spend rather than save, did mean, surely, that the extortion to which the records bear such eloquent witness was less likely to have impaired the community's aggregate capacity to grow food and wage war than to have increased social mobility here and there, shifted the balance of political advantage in certain places, and sometimes, perhaps, altered the way in which the burden of taxation fell upon the various groups at risk.

Moreover it should not be forgotten that purveyance and taxation took money and goods from villages which may very well have had some of the pressure on local food supplies relieved by the commissioners of array. In a world in which so many were superfluous, in the sense that nothing worth

38 A. R. Myers, ed., The Household of Edward IV (Manchester, 1959), pp. 89f.

reckoning was added to the work of farm or workshop if they no longer took any part in the doing of it, many villages may very well have met the commissioners of array with pleasure rather than foreboding. No doubt key men sometimes went. But the art of tricking or beguiling the commissioners into taking men whom everyone was delighted to spare did not originate with the suborning of the egregious Mr Justice Shallow. And once they had gone, the villages that the commissioners had relieved were doubtless in a better state to endure whatever the purveyors, and even, perhaps, the tax-assessors, had in store for them than they would have been otherwise. If the armies thus raised then went where the king's enemies could be laid under contribution for food, shelter, and all the comforts of military life, the relief experienced by the villages from which the commissioners had recruited their tally of conscripts was shared in some degree by all the villages that were subject to royal taxation and purveyance.

VI

With the coming of deflation in 1333, however, times changed for the big landlords. They encountered unexpected and indeed unprecedented difficulties. With the late fourteenth-century fate of the big estate only half a century away historians have often been tempted to conclude that the difficulties that were eventually to wreck the big estate were already undermining it at this time. When there were difficulties for the big estate before the Black Death, it is indeed generally at this period that they are to be found. And it was at this period that people complained so circumstantially that markets were idle because goods, though abundant, could not be sold.

Much speculation has been excited recently by this extraordinary period. Prof. Fryde, M. Contamine, and Dr Maddicott have all produced evidence to show that both the principal belligerents caused domestic shortages by exporting coin to pay for the war.[39] If coin shortage caused the deflation nothing is more likely than that the war was to blame. Edward III did not scruple to sacrifice anybody or anything to promote the success of the war and keep his allies sweet. He taxed and borrowed as much as he dared for as long as he could. The crisis that culminated in 1341 sobered him somewhat; but the years of intoxicating freedom from accountability were not finally over until 1352, when the last of the English wool syndicates collapsed. And before he was checked Edward had sent vast subventions abroad.

If these subventions had created the shortage of coin that was responsible for deflation, however, we still have to ask how they brought it about. The chronology is not wholly satisfactory because the deflation started before the

---

[39] Fryde, *loc. cit.*, pp. 256–7; Maddicott, *loc. cit.*, pp. 48–9; P. Contamine, 'La Guerre de Cent Ans en France: Une Approche Économique', *Bulletin Institute Historical Research*, vol. xlvii (1974), *passim.*

war did. Nor is it clear as to why the shortage of coin persisted for so long. Those who were caught short by low prices included most of the larger institutions and estates, all of which spent lavishly, in better times, on ornaments of gold and silver. These ornaments in deflationary times were worth, in real terms, much more than they had cost. In such circumstances how many necessitous landowners would, or indeed could, have resisted the temptation to part with their inheritance of precious things, and thus augment the money supply not without profit to themselves?

Nor was this the only, or indeed the principal, way in which fourteenth-century England could have relieved a general deflation caused by shortage of coin. The deflation presumably stimulated foreign demand for English wool at a time when it kept native demand for imports low by reducing the money profits of farming. In normal times such changes in the pattern of foreign trade should have brought coin flooding into the country, raising prices and thus restoring the former equilibrium.[40] But times were anything but normal when the king compounded the problems the war created by plunging disastrously into the wool trade, and when ransom and loot flowed to and fro in movements whose magnitudes we are in no position to assess. Consequently, we have a long way to go before we can confidently blame the war for the deflation of 1333–51.

If, however, the war did in fact cause or accelerate the deflation then it seems that any hardships the economy may have had to endure as a result of the wars of the late thirteenth and early fourteenth centuries were more likely to have been due to monetary disturbances than to the real costs of raising armies, conducting military campaigns, and fighting battles; for the deflation of 1333–51 appears to be all that is left of those possible consequences of the wars of the period to which we can attribute a disruptive or debilitating role.

From the landlord's point of view the chief result of the deflation of 1333–51 appears to have been that landlords lost the initiative that the shortage of land had given them for so many years, despite the fact that land remained as hard to come by as it had ever been. When markets could no longer be cleared at high prices they were cleared at low ones instead. So much is perfectly plain from the price material. Low prices meant that landlords could no longer afford the wage rates they had been paying hitherto. Does this not mean that wage rates followed prices down – no doubt after a painful interval? They could hardly have done otherwise with population pressures causing fierce competition for work; and the wage material certainly suggests they did. Lower wage rates presumably enabled

---

[40] Some of those who worked at the Mint certainly thought, in 1381, that the outflow of currency of which so many then complained was due to an unfavourable balance of payments: A. E. Bland, P. A. Brown, and R. H. Tawney, eds, *English Economic Documents* (1914), pp. 220–3. Coin exports by Edward III would not have caused as much inflation abroad as they caused deflation at home because the Continent was in every sense so much bigger than England at the time.

landlords to endure their afflictions more stoically. But what happened to contractual obligations like rent, which were hardest of all to adjust to sudden changes, but impossible, in circumstances of deflation, to enforce? Did farms and cottages stand empty, with evicted families grouped pathetically outside, exposed to wind and cold, because landlords would not tolerate unpaid rents and creditors unpaid debts?

If landlords and others had, in fact, foreclosed upon defaulters, in such conditions, would it have done them any good? Where could they have turned for better tenants or more reliable recipients of their credits? The problem was a perennial one. When the celebrated Coke estate suffered a similar rash of defaults during the depression that followed the Napoleonic war, the agent was eventually instructed to find new tenants, and asked himself, when he had done so, '. . . will the new tenants (at reduced rents) be enabled to fulfil their contracts, and stand their ground, at the present prices of produce with the same weight of taxation, I give a decided opinion that they will not, indeed it is utterly impossible that they should do.'[41]

No doubt some of those whom war had enriched, either in battle or as a result of campaigns of extortion conducted in more congenial domestic surroundings at the expense of adversaries who could not offer much resistance, were well able to snap up some of the tenancies that others were too short of cash or credit to be in any position to hold on to or compete for. But, for the rest, what could landlords and other creditors have done apart from adapting themselves, however reluctantly and belatedly, to the novel realities with which they had to cope?

They might have resorted to barter. But we have no reason to believe that barter dominated the economic affairs of the big estate-owners in these decades. They might have revised their terms. Some certainly did, only to regret it bitterly, no doubt, when inflation returned in 1351. Most, however, seem to have done nothing, which is the incorrigible response to adversity of everyone who firmly believes that trouble cannot last. This meant, in effect, that the real burden of contractual obligations which could not be discharged was shifted forward in time so that those with resources to spare found themselves taking more and more of their income by instalment. The grip of the creditor classes tightened, but what they held in their grip were mostly promises. Some landlords did indeed decide to give up the cultivation of their demesne lands, in whole or in part. But the choice was not yet a clear one because, in deflationary conditions, an income in kind was more dependable than one that was supposed to be paid in money and, therefore, might very well not be paid at all.

These unusual circumstances may very well have had more unexpected and even disquieting consequences for the landowning classes than those that followed naturally from the reduction of their power to spend. At a period when the tenantry was not even paying all its dues in full except in

---

[41] R. A. C. Parker, *Coke of Norfolk* (Oxford, 1975), p. 150.

promises, or perhaps in kind, it was surely impossible to transfer the real costs of war to the tenantry as it had been possible to transfer them when buoyant prices had rendered the landlords' control of economic affairs unchallengeable. Those who were charged with the responsibility of finding money and provisions and equipment for the king's war no doubt found it harder than ever, during the deflation, to raise what was required without demanding more than it was customary to do from those who had most of everything.

. Does this not mean that deflation gave rise to a paradoxical situation as a result of which the real burden of paying for the war, at a time when war costs were at their greatest, fell with more than usual weight upon members of the political classes? And if it does, have we not here an explanation of why the disastrous opening years of Edward III's continental enterprise provoked such passionate and rancorous opposition? Was Edward looking back to those days when he made tax concessions in 1357 'on account of the various adversities which . . . the middling men of the realm have long undergone'?[42] Prof. Miller and Dr Maddicott believe that we can hear the authentic voice of the poor in the comminatory mutterings enshrined in a set of verses written in 1338 or 1339 when the crisis was approaching its climax.[43] But this work, as Dr Harriss has pointed out, 'is no mere lament or tirade; it is a coherent indictment . . . Both in language and argument it strikingly anticipates the petitions of the Commons in the Parliament of 1340 . . . [and] thus reflects the mood of the lesser landowning classes.'[44]

In short, the wars that began in 1294, remarkable perhaps for terminating a prolonged interlude of military inaction, were not remarkable for rendering difficult conditions intolerable for the overwhelming majority of ordinary men and women by imposing upon them a burden of charges which they simply could not bear. England could take in its stride wars fought as they were fought in the Middle Ages. No doubt costs bit deeper at some moments than at others. And no doubt the poor felt their effects first and most cruelly. But costs were never the burden they seem to have been, and were sometimes met, perforce, by those who most confidently reckoned to evade them. If the wars caused death by starvation and disease to be more prevalent than before they did not alter the structure of society by doing so. There was always, in these years, a seemingly endless succession of people to take the place of those who died. Consequently, political crises did not mirror economic crises. And when it went well war was justified in everybody's eyes.

[42] G. L. Harriss, *King, Parliament and Public Finance in Medieval England* (Oxford, 1975), p. 345.
[43] Miller, *loc. cit.*, p. 26; Maddicott, *loc. cit.*, 65.
[44] Harriss, *op. cit.*, p. 251.

The Black Death

The fourteenth century was a century of violent contrasts. Unparalleled military triumph was followed by humiliating military failure and defeat. Kingship was raised to a culminating point of glory by Edward III who was, for contemporaries, the embodiment of the feudal virtues, only to be disgraced by a successor, his grandson Richard II, who had to be bundled off the stage amid scenes of public scandal and private degradation which moved one modern writer to conclude that 'in the end the case for deposing him looked stronger than the case for deposing his great-grandfather'.[1] And the century witnessed, in the unprecedented famines and epidemics that marked its course, an assault on the social system at its base which was infinitely deadlier than any which it had sustained at its apex by way of military loss or political subversion. Yet the result of this assault was to inaugurate a century of prosperity for the vast majority of the population, the like of which was not to be known again for generations to come.

The new age, which was not without its problems for contemporaries, is not without its problems for us. Everyone knows that the extraordinary reversal of the established order of things which inaugurated this new age was caused by the decline of the population. But no one is quite sure as to when that decline began. It is tempting to look back on the succession of famines and pestilences that marked the course of the fourteenth century, as Mr Saltmarsh once did, and see the recuperative vitality of the population progressively weakened by loss and debility.[2] But the statistics of wages and prices make it very difficult to credit this plausible account of what happened. If the population had declined substantially as a result of either the famines or the early visitations of bubonic plague then land should have lost value as its scarcity diminished. As rents fell, dragging prices after them, wages should have risen. Many years ago when Prof. Postan formulated his revealing analysis of the labour market, he warned those who would use wage statistics as a measure of population decline to beware of the exaggerated response of wage-rates to such decline.[3] He pointed out that falling rents attract wage-earners into tenant-farming with the result that the supply of

---

[1] M. McKisack, *The Fourteenth Century, 1307–1399* (Oxford, 1959), p. 497.
[2] J. Saltmarsh, 'Plague and Economic Decline in England in the Later Middle Ages', *Cambridge Historical Journal*, vol. vii (1941).
[3] M. Postan, 'Some Economic Evidence of Declining Population in the Later Middle Ages', *Economic History Review*, 2nd ser., vol. ii (1950), pp. 243–4; *The Medieval Economy and Society* (1972), p. 106.

wage-earners is depleted more sharply than the supply of labour, with dispro-portionate effects upon the wage-rate. But the statistics of wages and prices do not indicate by the slightest movement that there was any change in the relative scarcities of land and labour until very near the end of the century.

The fourteenth century produced two prolonged periods of inflation separ-ated by a period of severe deflation in the decade or so before the Black Death. The exigencies of war finance make it very likely that these general movements were monetary in origin.[4] But whatever the monetary factors may have done to the general level of wages and prices, the evidence shows unequivocally that they had no effect whatsoever on the relativity of wages and prices.

The widespread prosperity for which the new age is celebrated, since it depended upon land being abundant, and hence cheap, was enjoyed at the expense of the propertied classes whose affluence, when it was unassailable, depended upon land being scarce, and hence dear. Cheap land spelt ruin for demesne farming because demesne farming battened upon cheap labour; and labour was only cheap when land was dear. By the last decade or so of the fourteenth century the bankruptcy of demesne farming is plain for all to see, even if foreclosure had not yet terminated the business life of all demesne farms. And the cheerless end to the century has cast a melancholy retrospec-tive light upon the rest of the century, which is generally depicted in terms of the outcome of the struggles that marked its passage. The belief that the fourteenth century saw the beginnings of a silver famine, for example, must surely owe the vitality of its subterranean existence in the guarded footnotes of many writers on fourteenth-century problems to their immovable convic-tion that the fourteenth century was a century of low prices in which de-mesne farming was unable to pay its way. And even in the most distinguished quarters the conviction that prices for farm produce were only high for short periods and exceptional reasons is profound. Prof. Postan, commenting upon the Winchester wage material compiled by Lord Beveridge, remarked that real wages after the Black Death failed to rise as much as money wages did 'owing to a brief spell of very high agricultural prices on the morrow of the pestilence.'[5]

In fact the fourteenth century, when compared with the century that preceded it and the one that followed it, was a century of high prices. Out of the exiguous evidence at his disposal, Mr Farmer has constructed a series for the principal grains which shows very clearly that early fourteenth-century

---

[4] Thus the deflation occurred when the mint was particularly active and debasement had added to the other influences at work: J. Craig, The Mint (Cambridge, 1953), pp. 63–4 and Appendix I. At this period, moreover, nearly all the mint coining was done with imported metal: H. A. Miskimin, Money, Prices, and Foreign Exchange in Four-teenth-Century France (New Haven, 1963), p. 97. In short, everything made for infla-tion except for the need to export huge quantities of coin in order to defray the costs of war.

[5] Postan, 'Some Economic Evidence', p. 226.

prices were substantially higher, on average, than they had ever been in the period since 1208 when his series begins.[6] Prof. Phelps Brown, basing himself on the researches of Thorold Rogers, and calculating the price of a composite unit of consumables from them, comes to a similar conclusion.[7] His index starts in 1264. From then until 1309 it fluctuates about a level which is low by subsequent standards, and does so in a way which is perfectly consistent with the kind of disturbances normally caused by harvest glut and harvest failure. In 1310 Prof. phelps Brown's index rises sharply to a new plateau upon which the harvest failures of 1315 and 1316 plant spectacular peaks. Thenceforth high prices were the rule rather than the exception until 1334. With the gathering-in of the 1333 harvest the index falls and thereafter fluctuates about the levels of the thirteenth and very early fourteenth centuries, and does so as it did at those earlier periods. This period of low prices ended in 1351. And from 1351 until 1376 prof. Phelps Brown's index suggests that prices were generally higher than they had ever been, even in the previous period of high prices, though the peaks of 1370 and 1371 were lower than those of 1316 and 1317. The first really good harvest in all that long period came in 1377. In 1378 prices came tumbling down as they had not done for nearly thirty years. Thereafter for the rest of the Middle Ages prices remained low or fairly low except for years like 1391, 1401, 1410, 1417, 1430, 1438, 1439, 1440, 1482, 1483, and 1484, when the index shows that Prof. Phelps Brown's bundle of consumables was dear or very dear.

No one can study the careful work done by Mr Lennard, Lord Beveridge, and Mr Farmer on the manorial records from which such figures as these are derived, without becoming intensely suspicious of confident generalizations about economic conditions which depend solely upon the statistics that can be got out of such records. But the movements of prices suggested by the statistics are not without corroboration. The annual value of land, in the form of rent, is bound to reflect the prices obtained for the chief products of land, however imperfectly it may do so in practice. 'The general impression left by the sources,' says Miss Harvey 'is that rents were not moving much at all in the first half of the fourteenth century,' though some 'annual payments for contractual and customary tenancies . . . were still rising down to 1330, and on some estates the rise continued longer.'[8] It was, she adds, a period when the colonization of new land had not altogether lost 'the impetus of its earlier expansion'.[9] On some of the bigger estates, indeed, fluctuations of

[6] D. L. Farmer, 'Some Grain Price Movements in Thirteenth-Century England', *Economic History Review*, 2nd ser., vol. x (1957), p. 218.

[7] All references to Prof. Phelps Brown's work are to the two articles he wrote with Sheila V. Hopkins and published in *Economica* for 1955 and 1956. They are reprinted in E. M. Carus-Wilson, ed., *Essays in Economic History*, vol. II (1962). The year is that of the calendar year following the harvest. Mr Farmer's year is the year in which the harvest was gathered.

[8] B. F. Harvey, 'The Population Trend in England Between 1300 and 1348', *Transactions of the Royal Historical Society*, 5th ser., vol. xvi (1966), p. 39.

[9] Harvey, *loc. cit.*, 41.

prosperity seem to fit the movements of Prof. Phelps Brown's index very closely. The chronology of such fluctuations on any one estate will not necessarily synchronize perfectly with that of others if only because local conditions and individual circumstances varied so much that any particular estate is as likely to be an exception to the rule as an illustration of it. Moreover there is a taint of circularity in using manorial sources to support the contention that the evidence of price fluctuations drawn from other manorial sources is to be trusted. Nevertheless some remarkable exemplars of competent farming organization contrived to hit a bad patch in the third and fourth decades of the fourteenth century, when Prof. Phelps Brown's index falls, after having enjoyed an exceptional burst of prosperity in the earlier decades, when it was high. This is what happened at Ely and Canterbury, and indeed on many other ecclesiastical estates.[10]

With the arrival of bubonic plague, price history enters upon a new period. It was apparently a prolonged period of altogether exceptionally high prices. If Miss Harvey were to pursue her investigation of rents into the second half of the fourteenth century she would presumably find that in this period of sustained high prices, as in the previous one, rents, if they moved at all, again moved upwards. It is certainly difficult to see what else they could have done. Corroborative evidence, however, is hard to come by. The study of manorial history after the Black Death has not attracted anything like the host of scholars that its study in the century or so before the Black Death has done. And because comparatively few have had the courage, or the fool-hardiness, to toil in upland fields when there were easier lands to cultivate, their findings must be treated with correspondingly greater reserve. Yet many of them have remarked upon the rapidity with which demesne farmers recovered from the pestilence and managed to keep going, not perhaps without difficulty, until the third quarter of the century. And Dr Holmes, whose survey of the estates of the higher nobility concludes with a study of the economy of the inheritance, finds that 'income in the 1370s is generally not 10 per cent lower than it had been in the 1340s.'[11] Dr Holmes makes large claims for the implications of this remarkable bouyancy of income which go to the heart of the problem posed by these high prices. 'By main-taining his income at the old level,' says Dr Holmes, the noble landlord 'was seizing a larger proportion of the decreasing product than he had had before . . . and this may still have been the case if the national income had declined less than the population.'[12]

Unfortunately the value of his conclusions is impaired by the limitation of

10 E. Miller, The Abbey and Bishopric of Ely (Cambridge, 1951), pp. 81, 105; R. A. L. Smith, Canterbury Cathedral Priory (Cambridge, 1943), p. 143; D. Knowles, The Relig-ious Orders in England, vol. I (Cambridge, 1950), p. 47.
11 G. A. Holmes, The Estates of the Higher Nobility in Fourteenth-Century England (Cam-bridge, 1957), p. 114. Dr Holmes gives a useful list of the more notable work done by others on pp. 85–6.
12 Holmes, op. cit., p. 115.

his sample. For purposes of detailed investigation of the economy of the estates of the higher nobility, Dr Holmes has used the records of only one estate, and that an estate whose chief landed interests lay to the west of the kingdom rather than in the main centres of population. Some of these interests, indeed, lay in or near regions where scholars are now finding evidence of manorial prosperity at times when manorial farming was moribund elsewhere.[13] But it would be idle to pretend, in the present state of our knowledge of manorial farming in the aftermath of the Black Death, that we can get any farther than Dr Holmes has got in strengthening the case for believing that the money incomes of the larger corporations and the more exalted aristocratic families had not seriously declined as a result of the Black Death and thereby corroborating the price evidence out of which Prof. Phelps Brown has constructed his index.

Dr Holmes has raised a fundamental problem, however, which points the way to the next line of investigation. If it is true that the money incomes of the bigger landlords were not seriously diminished by the Black Death, is it also true that with population in decline these money incomes commanded a greater share of the aggregate resources of the community than they had done hitherto? Is it in fact the case that landlords, after the Black Death, were able to get tenants for their land, and paid work from the retinues of labourers, craftsmen, and professional people of all degrees whom they were in the habit of employing, on terms which were, from their point of view, very much better than before? Surely it is not. Certainly they got tenants on terms which were at least as good as they had been before the Black Death. The exceptionally high prices that prevailed for so long after the Black Death were bound to have kept rents up; and the astonishing rate at which things got back to normal on most of the estates which have been investigated indicates pressure from those who wanted tenancies rather than from those who wanted tenants. But in other respects the outlook was not perhaps quite so auspicious for the landlords. If manorial income were more or less what it had been, prices were not. Consequently, if Dr Holmes is right in thinking that manorial income did not change very much as a result of the Black Death, then he must surely be wrong in supposing that it bought more than it had done before the Black Death. For income had not kept pace with prices. The items that enter into Prof. Phelps Brown's index are limited to things that sustained life at a very low level, and manorial lords are not likely to have confined their spending to these. High corn prices, however, suggest that the prices of other farm products were high rather than low at this period. Moreover, many of the things that manorial households required in order to support their comfort and maintain their dignity incorporated a good deal of labour in their preparation or manufacture. And contemporaries

---

[13] J. Hatcher, *Rural Economy and Society in the Duchy of Cornwall* (Cambridge, 1970). Mr K. Brown of the Northamptonshire Record Office who is preparing a London M.Phil. on the Luttrell estates has found a similar buoyancy in Somerset.

were in no doubt as to what was happening to the pay that labourers, artisans, and others were demanding for the work they were required to do: they were convinced that pay was soaring. If Dr Holmes is right, therefore, about manorial income, then that income, far from enabling manorial lords to increase their share of the community's resources, in fact barely sufficed to give them as great a share of those resources as they had enjoyed before the Black Death. But had manorial income stood still? If it had, then it was not the prices that manorial farmers were getting for their crops that prevented them from increasing their share of the community's resources. Something else was keeping manorial income down. And, as contemporaries clearly saw, this was the problem of the wage-rate.

The wage-rate responded to influences from all but the most inaccessible recesses of the medieval economy. Many factors, no doubt, made its response sluggish or imperfect. But some response the wage-rate was bound to make. Even when the land was so densely populated that there were more villagers than tenants for the available farms and allotments, those who made up the surplus had to sleep somewhere, and had to eat and clothe themselves. And unless we postulate a teeming underworld of poaching, stealing, squatting criminals in every overpopulated medieval village, must we not assume that landless villagers paid for the accommodation they occupied and for the necessities they consumed? They paid, presumably, by earning. And if that is what they did then their pay was bound to leave its mark upon the markets in which they bought goods and services – as it was bound to leave its mark upon the markets in which they sold their labour. In this respect barter had the same effect as pay. And the repercussions of their entry into these markets, or their withdrawal from them, were bound to be felt, in some measure, far and wide. Even when work was done in order to discharge obligations of tenure the labour market felt the consequences, especially when the work was done not by the tenant or his family but by a labourer paid by the tenant to substitute for him. How much was done in this way we cannot hope to know. But the Poll Tax returns for 1379, when the tax was graduated, give some indication of what may have been common practice in earlier days when labour was cheap, by revealing the numbers of ordinary villagers who had labourers living with them as servants, many of whom were presumably available for such work.

If prices are hard enough to establish, however, wage-rates are infinitely harder. Lord Beveridge was reasonably confident that the wage-rates he collected for certain classes of day-labour on the manors of the bishopric of Winchester in fact reflected the whole of the remuneration paid to those who were employed.[14] But most of the wage-rates that survive are the rates that were paid by institutional employers with far more to offer their regular

[14] W. Beveridge, 'Wages in the Winchester Manors', *Economic History Review*, vol. vii (1936), p. 23. Lord Beveridge's figures (with others) are tabulated by Prof. Postan, 'Some Economic Evidence', p. 233.

employees than high wages or food and drink. And the best attested series
are the ones that Prof. Phelps Brown has incorporated into his tables. These
are wage-rates paid to building workers, most of them regularly employed by
large institutions for the multiplicity of jobs that go under the heading of
maintenance. Consequently the conclusions to be drawn from the wage
material must be drawn even more tentatively than those to be drawn from
the price material.

Nevertheless, some striking things emerge. 'From 1290 to 1379,' wrote
Lord Beveridge, 'money wages and the price of wheat move decade by
decade always in the same direction, rising and falling together.'[15] The price
of wheat may not be a very significant index of the well-being of a society
which had not yet reduced the wheaten loaf from the dignity of being
something that was aspired to as a luxury to the ignominy of being an item of
food that everyone demanded as a necessity. But a glance at Prof. Phelps
Brown's index of the purchasing power of the building worker's wage-rate in
terms of a group of commodities of which wheat was only one, shows that
Lord Beveridge's conclusion, based on rates paid to similar classes of workers,
was not at random. Indeed, to the extent that we can trust the figures we
have got, it looks as if real wages were held more or less steady for three-
quarters of a century during which there were two prolonged periods of high
prices and numerous famines and pestilences. Considering the notorious
inelasticity of institutional wages paid to maintenance staff this result is
surely extraordinary.

The fourteenth century seems to have been quite exceptional in wage-rate
history for the way in which the wages of building workers and the trend of
prices fluctuated together. When prices rose wages rose, and when prices fell,
as they did in the decade or so before the Black Death, so did wages. In an
episode of wage-rate history which Lord Beveridge remarked upon,[16] and for
which Prof. Phelps Brown could find only isolated parallels in fairly recent
experience,[17] the wage-rates paid to building workers in the third and fourth
decades of the century actually fell. If wage-rates which were normally much
less flexible than others could show such astonishing sensitivity to general
movements, what of wage-rates in other occupations, and what of payments
made for piece-work? The presumption must be that these were even more
volatile. Perhaps many were. But there is evidence of cross-currents. At
Winchester the piece-rates paid for threshing and winnowing did not fall
when day-rates fell, so that these harvesting operations were a greater burden
to the estate on the eve of the Black Death than they had been earlier in the
century when prices were high. But with inexplicable perversity these piece-
rates failed to rise as decisively as day-rates did on the morrow of the Black

15 Beveridge, loc. cit., p. 31.
16 Ibid.
17 Carus-Wilson, ed., op. cit., p. 174.

Death, thus compensating Winchester handsomely for previous aberrations.[18]

With the arrival of the Black Death wages rose once more. Contemporary outcry prepares one for a truly spectacular rise. But the figures do not tell a story which is in any way consistent with the volume of the outcry or the circumstantial detail of the chronicled horror. Wages certainly rose, and sometimes rose sharply. But Lord Beveridge and Prof. Phelps Brown are agreed that wage-rates did not soar. After the first shock of the pestilence was over, what was most remarkable about the wage-rates was the way in which they drifted steadily upwards, particularly in the sixth and seventh decades of the century, and continued to do so even in the fifteenth century. At Winchester, indeed, where the rise was generally less dramatic then elsewhere, the drift went on until the middle of the fifteenth century.

If these figures are to be trusted, demesne farmers were undoubtedly paying more for labour after the Black Death than ever before. But they were also getting better prices after the Black Death than they had ever seen before. The rise in wages meant that demesne farmers who were very dependent upon wage labour, as many were, could not make profits which were commensurate with the prices they were getting. Not all demesne farmers, by any means, were caught in this predicament. And those whose customary tenants normally provided much of the labour with which the routine work of demesne farming was done were obviously, to that extent, better off than those who had few tenants, or none, discharging part of their obligations of tenure in service. So complex was the structure of the manorial labour supply, however, and such is our ignorance of the relative importance of the different types of labour available on all but a handful of estates, that it is impossible to speak except in the most general terms about such things. But even those demesne farmers who had to watch their wage-bills, because wages entered substantially into their total costs, found that the rise in wages was not sharp enough to eat into profits. In this respect the evidence of wages and prices bears out the impression of buoyancy rather than stability of income which several scholars have brought away from their investigations of big landed estates at this period. For the wage-unit calculated by Prof. Phelps Brown was worth no more in this period of high prices than it had been in the previous period when high prices were matched by high wages.[19] Consequently, the evidence of manorial history, slender though it may be for this period, and the conclusions to which the statistics apparently lead, suggest, when taken together, that the Indian summer of demesne farming occurred, not in the early decades of the fourteenth century, but in the

[18] Beveridge, loc. cit., 26. Dr Titow has some harsh things to say about these findings. J. Z. Titow, English Rural Society, 1200–1350 (1969), p. 46, n. 9.
[19] Unfortunately, Prof. Phelps Brown has not calculated the value of the wage-rate for the years 1351–9. But he has tabulated the money wage-rate; and this shows no dramatic departure from the trend that we see once the series is resumed in 1359. The Beveridge material confirms this impression.

period of much-publicized difficulty that followed the introduction of bubonic plague into England, when it lasted for at least one decade, and may
have lasted for two.

It was not an untroubled Indian summer, but then the fourteenth century
was not an untroubled century. And it started imperceptibly enough, in a
minor key. Bubonic plague arrived in England during the high summer of
1348. Either that year's harvest was gathered in normally, or it was such a
successful harvest that not even epidemic bubonic plague could prevent
enough of it from being gathered in to provide for all needs in 1349: for 1349
was a year of low prices.[20] And the harvest of 1349 was collected adequately
enough to provide for survivors without difficulty: for 1350 was also a year of
low prices. Then the harvest failed, or the harvesters failed: for 1351 was a
year of scarcity. Scarcity is a relative term. Prices rose in 1351 to the level of
1272, 1295, 1310, 1315, 1324, 1331, 1332. They did not rise as high as they
did in 1316 or 1317. They did not even rise as they rose in 1318, 1322, and
1323, years which are not often mentioned in connexion with exceptional
hardship. In 1352, as a result of the 1351 harvest, prices really soared. But
they got no higher than they had done in 1323, and returned next year to
the level of 1351. Two fairly adequate harvests followed, and then a succession of bad ones which drove prices up until the second pestilence again
made them soar.

The second pestilence arrived in 1361 and persisted throughout the winter
in certain parts of the country. It or something else certainly upset the price
level: for famine prices prevailed in 1362, 1363, 1364, and even in 1365. If
the price index is rightly linked to the pestilences, then pestilence left a far
deeper mark in 1361–2 than it did when it first devastated the country in
mid-century. High prices were now the rule, and the third major epidemic,
which started in 1368 and persisted into 1369, occurred when high prices
were rising in a crescendo to a peak in 1370 when prices were higher than
they had ever been except for the terrible years of 1316 and 1317. To
contemporaries this rather than its successor was 'the great dear year'.[21] The
following year was as bad as 1352 and then the index falls to a level which is
high by the standards of earlier and more fortunate decades, but not by more
recent experience. Then came the harvest of 1375. It was the best for
twenty-six years. And it was a portent. The Indian summer was struck by its
first frost. And frost was followed by the swift onset of winter. A new age of
low prices began. And for the first time in the fourteenth century money
wages did not conform to the movement of prices. Low prices did not bring

[20] Knighton certainly thought it was a good year. R. B. Dobson, *The Peasants' Revolt of
1381* (1970), p. 61.
[21] The phrase was used by a chronicler with reference to the year 1371. C. Creighton,
A History of Epidemics in Britain, vol. I (Cambridge, 1894), p. 215. It may be that he was
correctly reporting local experience rather than making a mistake or exposing the
limitations of the price material.

wages down as they had done in the 1340s. On the contrary wages continued to rise, with ominous consequences for demesne farming.

Demesne farmers, however, were not without the means with which to protect themselves from the untoward consequences of having to employ men whose exorbitant and incorrigibly insistent demands for higher pay threatened the economy of their estates. They had the labour legislation of 1351 as subsequently refined and amended; and they had the courts of the Justices of the Peace. It was up to them to invoke the legislation and make use of the courts. Much thought has been given to the problem of deciding how energetically the labour legislation was enforced. There is, in fact, evidence of enforcement at all periods of the later Middle Ages. But when prices were high the incentive to enforce was weakened by the knowledge that rising costs could be passed on. Only when prices fell did employers look to their duties and responsibilities as loyal subjects and make shift to enforce the laws that their king and those who did his business in parliament had enacted. The mid-seventies were surely the years when employers were re-called to a sense of their duties. It was unquestionably then that they them-selves felt the need to have the labour legislation enforced as never before. For it was then that parliamentary agitation over the problem of labour reached its climax.[22] And it was then that those emotional charges were generated which produced the most spectacular expression of popular revol-utionary fervour in English history.

Peasant unrest was no novelty in medieval society, as Prof. Hilton has shown.[23] It is tempting, therefore, to see the rising of 1381 as the culmination of generations of oppression. Perhaps something of the bitterness engendered by the intermittent struggle to enforce the legislation of 1351 in the fifties and sixties gave it an added impetus. But the rising was marked by an extraordinary lack of bitterness. Restraint was its outstanding feature. And when it was over, retribution was neither wholesale nor vindictive. It is fashionable in some quarters to dismiss the rising as an event without signifi-cance, and in others to invest it with a momentousness it surely cannot justify. The divergent course of prices and wages in the third quarter of the century, however, suggests that whatever else the rising expressed, trivial or profound, it expressed as plainly as anything could the exasperation pro-voked by the first unwaveringly resolute attempt ever made to get the legisla-tion of 1351 enforced.

Whether it achieved its immediate objectives or failed miserably is beside the point. The fourteenth century was the century when wages rose without seriously diminishing the profits of demesne farming because prices always

[22] W. Stubbs, The Constitutional History of England, vol. III, ch. xxi, and C. Petit-Dutaillis, Studies and Notes Supplementary to Stubbs' Constitutional History, vol. II (Man-chester, 1914), p. 263, both noticed how the agitation grew as the century wore on. See also Dobson, op. cit., pp. 72–4, 76–8.

[23] R. H. Hilton, 'Peasant Movements in England before 1381', Economic History Re-view, 2nd ser., vol. ii (1949), reprinted in Carus-Wilson, ed., op. cit.

managed to rise in proportion to wages and thus more or less offset the potential gains of labour. By the last quarter of the century this age of equipoise was over, and demesne farming was condemned to the anguish of transition and supersession. What the rising did, whether it succeeded in the narrow sense or not, was to proclaim the passing of one age and the inauguration of its successor.

Demesne farmers, however, refused to acknowledge the passing of their age by giving up without a fight. Moreover, as the century wore on the crisis deepened, for wage-rates continued to rise and prices continued to fall. Consequently, after the rising of 1381 had been suppressed demesne farmers clamoured for more effectual labour legislation and stricter enforcement with as much vehemence as they had done in the years immediately before it. And at this juncture the king did not answer their clamour, as his grandfather had done, by reminding them that if the guilty went unpunished the fault was not in the law but in themselves. At this juncture he responded, as he did in 1388,[24] with fresh legislative and administrative ingenuities, and showed himself to be ready to look for conspiracy in the unlikeliest places, as he did in 1389, when he authorized a thorough investigation into the guild movement.[25] The king who did these things was in no way the equal of the king who had rebuffed the fathers of those who now turned so importunately to the government for help. But times had changed as well as kings. Times indeed had changed very much more even than kings. And they had changed, apparently, in the last quarter of the fourteenth century, long after the age of widespread and disastrous famine had come to an end, and a score of years and more since epidemic bubonic plague had first struck its seemingly fatal blow at the foundations of the English social system.

The result of these dramatic changes in the relationships of wages to prices was to ruin demesne farming. The records are full of it. They make sombre reading. In earlier periods, before the Black Death as well as after it, when the records told of unfilled vacancies and terms offered which were unsatisfactory from the landlord's point of view, they did not necessarily tell of a countryside from which the life was ebbing away.[26] By the late fourteenth century that is exactly what they do. By then, as never before, they are full of despondent reckonings of decayed rents, abandoned holdings, and demesne farms surrendered to tenants on almost any terms they cared to offer. The big demesne farmers who had weathered so many storms could not weather this one. For them it was the end. And their failure is at once reflected in the movements of prices and wages and explained by them.

This is surely the nub of the problem. If the movements of prices and wages reflect and indeed explain the dissolution of demesne farming that

24 Statutes, 12 Ric. II, c.3–10.
25 Toulmin Smith, ed., English Gilds (1870).
26 A. R. H. Baker, 'Evidence in the Nonarum Inquisitiones of Contracting Arable Lands in England during the Early Fourteenth Century', Economic History Review, 2nd ser., vol. xix (1966); J. Z. Titow, op. cit., p. 94.

took place at the end of the fourteenth century, then how can we ignore them when they seem to reflect and explain the continuing prosperity of demesne farming in the decades that followed the famines and later the pestilences?

To judge by the sensational behaviour of prices, the early fourteenth-century famines were the most staggeringly desolating ordeal by natural disaster that western Europe had ever been called upon to endure. But to all appearances they did not relieve population pressure. Rents did not fall as land was thrown on the market. Wages did not rise as survivors withdrew their labour in favour of life on the land as tenant-farmers. If Dr Titow is right in thinking that soil productivity was declining at this period,[27] then it is not difficult to find one reason why the famines failed to relieve population pressure: as the pressure fell, the capacity of the land to support population fell too. But is this the main reason? If it is, then how are we to explain the recovery that followed the Black Death? Are we to postulate a progressive deterioration of the soil in order to explain why the stupendous losses recorded by manorial officials in different parts of the country, after the Black Death, did not have the effect that we should have expected them to have had on wages and prices? Or was the Black Death perhaps, in spite of everything, not as bad as it was made out to be?

Contemporaries were shocked so very much more deeply by the Black Death than they had been by the famines that we are disposed to take it for granted that the Black Death was a greater scourge than the famines. But people were prepared to be demoralized before the Black Death actually reached the shores of England. Contemporary dread of plague had already been magnified by rumour before it was confirmed by experience. The Black Death travelled swiftly enough. But it took longer to sweep Europe than travellers took to carry advance news of its coming. And their accounts, no doubt, lost nothing in the telling. Certainly its arrival found the Council more or less prepared: for within a remarkably short time the Council had an ordinance ready imposing a code of conduct upon all with labour or goods to sell. The Ordinance of Labourers was promulgated on 18 June 1349, about a year after the arrival of the Black Death, but only a matter of months after it had developed into a threat to the entire nation. And this time the entire nation meant everybody. Plague broke down the barriers of class as famine could never do. Famine spared the clergy. Plague did not. Many clergymen died, no doubt, because their duties took them into the plague-infested homes of their parishioners. But many clergymen were absentee incumbents. The bishops' registers, in which institutions to vacant livings were recorded, did not distinguish between those who died in the midst of their parishioners and those who did not. But it is not unlikely that the toll of clergymen tells something of the toll that plague took of the middle classes generally. Parliament, for example, did not stand prorogued when famine stalked the land.

27 Titow, op. cit., p. 53.

Members of Parliament bore the sufferings of the poor with altogether exemplary fortitude in 1316, 1317, and 1323, and carried out their parliamentary duties undismayed. When plague struck, however, matters were very different. Parliament did not meet; and the normally impassive routines of law and administration were temporarily suspended.

What is more natural than to assume that the mortality of parish priests, the consternation of chroniclers, and the unprecedented interruption of normal processes of government are conclusive evidence that plague was deadlier than famine? But does the clerical evidence really justify us in drawing any other conclusion than the somewhat otiose one that famine respected the moneyed classes and plague did not?

The most recent treatment of these perplexing problems raises all the difficulties in an acute form because it consists of yet another attempt to worry the truth about the population movements of the fourteenth century out of the Winchester material. Dr Titow, who has made the attempt, has compiled a list of the heriots levied on five Winchester manors and a list of the tenants of Bishop's Waltham which was one of them.[28] He has found that the heriots indicate a death-rate in the year 1348–9 of at least 50 per cent and that at Bishop's Waltham the death-rate was 65 per cent. Dr Titow assumes naturally enough that the general population of the villages concerned succumbed to plague at much the same rate as the Winchester tenants did. At Bishop's Waltham, however, vacant holdings were taken up by survivors with so little delay that he is driven to the conclusion that the Hampshire countryside, on the eve of the epidemic, was teeming with people. The countryside would certainly need to have been teeming with people if a local population which had been reduced to 35 per cent of its previous size were nevertheless capable of supplying not only tenants for vacant manorial holdings but also wage-earners for all the multitude of jobs which had to be done on the estate at Bishop's Waltham, and of doing so on terms which were not very different from what they had been before.

It is arguable that Bishop's Waltham was exceptionally unlucky in 1348, and that its vacancies were filled by enterprising peasants from neighbouring villages which had been more fortunate. Dr Titow's impression is that Bishop's Waltham was not exceptionally unlucky; and his heriots seem to bear him out. And yet in the decade or so that followed the 1348 epidemic Winchester wages and prices behaved in very much the same way as the wages and prices collected by Thorold Rogers. How are we to reconcile a pattern of behaviour which displays none of the striking changes in the relationships of rents and prices to the remuneration of labour that sensational losses of manpower should produce, with a general mortality as severe as that demonstrated by Dr Titow?

Nor is this the end of the difficulties. One of the most extraordinary things about the Black Death is how little effect it seems to have had on the social

---

28 *Ibid.*, pp. 69–70.

and economic life of the country despite the tremendous mortality that is recorded in the random sample of manors which have been investigated in depth. Why was the country not enfeebled or at any rate unnerved by its losses? How can we explain the undiminished flow of wool exports that we find as soon as the farmers who took over the wool customs in 1343 had restored them to the king's administration in 1350?[29] How can we explain the dazzling career of expansion that cloth exports embarked upon in 1354 after a brief reversal of fortune for which the state of the foreign market was, apparently, as much to blame as anything else?[30] And how can we explain the early resumption of the French war with such ferocity and tenacity? Can we really believe that two countries which had just been weakened irreparably by the loss of one-third or perhaps one-half of their manpower could then fly at one another's throats again as they did so soon after their losses had been sustained? Both sides had been glad enough of a respite from mutual destruction in 1347 when plague was not even a traveller's tale and when both sides were glutted with idle hands with stomach enough for any adventure. Why were they so keen to renew the quarrel when their lands had been as wasted by plague as the manorial evidence seems to tell us they were?

The problem of population trends bristles with difficulties however it is tackled. But the difficulties are fewer if we project the age of decline into the last quarter of the fourteenth century than if we insist upon leaving it where it has always been. Everything that we know about the social and economic history of England makes more sense if we no longer postulate paralysing devastation at mid-century followed by a pause which is a quarter of a century long during which nothing happens as it should and everything seems to carry on as usual, until, suddenly and inexplicably, everything happens as it should and nothing is as it was.

Mr Saltmarsh, who recognized the pause for the problem it is, also propounded a solution to it by taking seriously Langland's remark that the plague was like the steady drizzle of rain upon a leaking roof. He conceded the recovery of the fifties but saw the permanent infection that the Black Death introduced as starting a slow relentless attrition of the country's human resources in recurrent outbreaks of plague. 'One great disaster if once over and done with, may be followed by confident recovery; a disaster that recurs and recurs again is far more discouraging.'[31]

This may be so, but a plague which removes between one-third and one-half of the population cannot be followed by confident recovery in Mr Saltmarsh's sense until the survivors have produced a new generation numerous enough to take the place of those who died. Even if they set about the agreeable duty of providing for the future in this way with all the alacrity

[29] E. M. Carus-Wilson and O. Coleman, *England's Export Trade, 1275–1547* (Oxford, 1963), pp. 46ff.
[30] E. M. Carus-Wilson, *Medieval Merchant Venturers* (1954), p. 246.
[31] Saltmarsh, *loc. cit.*, 37.

that the crisis demands, the replacement generation cannot be ready to earn wages and occupy land for many years. Meanwhile, the deficiency of wage-earners and tenants must inevitably transform the relationships of land to labour along the lines elucidated by Prof. Postan. Mr Saltmarsh meets this difficulty by pointing out that fourteenth-century England had large reserves of younger sons, poor relations, and squatters, who were only too eager to seize the opportunities that a sensational demographic crisis threw their way.

But the difficulty remains. If replacement were so easy how are we to explain the subsequent decline? Are we to throw the main burden of proof on to subsequent outbreaks of bubonic plague? Plague did not return for ten or eleven years after the first outbreak. During this interlude survivors were no doubt busy making up for the losses. We have no reason to believe that marriage rates fell at this time. The likelihood is that they rose. And if we are to assume that there was more room for everyone than before, then we must also be allowed to assume that everyone fed better and died less readily than before. Consequently the population that faced the second pestilence was not the devastated population of 1350 but the population that ten years of breeding by the available female survivors of the first attack could produce and better feeding could sustain. What we know about the second pestilence, however, does not compare with what we know about the first. There are scarcely any investigations of manorial losses comparable with those that have been done for the earlier outbreak. And failing such investigations there is nothing better to turn to than the equivocal testimony of the institutions to vacant livings. This shows, for what it is worth, that the clergy escaped much more lightly at the second attack than they had done at the first. But the price material shows that prices shot up in 1362, as we have always been wrongly led to believe that they did in 1349 as a result of the chaos that reigned on the morrow of the arrival of the Black Death. And then wages conformed to the new level of prices without, apparently, closing the gap between them. 'In spite of the continuous drain of population . . .' commented Dr Page in her review of the Crowland evidence, 'the supply of men seemed limitless.'[32] The wage and price material certainly appears to bear out her findings.

The second pestilence was then followed by others. But the evidence for these is no longer derived from either manorial fines or clerical lists. Henceforth we are beyond the help of such statistics. We are thrown back upon the chroniclers. And in order to make his point about the cumulative effects of recurrent plague Mr Saltmarsh is reduced to speculating about wage-rates and prices in exactly the same way as everyone else is.

But the wage-rates and prices cannot help Mr Saltmarsh's case without at the same time spoiling it. For it is the extraordinary behaviour of wage-rates and prices in the fifties and sixties that creates such difficulties for Mr Saltmarsh's belief in the malignant power of the Black Death. If he is right in

[32] F. M. Page, *The Estates of Crowland Abbey* (Cambridge, 1934), p. 152.

thinking that deficiencies of manpower in that period were made good from the reserves of manpower that the population normally carried, then we must ask what kind of reserve of manpower it is which can shift from doing no one knows what to occupying anything up to one-half of the tenancies in the kingdom and presumably to taking over a similar proportion of the wage-earning jobs without noticeably affecting rents, or prices, or rates of pay? Are we to assume the·existence of extended families in the early fourteenth century large enough and numerous enough to account for the feeding, clothing, and employment of a very substantial proportion of the total population without reference to the market; extended families, indeed, which were so organized, if that is the word, that members who were kept alive in this way never did anything that released other members for work in the community at large which they could not have undertaken but for the family help they received?

Anything less than absolute segregation from the market, in this sense, will not do. If these phantom presences actually released others for productive work in the economy then their own work, whatever it was, would have been as much a part of the productive system as the unpaid domestic work of women always has been. And if it had been as much a part of the productive system as that then drastic loss of population which made it harder to provide such work would have altered the supply of labour to the market in such a way as to dispose of any problem of stable wage-price relationships in a century of unprecedented famine and epidemic bubonic plague. Such people were a reserve. They added nothing to the wealth of the community as the market measured these things. What they subtracted from it in order to survive they subtracted from their families and neighbours in ways which the market was not sensitive enough to register. And when the population was struck by famine or pestilence they took the places of those who had perished in an orderly succession that left the world of markets and land tenure virtually undisturbed by the losses the community had sustained.

Can we really believe in the existence of this submerged and pullulating throng which, like the stars that were visible to astronomers only in their effects upon the orbits of neighbouring bodies, can be perceived only in the influence it exerts upon other factors at times of crisis? If we can then the Black Death provides us with a plausible example of the phenomenon of which Prof. Arthur Lewis has given the classic exposition: the phenomenon of an economy in which labour is so plentiful that its marginal productivity is negligible, or nil, or even negative; an economy in fact which has nothing to lose in productive power if its surplus manpower is removed, and indeed something, perhaps much, to gain.[33]

All our difficulties with the evidence disappear if we take it that the

---

[33] W. A. Lewis, 'Economic Development with Unlimited Supplies of Labour', *The Manchester School*, vol. xxii (1954), reprinted in A. N. Agarwala and S. P. Singh, *The Economics of Underdevelopment* (Oxford, 1958).

immensely heavy mortality caused by the Black Death was quite incapable of altering the social and economic relationships of the community or of impairing its capacity to produce and distribute goods and services because so much of the population was surplus by the fourteenth century that the early famines and the mid-century pestilences were more purgative than toxic.

Does this mean that the Black Death must forfeit its status as a formative influence in economic history as the price for retaining its reputation as a formidable scourge? If mid-century England were so full of people that a loss of at least one-third of the population was insufficient to change the relationships of land to labour, then the Black Death can tell us something important about the depths of poverty that large sections of the community had plumbed in earlier decades. It can also tell us something about the structure and size of the extended family, and about the immense significance of such families in the demographic history of the thirteenth and fourteenth centuries. But can it tell us very much about the loss of population that we see in the dramatic inversion of wages and prices in the mid-seventies of the fourteenth century, and in the tumultuous popular response to the legal and social pressures that the landlords applied thereafter?

The chief economic problem of the fourteenth century remains a population problem even when we have shifted it from mid-century to the seventies. And striking changes in the relationships of land to labour, such as we find in the seventies, seem to call for explanation in terms of a sudden irruption of epidemic disease rather than in terms of changes in the social customs of the community.[34] Moreover, changes which continued for so many years that the relationships of wages to prices were not stabilized until the second or third decade of the fifteenth century presuppose an epidemic disease or perhaps a series of different epidemic diseases which overwhelmed the recuperative powers of the population as Mr Saltmarsh thought the Black Death did.[35]

But was it Black Death that devastated the late fourteenth-century community? The problem is mainly a problem of epidemiology. And Prof. Shrewsbury, whose massive study of bubonic plague in England has recently appeared, believes that a very great deal of epidemic disease in later medieval England was not bubonic.[36] For this belief he has been learnedly taken to

[34] Plague did not, apparently, search out the children. See below, n. 37, op. cit., p. 209. Some chroniclers thought it did, in 1361 and 1369. See J. C. Russell, Medieval British Population (Albuquerque, 1948), p. 229. They did so, presumably, because children were so much in evidence as a result of the birth- and death-rate changes brought about by the first plague.

[35] The period during which wages and prices somersaulted was also the period of the notorious Poll Taxes. The main theme of all who write about these taxes is evasion. See, for example, Dr E. B. Fryde's introduction to Charles Oman, The Great Revolt of 1381 (Oxford, 1969), pp. xv, xviiff. But if this were the period when population loss was at its most dramatic, then the records to which the Poll Taxes gave rise are open to a somewhat different line of interpretation.

[36] J. F. D. Shrewsbury, A History of Bubonic Plague in the British Isles (Cambridge, 1970).

task in the *Historical Journal*.[37] But what Prof. Shrewsbury has been at pains to point out is that bubonic plague, to be epidemic, requires a density of population which is normally found only in towns. By the seventies recurrent visitations of bubonic and pneumonic plague had presumably kept the surplus population from recovering even if it had done no more than that. Was the rural population by then still dense enough to satisfy the conditions required by bubonic plague if it were to be able to sweep through the countryside and devastate its population? The only clue we have to the answer to this question is the opinion expressed by those who have scrutinized the chronicle literature that, as time passed, bubonic plague was confined more and more to the towns.[38] This bodes ill for the future reputation of the Black Death; for if it is ever to be restored to favour as a dynamic force in fourteenth-century history then it is in the 'seventies, rather than in the mid-century decades that it has dominated for so long, that the Black Death must be found a tenable position to occupy.

[37] C. Morris, 'The Plague in Britain', *The Historical Journal*, vol. xiv (1971), pp. 205–15.
[38] J. M. W. Bean, 'Plague, Population and Economic Decline in the Later Middle Ages', *Economic History Review*, 2nd ser., vol. xv (1963), pp. 427–31.
  Questions as to the nature of the plague have been raised, more recently, by a zoologist. See Graham Twigg, *The Black Death: A Biological Appraisal* (Batsford, 1984).

The Hundred Years' War:
Costs and Profits

Nowadays when we submit all things to ordeal by arithmetic it is, perhaps, inevitable that someone should try to calculate how much war took out of the medieval economy. War, which destroys resources as well as diverting them from other uses, also expedites developments whose benefits may make some reparation for the damage it does and for the interruption of the ordinary pursuits of life it causes. Consequently it is also inevitable that, with their sums done, historians should be irresistibly tempted to comment upon the losses incurred, or the gains made, and to speculate as to the economic effects of war on society.

Losses, however, once they have been marshalled into columns and added up, have a way of looking excessive. Consequently thinking about social activities in terms of what they have cost soon carries a perfectly innocuous investigation of patterns of expenditure, by imperceptible degrees, into the drawing up of an indictment of a way of life. Those who count the cost may not draw up the indictment. But when the costs are the costs of waging war it is exceedingly difficult for a twentieth-century reader who is told of hosts of men and quantities of material withdrawn from peaceful pursuits, to condone the purposes to which they were then committed. When remote and ancient quarrels are distilled into a story of treasure squandered or spoils won, what can the modern reader do but call down a plague on both houses?

Current inquiries into the costs of waging the Hundred Years' War depict the effects of war on the medieval economy of England in what seem to be very different ways. To Professor Postan the Hundred Years' War witnessed the victimization of England by its ruling classes. The war was a misfortune even when it was not an unqualified waste, and the excitement, adventure and spoil it afforded were merely incidental to the boredom, horror, pain and loss for which neither the excitement and adventure nor the spoil could possibly have compensated adequately.[1] To the late K. B. McFarlane the war was a splendidly successful business enterprise for the English, in which a people in whose veins coursed the blood of Frobisher and Drake, displaying

1 Professor Postan has written two articles on this subject. One appeared in *Economic History Review*, vol. 12 (1942), the other in *Past and Present*, vol. 27 (1964). They have been reprinted in M. M. Postan, *Essays on Medieval Agriculture and General Problems of the Medieval Economy* (Cambridge, 1973).

its incorrigibly buccaneering spirit, for the first time put forth its incomparable powers to resounding effect.[2]

At first glance there seems to be little enough in common between these two views of the Hundred Years' War. And yet by the modern standards to which they both appeal there is, in fact, not much to choose between them. They both appeal, fundamentally, to the arbitrament of the balance sheet; and the balance sheet can measure only 'things that you can touch and see'. Professor Postan had no hesitation in seeing the war as a vast diversion of resources from better uses: if there had been no better uses it would have been pointless to regret the uses to which such resources were actually put. And if McFarlane took a different view by contending that the Hundred Years' War was a profitable excursion abroad for the English he did so only because everything seemed to indicate that English pleasures were paid for by the foreigner. In short, whether we are asked to believe that the Hundred Years' War was some sort of mischievous interruption of the otherwise more or less tranquil development of English economic life or that it was a kind of business which was run at a loss only by the competitor that went to the wall, the dispute between the two historians who have made most of the running hitherto is about nothing more complex or exalted than the returns made on a rather special kind of commercial venture.

There is surely something paradoxical, however, about speaking of the costs or the effects of medieval warfare in such terms. The implication of doing so is that war, far from being a normal feature of social life in the Middle Ages, was an aberration of conduct which diverted people from nobler, or simply more practical and useful purposes, with ruinous or at any rate unproductive consequences. It is certainly true to say that medieval warfare was, at times, expensive. Sometimes it cost a good deal more than it had been expected to do. And the results it achieved, which posterity can so readily misprize, often falsified the hopes of those who had embarked upon it. But neither cost nor the frustration of hope is commonly taken to be conclusive as a condemnation of any particular social activity. Religion was also expensive in the Middle Ages. Religion could also put those who built or endowed in its name to a great deal more expense than they had bargained for. And the results achieved, as generations of scandalized reformers reminded generations of profane and sacrilegious contemporaries, were very often profoundly different from those intended or anticipated by founders and other benefactors. We have as yet no figures for all the prudential investment in spirituality made in the course of the Middle Ages. No doubt the necessary calculations will soon be to hand. When they are, shall we be invited to see medieval religion as yet another diversion of resources from we know not what and another deflection of the course of social development from we know not whither?

[2] K. B. McFarlane, 'War, the Economy and Social Change', *Past and Present*, vol. 22 (1962). See also his *The Nobility of Later Medieval England* (Oxford, 1973).

Contemporaries in the Middle Ages were often as blisteringly critical of the Church as they were of the practice of war. But that does not mean that the Church was not an integral part of medieval life. Everyone knows that it was. To call the money spent on it a waste is merely to confuse ends with means. And if we refuse to acknowledge that war was as integral to medieval life as religion, we surely run the risk of depriving ourselves of the opportunity of seeing life as many of the most representative members of the community saw it in the Middle Ages.

It is, after all, a very modern taste that deprecates war as a waste and a misfortune. Until it became too dangerous an amusement for unrestricted self-indulgence, war provided everything that other social activities, religion alone excepted, could offer only in an adulterated form, or in small doses, or with essential elements withheld. In the Middle Ages, indeed, far from being a cost which had to be met, war was the supreme expression of the social purposes for which the military aristocracy existed. To speak of the costs or the effects of war in the Middle Ages, to argue that one war was good for England because England won it, and another bad for England because England lost it, is hopelessly to misunderstand the significance of war in the Middle Ages.[3]

Fighting was not an interruption of medieval social life, or a smart way to get rich, though many people's lives were interrupted by it and some did get rich as a result of it: fighting was the chief way in which leading, and, in this respect therefore representative, members of society found fulfilment at that period. If medieval social life were ever interrupted that was surely when long periods of truce or formally concluded peace rotted the morale of men who had been bred and trained for war and whose social function was only truly expressed in war. This was not because such men were romantically dedicated to the abstruse and convoluted tenets of chivalry. What they felt and lived by was something that was far closer to the code and enthusiasms that Winston Churchill portrayed in his account of his early life. War was the supreme adventure and the sternest discipline. Adversaries were encountered without hatred or enmity, only with professional appreciation of their skill or resource and professional respect for their courage or address. Peacetime, when it did not serve some professional or political purpose, was merely a wearisome break, a demoralizing interlude which had to be got through somehow without loss of spirit or skill, self-respect or honour. To judge by the money spent on war by Henry III, his reign was such a period of stultification for the military spirit. And when his son came to the throne determined to be a great king he set out to make himself great as a soldier and a monarch. We do him a profound injustice when we remember him chiefly as a law-giver.

Indeed a fit man in the prime of life with the military skills at his fingertips

3 M. McKisack, *The Fourteenth Century* (Oxford, 1959), pp. 249–50. See also M. H. Keen, *The Laws of War in the Late Middle Ages* (London, 1965).

and comrades in arms upon whom he could really depend only when things
went well had no choice but to live life as a succession of medieval kings
tried to live it, and as Edward III lived it with such transcendent success that
he became the embodiment for succeeding generations of everything that
imparted lustre and distinction to medieval kingship. In a medieval society
what else was a king for? What else could he do but aspire to lead his men as
Edward III did?

Modern government is so preoccupied with welfare that we cannot without effort recall a time when there was little or nothing that government
could do to cure the sick, employ the idle, or feed the poor, and when,
furthermore, any attempt to do so that went beyond the most perfunctory
gesture of commiseration was bound to court serious political trouble. The
vast mass of the population was well beyond the circle of politics. Providing
for it could have been done, if at all, only at the expense of the political
classes. That would have meant political suicide. The population that
swarmed and pullulated outside the bounds of the community of the realm
was not, however, without its political influence. By way of riot and insurrection it made its inchoate but menacing presence felt. And the king in
conjunction with his lords and commons had to do what they could to
contain it without sacrificing the essential interests of those who mattered
politically. Consequently nothing was ever done that could have been left
undone without reckless imprudence; every concession was soured by apprehension; every assertion of public interest sharpened by suspicion. Fear of
what the hungry masses might do runs through all the legislation about the
pricing of food; and anyone who looks for a medieval poor law policy which
is anything more exalted that a question of police powers and police duties
will quickly be disabused of any fanciful notions he may have entertained by
the spectacle of a succession of timorous and palpitating governments con-
demning the playing of games on Sunday as a pretext for conspiracy and
suspecting the gild movement, which in fact organized the most respectable
and prosaic members of the working classes and the humbler members of the
bourgeoisie, as a cover for sedition.[4]

If political wisdom counselled the most extreme moderation in considering the welfare of those outside the world of politics, religion in the Middle
Ages exerted no countervailing influence. The care of the poor and needy
did not rank high enough amongst the forms of atonement consecrated by
the Church to the expiation of sin to attract substantial benefactions or
serious interest. Almsgiving was certainly encouraged. But it had neither the
sanctity nor the efficacy of prayer. Medieval religion was profoundly preoccupied with a personal salvation which was to be procured by prayer. Prayer was
offered and lavishly paid for simply in order to save the soul of him who

4 *Statutes of the Realm* 13 Ric.II.1.C.13; 17 Edw.IV C.3; 1 Hen.VII C.7; 3 Hen.VIII
C.9; Toulin Smith, ed., *English Gilds* (London, Early English Text Society, o.s., 40,
1870). Statutes of the Realm 15 Hen.VI C.6, renewed 19 Hen.VII C.7, and *Rotuli
Parliamentorum*, IV, p. 507.

prayed or endowed others to pray for him. Grants for alms-giving, compared with those made for prayer, were consequently meagre, fitful and capricious. How could it have been otherwise? If alms were given so as to improve the spiritual chances of the benefactor rather than the lot of those who received them, what else could a sensible man do but put his money where it would do him the most good? Accordingly the visible Church was, more than anything else, a gigantic engine dedicated to the transmutation of income into prayer.[5]

Life was not made easier for a medieval king simply because he was not required either by religion or by more worldly considerations to devote himself to the welfare of his people. The pressures upon him were often intolerable. Whatever the political theorists may have decided about his place in the structure of things, the public records show that his contemporaries regarded him, above all, as some sort of well from which patronage could be pumped inexhaustibly, and bear witness to their appetite for anything and everything that could be got from him and from one another. His public life was dominated by the quarrels of insatiably clamorous contestants for his favours, between whom he was obliged to arbitrate to such effect that he neither antagonized influential supporters nor deprived himself of the indispensable landed wealth upon which his own authority was necessarily founded. In addition he was driven by social pressure, if not by temperament and training or by more prudential considerations of self-interest, to provide his mettlesome aristocratic peers with an outlet for their martial qualities and skills which would enable them to fulfil their highest ambitions. Ambitions such as theirs when frustrated abroad quickly turned treasonable at home. Civil war was the retribution visited upon the medieval king whose foreign policy did not fix the gaze of his aristocratic feudal host on objectives which discharged the frictions generated by life and politics elsewhere than at home.

Thus to give the wars of the fourteenth and fifteenth centuries a special significance by singling them out for separate designation as the Hundred Years' War is to convey the entirely false impression that these were years of war when they might have been years of peace. The Hundred Years' War did not squander assets that might otherwise have been husbanded. It was the war that was fought instead of the war that would otherwise have been fought. When Englishmen were not fighting on the continent they fought at home or elsewhere in the British Isles. Powicke once suggested that the true cost of the Normandy connection established by the Conqueror was the diversion of energies from the conquest of Ireland and the Scottish Lowlands.[6] But for the Normandy connection perhaps those intractable problems would have been solved, at least to English satisfaction. Once solved,

---

[5] J. T. Rosenthal, *The Purchase of Paradise* (London, 1972); A. Hamilton Thompson, *The Organisation of the English Clergy in the Later Middle Ages* (Oxford, 1947).

[6] F. M. Powicke, *The Loss of Normandy* (Manchester, 1913), p. 448.

military ambition would infallibly have found something else upon which to fasten: it was in the very nature of medieval society that it should have done so.

Nor was there anything special about the Hundred Years' War in other respects. The endeavour to give some semblance of unity to the campaigns mounted between 1337 and 1453, however, means that less prominence is given than should be to the long periods of truce and quiescence that alternated with periods of fighting even at times when much fighting was being done. It also means that we find it harder than need be to set the fighting of those years in the context of that succession of wars in France and with France, inaugurated by the Normandy connection, which pursued their sometimes desultory, sometimes tumultuous course through the medieval centuries and into the sixteenth century, dying down before the end of that century except for fitful outbursts of antagonism, only to blaze out again in the eighteenth century on battlefields all over the world. Nothing new occurred in 1337 or in the immediately preceding years. Nothing ended in 1453. Dr Fowler in his thoughtful and illuminating study of the period has expressed the belief that Edward III's claims 'inaugurated a new period in Anglo-French relations' and rendered it 'impossible for a lasting peace to be made' until those claims had been quietly dropped so that the Treaty of Étaples could lay 'the foundations of a more permanent settlement' in 1492.[7] Yet Étaples did no better than the Treaty of Paris by which Henry III and Louis IX had come to terms in 1259. Henry VIII revived the old quarrel in 1512 and 1522 as resolutely as Edward I had done in 1294. Both fought costly and ineffectual campaigns after which France ceased to be a major preoccupation for some time to come. And if England turned to other matters in the course of the sixteenth century she did so not because of the efficacy or finality of treaties, Étaples or any other. She did so for very different reasons to do chiefly with the growing problem of Spain.

In the story of the development of warfare and of the social and economic burden of warfare the Hundred Years' War has always taken its place as a milestone along the road that leads to total war. And yet there is no reason to believe that the Hundred Years War was particularly expensive. The calculations of costs running into millions of pounds, with which McFarlane and Professor Postan have attempted to chasten and even perhaps to shock us, are immensely impressive. But they represent costs incurred in the course of more than a century of war-making. And they represent costs calculated in money instead of in feudal or communal services performed. The Hundred Years' War was fought by contract armies instead of by unpaid hosts. A paid army does not cost more in men and materials than an army which serves because it has an obligation to do so, but it looks more expensive, particularly when records of its costs happen to survive in comprehensive detail. Moreover armies were still absurdly small. And if the cost of equipping a

---

[7] K. Fowler, *The Age of Plantagenet and Valois* (London, 1967), pp. 14–15.

fully-armed knight had risen sharply over the years, the cost of equipping the other branches of the armed forces had not risen to anything like the same extent.[8] Furthermore campaigns were still not only few but brief. And the damage done, whatever chroniclers and petitioners might say, was limited, as before, because there was so little to destroy that could not be quickly and easily rebuilt or made good.

If the Hundred Years' War introduced anything new into European war-fare it was perhaps a facility for spreading the costs of war far beyond the confines of the area of conflict or the range of those who shared an obliga-tion to support the contending parties financially if not in other ways. It was some measure of the growing interdependence of the regions of Europe, for certain purposes, that the belligerents found they could reduce the direct impact of war upon their economies by inflicting some of the burdens of war upon people who were not directly involved. The English wool trade, for example, although severely taxed by the 1330s, maintained its export vol-ume undiminished until the final quarter of the century.[9] It is not unreason-able to conclude from this extraordinary inflexibility and tenacity, as McFarlane did, that a Parliament in which wool-growers were always a substantial if not a dominant political force would never have allowed taxa-tion of such severity to stand if it had found that wool prices had dropped as a result of it.[10] This meant, in effect, that Polish landowners and eastern potentates who bought cloth made out of English wool, by submitting to the payment of higher prices, were inveigled into making a contribution to the costs of a war in which they took no other part and whose issues were of no interest or concern to them.

Since Burgundian and Spanish wools were as highly esteemed as English by those who used them, even if they were not valued quite so appreciatively by contemporary Englishmen,[11] presumably those who were able to tax the trade in Burgundian and Spanish wools of such quality soon found, as the English did, that the trade did not immediately suffer when they taxed it. They seized the opportunity, perhaps, to pass on some of their war costs, as the English did, by making exalted personages in distant lands pay for their exotic taste in cloth by supporting western European wars.

The international mercantile community was also laid under contribution by the chief belligerents. It bore the brunt of the losses incurred by those who lent with profligate abandon to both sides in the early years of the war only to find themselves disastrously weakened or utterly ruined when their royal debtors defaulted on their loans.[12]

[8]   McKisack, op cit., pp. 238–41.
[9]   E. M. Carus-Wilson and O. Coleman, England's Export Trade 1275–1547 (Oxford, 1963).
[10] K. B. McFarlane, The Nobility of Later Medieval England (Oxford, 1973), pp. 39–40.
[11] E. Power, The Wool Trade (Oxford, 1941), pp. 13–14.
[12] M. Postan, E. E. Rich, E. Miller, eds, The Cambridge Economic History of Europe, vol. III (Cambridge, 1963), ch. 7.

But the cost of the war to those who took part in it was chiefly circumscribed by the inability of governments to raise money with which to fight it.
It is tempting to believe that England and France were bankrupted once royal
pockets had been emptied by the cost of supporting allies and mounting campaigns. Treasuries, however, were exhausted very much sooner than communities because medieval kings never succeeded in finding ways in which to
tap the real wealth of the communities upon which they called so often and
so urgently for money. Edward III and his French adversaries had an easier
task, in this respect, than any of their medieval successors. Population pressure upon available resources provided their recruiting sergeants with an endless train of eager volunteers and rendered the landowning classes amenable
to their repeated calls for financial support. In England these calls were made
in Parliament. And Parliamentary taxation usually meant a tax on movable
property. Throughout the later Middle Ages this tax was levied on towns and
villages at rates settled in 1334, when the liability was expressed as the communal responsibility of the town or village for a fixed sum instead of as the individual responsibility of the taxpayer for a sum which varied with the value
of his movable property. With the local liability fixed in this way the government left problems of individual assessment to local authorities. In theory, no
doubt, landlords contributed wherever they had possessions and according to
their local means. In practice when land was scarce they were able to raise
rents, in order to compensate themselves for any contributions they were obliged to make, without the least fear of losing tenants. When land was abundant they could not. By the last quarter of the fourteenth century, therefore,
when pressure on resources had been altogether relaxed,[13] the recruiting ser-
geant began to have a harder time of it and, as rents dropped, Parliament
began to grudge every penny of taxation, which its members plainly saw was
no longer to be passed on in higher rents but was, if anything, to be digested
in lower ones.[14] No wonder Parliament grew more refractory and resorted to
poll taxes when the King asked for more!

Not that Parliament, or indeed anyone else, minded paying for successful
war. No one objected to paying for the campaigns that culminated in the cap-
ture of the king of France. And many years later, in very different circumstances, no one seriously objected to paying for the war that Agincourt
vindicated and the colonization of Normandy crowned. It was abject and irre-
deemable failure that the country would not stand for. By the end of his reign
Edward III had let slip all and more than all he had gained in his years of
glory. The Good Parliament was the vengeance that the political classes
wrought upon him for the blighting of their hopes and the discomfiture of
their expectations. After his reign, as rents fell, natural mortification at the
failure of the military was aggravated, so far as Parliament was concerned, by a
growing recognition that taxation to pay for the war was becoming, increas-

[13] A. R. Bridbury, 'The Black Death', *Economic History Review*, 2nd ser., vol. 26 (1973),
also above, pp. 200–17.
[14] A. R. Bridbury, *Economic Growth* (London, 1962), p. 96.

ingly, a burden to be shouldered by those who granted it. Greater reluctance, henceforth, to support inept or ineffectual leaders did not mean that the country was exhausted. With taxation becoming ever more progressive this was very far from being so. Still less did it mean that the political classes had been suddenly afflicted by compunctuous visitations of conscience over the widows and orphans. The fourteenth century had supped full with horrors: it had known unparalleled famine and pestilence of unexampled frightfulness and pervasiveness. Death was too close in the fourteenth century to permit the fostering of the kind of squeamishness that any such fit of conscience would imply. French chroniclers execrating the English for cutting murderous swathes across the countryside of France in the course of their *chevauchées* exploited the turpitude of brutal and licentious soldiery to the limit of their powers. But the most notorious of those *chevauchées* occurred during the period when pestilence was still spreading its desolation far and wide. The chroniclers were not above imputing to the English what should have been laid to the account of natural forces; but the men who lost their nerve in England, if any did, were much more likely to have done so because they found themselves paying more than they thought they should have done for military expeditions which always seemed to end in humiliation and disaster than because they were sickened at a time of widespread pestilence by the infamous things that Englishmen had done in France.

Moreover even when Parliament conceded money for the waging of war, even when it made what was, by the standards of previous decades, the most generous provision for the king's needs, the funds it placed at the king's disposal bought much less than they used to do because rising wages ate into the army contractor's appropriations as they ate into the demesne farmer's arable profits. Calculations of the costs of the Hundred Years' War have so far ignored the momentous changes in the purchasing power of money that took place in the last quarter of the fourteenth century, although these changes may have done as much as anything else to make it harder for the successors of Edward III to raise armies and fight campaigns as he did.

Nor are the ramifications of the attempt to assign a sensible meaning to the notion of cost in connection with medieval warfare yet exhausted. Both McFarlane and Professor Postan align the adversaries as if they were the adversaries of later wars and speak of France as abroad and of damage done there in the course of the war as if it were always different from damage done to England when the French sacked the ports of the south coast. In doing this, however, they are surely committing a most extraordinary solecism. Many years ago Plucknett warned us to remember, when thinking about the Lancastrian constitution, that 'the later splendours of the constitution have been reflected backwards upon the fifteenth century, throwing certain features of it into undue relief and enveloping the whole structure with an appearance of maturity and completeness which is in fact illusory'.[15] If the

---

[15] T. F. T. Plucknett, 'The Lancastrian Constitution' in R. W. Seton-Watson, ed., *Tudor Studies* (London, 1924).

English constitution were feudal in the fifteenth century, when the most distinguished of the king's judges could reasonably argue that Parliament was an hereditary court and taxation the profits of a franchise, so was the political geography of Europe. By the end of the Middle Ages England was, despite the lawyers, very much more than a congeries of feudal dependencies loosely held together by bonds of allegiance to a king. But in this respect England was unrepresentative of Europe. The other regions of Europe were very far from coalescing into entities which were more than geographical expressions. In France deep antagonisms threatened, on many occasions, to produce a very different political map from the one with which we are familiar. We lay stress on the unifying achievements of later medieval French kings because we know that they endured. But contemporaries knew only that large segments of some of the richest regions of what were later to be integral parts of France had descended to the kings of England by inheritance and were enjoyed by them, without impropriety or illegality, as parcel of their demesne. Gascony was as much part of their inheritance as Kent or Yorkshire. No county of England could be declared forfeit for breach of feudal law as the king of England's French possessions could be, and were, from time to time. In this sense possessions held of the king of France were less secure than those held by the king of England because he was king and for as long as he remained king. But in all other respects the king's French possessions were his to enjoy as fully and freely as any possessions which an ordinary vassal held of his lord in the ordinary way could be.

Does it not follow from this that when English captains and their men made free with the property of those who dwelt upon land to which the king of England had what he claimed to be a clear title they were in fact enriching themselves at the expense of their liege lord and his tenants no less when that land happened to be in France than they would have done if they had looted and ravaged parts of England and had thereby diminished the profits that the king and his tenants normally derived from the districts they had wasted? If we are to set gains against losses in calculating the costs of the Hundred Years' War dare we ignore the fact that political geography was feudal in the Middle Ages? And if we are to take this factor into account how many of the gains that McFarlane so confidently placed to the credit of the successful captains who returned laden with booty from the French wars should we not transfer to the debit side of the balance sheet because their gains were made, according to this way of looking at them, at the expense of their king and their king's men? In this sense the Hundred Years' War had an affinity not so much with a war of nations as with a civil war in which every attempt to crush his opponent compels each of the rivals to inflict hardship and damage upon the possessions for which he is contending.

Even this is not the end of the matter; for the king of England's possessions in France were subject to violent fluctuations. Over the centuries he acquired a succession of dissolving empires of immense size and prodigious wealth, each one of which was hardly won before it was fragmented and then lost. Which empire, or which moment of empire, should we select as the basis for our calculations? Moreover his title was constantly in dispute. Whose version of his rights should we accept for purposes of assigning profit and loss?

If the attempt to calculate the costs of the Hundred Years' War lures us into a morass, what are we to make of current notions of profits as applied to medieval warfare? People were perfectly clear in their own minds, in the Middle Ages, as to what war profits meant and knew when they had been made and when they had not. For them war profits meant the transfer of property from loser to winner in the familiar forms of plunder, ransom, office, rent, indemnities and the like. McFarlane and Professor Postan, however, have both searched for the possibility of something more than personal advantage in the successful prosecution of the Hundred Years' War. They have looked for something that might have added to what McFarlane called 'the wealth of England'[16] and Professor Postan specified as 'material additions to manpower, or to capital assets in real terms, or to consumable commodities'.[17]

McFarlane's belief that transfers of wealth brought about as a result of the waging of a successful war enriched not only those who had won a fortune on the battlefield but also the community to which they belonged surely cannot survive Professor Postan's demonstration that the command of purchasing power which their success gave them did no more than buy them a place in the social system which existing incumbents could no longer afford and aspirants to social preferment who had not perhaps done well out of the war could not hope to acquire against their competition. Professor Postan's 'circular tour of rural wealth' brought about many changes in the nomenclature of county families which have no doubt delighted genealogists. But it is difficult to see how such changes increased or could possibly have increased the wealth of England, or indeed could have diminished it if it could be shown that the balance of advantage in these matters had in fact lain with the French. If there had been widespread unemployment in later medieval England then the flow of money introduced into the economy by those who had made war pay, by raising profits, might have created work for workless men and women. But whatever problems later medieval England may have had, unemployment was not one of them. Of course the victors returned laden with trophies. But even if we concede to McFarlane the point that Professor Postan contested, namely that the spoils of war fell mainly to the English 'for the simple reason that the war was fought almost exclusively on . . . [French] . . . soil',[18] it is still a very whimsical conception of national wealth that sees an enhancement of the productive powers of the com-

---

[16] K. B. McFarlane, 'War, the Economy and Social Change', *Past and Present*, vol. 22 (1962), p. 10: 'This early essay in "colonialism" increased the wealth of England'.

[17] M. M. Postan, *Essays on Medieval Agriculture and General Problems of the Medieval Economy* (Cambridge, 1973), p. 69.

[18] K. B. McFarlane, 'War, the Economy and Social Change', *ut supra*, p. 9.

munity in the store of plate and jewellery and other baubles that the English brought back from France.

And if we are asked to believe that success in the Hundred Years' War could have enhanced the productive powers of the economy of the side that won, in the terms that Professor Postan has specified, then we are being asked to believe that war in the Middle Ages was capable of conferring advantages which simply did not exist in the Middle Ages for anyone to enjoy. Any additions to England's manpower, as a result of success in war, unaccompanied by other changes in the structure of the economy, would merely have had the effect of depressing wages and perhaps of hastening the advent of a period when a glut of labour would once more reduce the ordinary villager to indigence as it had done in previous centuries. Nor was there any item of capital equipment which could have been transferred from vanquished to victor in order to raise the productive capacity of the victorious economy. There were no technological short-cuts to wealth and power for medieval economies, no production secrets to conceal, no discoveries in farming to withhold.[19] As to 'consumable commodities' these could only have enriched communities rather than individuals if victor had compelled vanquished to pay tribute as the provinces of the Roman Empire had once paid tribute to Rome. But medieval kingdoms were not organized on Roman lines. It would never have occurred to those who ran them to attempt to exact communal tribute in the Roman way. Throughout the Middle Ages the profits and losses of war remained, therefore, very much a matter of personal luck and individual responsibility.

What are we to conclude from all this, then, if not that the Hundred Years' War was merely a series of episodes in the history of medieval warfare which were not conspicuously different from previous episodes or other contemporary episodes of that history, and that the prosecution of war was as profoundly characteristic of the institutional pattern of medieval society as was the patronage vouchsafed to the Church, to which respect was paid and tribute given, from which wealth was drawn, and by means of which power and prestige were conferred and confirmed? Indeed in a society which, in fact, raised those who fought to the highest places in the kingdom and gave the Church the privilege and duty of praying for their souls, there can be no doubt surely as to whether the soldier or the clerk, illustrious exceptions apart, enjoyed greater social esteem. In such a society making war did not waste resources: it employed them. And the quest for costs in connection with social activities of such a nature is bound to lead to unfathomable and inextricable problems. Driven by the importunities of those who are consumed by a passion for calculating things, historians who embark upon such quests soon find themselves asking questions about the past which can only be answered by remaking the past to suit their questions.

[19] A. R. Bridbury, *Economic Growth* (London, 1975), new introduction.

New Introduction to
B. L. Manning's *The People's Faith*
in the Time of Wyclif

When we ask what medieval people thought about the purpose of life and how their thoughts affected their conduct, we ask some of the most interesting and perplexing of all the questions we could ask about the past. But the answers elude us. Studies of medieval thought, though numerous enough to be a drug in the market, assume that we shall understand the thought of the medieval world when we have understood what its professional thinkers had to say about it. Studies of the innumerable religious orders and foundations that served the needs of those who were dedicated to the cure of souls and the life of prayer, assume that we shall perfectly understand how the tremendous machinery of ecclesiasticism performed the functions for which it was ostensibly designed when we have celebrated the expansion and prosperity of these orders and foundations, deplored their moments of spiritual frailty, and regretted the comparative penury to which a few of them were sometimes condemned.

It is very much a donnish conceit to suppose that ideas rule the world. But is it true to say that the thoughts of ordinary men and women, humble or exalted, were nothing more than garbled versions of the cerebrations of theologians and philosophers? Was there, indeed, ever a time, in the Middle Ages, when the thinkers could agree and when, therefore, the church could formulate a set of doctrines which would command universal assent? The unity of Christendom, in these as in so many other matters, is surely a fiction which cannot survive examination. And if those whose thoughts dominated academic discussion were of many minds upon vital issues, what of the institutions through which the great truths were mediated to the mass of the laity? What thoughts about the purpose of life and the destiny of man percolated through the filter of ecclesiasticism to those who were deemed to have been divinely appointed to work and fight rather than to think and pray? Was it due to the immense labours of those who served the ecclesiastical machine that, in spiritual matters, the medieval church could 'maintain a hold so hardly won in earlier times, so easily lost in our own'?[1] Or was the medieval church merely an illustration of the truth that, in the late Dean

---

[1] F. M. Powicke, *The Christian Life in the Middle Ages* (Oxford, 1935), p. 9.

Inge's sour words, 'the powers of evil have won their greatest triumphs by capturing the organisations which were formed to defeat them'?

Stripped of its sophistries and involutions the Christian message held out a prospect, for those who submitted to the teachings of the medieval church, which was utterly cheerless. Conceived in sin, brought forth in suffering, the medieval Christian dwelt all the days of his life in circumstances in which he found himself irresistibly provoked to breaches of the most solemn commandments of his maker. So hopeless was his condition, indeed, that his chance of salvation was universally agreed to be no better than his chance of riches won on a gambler's throw, and, according to some authorities, no less arbitrary.[2] The Ages of Faith demanded an unflinching hopelessness of those who followed the argument with care and accepted its implications without question. But did ordinary men and women follow the argument and accept its implications? if they did were their lives made darker than ours thereby? Did they behave better, by their own standards, than they might have done otherwise? Or did hopelessness about their destiny tempt them to abandon themselves to whatever took their fancy in the meantime? And what if they did not understand the teachings of the church, or were not taught what the church had to say, or did not believe what they were taught?

Some chance remarks, the history of ecclesiastical recrimination and anathema, scraps of scurrilous verse, a few lines of contemptuous parody, are all that remain to suggest that the doctrines of the medieval church and the teaching afforded by those who served it left the common man as bewildered and disconcerted as we are left today by the eschatological forebodings and doctrinaire prescriptions of our economists. And if this parallel is not altogether inappropriate would it be unreasonable to pursue it further and suggest that the true function of religion in the Middle Ages was to provide the idiom in which people commonly expressed themselves much as the true function of economics is to provide the idiom in which we express ourselves today?

We believe devoutly in economic growth. Yet we do all manner of things that slacken the rate of growth. We insist on differentials. We strike. We go to war. We have more children than we can afford. And we spend our money in ways which cannot possibly help us to grow richer. Does this mean that we do not really believe in economic growth? Or that we believe in it only upon terms? Or that we believe in other things as well? Economists are, for some purposes, our parish priests. But we cannot often understand what they say. Moreover no two economists ever quite manage to agree upon their interpretation of any public issue. And when they commit themselves to a prediction things frequently turn out very differently from the way in which even the most discerning of them had expected. Nevertheless we invariably set our problems in a framework of economics.

[2] G. G. Coulton, *Five Centuries of Religion*, vol. 1, chapter 5 and Appendices (Cambridge, 1923).

Did ordinary medieval people, perhaps, feel something like this about the doctrines propagated by the church? Were they as bemused and even incredulous as we are? Did they seek refuge from thought in the comfort of slogans as we do? And was their conduct of life as little affected by the dark threats of their priestly mentors as ours is by the comminations of the economists? It may be that we can never answer such questions. But amongst the first enquiries we must make in any attempt to do so is the one we must make in order to find out what the medieval church actually succeeded in conveying to its lay congregations by way of instruction and example. Every such enquiry must begin with the encyclopœdic work of G. G. Coulton and with the more recent reflections of Dr Moorman.[3] But no less valuable and revealing is this learned and sometimes devastating survey of what was often taught, when anything at all was taught, and what was often believed, when anything remotely Christian was believed, at a period which was as Christian and as uncompromisingly orthodox as centuries of strenuous and unremitting effort could make it. *The People's Faith in the Time of Wyclif* is the best short introduction there is to the baffling and intriguing problems of social history with which it deals.

---

[3] J. R. H. Moorman, *Church Life in England in the Thirteenth Century* (Cambridge, 1945).

Markets and Freedom in
the Middle Ages

When we select an institution for historical investigation, we inevitably take it out of context. Indeed the very idea of an institution as a separate organism isolates a group of activities from the social process to which it belongs and does violence to its nature. There are, of course, immense advantages to be gained by studying any organism without the distraction of seeing it as part of something more complex. But anything abstracted from the totality of events is bound to be distorted, if not falsified, by such a procedure. This applies with particular emphasis to markets, because regular and mutually beneficial exchanges between consenting parties cannot possibly take place unless an irreducible minimum of appropriate political and social conditions permit the making of such exchanges. And it is by no means self-evident that medieval authorities saw their responsibilities in terms of encouraging such exchanges, particularly if it meant doing so to the detriment of their other obligations and interests.

This was partly a question of practical politics. Medieval politicians had the problem familiar to politicians in all ages of having to yield to pressures they could not resist without giving more offence than they cared to provoke. The statue book is full of concessions made to this interest or that which, taken together, add up to a farrago of contradictory policies as inextricable as those of any government's today. But this is not the only reason, or indeed the most significant reason, why medieval political authorities did so much less than we might think they ought to have done to promote exchanges of goods and services. They failed to do more because they did not take the same view as we do of the importance, not to say the sanctity, of markets and of the value of promoting market facilities.

Where they differ from ours it is tempting to conclude that medieval values were either higher or lower than ours, so that when it is not being commended for its exalted ideals, medieval society is commonly disparaged for its failure to live up to ours. But medieval society had its own values, and for these it is not answerable before the bar of any historical court of moral judgement. Social commentators may be forgiven, perhaps, for perceiving the world's history in terms of an evolutionary development in which past events are valued according to the contribution they can be said to have made to the achievement of what is thought to be best about present society. But any survey of past ages which gives prominence to those aspects of the past which can be made to wear an appearance of modernity and which, as a result, treats everything else is quaint or reactionary, is bound to hold up a distorting mirror to history. This does not mean that we ought never to go to the historical record, such as it is, in order to find out how something which interests us has evolved over time. When we ask about the development of Parliament or the evolution of steelmaking, we need make no anachronistic assumptions about the importance of Parliament to political society or the significance of steelmaking to the economy in earlier times. We distort history only when we assume that the things that interest or concern us had, or ought to have had, as much significance for our forebears; and we falsify history when we then proceed to judge men and societies by standards they never dreamt of observing and would have repudiated utterly had they been presented with the opportunity of making a choice between their standards and our own.

The values of past ages cannot be judged in this way. They are sacrosanct and beyond dispute because life at any time is its own justification. Life may be said to look to the future, at any particular moment, rather than remain imprisoned in the present, in the sense that the biological and evolutionary system is arranged so that each generation is responsible for the creation of its successor. But it does not look to the future in the sense that it finds its spiritual justification in the contribution it can make to the formation of that particular pattern of social organisation and that particular system of values which any one group of historians at any one phase of history happens to approve of and support. The conceit of supposing that the past culminates in the present afflicts economic historians even more than others, because as a result of twentieth-century material success, they can patronise the past, not only with hindsight and that confidence in their own moral standards which are the common prerogative of all historians but also with that sense of superiority with which the rich invariably contemplate the life of the poor.

This problem is presented to us in an acutely aggravated form by the question of markets and their relationship to freedom in the Middle Ages. Markets occupied an altogether different position in the hierarchy of medieval social values from the exalted one to which we assign them today; and freedom meant something entirely alien to our ways of thinking. Indeed we can tell that there was something very different about medieval attitudes to markets by looking at their attitude to freedom. Acton's preoccupation with history as the story of how men struggled towards political liberty would have meant nothing to the reflective minds of the Middle Ages; and the idea that certain institutional arrangements, introduced then, may have laid the foundations for what we call our liberties, would have filled them with dismay. When medieval people spoke of freedom, particularly in connection with trade, they meant what we should mean by privilege. They meant a right, incorporated into a charter or engrossed in a licence, which emancipated a named person or institution from an obligation; or entitled such a person or institution to enjoy certain lucrative perquisites or advantages to the exclusion of everyone else. The freest man, according to medieval ways of reckoning such things, was the most privileged, according to modern Western ways of thinking.

When we look at the Middle Ages we must be prepared to see a world in which the words used are familiar but the ideas expressed are foreign to our experience and often uncongenial to us. We can see this fundamental difference of outlook in questions of what we call welfare. On the face of it, medieval governments were intensely concerned about the welfare of the commonwealth. No one can turn the pages of the statute book, or examine the petitions presented in Parliament and answered in the king's name, without being impressed by the constantly reiterated expressions of solicitude for those in want, by the endless and apparently anxious search for equity in the relationships of man with man, and by the unwavering determination of those in authority at every level to do whatever possible to provide conditions in which life could prosper for members of every social class and group. If we were to take such expressions of concern at face value we might be tempted to compare them with those made today and conclude that there was not much to choose between the social ideals of then and now.

But we should be quite wrong to do so. The Middle Ages were wholeheartedly committed to the belief that the classes in society should be preserved in their due separation. Indeed they went further than that. They were determined to preserve the commonwealth intact; and by the commonwealth the Middle Ages meant, not the sum total of all who lived in a certain area, nor even the sum total of all who dwelt within certain lordships and acknowledged, however indirectly, an allegiance to a particular sovereign prince or king. They meant the federation of those whom lordship itself linked with the king, wherever that lordship happened to be, at home or abroad. National frontiers, as we understand them, meant nothing to members of the commonwealth. Those who belonged were thoroughly cosmopolitan in lifestyle, in culture, in language, in family ties, and in personal loyalty and political allegiance. Xenophobia was strictly for the lower classes. To medieval ways of thinking, membership of the commonwealth depended, not upon having a soul to save or a home and livelihood where the king's writ ran but upon having a material and social stake in society. At bottom, the commonwealth consisted of those who possessed property and exerted influence. It consisted of what we should now call the establishment. And establishment attitudes to problems of welfare were, to say the least, pragmatic. Attitudes to the poor were, in fact, as ambivalent as they were to women. Poverty was not the intrinsically manageable problem it is now thought to be. Poverty was blessed; but it was also a huge, permanent and potentially overwhelming political problem. It was sensible, therefore, for the sake of peace here and salvation hereafter, to make some attempt, however perfunctory, to relieve an infinitesimal fraction of the poverty that seethed and pullulated all around, and prudent to remember that, fundamentally, poverty was, from a political point of view, a matter of law and order, and should always be treated as such. Like women, whom the Middle Ages saw as a diabolical blend of Eve the Temptress and Mary the Mother of God, the poor were a necessary evil, a perennial threat, and a fateful embodiment of prophetic truths.

It is entirely in keeping with this attitude to welfare that medieval society should not have condemned out of hand the use of money to solve all kinds of social problems and expedite all sorts of issues of policy which we have withdrawn from the market-place. In a society whose overriding purpose seems to have been to promote the interests of members of the establishment, patronage inevitably dominated the political scene. Patronage was largely a matter of mutual aid. But money had its part to play. Indeed the landed estates which supplied the material basis for personal influence and were the material reward for success in the power-game, had the important obligation of supporting the family and a miscellany of other dependants. The revenues of these estates were employed, accordingly, in a variety of ways which may strike us as, by turns, whimsical and culpable. For money ransomed prisoners of war, purged sins, and redeemed innumerable transgressions of the criminal law which we should not consider to have been properly punished without the public humiliation of the transgressor. Everything could be bought; or to put the matter more exactly, everything had a price and some part of that price could be paid in money. Justice could be bought: that is to say, either by purchase or other forms of suborning, courts of law could be made to work in the interests of those who had every reason to expect that their influence and authority entitled them to satisfaction when they submitted their disputes to the formal arbitrament of the law. By the same token, Church livings could be bought; even remission of taxation could be bought. Above all, licences and charters of various descriptions could be bought, authorising their possessors either to ignore bans and restrictions, or to impose them upon others, so as to limit access to lucrative sources of income and profitable occupations. And the work of those who superintended or merely assisted in the running of the administrative machinery that controlled and regulated the flow of demand and supply in this quarter of the service sector of the economy, that too could be bought; so that those who paid could dispatch their affairs, whilst those who could not, found themselves, like the suitor in Spencer's Mother Hubberd's Tale, condemned

> To fawn, to crouch, to wait, to ride, to run,
> To spend, to give, to want, to be undone.

It is indeed some measure of the strangeness, to modern ways of thinking, of medieval standards of behaviour and social custom, that whereas patronage was tolerated, if not sanctioned, in the Middle Ages, usury was universally deprecated and formally anathematised. The subsequent history of these two social institutions illustrates the capricious fate of moral imperatives; for the moral stature of usury has risen over the centuries as that of patronage has sunk. Banking now stands high in social esteem and the exercise of preference has been discredited, but like usury in the Middle Ages, not extirpated. If some medieval bankers managed to live down their disreputable and clandestine activities, that was usually because fortunes made by way of foreclosure soon matured into genteel acceptability as rapacious usurers concealed the shabby origins of their wealth in the county families they founded.

Loans which made money for the lender may have been condemned by canon and statute law. But at a period when reserves were pitifully small in relation to the risks undertaken, even by those who were engaged in pursuing the homeliest and most necessary occupations, large numbers of people who were neither so poor that no one in his right mind would lend them a penny except out of compassion, nor so rich that creditors fell over one another in their eagerness to be the one to do them a favour, found themselves in the hands of the moneylender. Indispensable though their services may have been, those who made some part of their living by lending were as morally opprobrious to the Middle Ages as landlords are today.

Did this mean that the Middle Ages ran short of loanable funds for investment purposes, and that many people starved or endured greater privation than necessary, because many of those who were affluent enough to be able to lend, felt they ought not to lend for gain and saw no point in taking a risk without making a profit? No doubt there were some who took this view and deprived the economy of investment capital thereby. But the dilemma of the usurer raises wider issues than that of usury, because it raises the perennial problem, for governments as well as for individuals, of reconciling theory with practice, of taking the hopelessly quixotic witness of the world's prophets and making political or personal sense of it. The world's work must be done despite the shrill vociferations of its ideologues. Whenever their extravagant demands and apocalyptic hopes have been seriously heeded, the world about them has either dissolved into an anarchy of unappeasably conflicting idolatries, or rigidified into some sort of social crustacean.

Medieval merchants were peculiarly vulnerable to attack, because the climate of opinion, in the Middle Ages, was not favourable to those who made profits or accumulated wealth from trade. The acquisitive appetites, however, continued to be active enough, in those centuries, to earn their rating as a popular theme of pulpit commination. And the evidence certainly shows that medieval people needed no tutelage in the handling of economic affairs. The king's preoccupation with commerce as a source of revenue, or as a weapon of economic warfare, does not mean that medieval kings were 'innocents abroad' where money-making was concerned. Politics are about sharing, not creating, wealth, so that records of political activities are bound to give a misleading impression of royal attitudes to commerce. In fact when medieval kings saw a good thing, such as the potentialities of the tin-mining industry, they responded unhesitatingly to its needs. In effect they suspended the feudal system for the sake of tin miners so as to attract labour to the mining areas, promote output, and thus swell the harvest of taxes that they cropped from this source. And others acted in like manner when occasion offered, Churchmen with no less enthusiasm and alacrity than the laity, founding towns as speculations in real estate, promoting colonisation by conceding preferential terms for initial periods of tenure, procuring charters for markets, and so forth.Even when we find that, beyond a certain point, medieval people seem to have lost interest in the kind of sedulous devotion to hard work that was later to be propagated as a sacramental duty, they may well have done so, not because they lacked tenacity or even because they felt some compunction about profit-making, but because they saw very clearly that, in an economic environment in which marriage and patronage were far more likely, at every level of society, to further their ambitions than the most pertinacious application to their callings, they would be much better employed in devoting themselves to those commercially sound, but in the narrower sense, uncommercial activities in which the comparative return to effort was greater.

Nevertheless merchants found themselves in a dilemma in the Middle Ages which was none of their making. What they did was useful and even necessary; and sooner or later everyone in the community discovered for himself that this was so. But their occupation was suspect and its rewards were disreputable. This may not have worried some men. But is it not possible that social disapprobation acted as a brake upon enterprise and effectually constrained merchants who might otherwise have thrown themselves uninhibitedly into their work, with incalculable consequences for market forms and marketing techniques?

This may seem to be a curious construction to put upon the meaning of the concept of freedom in the context of markets; but social constraints, though intangible, are often decisive. And the moral dilemma of the merchant was shared in the Middle Ages by many others. It was shared, for example, by Churchmen. Success had transformed the Church from a struggling, penniless band of outcasts into a dominant authority of inconceivable affluence and incomparable power. Its organization and leadership called for administrative and political talent of the highest quality. Those to whom the running of this extraordinary institution was entrusted were under some sort of compulsion to conduct the business side of things as well as they could. When they did so, they conducted the business of the Church in ways of which we heartily approve because they are the ways in which we believe that business must be done if it is to be done as well as possible. But doing the work in this fashion meant transgressing many of the canons by which priests of the Church and dignitaries of the ecclesiastical establishment were supposed to conduct themselves. Doing it in any other way meant clearer consciences for them, perhaps, but loss and vexation for the immortal institution of which they were only briefly honoured trustees.

Nowhere in medieval history can we see the relentless pressure of this dilemma more vividly depicted than in the history of the Church. Throughout its medieval history, the conduct of those who governed the Church and carried out its spiritual obligations, provoked successive reform movements whose inspiration was the wrathful indignation expressed by contemporary critics with what was done in the name of the Church by its leaders. These reform movements are undoubtedly some measure of the compromises that temptations of flesh and spirit betrayed such leaders into making. But recurrent efforts to restore the church to a pristine purity of conduct and purpose which, even in the segregation and placidity of the monastic round, it invariably failed to sustain, indicate that what was being pursued was not so much an ideal as a chimera. Consequently these reform movements are more significant than they would have been even if they had really stood for nothing more than the periodic revolt of public opinion against the excesses of self-indulgent or self-seeking careerists. They are in fact some measure of the compromises that unworkable ideologies forced upon a succession of more or less able men who neither rose very high above nor sank very far beneath the common level of humanity in matters of morality and responsibility, and who were saddled with the problem of reconciling the realities of business and politics with the uncompromising doctrines of which they were at once the custodians and the appointed exponents.

Did considerations such as these deter men of the highest moral integrity from accepting posts of responsibility in the Church, so that as a result of the radiant spirituality of its message, the Church was condemned to dependence upon men of inferior moral stature for its leadership?

Commerce and politics, however, were not the only indispensable social activities for which the Church had no decent and honourable place in its scheme of things. Marriage was another; and the history of medieval attitudes to marriage may provide us with a clue to the way in which ordinary men and women came to terms with the forbidding austerities of doctrines which seemed to condemn everything that made life possible as well as pleasurable or even tolerable. In an ecclesiastical system served by a priesthood dedicated by the most solemn vows to invincible ignorance of the married state, and neurotically obsessed by the idea of chastity to the point of believing and inculcating the belief that propagating the species was irrevocably tainted by concupiscence, marriage was inevitably judged to be a second-best state for spiritually second-rate people. This belief haunted some married people just as the spiritually-defiling activities associated with commerce haunted some merchants. Those who renounced marriage, or commerce, for a life consecrated to prayer and self-denial, were rapturously applauded. Those who did not but felt that they should have done so, led profoundly troubled lives, knowing that they were jeopardising their souls by succumbing to temptations which better men had been able to resist. Those who repented of their lives in this way often revealed their afflicted consciences in their wills. But theirs was not the normal reaction. The majority of married people, like the majority of merchants, made dispositions of their effects which, without casuistry or hypocrisy, betrayed no hint of remorse for their status in society and expressed no desire to make reparation for their choice. And they were able to live and die with pride in the dignity of the social positions they occupied because pragmatic Churchmen knew that social necessity had a stronger claim than abstract doctrine. 'In my father's house are many mansions' may not have been a notably popular text for medieval theologians; but it was, perforce, a commonplace theme of medieval ecclesiastical policy.

The problem of accommodating ideals to the realities of daily life creates difficulties for any society which lays down strict rules about human behaviour based on a flagrant misreading of human nature. We know these difficulties today as well as they knew them in the Middle Ages. They are the difficulties, for example, that we all have with competitive theory. Competition requires that governments should hold the ring not the whip hand; that consumers should be collectively sovereign but individually devoid of bargaining power in the market; that factors of production should be valued at prices which reflect their scarcity and opportunity costs; that foreign trade should be altogether unimpeded; that all prices, including interest and exchange rates, should be allowed to fluctuate freely so as to clear the market. But conditions such as these carry ingenuousness to the far limit of political recklessness and absurdity. Strictly adhered to, competitive conditions will inevitably, in the course of time and change, sacrifice all coherent groups and interests, all associations of workers and employers, all party machines with their commitment to particular regions, particular industries, or particular classes, and will do so, perhaps, at the dictation of consumers in remote markets who are no less indifferent to, than they are oblivious of, the social and political consequences elsewhere of their vagaries of taste and changes of need. A government which was heedless of these consequences could not hope to last. Competition in the market-place can be a recipe for disaster in the polling booths, if not at the barricades. Hence in the last analysis all governments are mercantilist and protectionist, however rugged the creed of individualism they may preach, because governments cannot afford to offend their supporters even when the interests of their supporters run counter to the interests of the community at large.

At the political level, the modern problem is somewhat different from the medieval one. Modern governments with their commitment to economic growth, find, nevertheless, that they cannot hope to survive unless they make concessions to political realities which may render nugatory their best efforts to achieve what they acknowledge to be one of their highest purposes. Medieval governments had the same problem in reverse. They had to find a place for market operations which gave far more latitude to those who worked in the market-place, and to those who used the services offered there, than a strict interpretation of what the Church said about such things would have allowed or a strict adherence to those social ideals which required everyone to know his place and keep to it, would have conceded.

At the personal level, the problem is always the same. Those who touch pitch, said Innocent III, must defile themselves. But how is pitch to be handled if everyone who could handle it is so fastidious, so spiritually self-absorbed, so careless of the social consequences of not handling it, so deficient, in fact, in the ordinary social virtues, that no one with the necessary skill or flair is to be found who is prepared to tackle the degrading work of coping with the practicalities of organising and running society, because

work of that kind contaminates the soul? Moreover, those who find themselves, for whatever reason, pitchforked into such morally risky occupations,
inevitably fall prey to censure and misrepresentation, however honourably
they endeavour to conduct themselves, because the rules are not devised
with these occupations in mind. Consequently it is easy to find fault with
those who are successful in such occupations because those who are successful are bound to have broken the rules.

Some of the best minds of the Middle Ages struggled with this problem.
But not all of those with extensive experience of practical affairs shared
Innocent III's dark thoughts about it. According to his first biographer,
Anselm saw no difficulty, for any man whose conduct was wholly governed
by what he knew to be right, in reconciling the demands of the spirit with
the demands of the world. Perhaps there was no problem for him. But even
Anselm had to be forced to accept promotion; and when asked to explain
how a man dedicated to the life of the spirit could be expected to cope with
the business affairs which promotion brought with it, took refuge in the sort
of foolish allegory that achieves its effect by assuming away the problem to
be solved.[1]

For many people, however, in the Middle Ages as at other times, the
problems of conduct raised by the official canon were problems created by
the canon rather than by their conduct. Authorised social values are always a
poor fit because society is infinitely more complex than its prophets and
analysts allow for. Such values invariably need modifying and supplementing
therefore, informally if not otherwise, so as to allow for the kind of problems
that it never occurred to those who formulated the rules to take account of.
And those who live by other rules than those laid down in the official canon,
compensate themselves for the sense of alienation they might otherwise feel,
and screen themselves from the pain and humiliation to which they might
otherwise be exposed, by forming themselves into unacknowledged coteries,
closed societies perhaps, silent passive-resistance movements, within which
they can keep one another in countenance by providing comfort and recognition for all who think or behave as they do. Consequently society is
divisible not only by class but also by groupings which cut across the lines of
class and turn society, from that point of view, into a federation of what are
tantamount to freemasonries whose bond, in every case, is common problems and experiences; and whose conventions of behaviour are those that are
accepted and respected by everyone who values his association with others of
his kind.

The Jews were a special case in the Middle Ages; but they were also an
extreme example of this kind of functional bond. They were able to
specialise very profitably in usury, by forming an irredentist group in society,
since their values made them utterly indifferent to local standards of conduct, and local beliefs and inhibitions, wherever they found themselves in

---

[1] R. Southern, ed., *The Life of St Anselm* (Oxford, 1962), pp. 74–7.

Christian Europe. Eventually, this indifference and their incorrigibly alien behaviour and outlook made them intolerable nearly everywhere within that region. But other groups, which had evolved out of shared Christian traditions and common racial origins, were able to thrive in conditions which, in the end, defeated the Jews, who had formed ganglions of unassimilable irritation in a social system which was simply incapable of accommodating their flagrantly antagonistic values.

Those who married, in a society which, at the highest level of spirituality, spoke slightingly of marriage, formed the largest movement of passive resistance of all, and were able to offer support and reassurance, more perhaps by example than by any other means, to everyone who, by marrying, found himself at odds with the central orthodoxy of a Church which made contemptuous provision for those who were too frail in body and mind to abjure marriage in favour of a more exalted and ennobling condition. Those who enabled society to accomplish a simulacrum of its political purposes instead of running into the sands, as it assuredly would have done if they had heeded Anselm's advice, were able to turn to others of their kind for consolation and strength when they were publicly traduced for their failure to adhere to the abstract stipulations of the currently fashionable writers of didactic treatises and manipulators of scriptural theorems. And those who transacted the commercial business of society could protect themselves from the dangerously isolated and vulnerable position in which their work often placed them, by forming those associations with which we are all so familiar, and which, from this point of view, were not so much conspiracies against the public as refuges from an uncomprehending and hostile world.

Unless we postulate the existence of a whole series of sub-groups in society we shall find it very hard to explain how men and women, who lived in a social system which explicitly discountenanced so many of the necessary and wholesome activities of mankind, were able to defy the system, not furtively and shamefully, but with confidence and dignity. Indeed it would be straining credulity to the limit to claim for the Middle Ages that human behaviour was so profoundly affected by the formal doctrines of the Church that markets and the men who served them were radically altered in character as a result of the pervasive influence of the refined spirituality of those centuries. On the contrary, the most striking features of the economic institutions of medieval life is how like they were to those that we find both earlier and also later in European history. There seems to have been a sort of timelessness about the basic conditions of life over a very long period of history, a fundamental sterility, or perhaps, an immovable torpor, which seems to have set firm limits to what economic development could achieve and militates against the notion that medieval spirituality emasculated the economic potential of the times.

Thus the horse was the fastest means of communication, as the ox was the most powerful source of traction, in Julius Caesar's time as it was in Napoleon's. Before the canal age, conditions on roads and rivers had remained virtually unchanged since men had first colonised the region. Only the building of bridges had marked a significant advance; and that advance had been made earlier rather than late in historical times. By the Middle Ages we hear much about the inadequacy of bridges; hardly at all about the want of bridges. Coast trade is a closed book to historians. Foreign trade is not. But we learn nothing from the records of foreign trade which might lead us to suppose that there were any revolutionary improvements in shipbuilding or manning levels; merely the adaptations required as trade patterns shifted marginally.

The striking fact about communications systems in these centuries is that they do not develop. And their failure to develop is symptomatic of a deeper changelessness. Transport costs enter into all costs. Societies which cannot reduce transport costs are condemned to a regimen of narrow markets and restricted growth.

We see this narrowness and the restrictions, so far as medieval conditions are concerned, in the organisation and structure of medieval business. Both in technology and organisation, the making of commodities based on the commonest materials, such as wool, leather, iron and wood, was carried on then, and until comparatively recent times, in ways which would have been familiar to craftsmen and business men of the classical age. Farming techniques are notoriously slower to change than business techniques; consequently once the iron plough had displaced the wooden, we should hardly be surprised to learn that the farmer's round and the farmer's tools knew scarcely any improvement until market changes in the seventeenth century enabled the more enterprising farmers to suppress the fallow and embark upon a course of continuous and often rapid development.

The astonishing immutability of the established usages of economic life was reflected, as it was bound to be, in the social structure. Whether we examine Domesday Book or the sumptuary legislation of the mid-fourteenth century; whether we look ahead to the survey that Thomas Wilson drew up in 1600, or further forward still, to the calculations made by Gregory King in 1695, when times really were beginning to stir; we cannot help being struck more forcibly by the similarities than by the differences to be found in the social structure revealed in these very diverse compilations.[2]

Naturally there are difficulties about comparing surveys made for very different purposes and separated by a gap of centuries from one another. Nevertheless the broad conclusions to be drawn from such a comparison can scarcely be in doubt. At all these periods the social hierarchy was dominated by a landed aristocracy supported by a squirearchy. Merchants occupied only a minor and subsidiary place in this company. One reason for this was that the merchant disappeared in the gentleman as soon as wealth permitted men of business to acquire gentility. But the principal reason was that the profits

[2] *Statutes of the Realm*, 37 Edw. III c. 8 (1363) for the sumptuary legislation; Joan Thirsk and J. P. Cooper, eds, *Seventeenth-Century Economic Documents* (Oxford, 1972), VIII, for Wilson and King.

of trade made few great fortunes in these centuries, and that manufacturing made fewer still. Manufacturers formed no separate class in a world in which even the biggest of them merely exercised financial dominion over a series of small-scale enterprises organised on the basis of the putting-out of work. Putting-out meant low entry costs for industry, and low entry costs meant low profit margins.

Below these ranks, and sometimes in parallel with the wealthier merchants, came the lesser landed families, followed by several classes of tenant-farmers, some more independent and perhaps more affluent than the rest. In feudal times these classes included villeins and cottars with unique features about their terms of tenure which we do not find later. When we examine these terms, however, we find that they were so very varied in practice that it is often impossible to distinguish them from terms of tenure by lease or by copy of the manorial court roll; and that even when these terms really meant that villeins and cottars were actually being called upon to serve their lords as labourers, we find that they were not usually being depended on for skilled regular work on their landlords' farms, but merely for supplementary assistance.[3]

How much of this supplementary assistance they provided in their own persons we cannot tell. But below the level of the landed peasantry spreads the incalculable mass of the landless. The landless have virtually no history because historical records are almost exclusively preoccupied with the affairs of those with property. Even poll-taxes pass them by in silence because the landless are too poor to pay taxes. They emerge in later centuries because they arouse the curiosity of statisticians or the concern of poor-law administrators. But they are new only to history when they emerge in this way; they are not new as a social phenomenon. We can get some measure of their social significance in the Middle Ages at one moment only. It is at the moment when the Black Death devastated the English countryside. We can calculate the mounting toll of deaths by counting the succession of new tenants as they register their occupation of suddenly vacated holdings. Vacancies were nearly all filled, however; and vacancies went on being filled, without great difficulty, for a generation after the first visitation of the Black Death, despite subsequent visitations of comparable virulence. That they were filled is surely a tribute to the size of the reserve army of the landless, thanks to whom landlords were able to maintain their estates and their profits more or less intact until, and indeed in many cases, for some time after, the Peasants' Revolt. It was to this abject class of destitutes, moreover, that villeins and cottars presumably turned for help when they were called upon to fulfil their more laborious tenurial obligations, deputing them to do, for a pittance, the farm work they were reluctant to do in person.[4]

---

[3] E. A. Kosminsky, *Studies in the Agrarian History of England* (Blackwell, 1956); M. Postan, 'The Famulus', Economic History Review, Supplement no. 2, n.d.

[4] A. R. Bridbury, 'The Black Death', reprinted above pp. 200–17.

If the medieval countryside had indeed been choked with people as the Black Death evidence suggests that it was, then it would be wrong to think of the social structure as an edifice reared upon foundations of lesser small-holders. In a community with so many landless families,there was, presumably, throughout England, an even more extended social hierarchy in the village than the one that Dr Razi has revealed at Halesowen.[5] Villeins with full virgate-sized holdings formed a peasant aristocracy which looked down its nose at rung after rung of social inferiors, terminating at the bottom, not with cottagers, but with an even less-favoured group which doubtless even the cottagers could despise. Poverty in such circumstances was severe and incorrigible, being reflected in terms of tenure for land which left even the most favourably-placed villeins with much less of the net product of their farms than the size of their holdings might lead one to suppose that they enjoyed.

In England, before the Black Death, landlordism was not the cause of peasant poverty. Nor can landlordism take the blame for the narrowness of the markets patronised by the overwhelming mass of the people. Landlordism was the inevitable result of the conditions that prevailed at the time. Land reform is the cry of political activists throughout history. But land reform is always foredoomed because wherever the call is for changes in the laws of tenure, for the cancellation of indebtedness and for the redistribution of the land, reformers inevitably find, whenever they have dispossessed the landlord, that the sub-marginal peasant remains.

Seen in this light, feudalism was not, as it is so often made out to have been, a repressive system imposed upon the social structure, creating an environment in which everything conspired to obstruct development and paralyse enterprise. It was simply one of the forms that landlordism, particularly military landlordism, took when pressure on the land created scarcities that the social structure was bound to reflect. Consequently when certain prominent features of feudalism decayed, as they did in the fifteenth century, when pressure relaxed as a result of the Black Death, they did so because landlordism was temporarily on the defensive. By the end of that century, however, the Black Death had begun to lose its virulence. Thereafter feudalism was partially restored; and landlordism came back in strength; thus demonstrating that feudalism as a system of oppression was either unnecessary or unenforceable: unnecessary when land shortage dominated social relationships, and unenforceable when it did not. Serfdom, defined as a specific condition rather than used as a synonym for a state of general dependence or subjugation, only succeeded in shackling people when they had been immobilised for other reasons. And in the sixteenth century, landlords found other ways, or other names for traditional ways, in which to assert a power which they owed to circumstances and not to themselves.

The limitations upon development that we see illustrated in these various

5 Z. Razi, *Life, Marriage and Death in a Medieval Parish* (Cambridge, 1980).

ways imposed severe restrictions upon the range and scope of markets. Patterns of expenditure are determined by the distribution of income; and markets can do very little to work those miracles of liberation, with which they are credited by certain modern social thinkers, when prevailing conditions narrowly circumscribe variations in the distribution of income. These conditions, with one or two notable but temporary intermissions, endured for a very long time. For how long it is impossible to say. Historians make it harder than it need be for us to appreciate the timelessness of this phase of human experience because, if they are to hold children from play and old men from the chimney corner, they must depict the past as a drama, with movement, crisis and denouement. It is no accident that the word crisis, once the prerogative of the newspaper-headline writer, should have been borrowed by the historian who now features it quite regularly as the integrating theme of his narrative. The headline writer uses the word in order to arrest the reader's attention. At the heart of every successful news story lies a drama. Much the same is true of memorable stories about the past. But the urge to tell the story of the past so as to give evolutionary significance to everything that happens can easily tempt the historian into concealing the fact that many things can change without anything developing.

Strictly speaking, therefore, there can be no economic history of this long period, only an economic analysis of its prevailing features and a diary of events. The rise and fall of empires, the irrevocable disruption, through schism, of the institutions of ecclesiasticism, even the advent of radically new fashions in thought, seem to have made little impression on a succession of social systems in which farms, variously known as villas, colonates and manors, were fundamentally indistinguishable from one another in structure and operation. And the testimony of historians to the contrary, is bound to leave the reader nervously exhausted by a succession of inconclusive dramatic climaxes when he finds, after centuries of evolution, that society, at bottom, looks very much the same at the end as it had done at the beginning; when he finds, for example, that the peasants of Hardy's Wessex lived lives which differed only superficially from the lives lived by their forebears in Alfred's Wessex.

Society is always local in such circumstances. At best it may be federal. Consequently loyalties are usually circumscribed by family and lordship rather than enlarged by remoter allegiances to church and state. Politically, therefore, Europe in these centuries consisted of a congeries of tribal or near-tribal groups organised into a dissolving succession of wider, mainly dynastic, federations, and interspersed by city-states. Conquest somtimes extended the area of political control. But empires rarely survived their creators. Rome was the exception in this, not the rule. It was lucky in its timing as Napoleon was in his. It expanded into a political void, as Napoleon did. And it was lucky in having internal lines of communication. Its empire was organised round the perimeter of an inland sea. With the fall of the western Roman empire, the secret of empire-building in western Europe passed from the territorial successors of Rome to the Christian church, which maintained its universal dominion by taking the city-state as its model and spiritualising it into the diocese.

Naturally there were exceptional periods when social relationships were disrupted. Usually such periods are associated with population movements such as the Barbarian invasions or the Black Death. Subsequently traditional relationships reassert themselves; and when we can once more examine and analyse society we find that the realities of social life have not changed, however different the names of things may be.

The markets that characterised this long phase of human development were of two main types. One was local in range and narrow in provenance. The other was cosmopolitan and sophisticated. Inevitably these two main types of market interacted. In particular, they interacted when the products of local farming or industry entered into international trade. And the best-attested case of this is the medieval English wool trade.

The average medieval sheep yielded about 1½ lb of wool. This meant that it took 243 sheep to fill a sack of wool weighing 364 lb. At the height of the wool export trade some 30,000 sacks went abroad annually. This required the wool of over seven and a quarter million sheep. Only the very largest landed estates kept flocks which produced as much as 50 sacks of wool. Canterbury Cathedral Priory, one of the biggest of them, with about 14,000 sheep in the early fourteenth century, could and did. But there were very few estates in Canterbury's league. This meant that the export trade had to call on the resources of smaller farmers. To possess 200 sheep marked you out as a man of substance in most medieval social circles. But the wool of 200 sheep would not fill a sack. The export trade obviously had to reach deep into the farming community for its huge requirements. And the export trade was only one part of the wool trade. Everyone wore woollen clothing even though many wore only second-hand clothing. Clearly local farmers of humble status were making their tiny contributions, perhaps no more than a few pounds-weight at a time, through their local markets, to the huge tribute of wool that went abroad to pay for the food, drink, clothing, ornaments and the like, that diverted the tedium of life for the landed classes, or went elsewhere within the country to be made up into cloth for domestic consumption.[6]

Historians are always tempted to welcome any commercial influence that reaches into the recesses of the marketing system as an earnest of better things to come. But any exchange is not necessarily better than none. The landed classes whose needs were the main impetus behind foreign trade, and hence behind the most powerful of the forces linking local trade with regional and even national trade, generated these forces by spending the rents that deprived those who paid them of the means with which to bid for goods and services in local markets. Dispossessing the landowning classes, if such an idea had occurred to anyone in ancient and medieval times, would

6   A. R. Bridbury, 'Before the Black Death', reprinted above pp. 180–99.

not have proved to be the panacea that generations of more recent reformers have seen it to be, because the fundamental problem of mass poverty caused by high rents must be traced to the insatiable propensity of populations of every species to fill any area favourable to its occupation.

Trade raises productivity by way of specialisation and thus undoubtedly creates more wealth than it destroys. But in these periods transport costs severely limited the gains from trade. Moreover in conditions of labour abundance any gains from the specialisation of labour enriched neither the labourers nor their employers, nor even perhaps their employers' suppliers, all of whom competed for work on the keenest terms. Somewhere along the chain of supply certain international merchants competed on less onerous terms and took a greater share of the gains than they might otherwise have done, and certainly a greater share than ever fell to the regrators, forestallers and engrossers of notorious repute in internal markets. But there was enough competition even in the handling trade to ensure that a very great deal, if not most, of the gains of trade were garnered by those who entered the market as final consumers. In short, the spending of their incomes from rent did more for those who enjoyed the right to receive rents than for anyone else.

Thus for all the glamour of its achievements, long-distance trade, like so much else that was done for the landed classes, could do no more for the substantive development of successive economic systems than the building industry, whose most glamorous products also dominate our recollections of the outstanding achievements of past societies. Cathedrals were technologically the most sophisticated products of medieval industrial enterprise. Yet the skills developed by those who worked in the industry, the employment provided, even the product itself were, like the skills, employment and products of international trade, without beneficial ramifications for economies which were choked with labour, and in which, therefore, rent charges dominated income distribution.

It is for this reason, perhaps, that wherever we look in the historical record we find societies, otherwise primitive and even stagnant economically, which nevertheless supported a trading and even an industrial system as advanced as any to be found in the most progressive regions of Europe on the eve of the Industrial Revolution. Elaborate specialisation of function in producing hand-mirrors and similar baubles was, so far as we can tell, commonplace in Roman Italy. Trade routes which traversed ocean and desert, negotiated high mountain passes and marched across endless plains, were to be found in virtually all such societies. And we know from the detailed evidence that survives from the Middle Ages that such routes were used by merchants of many races and creeds; that freights were financed and insured by bankers whose methods of business would have excited the admiration of their nineteenth-century counterparts; and that goods were carried by ships and in caravans which ran scheduled services and achieved punctual delivery times at a multiplicity of markets and fairs throughout Europe and the Middle and Far East. But the extraordinary achievements of such international marketing ventures did nothing to rescue them from ultimate sterility.[7]

Wherever we find such hurryings and scurryings on behalf of the landed classes, we also find that urban development follows. Historical interest in markets had recently been supplemented by the study of towns. But the towns that grew out of a rack-rented countryside owed their development, if not their origins, to the same forces that created and promoted spectacular trade routes and the intricately specialised products that travelled along them. Some of these towns succeeded in swelling to monstrous dimensions; and historians are naturally tempted to see in them, as in other evidence of economic maturity, intimations of future achievement, engines of economic growth, milestones along the hard road down which economic progress had to be made. But the interest of all these developments for historians is to be found, surely, in precisely the opposite sense: in their sterile precocity, their absolute failure to carry any lesson or influence beyond the enclave to which they owed their existence, and also in their extraordinary capacity to reassert themselves whenever conditions favoured them. The reason why so much of the economic history of these ages gives the reader a sense of déjà vu is just because successive societies, however unrelated culturally or in other ways, seem to have been able to reproduce the skills of the long-distant merchant and the expertise of the specialist manufacturer, without borrowing or inheritance; and to have been able to build and run the huge towns from which such men so often operated with equal success wherever we find them.

The purchasing power that made possible these prodigies of commercial organisation did not depend exclusively upon the wealth of the landed classes. It also depended upon governments, because governments enter the commercial system as buyers in every age. And the bigger the political units controlled by governments, the wider the catchment area for taxation and the richer the government buyer. It is easy to understand why the Roman empire could build on such a prodigious scale. There was plenty of money from extensive imperial resources for investment in public grandeur. In the Middle Ages only the Church comprehended a realm of imperial dimensions. And it is easy to understand why the Church was able to out-build everyone else. Compulsory tribute flowed in from all parts of the Western world; and compulsory tribute was lavishly supplemented by voluntary contributions. Secular kingdoms, in the Middle Ages, could not spend on this scale. The incorrigible fragmentation of political society that was characteristic of the time meant that there were many governments rather than just a few, so that none controlled large resources. This curtailed foreign policy; for in the Middle Ages government stood, more than for anything else, for the pursuit of objectives abroad. At a time when the regions of Europe were all locked in a timeless vicious circle of low productivity, narrow markets, high rents and endless servitude, what else was there for governments to do?

---

[7] K. N. Chaudhuri, *Trade and Civilisation in the Indian Ocean* (Cambridge, 1985).

Domestic policy meant dispensing patronage to allies and friends and keeping the mass of the peasantry docile by treating welfare mainly as a problem of law and order. Everyone who could, gave alms. But sensible men knew the problem was not a simple one of maldistribution of resources, and gave alms, as we have seen, partly as an insurance against insurrection, and partly as a pledge of redemption in the world to come.

Curtailing foreign policy meant curtailing war. Despite its reputation, therefore, the Middle Ages was a period during which war was far less disruptive of peaceful pursuits than it could have been, at contemporary levels of technology, in different political circumstances. Countries had to be big before wars could be seriously destructive. Where countries were small, governments quickly ran out of money and hence out of men. When small countries, such as England and France were in the fourteenth century, attempted to fight a big war, they promptly went bankrupt, and having bankrupted everyone who might be able to lend them the money required for the prosecution of a big war, found themselves compelled to fight more modest wars thereafter. Exceptional wealth, as in the Italian city-states, was undoubtedly a substitute for size: wealthy communities could hire mercenaries in a world in which men were cheap. But this was unusual. During the Middle Ages, therefore, there were many small wars rather than few big ones. Long periods of peace were unknown because such periods required the undisputed ascendancy over wide regions of a single political power, such as Rome. Until trouble began to brew beyond the imperial frontiers, Rome maintained an order which was only broken when members of the ruling class, having destroyed all possible external opposition, fell out with one another. The multiplication of centres of political power, in the Middle Ages, set the stage for centuries of frequent wars but limited warfare.

Armies could still do a good deal of damage, however, notwithstanding the medieval limitations upon their size and strength. But damage, from an economic point of view, ought to be measured, not in terms of lives lost or capital destroyed, but in terms of the recuperative power of the social and economic system. Technology has been neutral, in this respect, more often than we always appreciate, because improvements in the means of destruction at the disposal of combatants, which have an immediate impact, are often accompanied by improvements in the means available to those who have to make good the damage done once the war is over, which may be just as important but not so obvious. In the Middle Ages, however, technology was neutral because improvements made in the techniques of fighting were not such as to make wars more destructive than they had been in earlier times. Other considerations were more important. The high level of self-sufficiency that spelt poverty for the mass of the people had the dubious advantage that it limited the dislocation that war could cause. And the low level of capital formation characteristic of such societies meant that there was very little to destroy. Scarcity, in such matters, makes everything there is correspondingly more precious. But there was nothing that men could not quickly replace. Manpower was the easiest of all to replace: there was no shortage of men. Homes, and therefore whole villages, could be rebuilt virtually overnight.[8] Oxen for ploughs, and seed-corn, were more difficult. But the records certainly convey the impression that recovery was never long delayed. When Edward III decided to keep the Scotch border quiet by devastating the countryside round about, he found that he could only do so by returning again and again to the area so as to keep recovery in check. The campaigns of 1334/5 and 1336, had to be followed up, therefore, by those of 1346 and 1356.[9] When the French attacked the leading towns on the south coast of England, in the fourteenth century, they were unable to check recovery in this way. Southampton, for example, was so seriously damaged by a Franco-Genoese fleet in October 1338 that the Italians, whose trade was vital to the port, took themselves off to Bristol until repairs, or the pacification of Italian fears, brought them back by the summer of 1341. With their return Southampton's trade, so far as we can measure it in the export figures, returned to normal.[10]

Effective contemporary propaganda, particularly in the form of French accounts of the devastation wrought by English armies in later fourteenth-century France, doubtless encourages us to believe that war could inflict permanent, or at any rate, serious material damage upon society. But if the evidence seems to show that it was unlikely to have been able to do so, because medieval warfare was generally small-scale and inconclusive, what the evidence cannot so easily show is the destruction of confidence that warfare can bring about. Confidence is harder to repair than homes. Those who spread fear and demoralisation, and thus increase the element of risk in holding markets and venturing capital in commercial enterprises, do far more damage than those who merely swoop and destroy without leaving their pray with lingering suspicions that they are able to return at will and do as much again. William the Conqueror's 'Harrying of the North' was clearly much more successful as a triumph of personality than as a punishment for insurgency.[11] And in medieval conditions it may very well have been the case that local violence, and even perhaps neighbourhood disturbances, particularly when these were the result of organised feuding could prove to be more damaging to economic life than formal warfare, in which armies so often consisted of little more than the combined retinues of their aristocratic leaders, and military operations were so often confined to casual skirmishing and raiding, that we are hardly justified in raising the manoeuvrings that took place to the dignity of campaigns.

8 W. Denton, *England in the Fifteenth Century* (1888); W. Greenwell, ed., *Boldon Buke*, Surtees Society, vol. 25 (1852) for the services of the villeins of Aucklandshire.
9 G. W. S. Barrow, 'The Aftermath of War', *Transactions of the Royal Historical Society*, vol. 28 (1978), pp. 124–5.
10 C. Platt, *Medieval Southampton* (1973), p. 111; E. M. Carus-Wilson and O. Coleman, *England's Export Trade 1275–1547* (Oxford, 1963).
11 W. E. Wightman, 'The Significance of "Waste" in the Yorkshire Domesday', *Northern History*, vol. 10 (1975).

Organised feuding was certainly a central fact of what we should nowadays deprecate as the hooliganism of the landed classes. When asked, by a nineteenth-century English traveller, how they spent their money, a Druze emir replied: 'we spend it on injuring one another'.[12] His reply would have appealed to representative members of the landed classes throughout medieval Europe. Nevertheless the disruptive effects of warfare, and of the anarchy created by warfare in its more informal manifestations as brigandage, piracy and feuding, were severely limited. Nothing illustrates this fact more vividly than the pattern of medieval political geography. According to that pattern England was the most progressive region in Europe, if we measure such things in terms of modern standards of nationhood; and the city-states were the most reactionary or even anachronistic elements in the political scene. Nowhere else in Europe did geography confer such advantages upon government as it did in England, where the land was flat, the area was small and compact, and the frontiers were sharply defined by the sea, if not always protected by it from the depredations of powerful neighbours. Offa's Dyke, completed at a time when England was far from unification, shows how important well-defined frontiers were thought to be, even then, by demonstrating what laborious efforts were made to secure them against the pinpricks of a weak neighbour.

These geographical advantages made it possible for the kings of England to wield immense power. Their control of the political and fiscal system was impressively effective and matured extraordinarily early. Abroad, medieval England had the reputation of dealing harshly with its kings. Perhaps Englishmen had to take their kings seriously because they were so much more powerful than rulers were elsewhere. Certainly English kings held by an unsecured tenancy. Between Hastings and Bosworth there were 19 of them, of whom no fewer than eight were either murdered or died, some in mysterious circumstances, as did William II, others just in time to avoid another sort of end, as did John. But they locked the social system together by providing the social hierarchy with a pinnacle and regulated the flow of patronage by redistributing the counters when they fell out of play. Nor was there anything factitious about their grip on English political life. The effective size of a political system can be measured by the degree of disintegration that sets in during periods of stress. When civil war broke out in England, the central institutions held firm. In France the story was very different. France was not merely England's nearest European neighbour; it was also, of all European countries, the one which was closest to England in political development. Yet in France civil war tore the country apart. Ireland, Scotland and Wales were always problem areas for England, but these were peripheral regions. Resistance to central authority in France often originated in the French heartlands.

Now this precocity in matters political might be thought to favour

---

[12] R. Owen, *The Middle East in the World Economy 1800–1914* (London, 1981), p. 19.

precocity in commercial and industrial affairs. Getting the political conditions right may not be a sufficient condition for economic advance; but, according to modern views on development, it is certainly a necessary one, England, to all appearances, fulfilled this condition in the Middle Ages. Did this in fact give England the edge over its rivals? To this question we are bound to give the answer that it did not. England may have been advanced politically, in the Middle Ages, according to modern ideas of political progress; but the most sophisticated commercial systems and the most highly developed industrial organisations were to be found where the political system accorded with classical notions of polity, namely in the city-states of northern Italy, the Low Countries and Germany, where the largest aggregations of mercantile wealth known to the Middle Ages were to be found. Quite obviously political fragmentation did not inhibit the growth of international banking; nor did it hinder the development of immensely successful industrial enterprises, particularly in clothmaking, based on extensive division of labour, long credits, distant markets and international raw material supplies.

What makes this evidence all the more relevant to the question at issue is the fact that, although the medieval world may have reproduced the city-state that was so familiar to classical times, it utterly failed to reproduce the comprehensive imperial control that gave the Roman city-state its incomparable distinction. In fact these medieval city-states, far from working together, or even tolerating one another, were constantly at one another's throats. Nor was that all. So far as a medieval city-state was concerned, all trade beyond its frontiers was foreign trade; and foreign trade, in the Middle Ages, was trade carried on virtually beyond the power of political authority. There was, it is true, an international law, rudimentary and undeveloped though it may have been. And there were treaties between powers. But, at bottom, retaliation was the only effective weapon to hand.

Nevertheless, as we can tell from many sources, difficult liquids like wine, bulky and delicate cargoes like wool, precious spices and textiles, metals, dyes, foodstuffs and an infinitely varied miscellany of other things, travelled regularly and extensively, by land and sea, throughout the Middle Ages, in war and peace, during periods when piracy and brigandage are said to have been rife and in quieter times. We can gauge how regular such travel could be by examining England's unique archive of foreign trade statistics. Such travel was not without risk, and hence cost; and such costs compounded all the other uncertainties of foreign trade: uncertainties about the reliability of ships and carts, about markets, about the condition of goods upon arrival at their destinations, about credit, about the foreign exchanges, about taxation, about commission agents, about the safety of goods which might be seized by foreign governments in retaliation for harm done to their citizens abroad, or in payment of debts incurred by fellow-merchants who shared nothing but a common nationality with those who were embroiled as a result of wrongs for which they bore no personal responsibility.

None of this appears to have inhibited the development of foreign trade in the Middle Ages, which changed direction and went through a variety of evolutionary phases that seem to indicate that the luxury markets with which the city-states were exclusively concerned were virtually unaffected by risk and uncertainty. Despite their extraordinarily elaborate specialisation, and hence dependence upon others, medieval city-states were able to cope with interruptions of flows of trade which ought to have played havoc with profits calculated on the basis of assumptions about prices to be paid for supplies and prices to be obtained for products, some of which had travelled from, or were about to travel to, the far limits of the known world. And yet exposed as they were, a great many of the leading merchants of the more famous city-states made more money out of commerce and industry than the members of any other communities of merchants to be found in medieval Europe.

The lessons to be learnt from the history of medieval foreign trade, about the influence of social and political factors upon economic relationships, are not without relevance to a study of domestic markets within a particular region. Even in England, beneath the carapace of national unity, feudal society reflected a social pattern which bore some resemblance to what prevailed internationally. Even in England, during the Middle Ages, each market, the preserve and prerogative of a manorial lord, stood to the rest as the potentates of rival feudal kingdoms did in the wider sphere of inter-national society.

Medieval markets were not always a matter of commercial activities which took place at certain times and places. They often consisted of current ideas about prices brought into equilibrium, or something like equilibrium, as a result of bidding and a response to bidding, which was unaided by the physical presence of participants at a known place and at an ascertainable time. Such markets were beyond manorial, and even beyond royal, control. The labour market was the outstanding example of this. Most markets, however, or more exactly, the markets we know most about, were to be found at established or appointed places and functioned at known times on recognised days. They were usually held on land. But a good deal of trade was done on board ships tied up at wharves at river-ports or sea-ports, or even anchored offshore or in mid-river. The famous galleys of Venice and Florence, for example, provided innumerable ports of call on their way north to the Low Countries, or on their way home, with all the colour and excite-ment of a floating bazaar.[13] Nor did markets always depend upon particular locations in quite this sense. Pedlars did a good deal of trade as they jour-neyed through the countryside and were so important even in London that fish salesmen were given a special dispensation to sell at will in the streets and lanes.[14] One man's trade done by chance encounter does not make a market. But in an economic system in which there was every material

---

[13] M. E. Mallett, The Florentine Galleys in the Fifteenth Century (Oxford, 1967).
[14] H. T. Riley, ed., Memorials of London (1868), p. 268.

inducement to substitute labour for capital in marketing, the pedlar was likely to have been an important element in distribution. We may surely assume, though we can never hope to prove, that pedlars went everywhere, plied a regular trade, maintained stable rounds, and even, perhaps, competed with one another for custom. Their work created an unusual sort of market by sophisticated modern Western standards, but it is difficult to see what marketing functions pedlars failed to perform.[15]

Much industrial work was sold speculatively in markets, either by craftsmen or their employers. Some, perhaps much, was sold by shopkeepers, stallholders and the like who had had no part in the manufacturing processes involved. But a good deal of industrial work was sold elsewhere than in markets by craftsmen who made to order. Again, a market for what they had to sell existed in the sense that known craftsmen were to be found, or craftsmen were to be found in known places, whose products could be had on terms whose limits were set by the easy availability of alternative supplies. Such products were not homogeneous; indeed the strength as well as the weakness of having something made to order was that in commissioning something that answered to your own particular needs you might very well find yourself lumbered with something that turned out to be not in the least what you had bargained for. But those who deal on these terms usually manage to make allowance for differences which were intended and disparities which were unforeseen, and of pricing things accordingly by reference to what is available elsewhere, Tailors, for example, were to be found everywhere in the Middle Ages: the Poll Taxes are full of them; and elsewhere, so far as medieval tailors were concerned, meant presumably what was available, ready-made or secondhand, in established markets. In such cases price formation depended upon a continuum of opportunities. In the last analysis, neither pedlar nor craftsman could impose upon his customer in normal circumstances because, by taking a little more trouble and incurring a little more expense, his customer could find something which was more nearly what he wanted in another place.

The market for labour was very much a market in this sense. Men were undoubtedly hired at fairs, as we can tell from the labour legislation.[16] But the impression one gets from the records is that relatively few were hired in this way. Manorial accounts do not tell us how hired labour was come by. But hired labour was very important in manorial farming; and since we do not hear of farm managers being paid their expenses for going to hiring fairs, the likelihood is that hired men were generally members of local families hired, so to speak, at the farm gate. And yet it would be quite wrong to say that

---

15 M. Spufford, *The Great Reclothing of Rural England* (1984) has recently attempted to sketch the later history of these 'petty traffickers'.

16 *Statutes of the Realm*, 25 Edw. III 2 c. i (1351). The statute actually required workers to foregather in the market towns, there to be hired publicly. But the contracts were to be for the entire year, so that it is likely that the words used were intended to apply to contracts made at the annual fairs rather than in the weekly markets.

there was no market for labour; for the manorial accounts show how quickly wage-rates responded to a general rise in prices and even to a general fall. Men voted with their feet. The labour market did not consist of a series of isolated pockets. We can tell that it did not from the problems created by the earliest exercise in the politics and economics of incomes policy.

When the Black Death seemed to threaten the labour supply, the king and his Parliament declared that no one should pay or demand wages which were higher than those current before the Black Death. An unsupported declaration of policy was likely to be fruitless, so courts of law were instituted to enforce the king's and Parliament's will. But more was required. This first exercise in incomes policy presently created the need for the first Settlement Law.[17] Members of Parliament, many of them no less important locally as landlords and farmers than they were influential as politicians, were forced to recognise that anyone who refused to pay more than statutory wages was bound to lose his labour because men who were offered such wages simply went elsewhere; and went, not just to neighbouring farmers, but away from the villages to which they belonged, to other districts where, presumably, they got work and pay with no questions asked. In this way wage-rates adjusted themselves in terms of supply and demand until they achieved some sort of equilibrium, and did so without benefit of formal marketing arrangements; and governments, in that characteristic way that governments in all ages seem to have, did their best to obstruct the path to equilibrium.

Other services, apart from labouring work on the farms, were also bought and sold without benefit of formal marketing. The range of such services, in an economic system in which labour was the cheapest factor of production, was immense. Most were provided, as many are today, by practitioners skilled, not only in their chosen callings, but also in the fine art of knowing what the market will bear. These have no special interest. But there is another group of services, some of which are no longer provided, others no longer paid for, as they used to be. This group includes all those services that expedited the processes of law and administration and provided loans for those who needed more money than they had got. The absence of formality in the arrangements made for the purchase of such services; the lack of uniformity in the services provided; and the clandestinity inseparable from the workings of markets which were either unlawful, like the market for loans, or were dependent upon conditions in which bids could be made, as they are at auctions, without arousing the competitive interest of potential rivals; all this means that we cannot possibly hope to find out how supply and demand were brought into equilibrium. Doubtless in such imperfect markets only a very rough and ready equilibrium was possible, with the equivalent of stocks being left unsold and consumers being left unprovided for, simply because the machinery of exchange functioned so badly. But

---

[17] *Statutes*, 12 Ric II c. 3 (1388).

markets are not important only when they work perfectly; nor are the important markets only the ones about which we are best informed.

All markets, whether domestic or foreign, depend for their survival upon the observance of certain norms of behaviour. Markets cannot function without a measure of confidence that merchants and merchandise will have safe passage wherever they happen to go; that contracts will be honoured, or if not honoured, then either enforced or compensated for; that dealings will be expressed in terms of a currency which, if not uniform and stable, will at any rate have the merit of being readily negotiable; and that weights and measures, if not standardised, will at any rate be familiar and acceptable to all the parties concerned. Fraud and collusion, if not kept within tolerable bounds, bring their own retribution in the end, because markets which became notorious for their cheats will not survive. Nor will they survive unless those who are enfranchised make some concessions to those whom they would rather exclude absolutely from the benefits of access to opportunities for profitable dealing, however unpalatable such concessions may be.

All these norms of behaviour were observed, by those engaged in foreign trade during the Middle Ages, not so much because governments imposed internationally agreed rules upon all who frequented the markets within their jurisdiction, but because of self-regulating mechanisms compounded of a balance of terror and a lively sense of mutual advantage felt by all members of the international mercantile community. Governments complicated and disrupted international mercantile relationships more than they promoted them, because foreign policy interests invariably took priority over other considerations.

Domestically much the same was true. Medieval markets operating within range of the authority of the kings of England were anything but free. Our earliest laws show English kings trying to force merchants to buy and sell before witnesses in authorised places.[18] Obviously there were many who preferred not to do so, and others with political influence who stood to gain by forcing them to inconvenience themselves, and hence their customers, by complying. Somewhat later, kings assumed the right to license markets; and licenses entailed the payment of a fee. Thereafter kings acted as willing instruments of the franchise holders' interests. They legislated against forestallers, regrators and engrossers, all of whom carried on their business outside the licensed markets rather than within them, and therefore to the franchise holders' loss. They legislated in favour of standardised weights and measures, though never with much success, to judge by the constant renewal the legislation required. But the enforcement of standards gave franchise holders a colourable excuse for imposing fines upon those who failed to conform. They sanctioned the foundation of innumerable craft associations in the towns, where so many of the country's markets were to be found; and

---

[18] I. Edward c. i, F. L. Attenborough, ed., *Laws of the Earliest English Kings* (1963), p. 115.

these craft associations promptly set about raising prices in the market-place by restricting recruitment, by limiting hours of work and by imposing quality controls which, in so far as they had any effect, reduced the supply of goods coming on to the market. And in the interests of law and order, they legislated to restrict the profits of bakers by requiring them, under supervision, to vary the weight but not the price of their bread so as to take account of variations in the supply of corn; and they legislated to restrict the profits of wine and ale sellers by having prices regulated locally, presumably on the grounds that disaffection was to be expected at all social levels if Englishmen were unable to get drunk without being fleeced.

But governments were by no means the only, or even perhaps, the main source of impediment to the operation of what we should recognise as a free-market system. Markets were profitable in the Middle Ages, not in the sense that anyone clever enough to attract trade to a particular centre could expect to make money out of those who came to spend and out of those who paid for stands or shops or for the services provided by inns or hostelries, but in the sense that trade and tradesmen were themselves fair game, legitimate victims of whatever depredations a franchise holder cared to visit on them. The countryside was a network of obstacles that trade had to surmount. There were tolls on goods entering and leaving markets; brokage was levied on sales; fines were imposed for breaches of regulations which had nothing to do with the maintenance of good order in markets; fees were exacted from those who used or were compelled to use communal services such as weigh-beams; and separate charges were made for the registration of bonds of obligation. Nor were these the only surcharges that franchise holders could impose on trade. Markets were, in the first instance, the property of those who were lords of the land upon which they stood. And such lords were at liberty to levy toll upon goods as they passed along roads and over bridges, along rivers and under bridges, within the boundaries of their lands.

Those who held market franchises had even more extensive powers. Indeed they enjoyed powers which were extra-territorial in the sense that they could enforce, or attempt to enforce, certain of their rights, over land that was not their own. This came about as a result of the nature of royal grants of markets. As a matter of abstract policy, that is to say, of policy with the politics left out, the king never knowingly granted a charter for a market which was to be sited in such close proximity to an existing market as to threaten its trade. Sometimes such eventualities could not be avoided. Towns might grow up side by side, as Wilton and Salisbury did. When that happened, each town depended upon having a market in order to survive. In such cases each market was assigned to a different day. This was a strategy with wider implications. In any particular region, the careful planning of markets for successive days, proved to be a boon to trade, and was recognised as such by everyone concerned, because it drew merchants to an area they might not have been so keen to visit had there been a clash of days or perhaps fewer markets within easy visiting distance. But many of these privileges and enforceable rights were likely to be extra-territorial in the sense that the catchment area for a particular market might very well extend beyond the territorial limit of its lord's lands. When neighbouring market lords fell foul of one another because one of them had allowed his market to trespass on days reserved for his rival's market, then the extra-territorial authority of market lords was plain for all to see: for the injured party had the right to seek the protection of the law in stopping what the offender was doing on his own land.

Some of these extra-territorial rights were very extensive and grievously harmful, because they enabled certain powerful franchise holders to shut down all rival markets within a stated distance for the duration of their own markets and fairs.[19]

The right to issue charters became important to the kings of England in the late twelfth and early thirteenth centuries, when a particularly sharp bout of inflation cut the real value of their revenues and drove them to search for sources of income which might help to restore their fortunes. The flood of charters that we find at that time, so often attributed to the growing prosperity of the age, may be interpreted equally well as the inevitable reaction of impecunious kings to an opportunity they had not previously needed to exploit. The flood created problems as well as opportunities for lords of markets. A chartered market was properly a market set up where it did not threaten an established market. But what was a threat? A flood of charters meant a flood of privileges; and privileges clashed. This created an anarchy of mutually incompatible claims and counter-claims. All manner of groups and many influential persons claimed exemption from dues charged by neighbours, rivals and the like. The situation was inextricably confused by the agreements entered into by particular places or persons. This in turn provoked litigation. A case law complicated the issues by urging the convention that earlier charters took precedence over later ones. And over the whole question, non-compliance, uncovenanted fees, power politics and patronage, exerted their familiar, and to us, insalubrious influence.

Exemption could be challenged on an infinite number of grounds. It could be challenged because it applied only to goods bought for personal use, not for trade; because it applied in markets but not in fairs; because it did not include trade in one particular commodity, which was always the commodity in question; because it extended only to the tenants of certain important personages; because it no longer had any validity since the place to which it had applied was no longer in the direct possession of the person who had obtained the exemption; because it was chronologically later than another charter conferring exemption on another group; because the privilege at issue had lapsed owing to the escheat of the land to the king; because it had lapsed through non-user; or because it applied to semi-finished but not to finished goods.

In such a labyrinth no one could be quite sure of where he stood. And

[19] E. Lipson, *The Economic History of England*, vol. 1 (7th edn) (1937), pp. 241–2.

what was worse, the local collector was king. What could a merchant do whose credentials were unexpectedly challenged? He could protest. But who would listen to him? A well-known merchant plying an established trade along familiar routes might be able to gather witnesses and prevail against wrongful demands for fees. But what if he could not? Wasn't a small toll better than confiscation? He had a choice, perhaps. If he were arriving rather than leaving, he could turn round and go home. But wasn't a small toll better than the loss of a day's, possibly a week's trading? Pay now and claim later must have been the motto of many merchants; and was it not, perhaps, their confidence that merchants preferred to pay that many toll-keepers exploited? Moreover, claims meant litigation; and litigation was no less of a gamble then than now; and whatever the decisions made they were no more likely to be observed afterwards than the rules they vindicated had been before.

There was another and perhaps even more powerful consideration. Markets were symbols of seigneurial power as well as sources of profit. It is arguable that they were more important as symbols than as profit-making organisms; for medieval markets were obviously much more than places for social foregathering and mutually beneficial exchange. They were places where privileges could be exercised and where privileges could be seen to be exercised. How important the exercise of these seigneurial powers was thought to be we can readily appreciate by following the fierce squabbles over trifling sums of money that some of the most powerful and influential landowners in the country engaged in. We can scarcely doubt from this evidence that prestige, not material interest, dominated their motives. Examples are legion and can be drawn from many spheres of life. Professor Southern in his survey of the medieval church, provides a very characteristic one from the papal archives of 1144. From this source we learn of a quarrel about a parish church in the diocese of Lichfield, worth perhaps £10 per year, which had been taken, by the exalted litigants involved, from Normandy to Rome, and from Rome to England, and which was then to be settled by representatives of an earl, an archdeacon, a Cathedral Chapter and two or three vicars or ex-vicars from both sides of the Channel, under the auspices of two English bishops acting with the Pope's authority.[20]

We make these struggles over status and power look ridiculous by concentrating upon the financial significance of what was at stake. But issues which were pursued with what looks like indefatigable litigiousness had other implications than financial ones. There was, as there always is in such cases, the question of precedents. A legal precedent, once established, though not irreversible, was a point gained. There was also the question of social strategy. The property you fail to seize or defend will fall into the hands of someone you would much rather deny it to. This was partly a matter of

[20] R. W. Southern, *Western Society and the Church in the Middle Ages* (Penguin Books, 1970), pp. 115–16.

prestige, and partly, again, a matter of scoring off others. We know these motives well in the sphere of international affairs. Why should we fail to recognise them in more homely settings? When America plunged into Pacific politics by acquiring the Philippines and Britain fought, only recently, to retain the Falklands, contemporaries witnessed pure examples of the genre. If we were to cost these excursions, we should arrive at results which were as ridiculous from the point of view of the material gains made by America and Britain as were those of the medieval litigants who pursued what they conceived to be their rights and interests beyond what we should regard as the limit of reasonable contention. But money was not the issue then any more than it is now. And if there is a difference between then and now, in such matters, then the difference is surely not to our credit; for there is always more point in squabbling over the spoils when there is little or no hope of increasing the size of the spoils-heap than there is when the effort put into squabbling could so easily produce a bigger heap. Consequently society was far more reasonably occupied in the Middle Ages in pursuing status rather than wealth than it is today when continuous economic growth produces greater wealth for comparatively little effort and improvements in status come only after strenuous exertion.

The impulse to maintain seigneurial rights at all costs and against all comers had to be disciplined and controlled, however, by the recognition that anyone who charged more than the market would bear stood to lose everything to the neighbouring rival who was content to charge somewhat less. We can read this recognition into virtually every complaint, and they are legion, that a franchise-holder's market rights are being infringed and his market's business is being diminished by a neighbour who is flouting chartered privileges and attracting merchants who used to frequent his market. The terms and the language of complaint may be medieval; but the tone of injured innocence stiffened by a suitable sense of outrage is one we all know well. It is competition that is being complained of; and competition, then as now, is always unfair, if not unlawful, when it threatens established interests.

Nor was this the only way in which we can see that medieval society was in large measure self-regulating. Successive English kings were gravely concerned about problems of law and order and created, in the course of the medieval centuries, an impressively complex apparatus of courts sustained by a variety of enforcement agencies which were themselves fortified by the lucrative practice of informing: in effect the putting-out system applied to social discipline. They even made provision for those who required special facilities for the quick and cheap resolution of mercantile disputes. We should be seriously mistaken, however, if we were to take these provisions at face value. The legal system consisted, after all, of a very small professional judiciary backed up by an amateur magistracy which ran a variety of local courts without anything like an adequate substitute for a police force.

There were obviously severe limitations to what could be accomplished by such a system; and indeed we should do the system a serious injustice if we were to assume that it failed in its purposes because it failed to accomplish what we should expect of it today. The law fulfils a social not an abstract function. It was important to medieval society as a means whereby men could adjust their relationships with one another without immediate resort to violence. At every social level the law courts provided a political arena and machinery for the arbitration of political, social and personal differences. Enforcement agencies filtered social discipline and political pressure through the system, sometimes by threatening court proceedings, and sometimes by making presentments. Procedural rituals in court offered opportunities for private negotiation between parties, and indeterminate court actions often signified settlements made out of court. Settlements may not always have been according to law. But they were triumphs of a sort if, through the mechanisms of the law, violence had been earthed instead of erupting into injury, damage, or seizure of property.

For the rest, the law was a form of outdoor relief for the landed classes who claimed most of the financial benefits of the system; and a gamble, a sort of informal lottery, for those for whom laws were mostly another kind of taxation. So far as most ordinary people were concerned, one either bought the right to ignore the law, or ignored it in the hope that one would never be caught, or if caught, merely cautioned or fined. It was the illegal parking syndrome. There were the unlucky ones, it is true, who were incarcerated in loathsome gaols or even hanged. But so far as markets are concerned, the system worked domestically as it did internationally, in the sense that intercourse between communities triumphed over a multiplicity of tiresome and frustrating obstacles.

It did not do so without cost. Crime had this in common with market franchises that it made conditions for trade more difficult than they would otherwise have been. There were limits, however, to what society would tolerate. The importance of franchises as a deterrent to trade was enormously diminished by widespread disregard of privileges, by failure to pay charges, by neglect of opportunities to impose them, and by skilful participation in the exemption game, in which all players were entitled to claim and counter-claim against franchise holders who clearly understood that competition between them could easily ruin the man who most stubbornly held out for what he conceived to be his rights. Crime was also contained within what medieval society could accept as reasonable bounds by social forces whose workings we can only follow when they surface in legal proceedings. Evidently these forces were tolerably successful; for most crime, as we see it in the records, was local and confined to familiars rather than general and anarchic. And we can measure their success, in other ways, by examining the expectations that lay behind certain established and well-known patterns of medieval behaviour.

The entire manorial system, for example, was organised upon the basis of everyone involved confidently expecting that money, goods and travellers, committed to regular journeys along familiar routes at ascertainable times of the year, would arrive unharmed and unmolested at their destinations. Manorial lords toured their estates for many reasons, not the least of which was that it was cheaper to move the household than the crops. But the chief product of the manor was, generally speaking, money not farm produce; and, as a rule, money could not be spent where it was earned. Consequently the roads were regularly used by manorial bailiffs or their deputies carrying money back to headquarters. It is certainly true that big consignments were escorted by armed men, as they are today. But the ordinary carriage of manorial rents and dues was not. If men had been hired for this purpose the costs would have been entered as a charge against income and itemised in the accounts. The fact that we rarely find such entries suggests that no special precautions were deemed to be necessary when fairly large sums of money were conveyed from manors to their manorial lords.

Markets and fairs were even more vulnerable than manorial cash to the attention of casual or organised brigandage. They were held at well-known places and at well-advertised times. Some of the biggest fairs were held in tiny places which, like St Ives in Huntingdonshire, were absurdly unsuitable from the point of view of security.[21] When they were in session they looked something like modern agricultural shows. But unlike modern shows, they lasted for weeks. Where everyone stayed is a mystery. Where valuable stocks were kept is another. The roads leading to such centres were probably crowded for days, before and after, with carts and animals loaded with precious, or at any rate, desirable things. The predictability of everything compounded the threat of pilferage or theft. Obviously marauding gangs and enterprising lone highwaymen were not the constant anxiety and imminent danger that we might have supposed they would be; for the big markets and fairs met and dispersed, year after year, and the violence that gets reported in connection with such occasions is generally the violence generated by heated argument over deals which have gone wrong rather than the violence of robbery.

Despite the wars, the civil unrest and the felonies, for which medieval England is still notorious in the historical literature, the evidence is overwhelming that the countryside was essentially tranquil. The toll books of the borough of Southampton, miraculous survivors of what may once have been a large class of records, show Southampton carters maintaining their uninterrupted itineraries throughout the fifteenth century, returning regularly for fresh loads, and taking them without escort to towns and villages all over the south of England.[22] The letters written by merchants and country gentlemen. some of them living, as the Pastons did, in what are supposed to have been very disturbed parts of England, bear out the message of the Southampton tolls. And when we consider the topography of the average English medieval town, what must strike us as forcibly as anything about it is that its defences,

---

[21] D. Usher, *Two Studies of Medieval Life* (Cambridge, 1953), draws an interesting portrait of medieval St Ives.
[22] O. Coleman, ed., *The Brokage Book of Southampton* (Southampton Record Society, 1960, 1961).

useful perhaps as a deterrent to wandering sheep, or as a formal warning to a trespassing vagrant, were hopelessly inadequate against anything or anybody more determined than that.

If, however, the countryside was as peaceful as it seems to have been, we are left with the problem of explaining how it was kept so. Certainly law enforcement is not the answer; for enforcement agencies lacked either the power or the will to do what had to be done in order to keep the peace. Indeed the habit of excusing anyone who was rich or influential enough to be worth favouring, from having to obey the law or accept the consequences of violating it, was one of the chief weaknesses of the system. It was mischievous according to the ethical standard that forbids a locksmith to sell a security system to one customer and the key to anyone with money enough to buy it. But in medieval circumstances it was one of the conditions upon which political stability depended. We must, of course, allow for the fact that life may not have been as peaceful in the Middle Ages as it would have had to be if it were to be judged peaceful by modern standards. And no amount of searching of the records can retrieve from past centuries contemporary notions of what constituted normal or tolerable behaviour, because what is taken for granted is never consciously expressed. Nevertheless whatever current medieval notions on the subject may have been, medieval society seems to have been able to maintain a remarkably elaborate network of communications; and did so presumably by exerting domestic and neighbourhood pressure upon deviants as well as by relying, more than we should today perhaps, upon self-defence and retaliation, resorting to the uncertain arbitrament of the law only in extreme or exceptional circumstances.

In these various ways, trade doubtless looked after itself within the country as it was forced to do, but with much less chance of success, internationally, where sanctions were fewer and weaker and conditions were therefore correspondingly harsher.

What then should we conclude about markets and freedom as a result of this somewhat prolix investigation of the social and economic environment in which markets operated in the course of the Middle Ages? Obviously it was not an environment in which markets themselves could function freely. A thousand obstacles, many formidable, others tenuous, impeded their activities at every turn. Nor was it an environment in which markets could have facilitated freedom of exchange even if they had been able to function with much greater freedom than they ever enjoyed. The social and economic structure of society determined income distribution, and income distribution, not market facilities, settled questions of purchasing power and patterns of consumption. Nor again was it an environment in which the activities of markets could have promoted political freedom, as we understand the term, however perfect markets may have been from the point of view of efficiency, and however favourable to exchange in terms of income distribution. And if it was not conducive to the growth of political freedom, the explanation is not to be found in some failure of the marketing system, but in our failure to understand that medieval people saw neither the individual nor political society in terms of the categories formulated by Locke.

Nor is there any reason why they should have seen either the individual or political society in Locke's terms. Increasing the efficacy of market mechanisms, and then proving the value of freedom of association by demonstrating how incomparably successful it is at making everyone better off, will not necessarily promote the cause of political freedom. To suppose that it will, or even could, is to substitute a materialist interpretation of history for a somewhat more agnostic and eclectic view which cannot rise to magniloquence but merely observes that if materialistic considerations had been paramount in human history then human history would have taken a vastly different course from the one that we can actually trace in the records. Wealth undoubtedly liberates. But wealth, like reason itself, supplies us with means, not ends. The market is not a politically creative leaven. Like education, it reflects social aspirations: it is never a prime mover in change. And medieval people would have been as unmoved by the suggestion that they ought to support political freedom because it pays, as most people are today.

English Provincial Towns in
the Later Middle Ages

Urban studies are very much the current fashion. But gloom pervades them. Towns are forever declining from some golden age in the distant and undefined past. Crises oppress them. Insoluble problems sap their vitality. If they are early into clothmaking, rural competition presently overwhelms them. If they have urban neighbours these soon supplant them, only to be overtaken in their turn by some local misfortune, as we are told that sixteenth-century Coventry was,[1] or by more general calamities. Once the theme has been proposed the evidence with which to support it seems to lie all about us. A grievance eloquently phrased, the lightest words of a passing traveller, a petition for relief acceded to by the king, evidence of falling property values or dilapidations – from insubstantial indications such as these, we may, apparently, draw sweeping conclusions about the economic fortunes of decades, sometimes of whole centuries, of urban history.

No argument in support of this defamatory campaign needs excessive scrutiny. If Hull declines it does so partly because York's decline in the fifteenth century has dragged it down. But if Southampton declines it does so in spite of Salisbury's rise to supremacy in clothmaking and its importance as an entrepôt for the region that uses Southampton as its port. Even Italian patronage of Southampton somehow counts against it. If certain towns are high in the tax lists that is because their tax is paid by one or two exceptionally rich men who happen to be citizens. But if townsmen are ever impoverished by the crippling obligations imposed upon them by civic extravagance that is because their rich fellow-citizens have bribed or bullied their way out of paying their share of a communal burden. If the towns are ruinous it shows in the decline of rents; but if merchants wax rich in them they demonstrate the quality of their commercial acumen by devoting substantial sums of money to investment in town property. 'Those who were pleading in 1474 that Cambridge was impoverished because craftsmen were leaving the town as scholars moved into it might not have cared to be reminded,' says Miss Coleman, 'that twenty years earlier the impoverishment of Oxford had been attributed to the withdrawal of scholars because there were no artisans.'[2] Urban historians are not always so fastidious.

[1] C. Phythian-Adams, *Desolation of a City* (Cambridge, 1979).
[2] D. C. Coleman and A. H. John, eds, *Trade, Government and Economy in Pre-Industrial England* (1976), p. 101.

The later Middle Ages may have been the one period before modern times when ordinary people could vote with their feet if they found that they could not vote with their hands. Yet we are asked to believe that in the towns of later medieval England generations of young men who were perfectly capable of making a success of commerce and industry wherever they went nevertheless submitted themselves to an oppressive regime in a faltering environment rather than strike out in more auspicious surroundings with better prospects elsewhere. Can we really believe that the provincial towns of later medieval England would have avoided the fate of Old Sarum if they had been as obstructive to ambition and as debilitated economically as they are so often depicted?

I

We cannot wonder that later medieval towns should have succeeded in conveying an impression of chronic shortage of population and irretrievable deficiency of revenue. They meant to persuade the king that their burden of civic obligations was hopelessly onerous and that the fiscal demands they had to meet were beyond their means. Towns were extremely well represented in parliament. Even when many of their seats had been taken over by lawyers and country gentlemen with little knowledge and less interest in their needs, the more influential boroughs continued to be represented by members drawn from the ranks of the more substantial citizens.[3] And these borough members made skilful use of their privileged access to the seat of political power. Newcastle complained of the Scots;[4] Shrewsbury of the Welsh.[5] East coast ports like Ipswich and Yarmouth complained of the effects of the sea;[6] south coast ports like Melcombe, Lyme or Rottingdean, of the French.[7] Towns which could hardly use these particular pretexts complained of impoverishment by fire, as Andover did,[8] or of the financial strain caused by the cost of maintaining their walls, as Norwich and Colchester did.[9]

On the whole the towns were very successful in their advocacy. The borough members, despite the dilution of their numbers by interlopers, were still formidable numerically. Their influence was by no means proportionate to their numbers; but the king, whose dependence upon the Commons for supply did not always end when the war was in abeyance, could hardly have failed to appreciate that, with a little discreet management, the borough

---

3   M. McKisack, *The Parliamentary Representation of the English Boroughs* (Oxford, 1932), ch. v, *passim*.
4   *Rotuli Parliamentorum*, iii, p. 518.
5   *Ibid.*, p. 618.
6   *Ibid.*, p. 514, Sc8/113, no. 5609; *Rot. Parl.*, iii, p. 620.
7   *Ibid.*, pp. 639; 618, 640; iv, p. 160, Sc8/24 no. 1170.
8   Sc8/90 no. 4477.
9   *Rot. Parl.*, iii, p. 637; Sc8/101 no. 5013.

members might be persuaded to use such influence as they had to make the passage of his business somewhat easier than it sometimes proved to be. Accordingly the petitions they submitted and the evidence they adduced in support of their appeals made a case which the king was, perhaps, prepared to find cogent. Whether their submissions impressed him or not, they unquestionably determined his policy; for he made large concessions to urban petitioners. And they have certainly impressed recent writers, who have taken the king's sympathetic response as proof that the towns were as poor and decayed as they had endeavoured to persuade the King to believe they were.

It is indeed very difficult not to be impressed by testimony which appears to offer indisputable evidence that the provincial towns of later medieval England were, in the words of an earlier statute of Henry VIII, 'fallen in ruin and decay and not inhabited with merchants and men of such substance as they were', and had become places where, in the words of a later statute of Henry VIII, 'in times past have been beautiful dwelling houses there well inhabited which at this day much part thereof is desolate and void grounds with pits cellars and vaults lying open and uncovered very perilous for people to go by in the night without jeopardy of life . . .'[10]

That the towns were much less populous than they had been is beyond dispute. When the population of England contracted as a result of fourteenth-century pestilence, towns lost proportionately more of their inhabitants than the countryside, partly because pestilence took, and continued to take, a heavier toll from those who dwelt in comparatively close proximity to one another in towns than it did from the more dispersed communities of village and hamlet,[11] and partly because towns no longer attracted surplus labour from the countryside once pestilence had emptied the farms.

When population pressure had filled the villages beyond their capacity to employ all the men, women, and children who needed work simply in order to survive, towns had lured the more venturesome of them, not because there was a mayor's mace in every ambitious peasant's wallet, but because there were opportunities for work in towns that the countryside simply could not match. This meant that when population pressure was at its most intense towns supported populations which may have been very much bigger than they needed to be in order to carry out the functions for which they had been developed. The outstanding topographical symptom of this elephantiasis was the extraordinary growth of suburbs. Dr Keane in an important paper has recently drawn attention to the impressive evidence of this development which has been accumulating almost unnoticed under our eyes.[12]

---

[10] *Statutes of the Realm*, iii, pp. 531, 768–9, 875, 959.
[11] R. S. Gottfried, *Epidemic Disease in Fifteenth-Century England* (Rutgers, NJ, 1978), pp. 138–42.
[12] D J. Keane, 'Suburban Growth', in M. W. Barley, ed., *The Plans and Topography of Medieval Towns* (The Council for British Archaeology, Research Report no. 14, 1976). When Parliament granted a ninth in 1340 it was specifically stated that merchants not

Once this pressure had subsided, however, there was so much to be done on the farms, and so much to be made out of farming, that towns lost this particular attraction. If young men and women left the farms for the towns, in the later Middle Ages, it was no longer in the spirit of ship-wrecked sailors struggling to a life-raft. By then they made the transition from countryside to town in the lively expectation that they were exchanging good prospects for better ones; and parliament which knew all about their power of choice and its consequences took a high moral tone with parents who encouraged their children to forsake husbandry for apprenticeships when husbandry was languishing for want of men.[13]

The towns were not replenished by such movements. It is very likely that merchants and craftsmen, taken individually, did a better trade in the later Middle Ages than their predecessors had done before the pestilences. After all, over-population is only another way of saying that people are under-employed; and, more fully occupied, fewer men and women could have done the work formerly done by many. But this did not fill the towns as they had been filled before. Whatever we may reasonably assume about the growth of effective demand as a result of the betterment of the condition of the people after the Black Death, we cannot reasonably assume that the economy needed towns as big as they had been in earlier days, or perhaps as numerous. Consequently when they claimed that houses, streets, and even, in extreme cases, entire quarters, which had once been crowded and full of life, were, by the later Middle Ages, empty and unfrequented, we cannot doubt but that the towns were describing things, substantially, as they were.

This means that obligations for the payment of fee-farms and parliamentary subsidies which the towns had incurred before the pestilences were not necessarily appropriate to the circumstances of the period after the pestilences when the towns were no longer choked with people. When full, the towns had been able to charge high rents, to impose innumerable court fines, and levy substantial tolls, not because their citizens and visitors were prosperous – far from it – but because there were so many of them that total receipts easily met standing charges and normal expenses. Later, if they were to meet claims upon them which had been fixed when population was in spate, they could have done so only by increasing individual contributions, because the taxable community upon which they relied had got so much smaller. This they did not do; and historians who assume that the citizens of later medieval towns would have supplied any deficiencies of revenue that arose from this cause, had they been able to do so, conclude from their conspicuous failure to raise as much as they were required to do that the

dwelling in boroughs should pay a fifteenth. Some, no doubt, dwelt in the suburbs. *Rot. Parl.*, ii, p. 112, printed in A. R. Myers, ed., *English Historical Documents, IV, 1327–1485* (1969), p. 440.
13 *Statutes*, ii, pp. 57, 157–8; also A. Abram, *Social England in the Fifteenth Century* (1909), pp. 22–3.

citizens of the provincial towns of later medieval England were, on the whole, as poor as the towns they lived in were decayed.

This is certainly the obvious conclusion to draw. But before we decide that it is also the right conclusion to draw, we must make sure that we are justified in deciding that taxpayers who failed to raise the levies to which they were committed failed to do so because the sums required were no longer within their means rather than because, like all taxpayers, they saw no reason why they should pay taxes which they could lawfully avoid.

The towns undoubtedly had a first-class *prima facie* case for relief. They did not need professional advocacy in order to be able to convince the king that they were emptier than hitherto: anyone who toured their streets could see for himself the deserted houses and abandoned streets. Nor did it require a statistician to point out to him that fewer citizens could not pay undiminished charges without putting their hands deeper into their pockets.

Moreover, there were other considerations. The chartered boroughs were more vulnerable to competition than they had been. When manorialism in the countryside was at its most demanding the towns were refuges from feudal importunity because their charters made them so. But in the later Middle Ages towns no longer required charters before they could expect to flourish. Their charters no longer safeguarded the older towns from unlicensed rivals. We can see from Quo Warranto proceedings how thirteenth-century towns trod upon one another's toes by encroaching upon one another's markets and by flouting one another's privileges. Did the burgess members of parliament recall these everlasting frictions and warn the king's advisors that any chartered borough which raised its taxes in order to pay the king's dues might find itself losing trade to neighbouring towns which had not followed suit, and then, perhaps, new blood, with the result that the king's revenues would be irreparably damaged? We know they told the king that the burden of taxation was the main cause of their distress. We know they complained that their citizens were drifting away. What more they said informally, after hours at Westminster, we cannot know. But we have no reason to believe that they failed to make a point as telling and obvious as that.

The king's concessions took many forms. Sometimes he reduced the fee-farms. Sometimes he granted remission of some fraction of the parliamentary subsidy. Sometimes he compensated a borough for the inadequacies of its taxable area by extending its jurisdiction into the surrounding countryside so that village peasants suddenly found themselves contributing to borough finances in such towns as Hull (1447), Coventry (1451), or Lincoln (1466), and in some cases even found themselves liable for civic office.[14]

Moreover, he did something else for the chartered boroughs, which had been done for some of them on occasion in the past,[15] about which little was

---

[14] *Victoria County History: Yorks. East Riding*, I, p. 4; *VCH Warwicks.*, VIII, pp. 40, 263; J. W. F. Hill, *Medieval Lincoln* (Cambridge, 1948), p. 281.
[15] Colin Platt, *Medieval Southampton* (1973), p. 120.

said and less is known: he allowed arrears of farm to accumulate with impunity until, like the debts of the nationalized industries, they had to be cancelled, only to accumulate inexorably once more. Madox gives an example of what may very well have been settled practice, but was most certainly not declared policy.[16] When Coventry was in arrears with its farm for a sum which was equivalent to nearly two decades of payments, the sheriffs of Coventry were instructed, in the year 1468, to distrain upon the land and goods of the mayor and men of Coventry. When they had done so, they returned that they had seized property of the mayor and men of Coventry to the extent that these persons had land or goods within the county. They valued what they had seized at 106s.

Anyone who turns over the pages of the Leet Book will know that Coventry was never at a loss to raise twice as much as it was required to pay annually for its farm, whenever it chose to make a gift or a loan to the reigning king. In 1471, only three years after the distraints, in addition to other heavy disbursements, it raised £200, which was equivalent to four years of its farm, in order to redeem its charter. At a time when loyalty and treachery were liable to change meaning overnight it had backed the wrong man. In 1524 its leading citizens paid more tax than almost any other merchants outside London.[17] Yet in 1468 this ridiculous sum of 106s was solemnly proferred, and, apparently, accepted without question or demur. Did observing the formalities of distraint exonerate the town from further probing of its financial affairs? presumably it did; for Coventry's burgesses continued to hand over to the king as gifts, or with culminating effrontery, as loans, the money they so punctiliously failed to pay in fee-farm; and Coventry's mayors continued to come and go in a steady and seemingly imperturbable succession.

II

The records of complaint and concession do not, by any means, make up, between them, a comprehensive register of the towns of England. There are significant gaps in the series; for debts which could accumulate without hope of redemption were not an equally serious problem for all towns. Ordinary chartered boroughs had no hesitation in urging the king to moderate his demands because, so they said, these demands bore so little relationship to their capacity to create wealth that they threatened to overwhelm them. Not all towns, however, were chartered boroughs; and not all chartered boroughs had the problem of the fee-farm. And when they had no legacy of inherited commitments against which to protest we cannot expect to find them

[16] T. Madox, *Firma Burgi* (1726), pp. 180, 217.
[17] M. D. Harris, ed., *The Coventry Leet Book*, pt. I (Early English Text Society, o.s., no. 134, 1907), pp. 37–8, 78–82, 125–9, 160–9, 174–80, 209–14, 236–42; pt. II (o.s., no. 135, 1908), pp. 370–1; W. G. Hoskins, *Provincial England* (1963), p. 73.

passionately proclaiming their weakness and impending collapse to the king, whatever their circumstances may have been in fact.

Any community which, by virtue of its economic functions, was a town in all but name, but which had no charter obligations to discharge and paid its contribution to the parliamentary subsidies at the rate at which it was assessed when it was deemed to be indistinguishable from any other settlement in the countryside, occupied a position in the world of later medieval England about which it could scarcely expect the king to express compassionate sympathy in the form of tangible concessions. Consequently, we cannot expect such places to make much of a stir in the public records. Yet there were many of them. It is now some years since Clapham demonstrated the vigour and variety possible in thirteenth-century manorial market towns which flourished with the aid of the very minimum of burghal privilege just below the level of formal civic status;[18] and Prof. Hilton has recently put together some suggestive evidence that what the tax commissioners of 1340 called *villae mercatoriae* formed an equally flourishing continuum in the later medieval hierarchy of towns.[19] Perhaps the most prosperous of these places were the cloth towns, such as Coggeshall or Lavenham. Who can say how large their aggregate contribution to trade and industry may have been?

Kindred to these towns were others which paid the parliamentary subsidies as towns, sent burgess members to parliament, but had no fee-farm for which to make annual penance in the later Middle Ages. These were the monastic and other ecclesiastical boroughs over which intractable ecclesiastical landlords had cast a spell of perpetual dependence.[20] History has dealt harshly with such landlords for granting facilities for trade to the urban communities on their estates, because trade was good for rents and profits, but for standing unshakably firm against any movement to elevate such urban communities into self-governing bodies in return for a fee-farm, because such movements threatened their share of subsequent improvements in rents and profits and compromised the dignity and honour of the church. But landlords who had clung so tenaciously to their rights were served out in full, in the later Middle Ages, when townsmen on ecclesiastical land, denied the privilege of farming their towns, found themselves untroubled by one of the chief legacies of the past against which so many chartered boroughs were driven, apparently by poverty, to protest.

One of the wealthiest towns in later medieval England, so we are told, was Salisbury. In law, Salisbury was the manor of the Bishop of Salisbury. Had the bishop granted his manor the full self-governing status its tenants had struggled so desperately to achieve in earlier days, successive generations of Salisbury notables would have had a fee-farm to answer for which no longer

---

18 J. H. Clapham, 'A Thirteenth-Century Market Town', *Cambridge Historical Journal*, vol. iv (1932/4), pp. 194–202.

19 R. H. Hilton, *The English Peasantry in the Later Middle Ages* (Oxford, 1975), ch. v.

20 N. M. Trenholme, *The English Monastic Boroughs* (Missouri, 1927).

corresponded with its size in terms of population, if not its wealth. But Salisbury, which the bishop had urbanized by charter, was not a self-governing community. Its citizens had no farm to pay. They discharged their obligations to their manorial lord simply by collecting and delivering to him whatever the year's trade had brought in. If receipts fluctuated, the fluctuations were the bishop's affair, not the town's. Since later medieval towns are reputed to have declined in prosperity as well as in size this means, presumably, that the citizens of Salisbury were requited later for the humiliation to which their predecessors had submitted in 1306 when the bishop won a famous victory over his insurgent tenants.[21]

If they were, then they had a curious way of celebrating it: for the fight for emancipation went on. And Salisbury was not the only ecclesiastical town in the later Middle Ages to carry on a hopeless and often costly struggle for emancipation with passion, and even with rancour, against a formidable adversary armed to the teeth with indefeasible legal rights. Exempt from the common lot, miraculously free from a burden of charges which so many later medieval chartered boroughs declared to be insupportable, Salisbury and other ecclesiastical towns apparently did not know when they were well off.

And their inexplicable pertinacity has another side to it. We hear about the plight of the chartered boroughs because so many of them were trying to persuade the king to lower their fee-farms. The ecclesiastical towns could not approach the king directly with a request for enfranchisement because this issue was one for their manorial lords to decide. But they involved the king in their struggles by conjuring legal titles out of nothing and testing them in the courts, or by provoking their lords into calling upon the king to keep them in order. They could hardly plead for a fee-farm, in such circumstances, on grounds of poverty, since poverty was the argument currently employed to secure wholesale remissions of fee-farm. Consequently, we can hardly expect to hear about the grievous condition of these towns in their submissions.

But can we doubt that pestilence emptied Salisbury as it emptied all the other towns of England? Can we doubt that Salisbury remained emptier than it had been before the pestilences even when it had recovered from the initial shock? We are often told that Salisbury was an exception to the rule that later medieval towns were in decline. Where is the proof of this? Whether we consider assessed wealth in 1334, or taxes paid in 1524, or even population size in 1377, there was always a whole range of towns in Salisbury's class. Many claimed to be impoverished in the later Middle Ages. Some are held up to us by historians as incomparable evidence of a general urban malaise. But if Salisbury were so exceptional why did it make no better showing in the statistics than they did? If the taxes they paid were so crippling how did these other towns manage to do well enough to rival Salisbury in wealth or size? Are we not left with the suspicion that the basis for the belief that Salisbury was exceptional in its prosperity, in the later

---

21 *Wiltshire Archaeological Magazine*, vol. xxxix (1916), pp. 203–19.

Middle Ages, is the circumstance that Salisbury was also exceptional amongst chartered boroughs in having no fee-farm to pay, and hence no excuse to plead for a reduction of its fee-farm on grounds of poverty?

III

At the other end of the range there were towns which claimed that what they were liable to pay in dues and taxes represented an altogether overwhelming and prostrating burden. These were the towns that suffered from the problem of the franchises. Many medieval towns contained enfranchised areas, or found themselves with franchises planted on their outskirts, or in their suburbs; and there is, perhaps, nothing which has contributed more copiously to the brooding and mephitic atmosphere of penury and neglect that hangs over the provincial towns of England, as depicted in virtually every modern account of their later medieval history, than the lamentations, protestations, and entreaties, uttered by those who spoke for places afflicted by what they alleged to be this special and disabling problem.

Franchises normally carried with them exemption from the duty of contributing to the more irksome civic charges. They were always a ganglion of irritation to town councils. We hear complaints about them in the thirteenth century, and even in the twelfth.[22] No doubt they were always envied and resented. But after the pestilences towns which included extensive franchises within their boundaries made the most of what they represented as their special misfortune. They claimed that they were doubly beset by having to meet customary liabilities with a population depleted, not merely by the mischances that all towns shared, but also by the migration of survivors from the unenfranchised quarters of town to those districts that enjoyed immunity from certain civic obligations.

The most notorious of these towns was fifteenth-century Lincoln. In central government records Lincoln appears with depressing regularity as one of the most necessitous of all the urban communities of England. It is often the focus of the greatest royal concern. It is, at one point, exonerated from payment of parliamentary subsidies for forty years. It is granted country parishes to the south whose taxable capacity is to help it with its desperate financial problems. It is also granted, in 1447, permission to acquire property in mortmain whose rents will enable it more easily to pay its way.[23]

A licence to acquire property may appear to be a whimsical, if not perverse, exercise of sardonic humour by the king, at the expense of a town which is acknowledged to be hopelessly sunk in debt. The petition that prompted the licence certainly explains a good deal. But it leaves us with

22 C. Gross, 'Mortmain in Medieval Boroughs', *American Historical Review*, vol. xii (1907).
23 Hill, *Medieval Lincoln*, pp. 272–3, citing CPR 1446–52, p. 80 (C66/464 25 Hen. VI pt. ii, m. 7).

problems as perplexing in their way as those it solves. It submitted that Lincoln was exceptionally disfavoured among towns because all the land and tenements in Close and Bailey, together with all the tenements of the Beaumont Fee with their appurtenances, amounting to half the city, were enfranchised and contributed nothing to the fee-farm, with the result that there were scarcely 200 persons in the city who were sufficiently well-off to be able to contribute to the charges.[24]

The petition did not claim, as we are often told it did, that there were only 200 citizens in the entire area that we are accustomed to visualizing when we think of medieval Lincoln. It claimed, quite simply, that the chartered but unenfranchised area had only got 200 sufficient citizens left. In 1421 trouble over the city's common seal brought 240 named citizens, and others not picked out by name, to a meeting.[25] Obviously there were so many more that the clerk gave up long before his list was complete. These were all presumably sufficient citizens: others would hardly have troubled themselves about such an issue. It is arguable that, between 1421 and 1447, pestilence had cut down their numbers. The Letter patent of 1447 recited that long-continued pestilence was one of the afflictions for which Lincoln had no answer. But it also mentioned that merchants were constantly leaving the city. We need not wonder that the Lincoln petitioners should claim that they were. Without some such claim Lincoln's attempt to get help with its fee-farm was exposed to the retort that loss of population was no worse for Lincoln than for other towns because Lincoln's farm was agreed to with the franchises in mind, since the franchises were already in existence when the charter was negotiated.

Nor need we puzzle as to where these merchants were said to be going. No formal statement by the town was enrolled on this point. According to Lincoln's historian, however, the enclave of Close and Bailey was obviously thriving commercially in the later fourteenth century. It was then that Lincoln's quarrel with the lords of its franchises became deeply embittered. It was also then that Lincoln increased the number of its bailiffs so as to spread the liabilities in case of civic default on standing charges. Moreover it was then that leading citizens took to offering large sums of money to be exonerated from civic office.[26]

The large sums are as puzzling as the mortmain licence. If later medieval Lincoln had really been split down the middle by the franchises then it would be reasonable to expect to find that Lincoln was a town which flourished in one quarter and languished in others; a town in which merchants could prosper, if they were careful, whilst the formal expression on the faces of civic notables reflected unappeasable anxiety and the civic tone was a disconsolate whine. But the citizens who bought exemption from office

---

[24] Sc8/121 no. 6024, printed in *Rot. Parl.*, iv, p. 313.
[25] Hill, *Medieval Lincoln*, p. 276.
[26] *Ibid.*, pp. 254–68.

carried on their businesses, presumably, in the unenfranchised districts; for those who were elected against their will were said to have fled to the franchises.[27] Why had they stayed so long if conditions in unenfranchised Lincoln were so bad and salvation so close at hand? Moreover the mortmain licence gave Lincoln permission to raise funds for the purchase of property with which to relieve the pressure of the fee-farm on civic funds. Yet this was of no interest or concern to those who had sought refuge in the enclaves of Close and Bailey. If so few remained, how did bankrupt Lincoln pay for the property it bought as a result of this licence?

The problem becomes even more perplexing when we discover that Lincoln's citizens managed to raise money readily enough when they saw a sound reason for doing so. They raised money, for example, to repave the streets of Lincoln and to rebuild its guildhall. Neither project was carried out at the time because the money was misappropriated. The commission empanelled to investigate the circumstances in which the money disappeared, was instructed, however, that 'great sums' had been raised for the purpose.[28]

Not all franchises were ancient. Some were recent. And the outcry against the new ones mechanically re-iterated the complaints raised against the old. In Cambridge, the sites acquired for King's College, and for student lodgings, were exempted by the king from payment of Parliamentary subsidies. The burgesses thereupon filed their objections. This exemption, they said, had thrown extra burdens on everyone else with the result that craftsmen were daily leaving town.[29] We need not take the disapprobation of the burgesses seriously. In Cambridge, as in Oxford, such displays of enmity were no more than passing incidents in the everlasting feud between town and gown. But they could hardly be more inappropriate than they were in the fifteenth century when lavish benefaction was transforming the physical appearance of the two university towns, creating thereby so much remunerative work that no established craftsman in his right mind was in the least likely to have turned his back on it all, simply to avoid paying a little more tax instead of a little less, always supposing that what the burgesses said about the tax burden had any truth in it whatsoever.[30]

IV

Even if we make an exception of the university towns, however, because we cannot believe that they declined when so much money was being poured into them for investment in buildings, and as income for those who worked in these buildings, the case for taking what other towns said about them-

---

27 *Ibid.*, p. 255.
28 *Ibid.*, p. 254 citing CPR 1391–6, p. 296.
29 *VCH Cambs.*, III, p. 13.
30 *VCH Oxford*, III and *VCH Cambs.*, III *passim*.

selves, at face value, is not a good one. Lincoln is only an outstanding example of a general problem. It is the problem of reconciling the urgent pleadings of the towns with the plain fact that the towns spent freely on a variety of things which, if we are to believe what they said, were well beyond their means.

Thus many of these hard-pressed towns embarked upon a policy of acquiring rents, in the later Middle Ages, in order to supplement sources of income traditionally appropriated to the discharge of such recurrent liabilities as the fee-farm. The policy was as widespread as it is well-known. And it is not a difficult one to understand. Town councils thought more naturally in terms of revenue appropriated to the payment of fee-farms than in terms of levying a rate for the purpose because fee-farms originally reflected the annual value of tolls, fines, rents, and the like, which, when conveyed by landlord to town, were subsequently expected to suffice for the discharge of the annual debt to the landlord. When they no longer did so, towns frequently complained, as Winchester did in 1410, that the revenues out of which the farm used to be paid were no longer adequate.[31] Winchester did not claim that it was too poor to make up the sum required, though by an understandable equivocation many towns doubtless claimed that they were too poor when what they really meant was that their appropriated revenues were no longer sufficient. Consequently, in looking for new ways in which to meet their standing charges, towns turned naturally to the acquisition of an income which could be appropriated to this purpose rather than to a general rate. And what, indeed, could be more fitting than that the wealthier citizens should donate, or sell to the town on generous terms, property whose rents would render the annual obligations more tolerable and perpetuate the memory of those who had made it possible to do so? But how could later medieval chartered boroughs, with their apparently intolerable fiscal burdens and their streets of decaying tenements, acquire so much income-generating property if their citizens had been as down on their luck as they said they were, and as we are so often told they were by modern historians?

Nor was this, by any means, the only way in which later medieval burgesses demonstrated their capacity for contributing handsomely to the costs of town life. This, after all, was the first age of incorporation; and incorporation was an expensive benefit.[32] Indeed, upon reflection, we may very well decide that it was more of a self-indulgent luxury than a benefit; for the grant of incorporation added far more to the lustre and prestige of a town than to its substantive power and influence. Incorporation was often accompanied by the grant of fresh privileges, or the concession of special rights. But these were accessory matters. A town did not have to be incorporated in order to be able to add to the number and value of its chartered franchises. Incorpor-

---

[31] Rot. Parl., iii, p. 641. Cf. a later petition in Myers, English Historical Documents, pp. 1096–7.
[32] M. Weinbaum, The Incorporation of Boroughs (Manchester, 1937).

ation certainly clarified what had been assumed, previously, to be the purport of the various clauses of borough charters. No doubt the law was becoming too complex for such matters to be left to chance. By the end of the four-teenth century most towns of any consequence retained a lawyer.[33] It was, perhaps, a sign that the law was already beyond the grasp of the untutored mercantile mind. But the lawyers were clearly making work for themselves rather than making themselves useful; for the urgent need of the age, so far as the towns were concerned, was for some form of protection for their officers against personal liability for civic debts. This the lawyers could not yet give them; and incorporation, as the Coventry example shows, still had a long way to go before it could protect mayors and aldermen from distraint.[34]

Nevertheless the burgesses of the biggest of England's provincial towns and sometimes of those that were most vulnerable financially, paid lavishly for the glamour of incorporation and, often enough, paid again for exemp-tion from the civic offices that made them liable for civic default despite incorporation. The evidence shows, in fact, that leading members of provin-cial town communities continued to seek exemption from office, not merely at first when the problem of accumulating debt was a new, or a fairly new one, but also later when the problem of civic debt was raised presumably wherever municipal affairs were discussed.

Those who were well-established in business when the towns were first made aware of the financial implication of population loss, had very little choice but to stay where they were and see the problem through. The records speak glibly enough of merchants drifting away. But a merchant who severs ties in this way probably forfeits capital and certainly sacrifices good-will. Wherever he starts up again, he does so at a disadvantage. If he stays where he is because the costs of going are certain and its advantages problematical, he does so because the municipal crisis hits him in mid-career. But what of his sons, or even more, what of the other young men who are not yet committed and therefore to some extent immobilized? Can we believe that successive generations of young men immolated themselves upon the altar of municipal extravagance by taking upon themselves burdens of office which they knew only too well had ruined their predecessors? Can we believe, indeed, that they did well enough in towns as destitute as later medieval towns claimed to have been even to contemplate the possibility of office? Yet on all sides, in the later Middle Ages, we see successive generations of

---

[33] This step was taken about a century later than it was taken by those with landed interests and regular business in the courts. J. R. Maddicott, *Law and Lordship* (*Past and Present*, Supplement no. 4, 1978), p. 12.

[34] W. S. Holdsworth, *A History of English Law*, vol. III (1909), pp. 367–9 shows that civic officials were protected from personal liability for certain corporate debts as a result of a judgement of 1442. But the evidence given by Madox is incontrovertible as to the personal liability of civic officials for debts owed to the king. A discussion of this point was recorded in the Year Book for 1429. Weinbaum seems to have overlooked it. See his *British Borough Charters, 1307–1660* (Cambridge, 1943), p. xxiv.

merchants pursuing successful careers in business, taking office, for whatever the repining the offices were filled, and retiring subsequently to the aldermanic ranks when active life was over, honoured and deferred to by all.

We do not require statistics in order to be able to show that this was so. But the freemen's lists have a significant contribution to make to our understanding of what was happening in the provincial towns of England at this period which it would be inexcusable to ignore. Naturally these lists must be handled with care. Should we want to know something about population size or occupational structure then, as Prof. Dobson has warned us, we had better approach them with circumspection.[35] But we must not conclude that the freemen's lists cannot answer any questions at all simply because they cannot answer all the questions we should like to ask of them. And if we want to know whether or not towns continued to attract burgess citizens after the major pestilences in the same sense and to the same extent as they had done before the pestilences then the freemen's lists, by telling us that there were often as many entrants later as there had been earlier tell us, in fact, something momentously important about later medieval towns. They tell us that in towns which were much less populous than they had been relatively more of those who lived in them, or merely worked in them, did so as burgesses.[36]

The sample extant, although random, is undoubtedly a poor one; but such as it is it confirms our expectations. It tells us that the abolition of land-hunger which, in the countryside, meant that the meanest peasant could aspire to a tenancy, meant, in the towns, better pay and conditions for the humblest wage-earners, and, for their employers, correspondingly higher remuneration and more exalted status.

If conditions of entry into the freedom had eased in the later Middle Ages so that the freemen's lists reflected changes of policy rather than changes in society then, naturally enough, the freemen's lists would tell us nothing of the sort. But the records do not tell of an easing of conditions of entry. If conditions of entry changed at all in the later Middle Ages they did so by becoming harder. Moreover when we find that the freedom of Norwich was sought, in the fifteenth century, by merchants who did not even live in Norwich and had no intention of doing so we are not entitled to assume, as one writer does, that Norwich had lost its power to attract new blood into the town. Since non-residence by freemen was nothing new in urban experience what these applications surely demonstrate is the extraordinary value set upon the freedom of Norwich by businessmen living in an age when feudal control of the countryside had virtually lapsed and unchartered towns were burgeoning.[37]

---

35 R. B. Dobson, 'Admissions to the freedom of the City of York in the Later Middle Ages', Economic History Review, 2nd ser., vol. xxvi (1973).
36 A. R. Bridbury, Economic Growth: England in the Later Middle Ages (1962), ch. iv.
37 C. Phythian-Adams, 'Urban Decay in Late Medieval England', in P. Abrams and E. A. Wrigley, eds, Towns in Societies (Cambridge, 1978), p. 179.

V

Are we not driven by all this evidence to the conclusion that despite the competition of other places and other occupations, life in the old chartered boroughs was still very sweet in the later Middle Ages; and that neither the costs that were inseparable from that life, nor the risks of office, deterred numerous young men from embarking upon careers which would take a few of them to positions in which they would have to spend freely and incur risks from which there was, as yet, no legal protection?

Prof. Dobson has recently drawn attention to what is perhaps the perfect illustration of the point at issue.[38] In 1518 William Dale, the junior sheriff of Bristol, complained to the court of Star Chamber that the sheriffs of Bristol were being ruined by the costs of office, with the result that their workmen were made idle and the town was depopulated. Dale alleged that 800 Bristol houses were empty at that time and blamed the bankrupting of successive generations of sheriffs for much of the trouble. Here we have all the classic symptoms of later medieval urban decay.

Fortunately for us, however, Dale submitted with his complaint a schedule of the charges for which the sheriffs were responsible; and still more fortunately we have the decision of the court. The decision was Wolsey's, so that we can be sure that his judgement reflected conventional medieval standards, and not some treacherous ferment of post-Reformation radicalism. From these documents it is perfectly clear, whatever else may be dubious or obscure, that Bristol citizens spent prodigiously, on feasting and junketing, as well as on liveries and ceremonial processions; and that Bristol's revenues were perfectly capable of meeting the normal charges incurred in running the town once these extravagances had been pruned. Wolsey disallowed many of these extravagances. But he allowed others to stand and therefore left the sheriffs with an annual deficit which, as someone commented at the time, 'is not for any honest person called to any worshipful room in any town to complain of': a sentiment, surely, with which every civic notable since would agree. Bristol in 1518, if we may judge by this case, was not a town ruined by crippling charges: it was a town in which extravagant men had simply over-spent themselves.

Whether over-spending was a singular predilection of the citizens of Bristol or a widespread characteristic of civic life, what we find elsewhere is unmistakable evidence that mercantile communities did not stint themselves. They indulged in lavish display of every description. Prof. Dobson has spoken of 'a veritable boom in the building or rebuilding of town halls within

---

38 R. B. Dobson, 'Urban Decline in Late Medieval England', *Transactions of the Royal Historical Society*, 5th ser., vol. xxvii (1977), p. 14, citing I. S. Leadam, ed., *Select Cases Before the King's Council in the Star Chamber*, II (Selden Society, 1911), pp. cii–cxviii, 142–65.

the largest [English] boroughs';[39] and if he hesitates to add to it a parallel boom in the renewal of urban parish churches, in the course of the later Middle Ages, he does so because the palpable evidence of perpendicular re-styling, with which every observant tourist is familiar, lacks precise dating. But precise dating only matters, in this context, if we have reason to believe that a substantial proportion of this perpendicular work was done after the phase of population loss, with which later medieval urban studies are pre-occupied, had come to an end. Can we really believe that it was? Prof. Dobson lists some of the most famous of the urban parish churches known to have been renovated or rebuilt in the later Middle Ages. His list could readily be lengthened many times even without venturing beyond the resources of the VCH.

Nor is it evidence against a boom in the rebuilding of urban parish churches that in towns like Winchester some were refurbished at a time when many others were ruinous. When the towns shrank many such churches, like the parishes they served, hung 'like a giant's robe about a dwarfish thief'. Others did not. These were repaired and renewed. We cannot take the fact that unwanted churches were abandoned as evidence of the vital decline of a town in which churches were cared for when they had congregations to serve. It would be a reckless presumption, in view of the impending publication of the second volume of the monumental history of Winchester that is so actively in progress, to be categorical about any aspect of Winchester's later medieval history; but when Furley states that Winchester derived a 'considerable income' from city rents acquired in the fifteenth century, he confirms suspicions that Winchester's unrepaired parish churches were not neglected because the citizens of Winchester were too poor to do anything about them.[40]

Those who found the money for town halls and parish churches, for the paving of the streets and, sometimes, for the improvement of the water supply and the upkeep of important bridges in the neighbourhood, did not confine their public works to the more sober preoccupations and the more prosaic needs of their fellow-townsmen. We have seen how the citizens of Bristol indulged themselves in public festival and display; and we can see from Mr Phythian-Adams' calendar of the communal year in later medieval Coventry that other provincial towns probably differed from Bristol in the scale rather than the range of their public ceremonies and convivialities.[41]

Those who spent so freely on public amenity and the communal life of towns are not likely to have denied themselves the public as well as the private satisfaction of a sumptuous, if not a grandiose, domesticity. If communal and public investment suggest that the towns of the later Middle Ages reflected the animation and vitality of the economy of the later Middle

---

[39] Dobson, 'Urban Decline', p. 7.
[40] J. S. Furley, *City Government of Winchester* (Oxford, 1923), p. 109 n. 1.
[41] C. Phythian-Adams, 'Ceremony and the Citizen', in P. Clark and P. Slack, eds, *Crisis and Order* (1972).

Ages, then private investment, in the form of houses and tenements of every description, could we but guess at its magnitude, might very well indicate how substantial was the personal wealth generated in the towns by the economy's multifarious activities. In aggregate, the private building and personal consumption that took place in later medieval towns probably far exceeded the poorly documented but clearly discernible expenditure on public building and communal affairs. We know next to nothing about such private building and personal consumption. But we are not entitled to ignore it, and by ignoring to discount it, simply because we do not know in detail how to assess it.

VI

What then are we to make of the urban protest movement which has so deeply impressed modern historians of later medieval towns? We can see how flimsy were the excuses that the towns sometimes offered in extenuation of their defaults; how sophistical their arguments; how fraudulent many of their claims, their recriminations, their alarmist predictions; how specious their abject entreaties. Was there no substance whatsoever in what they said?

The taxation evidence strongly suggests that the burden of standing charges carried by the chartered boroughs of England in the later Middle Ages was not what it was made out to be. If we take the parliamentary subsidies that the towns agreed to pay in 1334, when the assessments were revised for what turned out to be the last time, and divide them by the population figures returned by the Poll Tax commissioners of 1377, we get a dividend which seems to show that the burden of charges upon the chartered boroughs, when parliament granted the king a subsidy, represented a *per capita* levy upon the working populations of such towns of something like double the daily wage without food authorized for women harvesters by the statute of 1445.[42]

Table I gives the results for towns with an assessed value in 1334 of £500 and over.

It would be wrong to give the impression that everyone contributed when money had to be raised for a subsidy or a gift. At Coventry, where the Leet Book records the names of those who subscribed to loans and gifts to the king between 1421 and 1449, we can see that, generally speaking, 600 or 700 citizens raised all the money that was required.[43] At Salisbury the Ledger Books are less informative; but when lists of contributors are to be found they show that several hundred citizens paid for all. Clearly the burden of parliamentary subsidies upon the taxpaying classes was greater than it would

---

[42] *Statutes*, ii, pp. 337–9. This being a maximum rate implies, of course, that many women regularly got more.

[43] *Leet Book* as above, n. 17.

TABLE I

	1334 Assessments* (£s)	(pence)	Poll Tax† (1377)	Wealth per Taxpayer (pence)	Tenths per Taxpayer (pence)
Bristol	2,200	528,000	6,345	83.2	8
York	1,620	388,800	7,248	53.6	5
Newcastle	1,333	319,920	2,647	120.8	12
Boston	1,100	264,000	2,871	91.9	9
Yarmouth	1,000	240,000	1,941	123.6	12
Lincoln	1,000	240,000	3,412	70.3	7
Norwich	946	227,040	3,952	57.4	6
Oxford	914	219,360	2,357	93.0	9
Shrewsbury	800	192,000	2,082	92.2	9
Lynn	770	184,800	3,127	59.0	6
Salisbury	750	180,000	3,226	55.7	6
Coventry	750	180,000	4,817	37.3	4
Ipswich	645	154,800	1,507	102.7	10
Hereford	605	145,200	1,903	76.3	8
Canterbury	559	143,760	2,574	55.8	6
Gloucester	541	129,840	2,239	57.9	6
Southampton	511	122,640	1,152	106.4	11
Beverley	500	120,000	2,663	45.06	5

* R. E. Glasscock, 'England circa 1334', in H. C. Darby, ed. A *New Historical Geography of England* (Cambridge, 1973), p. 184.
† R. B. Dobson, *The Peasants' Revolt of 1381* (1970), pp. 55–7.

have been if it had been shared out in accordance with egalitarian notions of distributive justice. Nevertheless it was well within the means of those who actually paid. At a time when Coventry could not raise soldiers for the king without offering them 10d per day, the shopkeepers, merchants and leading artisans of the town were finding an average of about 3s each for the loans and *ex gratia* gifts which they were making to the king.[44]

Parliamentary subsidies were by no means an annual imposition. Moreover, in 1433 and 1446 they were permanently reduced. Fee-farms, however, were paid, or rather, were due, every year. On the whole they were comparable in order of magnitude with parliamentary subsidies.[45] On the evidence, therefore, we are surely driven to the conclusion that, however

---

[44] Ibid., pt. ii, p. 343 (1469).
[45] J. Tait, *The Medieval English Borough* (Manchester, 1936) tabulates early farms on p. 184. See also A. Ballard and J. Tait, eds, *British Borough Charters, 1216–1307* (Cam-

destitute the towns declared themselves to be, there were few of them so poor that they could not easily afford whatever they were asked to pay. Whether we see the king's demands in terms of the earning capacity of the working population of the towns, or in terms of what the taxpaying classes were actually called upon to contribute, it is impossible to see them as anything but a series of hesitant, even perhaps timorous, attempts to appropriate for his royal needs some modest share of the wealth that the citizens of the towns of provincial England obviously disposed of and spent. The volume of indignation and dismay generated by the annual liability of the fee-farm, magnified whenever parliamentary grants added their weight to what was so often said to be an insupportable burden even before these grants had augmented it, must surely be seen as nothing but a calculated, trumpet-tongued, and even perhaps, at times, a systematically concerted campaign to defraud the king of his meagre dues. And when we recall the violent and indefatigable campaigns waged, often at what looks like disproportionate expense in the courts, by the burgesses of the ecclesiastical towns in the later Middle Ages, we can readily understand that, in striving to end their miraculous immunity from the burdens of the fee-farm, they were not recklessly sacrificing self-interest to the pursuit of some ideal of independence, but merely attempting, at no very great cost to themselves, to clear their landlords' stewards and bailiffs from their streets.

If the towns could so easily afford what they so plainly resented paying, they may have had an additional motive for resisting the king's importunities, apart from the universal and perennial desire to pay as little tax as possible.

Contrary to widespread belief, oligarchic power was not easier to maintain in the towns of later medieval England than it had been in earlier days: it was harder. The competition of other places and other occupations made it so. And the efforts made in certain towns to restrict the franchise do not show that the grip of the oligarchs was tightening: they only serve to show what trouble the lesser citizens were giving. By the fifteenth century the direction from which complaint emanates is in striking contrast with that of earlier periods. In the thirteenth century, whenever urban complaint can be heard, it is the complaint of the lesser people, who say they are being exploited, that we hear.[46] By the fifteenth century, what is said to be in jeopardy is the authority of those whose rule was once virtually unquestioned. By then the lesser citizens are no longer protesting against wrongs: they are asserting rights. The distinction between citizenship meaning residence, and citizenship meaning scot-and-lot paying enfranchisement, has never been, perhaps, an easy one for ordinary men and women to grasp. With the lesser citizens emerging, if only fleetingly, from the sombre world of Karl Marx into what

bridge, 1923) and M. Weinbaum, ed., *British Borough Charters, 1307–1660* (Cambridge, 1943).
[46] E. F. Jacob, *Studies in the Period of Baronial Reform* (Oxford, 1925), pp. 134–7.

may have been no better than a simulacrum of the sunlit paradise of William Morris, the distinction was being blurred. In such circumstances, what was more likely to reconcile them to traditional usages in local government than success in inveigling the king into conceding relief from taxation which went off into the blue, so far as ordinary shopkeepers and artisans were concerned, and never did anyone any good that they could see? After all, the lesson of the Poll Taxes, so far as contemporaries were concerned, was, surely, that taxation did not have to be onerous to be thought intolerable.

VII

All this does not in the least mean that we must, henceforth, swing to the other extreme in our estimate of later medieval English towns, and visualize them as splendid places where fine streets of new or smartly renovated houses were dominated by imposing town halls and handsome churches. There was plenty of squalor intermingled with the splendour. The derelict and untenanted houses, relics of a more populous age, were not taken down. The empty streets were not cleared so as to serve some fresh and imaginative civic purpose. Who would throw good money after bad by clearing a site, or having the town clear a street, which had not earned its keep in the past and did not look like doing so in the future? When the early Tudor statutes declared that practically all the provincial towns of England were disfigured by derelict tenements and dangerous ruins they probably spoke as truly as statutes ever did. But squalor and splendour were not neighbours for the first time in the history of English towns. The two were juxtaposed in earlier centuries, when the tenements were pullulating slums, and the big houses testified, no doubt, to the awful power exercised by the mercantile oligarchs whose word was law then as it was not to be again until the sixteenth century restored earlier conditions to the countryside.

When we turn to the parliamentary subsidies for whatever assurance they can offer that this impression of later medieval urban prosperity and good living is not merely a delusion, we find that they seem to provide it in generous measure. We find that the share of the towns in the taxable wealth of the community had risen virtually everywhere by 1524 as compared with what it had been in 1334.[47]

Several scholars who interpret town petition and royal concession in sombre terms and invite us to endorse the cheerless conclusions that follow from doing so, have expressed incredulity at these findings. Prof. Dobson, following Willard, has offered the suggestion that urban taxpayers, despite the government's best efforts, were usually successful in minimizing their subsidy liabilities in 1334.[48] No doubt they were. But were they consistently

---

[47] Bridbury, *Economic Growth*, pp. 77–81.

[48] Dobson, 'Urban Decline', p. 19; J. F. Willard, *Parliamentary Taxes on Personal Property, 1290–1334* (Cambridge, Mass., 1934), p. 86.

more successful than those who lived in the country districts, and more important, were they more successful in 1334 than in 1524? Prof. Dobson does not commit himself on these crucial issues. But Mr Phythian-Adams, concentrating upon the 1524 subsidy, approaches the problem of differential bias in the records from another point of view. He contends that rich merchants with substantial landed wealth, who nevertheless chose to live in the provincial towns of England, inflated the 1524 urban figures 'to an unknown degree' by paying their subsidy contributions where they lived and not where their possessions lay.[49]

According to the statute that authorized the 1524 levy everyone was certainly required to pay where he usually lived.[50] And this was indeed in striking contrast with previous practice. Between 1290 and 1332 a taxpayer's moveable wealth was charged where it lay and not where the taxpayer lived.[51] And when the assessors were instructed in 1334 to make collective agreements with the towns and villages instead of empanelling juries to make individual assessments of each taxpayer's liabilities, they did so, as far as we can tell, without involving themselves in fundamental revision of established usages, in this respect as in others.[52]

But this change did not inflate the 1524 urban figures as Mr Phythian-Adams feared it might, because the tax rates made it extremely unlikely that a man with substantial landed interests would appear in the records as a wealthy townsman. Land and houses were not assessed on the same basis as moveables for the purposes of this subsidy. Land and houses were assessed on their annual value; but moveables were assessed on their capital value. No one paid on both. The assessors were instructed to charge each taxpayer on whichever class of assets gave the Exchequer the greater yield. With land changing hands at twenty-years' purchase, which seems to have been the current rate in the early sixteenth century,[53] a townsman who paid on his landed wealth instead of on his moveables would have had to have been very substantially invested in land before his income from land exceeded the capital value of his moveable goods.

Land paid 5 per cent on its annual value in 1524; moveables worth £20 and over also paid 5 per cent. A merchant with no more than £20 worth of stock was only in a very moderate way of business by the early sixteenth

49 Phythian-Adams, 'Urban Decay', p. 161.

50 Statutes, iii, pp. 230–41.

51 Willard, Parliamentary Taxes, pp. 154, 162 et seq. The 'form of the taxation' issued for the 1332 subsidy instructed juries to search out all goods liable for assessment 'en maison et dehors ou qu'ils fuissent'. Rot. Parl., ii, p. 447. This surely meant that they should not fail to look for such goods elsewhere than in the taxpayer's actual home, not that they should tax all his moveable goods, wherever they might be, at his place of residence.

52 Willard, Parliamentary Taxes, p. 57.

53 H. J. Habakkuk, 'The Long-Term Rate of Interest and the Price of Land in the Seventeenth Century', Economic History Review, 2nd ser., vol. v (1952), p. 45.

century. But if a merchant with £20 worth of stock were to qualify as a landowner for tax purposes, he would have had to invest well over £400 in order to enjoy an annual income from land which exceeded the capital value of what was, after all, a very modest stock of moveables.

The merchants whom Mr Phythian-Adams had in mind when he warned us of the influence of landed property on urban values, dominated the towns in which they lived and disposed of stocks of moveables which were worth many times more than £20. If they had paid their 1524 subsidy contributions on the basis of the annual value of their landed property then they would have been the peers of the leading county families of England. Can we really believe that men of such consequence would have been content to live the provincial life of the provincial towns of later medieval England when they might so easily have exchanged it for the patrician splendours and prospects of county society? Mr Phythian-Adams who sees most of the towns of later medieval England as sunless, dispirited places, ruinous and decayed, must surely wonder at the choice he believes they made, and indeed, at the capacity of such places to throw up a succession of outstanding businessmen, not just here or there, but in so many of the counties of England that we must distrust what the subsidy returns tell us about urban prosperity in 1524.

It is difficult to believe that this view of urban life in the early sixteenth century reflects things as they really were. Many merchants bought country property. They did so at all stages of their business careers, and for a variety of reasons. But nothing that we know about the conduct of business by active and successful merchants warrants the belief that they made a habit of locking up more than a fraction of what might otherwise have been their working capital in a form which rendered it useless for purposes of trade. When they did in fact buy their way into the life of the county they did so when they were ready to quit the life of industry and commerce; and when they were ready to do that they seldom lingered in the towns. We know that one or two immensely wealthy merchants who invested heavily in land nevertheless continued to live where they had made their money. Thomas Spring III was evidently one who did.[54] But one Spring does not make summer.

Mr Rigby's objections to the statistical findings derive, at bottom, from their failure to reflect the decline of towns whose misfortunes in the later Middle Ages are the common currency of historical debate. He gives examples to show the paradoxical consequences of believing what the statistics suggest. But the historians upon whom he depends have, as a rule, taken at face value everything that was said by townsmen about the hardships they were enduring, or done by the king in mitigation of these hardships. The result is an encyclopaedia of special pleading. By running through Mr Rigby's

---

[54] B. McClenaghan, *The Springs of Lavenham* (Ipswich, 1924), App. D. Lavenham, being a new town, was excluded from the urban list and therefore added its weight to the rural side of the equation in 1524.

examples we learn more about the present state of later medieval urban studies than we do about the later medieval condition of England's provincial towns.[55]

Lincoln was an obvious choice because Lincoln's devastating decline, although notorious in the historical literature, is not as conspicuous as it might be in the statistical calculations. Lincoln's exceedingly complex historical problems, however, discussed above, preclude us from making any confident judgements, henceforth, about Lincoln's later medieval fortunes. Grimsby's historian, having described Grimsby as 'a small town growing poorer' in the later Middle Ages, nevertheless makes no attempt to reconcile this dismal verdict with the town's evident success, also described, in attracting hosts of non-burgesses, who carried on their businesses in Grimsby as if they had been enfranchised, as well as in recruiting a succession of duly enfranchised citizens who were, apparently, perfectly willing to serve the town in official capacities, notwithstanding their liability for its public debts.[56] Stamford earns its place in this company because Dr Thirsk expressed the view that Stamford was destitute by 1500. The latest historian of its later medieval activities, however, noting Stamford's incorporation in 1462, and its substantial building and rebuilding of its public places, is convinced that the fifteenth century was a prosperous one for the town.[57]

Boston is another matter. The temptation to judge the prosperity of a port by the record of its foreign trade is very great; and Boston's foreign trade was certainly negligible by 1524. London had by then devoured Boston's foreign trade as it had devoured, or was devouring, the foreign trade of so many provincial ports. Are we to conclude from this that the regions these ports had once served henceforth enjoyed none of the benefits that foreign trade had once brought them? Surely not. Are we to assume then that links between London and the regions were henceforth overland? Surely not. No dramatic changes in transport technology had emancipated later medieval Englishmen from dependence upon water for cheap freight. Consequently, the decline of the foreign trade of the provincial ports of England did not necessarily diminish the importance of their shipping and commercial services. Trade with London superseded trade with Calais, Bruges, Middleburg or Amsterdam. The links were perhaps less exotic. It is arguable, however, that they were not less remunerative.

Hull's foreign trade record is a warning against any facile assumption to the contrary. Hull's foreign trade declined fairly sharply in the early fifteenth century; but the turning-point in Hull's prosperity came not then but in the

[55] S. H. Rigby, 'Urban Decline in the Later Middle Ages', *Urban History Yearbook* (1979), pp. 46–59. Detailed discussion of Mr Rigby's analysis seems to be out of place. If the subsidies are not suspect because they give the wrong answers there seems to be little point in discussing why they gave the wrong answers or how to make them give more plausible answers.

[56] E. Gillett, *A History of Grimsby* (Oxford, 1970), pp. 66, 63, 55–6.

[57] A. Rogers, ed., *The Making of Stamford* (1965), pp. 58–9, 42, 50.

1460s when burgess admissions, town rents, weigh-house receipts, and income from tolls, all fell to lower levels than hitherto.[58] If Hull declined thereafter we ought to suspect any explanation of that decline which attributes it to the subsequent erosion of Hull's foreign trade.

Having tried to show that the historical evidence discredits the statistical findings, Mr Rigby then turns to Dr Schofield's work on the geographical distribution of wealth to show that the changes in county ranking between 1334 and 1515 calculated by Dr Schofield are not reflected as they should be in the increases in the urban share of county wealth between 1334 and 1524.[59] Devonshire rose from thirty-fourth to eighteenth place in county ranking, according to Dr Schofield, but the share of Devon's towns in the taxable wealth of Devonshire grew more slowly than, for example, the share of Lincoln's towns in the taxable wealth of Lincolnshire.

The rank ordering of counties on the basis of single assessments made for taxation purposes is inherently suspect. Any particular year may be exceptional for certain regions. And there is always the problem of under-assessment. Dr Schofield assumes that this was a constant factor.[60] But Mr Hadwin, in an important paper, as yet unpublished, has shown how much volatility changing assessment practices caused in the rank ordering of counties between 1290 and 1334.[61] Over the long period that Dr Schofield surveys, how can we pick economic development from administrative caprice or short-lived triumph or disaster in appraising the changes in rank ordering that we find, without looking elsewhere than to these taxation records for enlightenment? Yet taxation records are invoked because they give promise of being able to decide issues which other types of historical record cannot easily resolve.

Dr Schofield's calculations show that Devonshire was the fastest-growing county in England in 1515. Mr Rigby argues that fishing, wool, clothmaking, and tin, provided the basis for this growth. He may be right. But how does he know? Fishing is an altogether unknown quantity, in Devonshire as elsewhere in England. If wool production grew or improved at this period, it did so without attracting comment from Dr Lloyd.[62] A dramatic expansion of clothmaking in later medieval Devonshire is something that has yet to be

58 Hull's foreign trade is displayed graphically by Dr N. Bartlett in 'The Expansion and Decline of York in the Later Middle Ages', *Economic History Review*, 2nd ser., vol. xii (1959), p. 28. For Hull's turning point see *VCH Yorks. East Riding*, I, p. 41.
59 R. S. Schofield, 'The Geographical Distribution of Wealth in England 1334–1649', *Economic History Review*, 2nd ser., vol. xviii (1965), pp. 483–510.
60 *Ibid.*, p. 497.
61 I am much indebted to Mr Hadwin for allowing me to see his calculations and for much enlightening discussion of the problems he is tackling. His work is now in print: 'The Medieval Lay Subsidies and Economic History', *Economic History Review*, 2nd ser., vol. xxxvi (1983), pp. 200–17.
62 T. H. Lloyd, *The Movement of Wool Prices in Medieval England* (*Economic History Review*, Supplement no. 6, 1973); *The English Wool Trade in the Middle Ages* (Cambridge, 1977).

substantiated. And if tin production increased in the final decades of the period, as it undoubtedly did, we may nevertheless question whether much of the wealth it generated was retained within the county, or indeed sufficed to account for the growth of Devonshire's wealth, as Dr Schofield has measured it, if it were.[63] Certainly Cornwall's output in 1334, nearly three times as great as Devon's in 1515, did nothing for Cornwall at the time, according to Dr Schofield's rank ordering, which deposits Cornwall, with the sluggards, at the bottom.[64]

Such calculations as Dr Schofield's are bound to reflect, as well as to breed, anomalies. But if parliamentary subsidies are not to be trusted for rank ordering, in the sense that we can never know without further investigation when to believe what they tell us, then why should we trust them to be able to measure changes in the urban share of county wealth between 1334 and 1524?

The answer is that we can no more trust an individual result in the one case than in the other. The same strictures apply to both; the same anomalies vitiate results. But there is safety in numbers. When we find, in county after county, that different assessors, each with his own weaknesses, eccentricities and predilections, his own family ties and social or political allegiances, had, more or less independently, compiled lists of taxation liabilities which show that the share of urban wealth in county wealth was greater in 1524 than in 1334, then we are surely entitled to presume that we are dealing with changes in economic conditions rather than with changes in administrative practice.

No doubt some of these results are wrong. No doubt others exaggerate or minimize the changes that took place. Others, again, presumably, tell us more about the world that was beginning, in 1524, to retrogress towards conditions as they were in 1334, than about the fifteenth century. But what the subsidy calculations seem to do, and indeed all they were ever intended to do, is to dramatize the fact that later medieval England, which possessed land and capital in abundance, and had completely industrialized its export trade by the end of the fifteenth century, was making a more energetic use of its urban network of industries and services than it had done in what were, from the point of view of economic growth, less fortunate times. Mr Rigby has devoted much ingenuity to manipulating the subsidy returns so as to make them fit the historical facts about the towns. But the facts about the towns are not what they seem; and the subsidies by reflecting things more nearly, perhaps, as they were, than as they were made to appear, surely tell us that the bustle and change to be found in the general run of England's later medieval provincial towns illustrate certain well-known truths about

[63] J. Hatcher, *English Tin Production and Trade Before 1550* (Oxford, 1973), App. A.
[64] Schofield, 'Geographical Distribution of Wealth', p. 504. Tinners were exempt from parliamentary subsidies: Hatcher, *English Tin*, p. 48. But this does not affect an argument about changes in the indirect effects of mining on wealth, and hence on taxable capacity.

economic development: that early steps in economic development take the form of increasing division of labour; and that market size, not population size, sets the limit to what division of labour can achieve.

VIII

Mr Rigby has concerned himself mainly with the fifteenth century. But other historians, persuaded that English provincial towns were sinking into economic decadence and physical dilapidation during the later Middle Ages, have confirmed their worst fears by recalling the terms in which certain statutes of Henry VIII's reign required the towns of England to remedy the appalling conditions to be found in many of their most important districts.[65] The re-edifying statutes, which tell of widespread, if not universal, urban dilapidation, seem to vindicate the belief that the intense depression that overwhelmed the towns of later medieval England was not easily dispelled even in the more genial climate of the sixteenth century. Virtually every town of any pretensions whatsoever was named in them. How can we resist the conclusion that they were all decayed?

By the time that the re-edifying statutes were enacted in 1535/6, 1540, 1541/2 and 1543/4, the towns of England were moving swiftly into a phase in which conditions were comparable with those that prevailed before the pestilences. Real wages had begun to fall significantly, and towns were resuming their function as havens where men might find work. It is perhaps no accident that pioneering a poor law was something that the towns did in the sixteenth century. Their doing so, however, does not prove that sixteenth-century towns were as impoverished as ever. It is not evidence of the poverty of towns that poor men should congregate in them. On the contrary, poor men congregated in the towns because they had every reason to believe that the towns had more to offer them than the country districts whence they came.

Prof. Elton in a recent examination of the problem posed by the re-edifying statutes cites a contemporary claim that, in many towns, houses were empty because rents were too high.[66] It is certainly very likely that urban rents were rising generally at this period. Rentals of borough property at Reading, Salisbury, King's Lynn, and Exeter, suggest that towns which were listed in the re-edifying statutes did not necessarily encounter difficulties in letting their shops and tenements at full rents, and indeed even when they surcharged them.[67] But if urban rents were sometimes high, or at any rate rising, what are we to make of the assertions in the statutes that the towns of England were decayed?

---

[65] For references see note 10 above.
[66] G. R. Elton, *Reform and Renewal* (Cambridge, 1973), p. 107.
[67] Borough MSS. Chamberlains's Accounts, *passim*.

The statutes pose a dilemma. Either the towns were declining, in which case there was no point in their councils seeking powers to enable them to take over ruinous tenements which their owners would not maintain or rebuild; or they were not, in which case it is hard to see why owners needed to be prodded or cajoled into doing what any landlord with half an eye to the main chance would have done in any case, eagerly and without prompting. Some towns actually put themselves forward for inclusion in these statutes. If their property were decayed because the towns were incapable of attracting citizens and trade, and this is the implication we are asked to accept, then what did these municipalities expect to be able to do with the tenements they had requisitioned once they had spent ratepayers' money in an uncharacteristic and, so far as the ratepayers were concerned, scandalously improvident way, upon the renovation of buildings which nobody wanted to lease at rents which would cover the costs of improvement and maintenance?

Surely we must look elsewhere for an explanation of these extraordinary statutes. The landlords of ruinous tenements were being required to do something under threat of confiscation, that no sensible landlord, in normal circumstances, would do if rents were depressed, and would fail to do if rents were buoyant. Were circumstances, perhaps, abnormal? Towns had been empty for many years. pestilence had shortened family dynasties as well as individual lives. Vacant lots or ruinous buildings were, consequently, scarcely worth the trouble of conveyancing.[68] Then the tide turned. Speculative opportunities occurred in towns which were filling up again. Those who would normally exploit such opportunities found themselves hampered by the problem of there being no clear title to the properties they wanted to modernize or rebuild. The statutes were a neat solution to just such a problem. They gave the boroughs, and hence the speculative builders, a clear right of possession if no one came forward to claim ownership.

But once busy speculators start chasing lost titles with the help of parliament and the town councils we are back again in a familiar world of overpopulated towns. The re-edifying statutes of Henry VIII do not tell of the incorrigible persistence of what we are encouraged to call urban decline or urban decay: they signalize the end of a period of spaciousness and promise in the history of England's provincial towns.

---

[68] Some towns already had rules about what should be done with ruinous or dangerous property that read very like the statutes. Possibly London's practices influenced legislation. Curiously enough, Waterford c.1300 made provision for compensating an heir, who turned up many years after he should have taken possession, for the period during which the town had made use of his unclaimed inheritance even to the extent of building on it. See M. Bateson, *Borough Customs* (Selden Society, vol. xviii, 1904), pp. 275–6, 278–80.

A Reply to S. H. Rigby on 'Late Medieval Urban Prosperity: the evidence of the lay subsidies'

Dr Rigby's preoccupation with the subsidies gives the wholly misleading impression that my intention in using them was to make them the basis of my argument. Extracting them and preparing them for use took many months because neither Glasscock nor Sheail had started his studies by the time I had finished with them. But they occupy only four pages of my book because I thought then, as I do now, that arguments whose validity depends upon these subsidies, with their obvious and often flagrant evidence of manipulation and fraud, are bound to be insecure. Mr Hadwin's recent investigations into the subsidies levied before 1334 brilliantly illustrate the manipulations to which they lent themselves. And the fraud is one of the commonplaces of historical writing.

Moreover they are poor evidence for another reason. They are much too far apart in time to be worth any greater attention than I gave them; for the time factor compounds all the other problems raised in using them. In particular, anyone who takes figures from one side of that immense divide and compares them directly with figures from the other side, does so at his peril.

Making such comparisons has, unfortunately, become a popular pastime, particularly with historical geographers. But its popularity has done nothing to enhance its respectability. I made such comparisons myself, in my book, and now regret having done so because they have attracted much more attention than they deserve and have diverted attention away from the method I devised, specifically, in order to avoid the dangers inseparable from direct comparisons. The substance of my findings is to be found, therefore, in Appendix II of my book where I compare the ratios of town to country taxation in 1334 with the ratios of town to country taxation in 1524. Rigby calls these findings impressionistic. And so they are; but not, I hope, in his pejorative sense. They are, I believe impressionistic in the sense in which actuarial statistics are. They register trends without saying anything about particular cases. And they tell us about relationships. They do not tell us about changes in aggregate levels of wealth.

Now the impression these findings convey is that of a society in which urban wealth, and hence urban activities, have come to play a more important part in economic and social life by the end of the Middle Ages, than they had done previously. If true, these are significant findings because towns, at bottom, are processing plants, and their prosperity, in an economy such as that of medieval England, was a reflection of prosperity beyond their boundaries. There is a movement, in current historical thought, to deny the close bond between town and country in this simple sense. If this movement should prove to be an attempt to find out which settlements had in fact served as towns for any particular region at any given period, then we must all wish it well. Anything that clarifies terms must be welcome. But if this movement should turn out to be an attempt to deny the central importance of towns to an exchange economy, then it is founded upon a basic misapprehension of their function, and should be deplored.

The discussion of urban fortunes in the later middle ages is notable for its presumption that towns must have been in decline then because everything else was. But was it? The whole economy had been swung out of its traditional orbit, at that time, by a pestilence which killed but did not maim, debilitate or paralyse; did not discriminate between the sexes; and did not attack any one age-group rather than another. High mortality rates, which ended all the overcrowding, were matched, therefore, by high standards of living: an incongruous, not to say unparalleled combination. As economic historians, we fasten eagerly enough upon evidence of improvements in the capital structure of any economy we happen to be studying, and dwell approvingly upon advances in its technology. But extraordinary changes in the human capital, such as we find in the later middle ages, we tend to dismiss as mere questions of welfare.

Malthus's comment upon the stunted growth of the sons of labourers, a commonplace, he declared, to everyone who lived much in the countryside in his day, finds no place in our discussions. Nevertheless later medieval England was full of people who were, by the standards of previous ages, bursting with health. Is it unreasonable to link this fact with the evidence I have adduced in various places to show that later medieval England did not wane or decline, and that its peasants' welfare was much more than that of a sated pig asleep in the sun?

If the presumption with which we start ought to be that the statistics of town wealth are more likely to be true than false, we are not therefore exonerated from subjecting them to searching scrutiny. This we can do in one, or both, of two ways. We can examine the statistics themselves in order to determine whether they reflect things more or less as they were, or exaggerate, or conceal vital information; and we can compare what they tell us about particular places with what we should expect them to tell us as a result of our knowledge of such places.

Rigby has tried to do both of these things. But in handling the statistics he has used two different arrangements of them without making it clear that the status of one arrangement differs profoundly from that of the other. Comparing the ratios, as I did in my Appendix II, is a very different exercise from that of comparing the sums paid in 1334 with the sums paid in 1524. That is what I did in my Appendix III, and is, as I pointed out at the time, a very much more hazardous thing to do.

The central problem set by these taxes is the problem of the possible under-assessment of the towns in 1334 and their possible over-assessment in 1524. Much ingenuity has been devoted to this problem since I published my figures; but every attempt to impugn the validity of one set of figures seems to provoke a countervailing suggestion whose effect seems to be to neutralize the first attempt. Nor is there any end, apparently, to a quest which is fatally disabled by the lack of corroborative evidence, independent of the figures, to which we can appeal.

My own feeling at the time was that I should do everything I could to minimize the trend in urban wealth so as to increase the credibility of the figures. Consequently I excluded from my 1334 list of towns all those places, chartered or otherwise, which were undoubtedly performing urban functions later but which were probably not towns in 1334 or were towns in name only. These places were then excluded from my 1524 list even though it was clear to me that by then they were not only towns in my sense but, often enough, towns of very considerable importance within their regions. Some very prosperous places, according to Appendix III, are therefore to be found on the rural side of the equation at both periods in Appendix II. I made it as plain as I could that a great deal of urban wealth had made its contribution to the rural wealth of England in my 1524 figures. Rigby, however, does not mention this as a mitigating factor on the other side when he speaks of the bias of the 1524 records.

I also mentioned, at the time, that the taxation of wages in 1524 added its weight to the rural side. Rigby says I did so because I had forgotten that most people lived in the countryside at both periods. I had not forgotten, and mentioned it because the virtual ending of servile tenure by 1524 meant that men who did not pay on their moveables in 1334 were nevertheless caught by the taxation of wages in 1524. Since there were many more wage-earners in the country than in the towns, it follows that the effect of taxing wages in 1524 was to add to the rural wealth of the counties rather than to the urban.

These 1524 figures have caused a good deal of trouble. Rigby concedes that we should no longer believe that the wealth of the towns was exaggerated in 1524 because rich countrymen were being taxed as townsmen; but he then, in effect retracts his concession by quoting with approval an article by Darby, Glasscock, Sheail and Versey, which reproduces this belief because it was published two years before the article in which I demonstrated its falsity appeared.

Another point about the 1524 tax which has caused Rigby concern is the question of the moveables of those with £20 worth or more. People in this category were charged at 12d in £ instead of at 6d which was the rate paid by those with less. If most of those who paid at this rate were townsmen rather than countrymen, then two things would follow. The first is that urban activities were obviously making substantial fortunes for certain members of communities which we are asked to believe were in dire straits at the time. And the second is that any assessment of the relative wealth of towns based on the sums paid rather than on the value of the moveables taxed, would be bound to exaggerate the wealth of the towns. Hadwin, who drew attention to this factor in an unpublished paper, also drew attention to the fact that, so far as his investigations have gone, this is not a factor of fundamental importance because the disproportion between urban and rural surtax payers is not very great. Rigby mentions the point at issue but not Hadwin's reservations about it.

When he turns to my Appendix III, in which I ventured to make direct comparisons of the sums paid by towns in 1334 with the sums those towns paid in 1524, Rigby turns, in the first instance, to the rural instead of to the urban figures, and makes a direct comparison between rural areas. On the admirable principle that what is sauce for the goose is sauce for the gander, Rigby sets himself to find out what happens when you take the payments made by the rural areas in 1334 and compare them directly with the payments they made in 1524. The result appears to be devasting. Even the most properous areas hardly grow at all in terms of the standards of growth achieved by the most successful towns. Does this tell us, after all, of a declining later middle ages, with the countryside growing poorer even more quickly than the towns in their midst? It does not. Rigby has confused aggregate wealth with wealth per head.

The loss of a substantial fraction of its previous population as a result of pestilence had unquestionably reduced the aggregate wealth of the economy. That is what Postan, and many others, have always understood to be the meaning of economic decline. And such a loss must inevitably show up in taxation returns which purport to reflect in their yield a faithful assessment of the community's aggregate wealth. That they do so in this way is perhaps more a tribute to their verisimilitude than a reflection upon their shortcomings. What it emphatically is not, is evidence of the impoverishment of those who were actually living and working in the countryside. The real wage evidence, whatever its deficiencies, bears incontestible witness to the fact that the decline of aggregate wealth was not proportionate to the decline of population. And the fact that so many towns were doing very much better than the country districts, according to this far from satisfactory way of using the statistics, is perhaps a vindication of the impression conveyed by the ratios set out in my Appendix II of an economy which was thrusting forward rather than stagnating or sinking into decline.

When he transfers his attention to particular cases, Rigby attributes to me remarks which I simply did not make. He says I argue that Devon did not prosper in the later middle ages. What I said was that he may very well be right in maintaining that it did, but that unsubstantiated assertion is not enough to establish its prosperity. He says that I now think that coastal trade provided Boston with an alternative to foreign trade which was equally remunerative. What I said was that Boston's foreign trade could very well have been conducted via London instead of with foreign ports at the time when the customs accounts show that Boston's foreign trade was in decline. Customs officers only took cognisance of what left a port when it also left the country, and of what entered a port when it also entered the country.

Consequently the decline of Boston's foreign trade, as reflected in the customs accounts, is not the proof that Rigby takes it to be that goods imported into England at another port, or destined for export from another port, were no longer using Boston's port facilities as much as ever.

Nor did I contend, as Rigby says I did, that Lincoln's franchises saved the town. Indeed I was at pains to point out how unaccountable was the behaviour of some of Lincoln's leading citizens if we make the assumption that everything that was progressive about Lincoln's economic life took place in those cramping quarters.

The mention of Lincoln raises once again the question of Rigby's handling of the statistics. Rigby manages to show how very different the economic fortunes of Lincoln appear to be if you compare the ratios of Appendix II, which indicate a healthy rise in the proportion of urban wealth to rural in the county of Lincolnshire by 1524, with the tax payments of Appendix III, which seem to suggest that Lincoln's record of growth was poor when compared with the record of more dynamic towns. Rigby finds these conclusions incompatible with one another; but he does so because he has ignored the clear warning I gave, when I published my results, that comparing ratios serves a very different purpose from that served by comparing urban payments in 1334 and 1524. The ratios tell of a region which was making comparatively more use of its urban facilities in 1524 than in 1334; and the payments evidence suggests that certain towns, of which Lincoln was one, changed at a much slower rate than others. No doubt certain older towns, with a long history of growth in the past, changed more slowly than other towns which had perhaps only recently emerged as important centres, or which had grown rapidly in this period for a special reason, such as cloth-making.

It so happens that Rigby has himself provided clear evidence of what I have in mind. In the current issue of *Midland History*, he has published an account of later medieval Boston which is, in effect, a commentary upon Leland's view of the city. Leland saw Boston's 'sore decay'; and Rigby uses the customs accounts, wrongly in my judgement, to demonstrate that the decline of Boston's recorded trade was tantamount to the decline of Boston's sea-borne trade. But Leland also noted Boston's 'fair dwellings' and the 'divers good ships and vessels' in Boston's harbour. Rigby confirms Leland's impressions by turning to the fourth year of the 1523 subsidy, which required those with moveables worth £50 and more to make a further contribution. He found that no less that ten Boston merchants qualified for this additional levy. Rigby's comment seems to be fully justified. 'Boston', he says, 'was still a major regional centre and the main market and only town of any size in one of the richest areas of early sixteenth-century England'. In terms of the subsidy statistics, Boston's increasing share of county wealth, taken in conjunction with the share of the other towns of Lincolnshire in 1524, is perfectly compatible with a record of growth which, like that of Lincoln itself, looks very poor, when measured by the Appendix III payments method, in comparison with that of Coventry or Lavenham or any one of a multitude of other towns whose expansion was at a far quicker rate in this period.

Rigby finds it difficult to visualize conditions, in the later middle ages, in which it could have been the rule rather than the exception for towns to have improved their economic positions. But the context within which life was lived at the time meant that no-one was obliged to live as the mass of the population was obliged to live before 1370. Consequently, rise and fall, prosperity and depression, take on an altogether different significance in the later middle ages to the one they had earlier or would have again later. Naturally there were casualties. Marginal areas which were virtually deserted lost their markets and towns as well as their fields and villages. And in other areas which were not deserted, markets and towns also disappeared. To some extent this was an optical illusion created by the charter evidence. The formalities of foundation created a record. But foundation is not a guarantee of subsequent development. Consequently what seems to have disappeared later may never have enjoyed a substantive existence formerly except as a hopeful speculation and a legal instrument.

But the transformation of life in the later middle ages undoubtedly provoked shifts in the urban pattern. As rents fell, so did fodder costs. Those who could only walk to market in Bracton's day were able to ride and carry goods for greater distances. This favoured some commercial and industrial centres and broke up many a tight little monopolistic paradise. Perhaps, handled with care and imagination, the tax figures may be able to tell us something about these and other cross-currents. They are not infallible. But whatever their shortcomings they do seem to be able to illustrate certain aspects of an extraordinary interlude in our history.

The Lisle Letters[1]

The Lisle collection is unique. In the Paston and Stonor papers we can follow the family fortunes of the county gentry; in the Cely papers we can trace the operations of a London business. But this is the earliest insight we possess into the inner workings of an aristocratic family of the first rank. Arthur Viscount Lisle was Henry VIII's uncle, the bastard son of Edward IV, whom Henry had drawn into the circle of his intimate friends and upon whom he had bestowed honours and responsibilities as well as friendship. In March 1533 Henry appointed him Lord Deputy of Calais, or Governor-General as we should call the post if it had been a modern one. In May 1540 Lisle was arrested and imprisoned in the Tower on suspicion of treason. The suspicion was subsequently proved to be unfounded; but Lisle died in the Tower before he could be released. His lands and moveables were restored to his family, but his letters and papers were not. They survived as state papers, and because they survived so does Lisle.

Virtually everything in the collection belongs to this period. There are some 3,000 items, three times as many as we possess in the way of letters and papers for the Paston family, though the Paston collection itself vastly exceeds in volume every other early collection of this class extant. This is not their first appearance in print. The Lisle letters were calendared with many passages printed *in extenso* in *Letters and Papers, Foreign and Domestic, of the Reign of Henry VIII*. But anyone who supposes that they can be used as calendared has only to try to do so in order to find out why they have been so neglected by modern historians. The Lisle letters were not so much calendared and printed as buried inaccessibly by the editors of *Letters and Papers*. One cannot be anything but profoundly grateful to the editors of these indispensable volumes for their toilsome work. But a very great deal of the interest, value and indeed intelligibility of a correspondence such as this lies in its unity. The editors of *Letters and Papers*, however, took the Lisle archive, preserved as a consecutive series, and scattered its contents amongst all the other state papers of these years, when it obviously warranted very different treatment.

Miss Byrne has now given the Lisle letters the treatment they deserve. But she has done infinitely more than put them into correct sequence and print them in full with the spelling modernized so as to remove an unnecessary barrier to easy reading. She has annotated them as fully as she can, and has

[1] A review of Muriel St Clare Byrne, ed., *The Lisle Letters*, 6 vols (Chicago, 1981).

provided a running commentary for them after the style of Carlyle's for Cromwell's letters and speeches. We soon get to know everyone who writes regularly; usually, as a result of the exhaustive researches of our indefatigable dragoman, we can guess why they have written and what they hope to gain by doing so.

This splendid six-volume edition is not, however, complete. The editor has not printed everything she has found. She has selected just short of 2,000 items for publication. Unpublished are most of the letters in French (nearly 500 of them survive), which arose out of Lisle's contacts with his French and Flemish neighbours; and most of the letters and papers, presumably about another 500 items, which arose out of the administrative problems of governing Calais. Of these, says the editor, 'typical examples will suffice'. It is a flaw in this incomparable work, however, that the editor does not provide a list, preferably an annotated list, of what she has left out, so that the reader may decide for himself how significant for his own purposes the editor's omissions may be.

By courtesy, the collection is known as the Lisle letters. But in fact we get the letters written by Lisle only when a draft letter survives in the files, or when Lisle writes to his wife, who then keeps the letters that bridge their brief periods of separation and restores them to the files when she returns to Calais. Otherwise, these letters are Lisle letters only in the sense that these are the letters, or a selection of the letters, written to Lisle and his wife during their memorable seven-year sojourn in Calais. In this respect the Lisle letters are very different from the letters of Pastons, Stonors, or Celys. When we turn the pages of these well-known collections we find them full of the correspondence written by members of the families to one another. When we turn the pages of the Lisle letters we find that, if the Lisle letters are anyone's letters, in the sense that they are the letters written by any one person, then they are surely the letters of Lisle's man of business John Husee, whose vivid and informative contributions form the backbone of the collection.

Husee's importance in the Lisle letters, indeed, provides us with an essential clue to their significance. For Husee proves to have been the very type of the alert, loyal and highly intelligent young man who, nowadays, is put in charge of the minister's 'private office', where he keeps an eye on the minister's diary, makes sure that the minister is kept informed of everything he ought to know, runs errands for the minister's wife, and does all the hundred and one things, some of them very homely and even menial things, expected of young men on the threshold of distinguished civil service careers who are told to look after the political heads of departments as one of their earliest responsibilities. Husee was a paragon for whom no legal tangle was too abstruse, no diplomatic mission too delicate, no practical problem of matching colours for a dress or of ordering a young lady's trousseau or a schoolboy's outfit, too taxing. And if Husee's duties call to mind the civil service they do so because so much of what Husee has to say in his letters, and indeed so much of what other correspondents have to say in theirs, provided Lisle with the background information and direct help he needed for the successful running of the Calais post. The Lisle letters are, in effect, the in-tray of a government department with the difference that, the department in question being situated abroad, the in-tray is inevitably swollen by the private correspondence dealing with family affairs that might not have got into it if the department had operated from London.

The Lisle letters give the impression, confirmed by other letters, that the middle ranks of society from which Husee sprang were producing swarms of young men like him. Versatile, resourceful and thoroughly well-educated, they provided wealthy and aristocratic families with services which we can best epitomize as secretarial, though few of them could write with such skill and charm as Husee, and fewer perhaps were called upon to perform quite such onerous and responsible duties. In an earlier age William Worcester provided Sir John Fastolf with the benefit of such services; and we can see from the Stonor papers that Harry Dogett, whom his employer addressed as 'my old friend', did as much for Sir William Stonor. Husee was not so much employed by Lisle as dedicated to Lisle and his family: pathetically anxious to please; devastated when he failed to do so; and on call at all hours, despite arrears of pay, rebuffs, and even ill-natured comments on his character and services (III, pp. 500, 505). Perhaps there were too many of these young men for their own good. William Worcester's complaint that he served like a slave at the plough was undoubtedly a reflection upon the man he worked for; but it may very well have been a comment also upon the state of the market for educated laymen, then as later.

With men such as Husee or William Worcester at hand it is scarcely surprising to find that aristocratic members of society did not as a rule put themselves to the trouble of writing their own letters. Lisle certainly did not; and in less exalted circles we find the Pastons and the Stonors writing their own letters only when there was nobody about to do their writing for them. Literacy was a necessary accomplishment at lower social levels than these, so that when education extended its influence it did so by spreading to higher classes long before it did so by plumbing the social depths.

Lisle desperately needed someone like Husee because he was not merely stationed at Calais: he was marooned there. He could not leave his post without express permission. Calais was promotion at the expense of exile. This meant that Lisle was obliged to correspond with people whom he would otherwise have made it his business to meet, and obliged to depend upon others, upon Husee above all, to be his eyes and his ears and to do things for him which he could no longer do for himself. His loss is our gain; for the letters are full of matters which we should not find committed to paper in other circumstances.

Lisle found his position intensely frustrating. By 1538 he confessed to the Earl of Southampton 'I assure you, I do live a worse life than the poorest soldier in Calais' (V, p. 139). His urgent recommendations for the reconstruction of the defences of Calais were constantly ignored. Was this vacillation or policy? Useful diplomatically though Calais occasionally proved to be, it was nevertheless something of a strategic and commercial white elephant. As an invasion centre for English expeditionary forces it could not compare with Harfleur, which threatened Paris and the heart of France. And as a wool market it provided second-rate facilities for a declining trade. Did the king in fact realise all this? He may have done so. But denied familiar access to the king, sick with hope deferred, is it not likely that Lisle would have endorsed wholeheartedly from his own experience what Keynes wrote about the infirmity of purpose that he detected in Washington during the Second World War?

> The situation [he wrote] is entirely fluid up to the last minute. Everything you are told, even with the greatest appearance of authority and decision, is provisional, without commitment . . . There is no orderly progression towards the final conclusion. . . . I liken them to bees who for weeks will fly around in all directions with no ascertainable destination, providing both the menace of stings and the hope of honey; and at last, perhaps because the queen . . . has emitted some faint, indistinguishable odour, suddenly swarm to a single spot in a compact, impenetrable bunch.[2]

Where his personal affairs were concerned, Lisle's close friendship with the king in earlier days left a warmth of afterglow that stood him in good stead during his exile. When he fell so far in arrears with his taxes that Sir Brian Tuke, the treasurer, was driven to remind him, in 1539, that anyone else would have incurred outlawry for debt these many years, Lisle knew, as Sir Brian knew, that while the king was Lisle's 'good lord', nothing untoward could possible happen to him. And when John Basset, Lisle's step-son, had his inheritance threatened, a word from the king sufficed to 'stop the course of his common laws' and thwart the ambitions of those eagerly expectant litigants, Lord Daubeney and the Earl of Hertford (V, p. 168).

We can best measure what absence from court meant for Lisle, however, in terms of the endless delays and inexplicable difficulties he was forced to endure during the scramble for the monasteries. The dissolution created a hectic gold-rush atmosphere at court. Lisle, isolated in Calais, had to write 'beseeching' Cromwell 'to help me to some old abbey in mine old days' (III, p. 296). Thomas Warley, another Lisle retainer, writing to Lady Lisle, made a somewhat imprudent, not to say quixotically tactless invocation to 'our Lord', by whom he meant God, 'to send my lord', by whom he meant Lisle, 'a good abbey or two for a commendam' (III, p. 297). And Husee asked for instructions about 'which abbey or priory to make . . . suit for' (III, p. 385). Lisle got his share of this mountain of ecclesiastical spoil: the Augustinian priory of Frithelstock as a gift in fee simple. It was an unusually generous benefaction. But Cromwell made him sweat for it. Nor did it satisfy Lisle, who then put in for the house of the White Friars in Calais. And there arose also the question of his pension. The pressure Cromwell was able to exert

---

[2] Quoted in Christopher Thorne, *Allies of a Kind* (Oxford, 1979), p. 115.

upon Lisle over these matters tells us better than anything else how Lisle's enforced absence from court affected his fortunes. Husee at one point put a price on it. Writing of Lisle's next posting, Husee says of one prospect: 'then should your lordship be nearer home . . . which I doubt not would be £1,000 a year in your way' (V, p. 444).

The court encircled the king as the living tissue encircles the tree. Government depended upon its organs of administration, and even of legislation, as the tree depends upon its wood – for substance rather than life. The court had no formal structure, employed no secretariat and enrolled no proceedings. Consequently we can know very little about its workings, except for such glimpses as we get in sources such as the Lisle letters. And what a minefield it was! When Lisle's step-daughters succeeded in obtaining court appointments Husee warned Lady Lisle that it was 'full of pride, envy, indignation and mocking, scorning and derision' (IV, p. 152). As well it might be when we recall the mean, avaricious, and ruthless expressions that stare out at us from the rogues' gallery of sketches that Holbein made of the men and women who thronged Henry VIII's court and who fill the pages of the Lisle letters. As the central focus of power and patronage in the kingdom, the court was a place where every man's hand was against every other's; where Macbeth's 'there's not a one of them but in his house I keep a servant fee'd' is borne out by what we learn about the planting or bribing of informers from the Lisle letters (IV, pp. 40, 61); and where the sworn adversaries of one moment are the firm allies of the next. When the Earl of Hertford had been choked off in his pursuit of the Basset inheritance, this was not the beginning of an undying feud with the Lisles; for the next thing we find in the letters is an offer by the Hertfords to take one of the Lisle daughters into their home and service (V, pp. 464–6).

We can tell how they esteemed the prizes they competed for by witnessing, through the Lisle letters, the humiliations these powerful and exalted suitors endured for their sake. 'Fashionable beggars', Halifax called their seventeenth-century successors. And begging takes time. 'This present day Mr Husee and I were at St James' in the morning by seven of the clock', writes Lord Howard to Lisle, 'as we be every day, or at the court, and never fail day, for that we would be dispatched' (V, p. 86). 'Sometime', writes Husee on another occasion, distilling bitter experience, 'one hour missing attendance . . . may hinder a month's suit' (V, p. 97).

It would be easy to write off this class and generation as unusually self-regarding, as one of Lisle's correspondents does. 'The bishops of Worcester and Salisbury have resigned up their bishoprics', he reports. 'They be not of the wisest sort, methinks, for few nowadays will leave and give over such promotions for keeping of opinion' (V, p. 576). Lisle himself knew all about the acquisitive instinct; for his position made him peculiarly accessible to the importunate suitor. Gifts poured in upon him; but there was almost always something more than impulsive generosity or warm friendship packed up with them; for Lisle had places in the Calais retinue to fill. Nevertheless, behind the seemingly abject compliance with the breach with Rome and the apparently spontaneous and uninhibited response to the opportunities created by the release of so much ecclesiastical property into the land market, we can perhaps discern, in the Lisle letters, a conviction, expressed by Shakespeare in the words he puts into Richard II's mouth, that the king knew best what ought to be done, that disobedience of his wishes was a sin as well as a crime, and that if it all turned out badly the king, and not his subjects, would carry a heavy burden of guilt for which he, and not they, would be answerable hereafter. We get the clearest indication of these un-spoken convictions from the letters in which Husee provided Lisle with a running commentary upon the drafting of the statement defining certain precepts of belief that Parliament passed as the Act of Six Articles. Trouble had brewed because reformers eager to use the breach with Rome as the prelude to radical reform in the Church, clashed with the king, who was determined to stop the Reformation in its tracks. The king took an active part in the work, and Husee's letters testify to the way in which everyone, however exalted his station, held his breath and waited to be told what he must think and do in order to conform with Church doctrine and practice as by royal will established.

Domestic affairs occupy much space in the letters. The Lisles were sub-stantial landowners and had to supervise their estates at a distance during Lisle's posting to Calais. Unfortunately, we hear virtually nothing about the problems of landlords in the letters. The accounts are sent to Lady Lisle for examination (I, p. 636), a choice which will surprise nobody who recalls how important women were in the Paston and Stonor households. Indeed, we are left in no doubt by the letters that Lady Lisle occupies a key position in the Calais household. Everyone who values Lord Lisle's goodwill knows that hers is vital if his is to be obtained. Husee writes to her constantly. So do Lord Lisle's close friends as well as suitors for his favour. And, like Paston and Stonor women, she dispenses medical advice which is gratefully received by her correspondents, doubtless on the ground advocated by Hobbes a century later, that the nostrums of a practical woman were infinitely preferable to the prescriptions of learned but inexperienced physicians.

Money was a perennial problem. Debts were for ever mounting as trades-men were kept waiting endlessly to have their bills paid. Thomas Betson, in one of his avuncular moods, warned Elizabeth Stonor against extravagance; but Betson's tone was nothing to Husee's when he was provoked to one of his more sanctimonious outbursts: 'Now may your ladyship see,' he writes, 'that ready money buyeth all things at advantage, and they that dealeth otherwise must take it at their price or go without it' (V, p. 59). Scrounging about for money was one of Husee's most distasteful tasks. He borrowed at court (III, p. 435), earned a rebuff on one occasion from the vice-treasurer who told him that he could not help Lisle 'of no man's money' (IV, p. 117), and found out at another time that the things the Lisles wanted were to be had on better credit in Flanders than elsewhere (IV, p. 77).

Virtually everything the Lisles needed came over from England, Lady Lisle, it is true, got her nightcaps from a Dunkirk nunnery which, at one period at least, sold its entire output for three months to a Spanish merchant, in much the same way as English nunneries had for many generations sold their wool clips for years in advance to the Italians (V, p. 388). But this seems to have been quite exceptional. The letters give the impression that London was where the Lisles expected to be able to supply practically all their needs. With the great centres of northern trade and industry only up the road from Calais, a preference for London markets and London crafts-men is one that the reader cannot fail to be struck by.

Education was a central preoccupation of the family. Lady Lisle had seven children by her previous marriage, Lord Lisle three by his. We hear very little about Lisle's three because they were all grown up by this time, but Lady Lisle's were still to be provided for. Miss Byrne has very wisely broken her rule of strict chronological sequence in order to group together many of the letters that bear on the subject of the education of these children. They are to be found in volume Ill; and they are worth a library of books on the history of education. There is a perennial quality about such letters. The clothes, the lodgings, the fees, the reports from tutors, the anxieties about health, comfort and pocket-money, all these matters are the common con-cerns of parents who send their children away from home for long periods. But the Lisle letters add a spice of their own. There was the unsuitable tutor, exposed as a result of Husee's investigations, who kept a mistress, 'a dun cow', as Husee put it, 'by whom he hath had five or six calves' (IV, p. 55). And there was the irrepressible James Basset, who smuggled out a letter warning his parents not to believe anything he had written in previous letters because these had been written under duress. (IV, p. 497). Lady Lisle had the matter instantly but discreetly investigated and got the immemorial answer to her agitated inquiries: 'Madam, I desire that you will not be moved with every word your son shall send you . . . Children complaineth other-while when a man doth most for their profit' (IV, p. 498).

Sending children away from home was condemned by the author of the *Italian Relation* as an English barbarity, and his strictures have stuck. What-ever its shortcomings, however, the practice never involved the sequestra-tion of the Lisle children from domesticity in institutions where they met only members of their own age and sex. The Lisle children were sent away from home in order to be placed in homes comparable with their own, where they were treated as members of the family. The girls came to regard the French families with which they lived as second homes, enormously ex-panded their range of contacts and made fast friendships. We hear rather less about the boys; but they seem to have been well looked after, on the whole, and received a polish which stood them in good stead.

Given the one-way characteristic of the Lisle letters, we cannot expect to hear a great deal about love and marriage in them. The Pastons with their tempestuous family quarrels and the Stonors with their lovers' idyll have spoilt us for anything less than lyrical poetry or melodrama in these matters. The Lisle letters, however, are pitched in a much quieter key. They tell us of much more choosing of marriage partners than we might have expected to find in view of the trafficking in marriage that was regular feature of the life of the times. Lisle himself, whose first wife was a baroness in her own right, chose a knight's daughter who was a knight's widow as his second wife, when presumably he could have taken his pick of nobler and wealthier women. And young people, so obviously trapped by the system, were in fact much freer from it than they seemed to be. The lesson of the crisis caused by Margery Paston's secret betrothal to the Pastons' general manager, Richard Calle, was that even the bishop of Norwich, who was dragged in to find some way of annulling their compact, was defeated by the Church's own rule about the sanctity of the plighted troth. Possibly the Lisle children were more docile than the Paston girls; possibly the Lisles by conforming to the current practice of sending their children where they would meet only suitable partners were vindicated in the event: for their children seem to have pleased themselves in this respect without displeasing their parents. At any rate, whatever the disabilities of the medieval system, the letters of the period, even the Paston letters, for all their beatings and scoldings of recalcitrant daughters, convey the impression that family devotion was neither less common nor more so than at other times. There was plenty of genuine affection expressed in letters in which, as with the Lisle letters, there was nothing to be gained by dissembling.

Letters in the Lisle collection were by no means confined to practical matters of business, public or private. Correspondents were chided for not writing, and they excused themselves for failing to do so in ways with which we are all familiar – a sure sign that letter-writing was a regular rather than an exceptional feature of life. And there was plenty of racy, even bawdy, chaff and mischief in them. The Governor of the Merchant Adventurers, a family friend, tells Lady Lisle that he writes to make her merry by day, leaving it to her husband to do as much for her by night (IV, p. 124). Lady Lisle's letters to Thomas Thirlby, though more delicate, are equally full of fun (V, p. 234), as are Francis Bryan's to Lisle (I, pp. 595–6). Gardiner, the bishop of Winchester, writing officially but as Lisle's old friend, to keep him informed of the prospects of war between France and the Empire, puts his news thus: 'We can write you no tidings but after such sort as one answered his friend that asked him whether it should rain or no that night'. And there follows a pleasant conceit in the form of a mock dialogue between the two (III, p. 290).

Never far away, however vivacious the chatter, were graver realities. There was the plague, to which people responded with the same helpless dread that they responded to the threat of polio before the days of immunization. 'Send over Mr Bassett', writes Husee from London to Calais, 'if they begin to die there, for they dieth not about Lincoln's Inn' (V, p. 85). On another occasion, when young Basset is lodged at Lincoln's Inn, Husee worries because 'they dieth daily in the city' (III, p. 527). And mingled with the gossip and banter and the talk about fashion and quails, is stark news conveyed without comment, of arrests and torture, of hangings and executions, and of the rebellion of the Pilgrims of Grace whose issue hung in the balance as letters

passed between London and Calais. And sounding like the tolling of a bell
through the correspondence came news of the monasteries as they fell, one
by one, beneath the hammer of the king's commissioners.

It is hard to exaggerate the importance of these volumes, and harder still
to give anything but the most inadequate impression of the pleasure and
profit to be got out of studying them. Miss Byrne has produced one of the
masterpieces of modern historical scholarship; and the Chicago University
Press is to be congratulated for having risen magnificently to the occasion.

Sixteenth-Century Farming

The sixteenth century is commonly depicted as the century during which the modern world emerged from the medieval. Those who divide history into stages of economic growth have usually found themselves in agreement, on this point, with those who divide it into periods of social and political change. According to this view the dissolution of feudal ties, the renunciation of allegiance to an oecumenical church, and the termination of a time-honoured method of expropriating the surplus value of labour made room for the emergence, in the course of the sixteenth century, of systems of thought and modes of action, in politics and administration, in production and distribution, in religion, science, and the arts, which settled the way in which things would develop until now.

The sixteenth century has been regarded for so long as the natural frontier between medieval and modern in English history that it takes an effort of thought to realize that it is in fact no longer the frontier it was. Paradoxically enough, the weakening of this established division owes much to the work done by historians of sixteenth-century affairs whose intention was to strengthen it. So provocative were the claims they made for sixteenth-century developments that they roused the indignant opposition of historians who had been placidly content, hitherto, to ruminate in pastures which were unquestionably medieval without troubling themselves in the least with thoughts which went beyond the bounds of their normal interests. Having asked for trouble, they got it. They found themselves being challenged on their own ground with the result that familiar landmarks are fast disappearing from the historical landscape, and a frontier which was once so firmly established is now, at last, on the move.

If we hear no more of the New Monarchy for the future that will be part of the debt we owe to the late K. B. McFarlane and to those who have followed where he led.[1] If we hear less than we did of the enormous accession of prestige and even of power that accrued to Parliament as a result of the use that Tudor monarchs made of it, we owe it to Prof. Roskell that we now see that the real break in the history of Parliament occurred very much later than the sixteenth century and in circumstances very different from those

---

[1] K. B. McFarlane, *The Nobility of Later Medieval England* (Oxford, 1973), p. xviii, and n. i. See also S. B. Chrimes, ed., *Fifteenth Century England, 1399–1509* (Manchester, 1972).

that prevailed then.[2] And if the administrative changes made by Thomas Cromwell have now lost the fresh gloss of novelty and modernity that they once had that is surely because medievalists such as Mr Harriss have shown that when all Cromwell's reforms had been accomplished the structure of government was not so very different from what it had been before his time.[3]

In economic history the outstanding issue that served to divide medieval England from modern was, for many years, the issue of commercialization. And whilst the medieval manor was thought to be synonymous with the medieval farm, its structure, in Tawney's phrase, 'a perverse miracle of organised torpor', it was not difficult to see English trade and industry, in the Middle Ages, as little better than a negligible quantity of variable but often dubious importance to the economy. The historical work done in the last generation or so on centuries which are indubitably medieval has made it impossible for anyone to hold this view with quite the old fortitude. The market so obviously exercised its influence upon the dispositions made by perfectly ordinary farmers, merchants, and manufacturers, that it is now impossible to believe that the medieval centuries were ever as innocent of commercialization as historians who looked back on them from the vantage point of the sixteenth century once imagined.

Nevertheless the belief persists amongst historians of the sixteenth century that the pace of economic life quickened at that time and that market forces penetrated more deeply and permeated more widely than ever before. And indeed everything conspires to fortify them in this belief. The language of the records, and indeed of people generally, though quaint to modern senses, is no longer stiff and crabbed. It is often fluent and melli-fluous. In poetry it soars. Politicians seem to speak in modern accents of modern problems. Economists write in familiar terms.

Appearances, however, can be deceptive. This is, after all, the first age of printing. It is therefore the first age in which we can hear the more vocal and literate members of society discussing their problems at length in records we can still pick up and read. When they discussed them in previous centuries we hear the commotion they made or provoked, if we are lucky, at one or two removes, and catch one or two of the words they spoke or set down. But nearly everything we know about them or their problems we know by inference and surmise. Inference and surmise are still important to the historian of sixteenth-century affairs. But the impact of printing is so tremendous that we cannot easily adjust to its novelty by making the sort of allowances for its testimony in the sixteenth century that have become commonplace in assessing the records of later centuries when printing is

[2] J. S. Roskell, 'Perspectives in English Parliamentary History', *Bulletin of the John Rylands Library*, vol. xlvi (1964), reprinted in E. B. Fryde and E. Miller, eds, *Historical Studies of the English Parliament*, vol. II (Cambridge, 1970).
[3] G. L. Harriss, 'Medieval Government and Statecraft', *Past and Present*, vol. xxv (1963). See also *Past and Present*, vol. xxix (1964) and xxxi (1965); J. Hurstfield, *Freedom, Corruption and Government in Elizabethan England* (1973), pp. 23–49.

taken for granted. Consequently the medieval politician, churchman, trader, or farmer is often credited, sometimes by the most distinguished scholars, with a simplicity of mind bordering on downright addle-pated ingenuousness unrivalled in later and better-documented centuries, and with a lethargy of spirit for which the justification appears to be nothing more substantial than the feeling that those who make so little stir in the records cannot be up to very much, either for good or ill.

All this has an important bearing upon the attitude of historians to sixteenth-century agrarian problems. In countries like sixteenth-century England, where farming was still the chief occupation of the majority of the people, fluctuations in the prosperity of farming were overwhelmingly important in determining the fortunes of the entire economic system. And historians of sixteenth-century farming, whatever their other disagreements, have always been unanimous in believing that sixteenth-century agrarian problems differed fundamentally from those that affected medieval farmers, and that sixteenth-century opportunities were incomparably greater than those that medieval farmers were offered, or indeed were capable of exploiting.

A medievalist who looks at the farming world of sixteenth-century England, however, cannot resist the impression of having seen it all before. Corn prices rise more or less continuously as they did, apparently, from the late twelfth century until the middle of the thirteenth century. The real incomes of those who work for wages fall as far below the heights achieved in the fifteenth century as they did in the thirteenth and early fourteenth centuries. And to judge by the crises that occur the economy seems to be having as much difficulty in feeding the population by the end of the sixteenth century as it had by the end of the thirteenth.[4] Rents rise as land runs short and some efforts are made to add to the cultivated area. If we hear less than we did in the thirteenth century about such efforts, that is surely only in part because thirteenth-century farmers, in this respect at least, kept better records than their successors. It is mainly, perhaps, because thirteenth-century farmers had already assarted every scrap of land that was capable of bearing a crop so that when their successors resorted to land at the margin they were generally going where others had been before.

The chief problem in the sixteenth century, however, as in the thirteenth, was not simply the shortage of land. It was the problem of competition for land which had other uses than the obvious one of growing corn. Much land in both centuries was devoted to sport. But a good deal of the land reserved for sport was not suitable for anything else, given the contemporary state of the arts. Consequently, the chief competitor for arable land was usually either sheep or cattle.

Farm animals were required, in those days, for all forms of traction, includ-

---

[4] The evidence is summarized in A. R. Bridbury, 'The Black Death', reprinted above pp. 200–17, and in Joan Thirsk, ed., *The Agrarian History of England and Wales*, vol. IV (Cambridge, 1967), ch. 9.

ing the pulling of barges. Their wool and skins clothed virtually the entire population. And their milk and meat supplied the community's demand for protein foods in a more palatable and concentrated form than peas and beans. In the sixteenth century, as in the thirteenth, the market for richer foods, better clothing, and even for traction in its many forms was severely limited. It was not limited because ordinary consumers were so unsophisticated that they had not yet acquired the taste for such things. Piers Plowman and the official records of his time show the ordinary villager avid for all the luxuries enjoyed by his betters and impatient to the point of insurrectionary violence to seize his chance of them. The market for these things was limited, in the sixteenth century as in the thirteenth, by the diminishing capacity of the ordinary Englishman to pay for anything but the most rudimentary means of satisfying his need for food, clothing, shelter, and warmth. The pressures that raised the price of land in these centuries drained the money from the pockets of the ordinary farmer and farm worker, and put it into the pockets of those whose title to land was secure enough to enable them to profit by such pressures. In both centuries the landed classes lived exceedingly well. In both centuries dairying and beef-cattle farming flourished by supplying their needs. In both centuries the authors of farming manuals encouraged them to make the most of their opportunities. But those who were in a position to take advantage of the chronic shortage of land were comparatively few, even if we include amongst their number their dependants and their servants of all degrees. Consequently, given the circumstances of the time, neither the traction needs of the economy nor its animal protein needs can easily account for the competition for corn land in either century. That privilege belongs to the sheep.

The keeping of sheep in a climate like that of England was to some extent a matter of necessity. Woollen clothes were, for most people, the simplest and cheapest way of keeping warm. How many sheep were kept for this purpose was, for most people, a matter of their standard of living. The poor made clothes last for much longer than the well-to-do, and patched and patched instead of buying new, and sold what they cast off to others even less fortunate than themselves instead of turning it into rags. When poverty receded the market for old clothes contracted. But the market for wool was not simply a market created by the need for warm clothes, however restricted by poverty or expanded by comfort that market might be. It was not even simply the market created by the extravagances of the wealthy. Exported raw or manufactured into cloth, it paid for all the imports that the well-to-do bought in greater profusion and with greater liberality as the price of land rose. Consequently, the demand for sheep pasture in England was in fact, in large measure, in both the thirteenth and the sixteenth centuries, a demand for the means with which to pay for the wine and furs, the exotic foods and spices, the linens and precious cloths, the gold and jewellery that provided the well-to-do with the refinements of foreign luxury which their buoyant incomes enabled them to enjoy.

At both periods this demand for land represented a formidable draft upon the scarce physical resources of the country. Historians of arable farming have made us very familiar with the deplorably meagre productivity of land devoted to corn before the seventeenth and eighteenth centuries. Animal productivity has attracted less attention. But animal productivity was also extremely low. England may have been famous for the quality of the wool grown by English sheep on English pastures. But enormous flocks required immense pastures in order to yield the clips that made English wool so famous.[5]

Contrary to widespread belief, however, the demand for wool with which to supply the export trade did not represent a more serious draft upon scarce resources in the sixteenth century than it had done in the thirteenth. In the late thirteenth and early fourteenth centuries, for which we have the earliest figures for exports, the volume of wool exported fluctuated between 25,000 and 35,000 sacks per year. In the sixteenth century, when nearly all the wool exported left England made up into cloth, the total quantities exported, raw and manufactured, rarely exceeded that volume except perhaps for a brief period in mid-century when currency manipulation created an altogether exceptional and artificial market for English woollens abroad.[6]

Indeed, it may be that sixteenth-century export requirements made fewer in-roads upon the landed resources of the country than they had done in the previous period of intense scarcity of land. Dr Bowden has reminded us that fleeces got heavier once enclosure had revolutionized farming.[7] Whether enclosure was widespread or not in the sixteenth century is a question which admits of dispute. But there can be no doubt as to the nature of its influence upon the weight if not the quality of the fleece, and hence upon the size of the investment required for a given volume of production.

In terms of labour employed the sixteenth-century export trade in cloth employed many more than the thirteenth-century export trade in wool had done. This no doubt generated more income in the export sector than ever before. But it made no contribution whatsoever to the acute and worsening problem of food supply that disquieted sixteenth-century statesmen and haunted ordinary sixteenth-century townsmen and villagers. The cloth exported from England did not help to mitigate the problem of land shortage

5   P. J. Bowden, 'Wool Supply and the Woollen Industry', *Economic History Review*, 2nd ser., vol. ix (1956).
6   A. R. Bridbury, *Economic Growth: England in the Later Middle Ages* (1962), p. 32, gives the decennial averages until 1540. See E. M. Carus-Wilson and O. P. Coleman, *England's Export Trade, 1275–1547* (Oxford, 1963). For the period 1544–61 see J. D. Gould, *The Great Debasement*, App. C. (Oxford, 1970). The London accounts for the second half of the century have been printed in triennial averages by F. J. Fisher, 'Commercial Trends and Policy in Sixteenth-Century England', *Economic History Review*, 1st ser., vol. x (1940), reprinted in E. M. Carus-Wilson, ed., *Essays in Economic History*, vol. I (1954). For the conversion rate of cloth into wool, see E. M. Carus-Wilson, *Medieval Merchant Venturers* (1954), p. 250, n. 2.
7   Bowden, *loc. cit.*

by laying other regions of the world under contribution for the corn and meat supplies that England desperately needed. The woollen cloth export trade was not, in that sense, the precursor of the export trade in cotton pieces that fed nineteenth-century England. Nor did the wages paid out to those who worked in that trade provide farmers with much incentive to raise output by increasing the productivity of the land. With population in spate those who worked in the cloth export trade were most unlikely to have been able to escape the misfortunes that overtook the vast majority of sixteenth-century wage-earners. To judge by the real value of its remuneration, there was, to all appearances, so much labour to be had in sixteenth-century England that wage rates were cut to the bone, so little land with which to combine it, and hence so few raw materials, that the output of labour was often, presumably, scarcely worth its cost, and consequently so little work for all who were looking for it that employment was often haphazard and irregular.

The plight of sixteenth-century labour was strikingly similar to the plight of labour in the thirteenth century. These surely were transcendentally the centuries of enforced idleness, when the problem of work, for the ordinary labourer or artisan, was not the tantalizing one of choosing which job to do, nor even the agreeable one of deciding whether to work or not, but the desperate one of finding any work whatsoever which paid well enough to enable a man to keep body and soul together. Tudor pamphleteers and Tudor legislation were full of complaint about vagrancy and the sturdy beggar. But what is a man to do but wander, and in particular wander towards London and the bigger towns, if he cannot get work where he is and knows that he cannot fare worse by making for places where there is much more going on than there is at home?

If thirteenth-century records are not so full of this problem as later ones the reason is much more likely to be that the records are less helpful than that the problem was less urgent. Where, after all, should we look for thirteenth-century complaint? In the pamphlet literature? There was none. In petitions to Parliament? It scarcely existed yet as a national forum for grievance and its redress. In the parish records? They have not survived. And yet the impression we get from the comparatively meagre freight of thirteenth-century town records which has survived the journey through time is that the town was as much of a raft to which the social flotsam clung in that century as it was in the sixteenth century.

The new towns that sprang up all over thirteenth-century England were certainly a tribute to the business enterprise of those who founded them and those who ran them. But the new towns that prospered filled up at an astoundingly rapid rate.[8] Those who filled them up were not burgesses. The

---

[8] E. M. Carus-Wilson, 'The First Half-Century of the Borough of Stratford Upon Avon', *Economic History Review*, 2nd ser., vol. xviii (1965); M. Beresford, *New Towns of the Middle Ages* (1967).

majority of those who lived in towns performed humbler offices than those of master-craftsman. Their reward, when they could earn one, was not a fee, or a return on management, or a profit on capital invested. It was never more than a wage and often enough, no doubt, scarcely more than a tip. In the circumstances of the thirteenth century can we doubt but that it was despair rather than hope that took such people off the farms and brought them to the towns? Some no doubt counted the days as they passed and waited for that liberating moment, after a year and a day, when their lords might pursue them no longer. But how many were of so little account whence they came that they were even denied the satisfaction of out-witting their pursuers, either because they were not missed or because none thought them worth the trouble of pursuit?

The towns were too small both in the thirteenth and in the sixteenth century to have been able to relieve more than a tiny fraction of the desperate social and economic pressure that we can discern in the surviving records. In these centuries most people were destined to die where they were born, many of them enduring a purgatory of want and unemployment, in the more or less brief interlude between birth and death, without having the chance or the desire to look elsewhere for relief. And this meant, in the sixteenth century as in the thirteenth, that the market for farm produce was severely restricted by the poverty of large sections of the community.

Markets limited as these were offered precious little incentive to the innovator and the improver. The price of corn may appear to have been high enough to stimulate enterprise, and the wage rate reasonable enough not to discourage it. But in both centuries rent entered so deeply into the ordinary farmer's costs as to increase the risks of farming to the point where very few were willing to add to their risks by embarking upon experimental changes, and fewer still had the means with which to do so once they had paid their rent. In both centuries security of tenure was seriously jeopardized. Death shortened every variety of tenure as famine and pestilence took their toll of an overstretched economic system; and landlords, with a prescient eye on the chances of renewing them upon terms which were ever more favourable to themselves, shortened leases. Moreover, as life got harder for the majority the burden of debt no doubt bore more heavily upon them. These are not the circumstances in which ordinary men take chances with new methods.

In the sixteenth century, as in the thirteenth, there were tenant-farmers who were in a strong enough position to resist all efforts by their landlords to raise rents.[9] There were some who were able to keep inheritance fines down. In the thirteenth century the landlord who imposed a variety of vexatious customary levies upon his tenants was often in a stronger position to raise the annual value of his property than the sixteenth-century landlord who did not. Accordingly the sixteenth-century landlord was obliged to depend upon

---

[9]   E. Kerridge, *Agrarian Problems in the Sixteenth Century and After* (1969); A. L. Poole, *Obligations of Society* (Oxford, 1946).

fines more heavily, perhaps, than his predecessor had done in order to recover past increases in value which he had been unable to recoup in other ways.

Whether the price of land rose annually, however, or at intervals, whether it was paid annually, or in lump sums, there can be no doubt as to its trend in either century. And neither the high price of farm products nor the low pay of farm labour is likely to have given ordinary tenant-farmers a margin, after they had satisfied their landlords, which was always big enough even for purposes of maintaining capital intact.

There were those who were not caught in this vicious circle. There were those who had virtually no rents to pay. And there were those who had their land on easy terms. Such people were under no necessity to cost their farming operations by making substantial allowances for rent in their calculations. Their takings less maintenance and running costs were therefore enormous. Farming kept them rich without their having to make any effort which was out of the ordinary. In the thirteenth century these fortunate few were mainly the great landlords. In the sixteenth century they were more often the affluent tenants of landlords who had lost the taste for farming and who were generous with their tenants, in the matter of rents and fines, sometimes to a fault.[10] In both centuries there were men of wealth and industry, whether they had their land on easy terms or not, who farmed well, made profits, and even experimented with improved ways of doing things. Were they portents or freaks? Did they lead where others should have followed? Or did they offer a solution to the agrarian problems of their age which was bound to lead to disaster?

The agrarian problems of the sixteenth century, in the sense that these were problems of maintaining and improving the fertility of the soil, were not unique to the sixteenth century. They may have been intractable in sixteenth-century circumstances but they were not insoluble because sixteenth-century farmers were ignorant or inadequate. And they are soon understood.

Most soils have reserves of all the mineral particles and compounds which are necessary for plant growth. But without organic matter these minerals cannot support plant life. The organic content of the soil, however, and with it the fertility of the land, can vary enormously. The balance between the rate at which organic matter is deposited into the soil, and the rate at which it is taken up and broken down into essential plant foods by the organisms that live in the soil, can rise to an upper limit or fall to a lower one. Pasture, unless it is grazed to extinction, will maintain its content of organic matter at the upper limit, more or less indefinitely. It will do so because grass, being a permanent crop, sheds organic matter into the soil continuously, from roots and leaves; and being a permanent crop restricts the supply of air to the soil

---

[10] Thus Thirsk, ed., *op. cit.*, pp. 345ff, and C. Hill, *Economic Problems of the Church* (Oxford, 1956), ch. 2.

organisms and hence the rate at which they can break down the grass residues and consume the food they provide.

Arable is quite another matter. On arable land the supply of plant residues is curtailed because the soil is only intermittently under crops. Moreover, the soil itself is much better aerated. Aeration stimulates the soil organisms to greater activity and fecundity. When the land is in arable they are stimulated in circumstances in which the natural replacement of what they take up is much reduced. This is the crucial factor because it is they, and not the arable crops, that then consume the lion's share of the organic foods in the soil. 'Much of our agricultural effort,' commented Sir John Russell, 'goes in sustaining the large and varied population of living things in the soil: we get only the by-products of their activity.'[11] Hence the organic content of the soil under arable can quickly fall as a result of the ravages of the soil organisms until a new low-level equilibrium is established between the organic matter available and the soil organisms it can support.

Whatever the arable crops grown the organic content of the soil can only be maintained at the level achieved under grass by feeding the soil with sufficient quantities of organic matter, or substitutes for organic matter, to compensate for this staggering loss of fertility. Before the nineteenth century farmers could compensate for the immense losses incurred by continuous tillage only by keeping animals on pasture and spreading their dung over the arable land. Farmers have always known that dung was the answer to their problem. The closes they so often cropped continuously in the Middle Ages were kept in good heart by a regimen of intensive dunging whatever may have been customary on the village fields.[12] Indeed dung was so often at the bottom of their arguments and quarrels that, as Maitland remarks somewhere, a good deal of legal history could be written in terms of dung. But the feeding that arable land required for continuous tillage imposed upon those who tilled continuously the necessity of keeping large herds and flocks of animals. And these animals had to be fed. During the growing season they needed grazing; and some of the crops grown had to provide their winter fodder. This meant that unless these animals had some commercial value apart from the value of their dung the cost of keeping animals for the purpose of restoring the fertility of the arable was likely to have imposed an insupportable burden upon the profitability of arable farming.

The feeding problem was in fact solved when farmers took to growing fodder crops, apart from hay, for their animals. And they did so not as a result of devastating revelations of the hitherto unsuspected value of these crops but as a result of changes in the market for animal proteins, for clothing, and for motive power. When they found that the market could take animal products at prices which made it worth their while to keep larger herds and

11 E. J. Russell, *The World of the Soil* (1961), p. 172.
12 W. O. Ault, 'Open-Field Husbandry and the Village Community', *Transactions of the American Philosophical Society*, n.s., vol. clv (1965), pp. 29–30.

flocks than ever before farmers found that they had the means with which to raise the productivity of arable to heights which had never been achieved before. The nineteenth-century chemist broke this particular bondage of interdependence. But in the absence of satisfactory substitutes for dung, revolutionary changes in the productivity of arable farming were indissolubly linked, in earlier centuries, to changes in the market for animal products.

Before animals were valued highly enough to be kept in such numbers, however, the problem of restoring the losses incurred in cultivating the soil had to be solved, or partially solved, in other ways. Rotating the crops so that the same crop is never grown in the same soil in successive years rests the land in the sense that different plants root at different depths, carry different diseases, harbour different parasites and insects, and vary somewhat in what they take from the soil. But all cropping is deleterious, and the simplest way to cope with the problems it brings is to forgo one crop in a series by fallowing the land. Fallowing, even without benefit of dung, can substantially increase crop yields as the Rothamsted experiments have shown.[13] The fallowed land having grown a grass cover will soon begin to regenerate naturally. Dunging it will hasten the natural process; and no doubt it always did so, for, in the days before tractors, even the poorest arable farm possessed some animals.

The longer the fallowing lasts the better. Indeed no method of enriching the soil with organic matter is more satisfactory than that of leaving it for several years under a cover of grass and clovers, or grass and some other leguminous plant. When land is cheap the farmer can afford to rest it, in this way, for years. The infield-outfield system which usually rested some of the land for successive years usually rested land which was cheap because it was poor, not cheap because it was good but abundant. Nevertheless it operated somewhat along these lines. If he is prepared to move at intervals no doubt the farmer can rest the land he has once cultivated for ever. In a country like England, however, moving was never a simple matter even when other men's rights did not stand in the way of it. In England, soil, temperature, and rainfall, being more or less exactly what arable farming requires, are also more or less exactly what forest requires. The farmers who moved from virgin site to virgin site in England in order to maintain the productivity of the soil of their farms, if they ever did so in any numbers, presently found the effort of clearance more than the extra yield was worth. And soon enough the growth of the population made it harder to move on, and in the end halted movement altogether.

In the end, therefore, the cost of fallowing was the value of the crop forgone. As prices rose, farmers were compelled to make nicer and nicer calculations of costs and returns in order to decide whether or not the extra cost of a longer fallow would be justified by the additional output at expected

[13] Rothamsted Experimental Station, *Report for 1968, part 2* (Harpenden, 1969), pp. 43–4.

future prices. And with present prices rising as they did in the thirteenth and sixteenth centuries, expected future prices were not always good enough to encourage them to postpone production today in favour of higher production tomorrow. No society in which poverty was as widespread and acute as it was in England in those centuries could afford to wait. The ultimate gain by so doing did not compensate for present loss. When starvation is never far away corn today has infinite value; corn tomorrow, however bountiful its promise, none at all. No doubt the three-field system made better use of richer soils than the two-field system by cutting down the proportion of cultivable land that was kept fallow. But it also increased current output when, perhaps, it might have been improvident to do so in a longer view. Every now and then we catch·glimpses of farmers breaking the rules and sowing the fallows.[14] No doubt they did so with the collusion of their neighbours. And in the circumstances of the thirteenth century what could be more likely than that they did so because they could see no future for themselves unless they got something out of the soil at once, leaving the future to look after itself? Thus the open-field system seems to have been the perfect answer to the need for compromise between resting the fields and starving the population by making the utmost use of scanty animal resources on fallows which lasted just long enough to add more to the productivity of the soil than they denied crops to a vulnerable community.

Field systems were endlessly different from one another. But in all the populous regions of England they shared the common purpose of rotating the crops and using the animal resources of the farm so as to restore some of its fertility to the uncropped land during its regular period of fallowing. When the fallowing was done in common by all who held land in the village, the rotation coincided with the field system in the sense that everyone fallowed the same field at the same time. Often this meant that crops were sown and harvested according to the large and simple divisions of the orthodox two- and three-field systems. Often enough, however, it did not. Sometimes the cropping unit was a group of strips within the field. When this was so crops might vary even though fallowing was still done in common. Sometimes, as in parts of Norfolk, Cambridgeshire, and Essex, where the common fields may have looked like common fields anywhere else, the fields had in fact altogether lost their functional importance and retained only a topographical utility as aids in locating the groups of strips, gathered into what were called *tenementa* in medieval Norfolk, which were the true units of the system for all farming purposes. Sometimes, as in many parts of East Anglia and the Chiltern region, the fields were so small and numerous that they had to be grouped together for fallowing purposes. In such cases, as the editors of the latest studies of these matters have concluded, 'it thus becomes more important to discover whether in any particular township a two- or three-course

---

[14] G. C. Homans, *English Villagers of the Thirteenth Century* (Cambridge, Mass., 1942), pp. 57–8.

rotation was practised than whether its lands lay in two or three or any other number of fields.'[15]

In fact, there was almost no limit to the degree of fragmentation that could have taken place. The pressure to share the fallow, and hence to compel farmers to join a communal system, was more likely to have come from farmers desperate for fodder for their animals than from farmers who were anxious to enrich their soils. This was so because fallows are not enriched merely by having animals consume the fallow growths and then return what they have eaten, as waste products, to the fallow soil. Animals can only enrich the fallows directly by dropping on them what they have eaten elsewhere.[16] Consequently, wherever the demand for fodder was low the demand for communal grazing was also likely to have been low, with correspondingly weakening effects upon communal routines of farming. In every case, however, from the simplest to the most complex, one consideration dominated all others. Wherever there was too little dung the arable had to be fallowed; and wherever the arable was fallowed the open-field system prevailed in essence if not in appearance.

The classical open-field system as depicted in the Orwins' study of Laxton manor did not spring to maturity in the dawn of history; and we are all substantially in Dr Thirsk's debt for pointing out that the open-field system, like every other social institution, has its history of development and adaptation.[17] But the tyranny of fertility loss has no history in this sense; and it would be a pity if the work of seeking out origins and tracing changes and variations in early field patterns and early systems of social obligation were ever allowed to obscure the fact that every field pattern and every system of obligation had to accommodate itself to the unrelenting demand of the soil for recuperative fallowing.

The open-field system, as finally evolved, may strike the casual observer as being, like the camel, the very definition of clumsy and inept committee work, an ignoble product of evasion and compromise. In fact, like the camel, the open-field system was perfectly adapted to the conditions in which it had to work. And it was extraordinarily flexible, lending itself to much variation, and even to the exacting requirements of market-gardening.[18] These obvious merits, however, have not sufficed to commend the system to writers of sixteenth-century farming history. In a century in which so much was astir, it was not to be believed that farming could have been impervious to the spirit of the age. Almost without exception, therefore, writers on sixteenth-century farming history have looked for changes in the routines of English

[15] A. R. H. Baker and R. A. Butlin, eds, *Studies of Field Systems in the British Isles* (Cambridge, 1973), p. 643.
[16] Russell, *op. cit.*, p. 201.
[17] J. Thirsk, 'The Common Fields', *Past and Present*, vol. xxix (1964).
[18] F. J. Fisher, 'The Development of the London Food Market', *Economic History Review*, 1st ser., vol. v (1935), reprinted in Carus-Wilson, ed., *Essays in Economic History*, vol. I, p. 142.

farming which were profound enough to be commensurate with what was going on elsewhere in English life. And they have generally found what they were looking for in the enclosure movement. Hence, until recently, virtually all interpretations of sixteenth-century agrarian problems have been, in effect, variations on the theme of enclosure.

Recent work, however, has had a devastating effect upon all such interpretations by subverting the foundations upon which they depended. In 1955 Dr Kerridge demonstrated that the returns made by the commissioners appointed to inquire into enclosure and depopulation in 1517, 1518, and 1607 are not to be taken at face value.[19] He pointed out that these returns were simply presentments made by juries, not judgements according to law; *prima facie* cases perhaps, but certainly not findings tested in the courts. Many of the returns of 1517 were, in fact, drastically revised in 1518; and of the returns to the inquiries of 1607 Dr Kerridge says that 'it is difficult to see how anyone could read, let alone transcribe or digest, the returns of the commissioners without being struck by the dubious character of many of the presentments'. Accordingly, when they were disputed in the courts many failed. Even taken at face value, however, the returns show that the juries could find nothing worse than a mass of trivial breaches of the law, whether in terms of acreages enclosed or houses destroyed. And when Prof. Beresford followed through the cases brought into the Exchequer as a result of the legislation of 1489, 1515, and 1536, he found that the cases disputed at court proved to be as trivial as those that the juries had presented.[20]

No doubt many notorious enclosers, with the means or the influence with which to silence those who should have enforced the law, escaped justice. Certainly the bigger landlords had no desire to see the law enforced and, as Prof. Beresford has shown, did little or nothing to assist the king by bringing cases to court. And when mutual interest brought encloser and enclosed into happy accord there was little risk that retribution would follow their infringement of the law. But neither Prof. Beresford nor Dr Kerridge attempts to restore the enclosure movement to the sixteenth century in this devious way. Having destroyed the validity of the view that new forces were undermining traditional routines and traditional relationships in the sixteenth century by means of enclosure, Prof. Beresford and Dr Kerridge then propose very different explanations of what was happening to English farming at that time.

After exhaustively analysing the mass of trivial cases brought before the Exchequer, Prof. Beresford was driven to conclude that the enclosure movement was virtually over before the government saw any need for public

[19] E. Kerridge, 'The Returns of the Inquisitions of Depopulation', *English Historical Review*, vol. lxx (1955). J. Martin, 'Enclosure and the Inquisitions of 1607', *Agricultural History Review*, vol. 30 (1982), pp. 41–8 points out that there were many more convictions than Kerridge realised. But he has nothing to say in contradiction of Kerridge's claim that breaches of the law were mostly trivial.

[20] M. Beresford, *The Lost Villages of England* (1954), pp. 116–17.

action to check or stop it. This view offers a curious twist to the orthodox story of the sixteenth century as a century of dramatic change in farming. In this version the sixteenth century becomes the first century in which the new techniques of farming can be given their head, and the fifteenth century is confirmed in its traditional role of preparing the way and suffering all the afflictions of an age of transition. But what is the evidence that the problem can be shifted backwards in this way? And what is the likelihood that enclosure was the natural solution to the problems of fifteenth-century farming?

Many of those who contested the charges of enclosure and destruction of houses claimed that what they did was done before any legislation had been enacted to forbid it. Prof. Beresford rightly places very little confidence in what could easily have been nothing but a trick of advocacy. But he takes very seriously a statement made by John Hales, who was an enclosure commissioner in 1518, and again in 1548, when his work provoked such an outcry that he felt obliged to answer it. In the course of this answer he threw out the comment that 'the chief destruction of towns and decay of houses was before the beginning of the reign of King Henry the Seventh.'[21] Prof. Beresford also takes very seriously the work and indeed the fulminations of John Rous, a Warwickshire antiquary who died in 1491 leaving amongst his papers a history of England which included a list of depopulated villages in south Warwickshire and its neighbourhood and a bitter denunciation of those whom he believed to be responsible for their destruction.

Both these men reported what they knew. Rous reported what he had certainly seen; Hales what he may have seen as he rode past the ruins of deserted villages, or what he may have deduced from a comparison of the places mentioned in the Hundred Rolls of 1279, which he cites in his defence, with the lists from which he presumably worked in 1518 or 1548. And what they said about the abandonment of large numbers of villages in the fifteenth century Prof. Beresford has corroborated in his comprehensive study of lost villages. Consequently, the facts are not in dispute. Hales offered no explanation of them. Rous blamed the encloser in terms which are to become very familiar to readers of the pamphlet literature of the sixteenth century.

The rabid sixteenth-century castigator of enclosures never saw depopulation without searching for a depopulator and never found a depopulator who was not also an encloser. But the great depopulator, as we now know, was not to be found in the ranks of the stock miscreants and racketeers of vituperative pamphleteering. Disease was a deadlier scourge of the commonwealth than the most rapacious speculator. It emptied the villages more quickly than the most ruthless encloser. In particular it emptied those villages whose life had always been precarious. This is the gravamen of Prof. Beresford's find-

---

21 E. Lamond, ed., *A Discourse of the Common Weal of this Realm of England* (Cambridge, 1929), p. lxiii.

ings. When the flood-tide of population engulfed the land, as it did in the thirteenth century, all manner of villages which had got themselves established where they never really throve managed to keep going and make their diminutive showing in the records. When the flood-tide receded, as it did in the fourteenth century, such villages were left stranded, their communities soon drained of all but a sorry remnant. When they were finally deserted their sites were never subsequently reoccupied. Like those new towns of the thirteenth century which scarcely survived their foundation, they had been built where they should not have been. Their fields never knew the plough again. When farming went on it had to go on as pastoral farming. No doubt when he got the chance to lease his fields to a grazier before the village community had quite disappeared the landlord was sorely tempted to evict those who remained. At Azerley in 1362 it was said that 80 acres 'are worth nothing as grassground or as anything else on account of the large quantity of grassground that there is in these parts'.[22] In a world where scarcity had suddenly turned into such abundance, what could a landlord do but take what he was offered and move his surviving villagers on?

But the average fifteenth-century landlord was not a depopulator. In fifteenth-century conditions he neither proposed nor disposed. With wages rising to famine heights and rents falling catastrophically, the landlord's characteristic posture was more akin to the propitiatory cringe that a generation of full employment has made very familiar to the late-twentieth-century employer. In this respect Rous was quite wrong to blame rapacious landlordism for what had happened. He simply let his feelings run away with him. If the fifteenth-century landlord enclosed he did so in a very different spirit.

Arable farming had certainly become a struggle against insurmountable difficulties for fifteenth-century landlords. The combination of low rents and prices with rising wage rates drove them out of the business. Many of them kept a home farm going for the sake of their domestic needs.[23] And some continued to maintain important sheep flocks. Indeed the Italians still thought it worthwhile to tour the English countryside in the fifteenth century, as they had done in the thirteenth, buying up the wool clips supplied by these big producers.[24] But what does this mean? Does it mean that demesne farmers, driven out of arable farming by changes in the structure of costs and prices which threatened to bankrupt them, had merely retained the lucrative pastoral interests from which they could still make money? Or does it mean that they had actually switched from arable to pasture in order to continue to

[22] Beresford, Lost Villages, p. 427, n. 39.
[23] A. Savine, English Monasteries on the Eve of the Dissolution, Oxford Studies, ed. P. Vinogradoff, vol. I (Oxford, 1909), 170, 171–2, 178.
[24] Bridbury, Economic Growth, pp. 29–30; E. Lipson, Economic History of England, I (7th edn, 1937), 145; K. J. Allison, 'Flock Management', Economic History Review, 2nd ser., vol. xi (1958), p. 100.

earn as much of a living as possible by farming in the only way that was left to them?

Historians are strongly disposed to believe that pastoral interests were very widespread in the fifteenth century as a result of the transfer of extensive resources into grazing. Observers like Fortescue and the author of the Italian Relation certainly saw England in the late fifteenth century as a thriving country given over to pastoral farming.[25] And if he kept more animals than before what is more reasonable than to suppose that the fifteenth-century farmer had every incentive to enclose his farm? The push of costs and the pull of agrarian reform, according to this view, conspired to prepare the way, in the fifteenth century, for the great achievements of the sixteenth. But was the market for animal products buoyant enough to support such a wholesale transfer of resources from arable to pasture? If it were not, then a headlong rush into pastoral farming, as prescribed by the new structure of costs, was as sure a recipe for bankruptcy as the most obstinate and unthinking determination to go on farming the arable could have been.

The population that survived the fourteenth-century pestilences was better fed and better clothed than it had been for a very long time, if ever. This meant that farmers, at this period, never had to want for plough-teams as they had done when poverty forced them to share plough animals with their neighbours. It meant that they could keep dairy herds and rear beef cattle to supply a market which reached lower down the social scale, perhaps, than ever before. It meant that they could reckon on a wool market made up of the demands of a community which cast off its old clothing with less hesitation than before and which was confirmed in its taste for foreign wares by the greater comfort in which so many of its members now lived.

All these calls upon the resources of the land, however, were easily met in the fifteenth century. The resources which had supported the huge population of the thirteenth century, albeit in straitened circumstances, and sustained the immense export trade in wool that thirteenth-century England had managed to carry on, were fully equal to the task of keeping a much smaller population better supplied with food and clothing, and of furnishing a much smaller export trade with the wool it required. We know that this was so because land remained cheap in the fifteenth century even when all the changes in markets that took place after the pestilences had worked their way through the economic system.

What does this imply if not that the sellers' market which had for so long sustained the farming revenues of the big landlords was henceforth no more to be looked for in wool than in corn? For the big landlords the risks of farming had increased all round. In such circumstances was it likely that those landlords who had persevered as wool farmers when the bottom had dropped out of the market for corn would have increased their investment in

---

[25] C. A. Sneyd, ed., A Relation (Camden Society, 1847), pp. 18–19; S. B. Chrimes, ed., Sir John Fortescue: De Laudibus Legum Angliae (Cambridge, 1942), pp. 67–71.

farming by adding to their flocks and enclosing their fields? Without a clear
market trend to guide their choice every consideration of prudence is likely
to have counselled caution. Some no doubt bought sheep in the unshakeable
belief that the wool market which had sustained the fortunes of their estates
so brilliantly in the past could not possibly fail to do so in the future. Others
no doubt enclosed in order to forestall any movement of wages which might
otherwise drive them out of wool as it had already driven them out of corn.
But whatever they did their influence on fifteenth-century farming was
bound to have been comparatively slight; for fifteenth-century farming was
dominated by the smaller producer.

The smaller producer had every economic incentive, in the fifteenth
century, to treat the cheap land he farmed as a disposable asset to be exhausted and then abandoned. The cheapness of land certainly gave him the
power to choose where to farm and to stipulate the conditions of tenure
upon which he would consent to do so. But it did not give him the urge to
keep moving. The strong impression that the records convey is that ordinary
farmers were more concerned to make the most of their farms than to make
the most of their situation by for ever moving on. Immensely favourable
conditions of tenure were proffered by landlords who had to make unparalleled efforts in the fifteenth century in order to secure and retain their
tenants; and the records, meagre at best, seem to indicate that their tenants,
having struck bargains with which they were reasonably content, then proceeded to dig themselves in for life. Leases lengthened, tenants added acre to
acre as and when they could, and the economy, if not the landlords, throve.

No one has yet done the work that will tell us how the smaller fifteenth-
century farmers reacted to their unprecedented circumstances and unique
opportunities. Can we believe, however, that they did nothing to improve
their farms? If they were not to be constantly on the move did they not have
every inducement to improve the condition of the soil and emancipate
themselves from the intolerable irksomeness of having to share essential farm
equipment with neighbours? Few things are harder to do amicably than to
share tools; and given the unpredictable vicissitudes of the English climate
few things can have generated more rancour and contention than the
necessity that compelled neighbours to take turns with the plough. Co-
operative husbandry may please the clubbable historian. It cannot have
pleased those who depended upon it for their livelihood. Would it be
stretching speculation too far, therefore, to suggest that one of the first calls
upon the spare cash of an improving fifteenth-century farmer was very likely
to have been for the purchase of draught animals for the plough?

The farmer who made himself independent in this way did more than
dissolve his partnership with neighbours. He in fact loosened the ties that
bound him to the routines of co-operative husbandry. These routines had
provided him with the use of a plough and a share of the village grazing. No
sooner was he master of his own plough, however, than he lost all interest in
sticking to a system which scattered the land of his farm in strips about the
fields. It was a system which made sense only when scattering the arable in

this way enabled those who shared a plough to save precious time by sharing boundaries as well, wherever their plough went. This need once dispensed with, nothing but habit barred the farmer's way to consolidation.[26]

Consolidation did not have to mean the putting together of all the strips of a farm wherever they might be. No doubt farmers experimented with consolidation, as they experimented with so many other things, by taking it up in stages. A cautious innovator could certainly expect to be able to reap many of the benefits of consolidation, without sacrificing any part of his share of the common grazing, by confining his consolidation to the putting together of all his strips in each of the fields. And perhaps that is what many did. What did such farmers do, however, when they made their farms bigger? Did they simply add arable acre to arable acre heedless of the sluggishness of the fifteenth-century corn market? Or did they diversify? The fifteenth-century market for meat, and wool and dairy products, was certainly good enough to make diversification a sensible alternative to corn. And diversification was not for them the gamble with market trends that it was for the big producer because when the market disappointed the small man his family could always live on what he did not sell.

Does this mean that Hales was right after all, as Prof. Beresford thinks he was, to contend that the urge to consolidate, and in the end to enclose, was strong enough in the fifteenth century to bring about all the changes in farming that historians have so readily ascribed to the sixteenth century and attributed to the work of the wealthier reformers? With rents as low as they were in the fifteenth century, and markets as subdued, is it likely that fifteenth-century farmers found it necessary to transform the agrarian system in order to prosper? Surely it is not. Moreover, the temptation to read too much into the changes that took place in these early centuries can easily betray us into forgetting how much unconsolidated and unenclosed farming seventeenth- and eighteenth-century improvers had to cope with. Unless we are prepared to postulate a farming world in these centuries in which land was scattered into strips and converted to co-operative husbandry at one period, in response to one set of market changes, and then restored to consolidated and enclosed farming at the next when markets had changed again, we must beware of making too much of these early stirrings of reform.

If the enclosure movement that Prof. Beresford and Dr Kerridge have finally banished from the sixteenth century can find only limited sanctuary in the fifteenth century, are we to conclude, therefore, that sixteenth-century farming was carried on more or less in the old way, without benefit of innovation or reform, once the stringencies of the thirteenth century were imposed upon it? The most recent attempt to redeem the century's reputation, in this respect, is in fact Dr Kerridge's. It is perhaps right that one who

---

[26] It is often contended that strips were scattered so that everyone might have his share of good land and bad. But it is difficult to see how such a distribution could have withstood market forces for so long if social concern had been the chief factor in maintaining it.

has done so much to deprive the century of its reputation as the century of enclosure should attempt to offer some reparation in this way. Dr Kerridge's view is that the sixteenth century was distinguished in farming history as the first in which farmers made widespread use of convertible husbandry. This system, which was to be found in the north-west and in scattered places elsewhere in England in the early sixteenth century, 'spread rapidly after 1560 and fastest between about 1590 and 1660 by which time it had conquered . . . half the farmland'.[27]

Convertible husbandry meant two things. It meant abolishing the traditional distinction between permanent pasture and permanent arable. And it meant keeping more animals. Under this system the plough was taken all round the farm. Breaking up the established pastures enabled the farmer to tap the stored fertility of fields which had been for long in grass. This raised arable productivity at once. Keeping more animals enabled the farmer to use the dung they produced by feeding on fields temporarily laid down to grass to put heart back into the arable. This dispensed with the need for a fallow and gave the farmer more as well as richer land for tillage. The problem of winter feed for the larger herds and flocks which supplied all this dung was solved by growing fodder crops in addition to hay.

The spring of the whole system was the pasture. It was the fertility reservoir. Dunging land, unless it is done at an exceptionally heavy rate, is no substitute for grass and legumes. Everything depended, therefore, upon the farmer's willingness to leave his fields in grass for several years so as to give them time to restore their organic content completely. During this period of rest they could be grazed with impunity, provided that they were not overstocked, because, in normal conditions, a field under permanent vegetation will shed plant residues fast enough to enable it to cope with the depletions caused by soil organisms and grazing animals and yet restore the fertility of the soil. This meant that the farm gave every appearance of being run more slowly than before whilst at the same time vastly increasing its productivity and hence its profitability in all departments. It meant, in a sense, the restoration of the two-field system in a version which was emancipated from the two-field system's dependence upon permanent pasture and fallow.

The new system was obviously an excellent one. But was it the system that the sixteenth century required? The community, in the sixteenth century, needed everything that the new system could supply. But it could afford very little of it, for the sixteenth century witnessed a progressive decline in average standards of living. 'The lowest point we record in seven centuries,' remarked Prof. Phelps-Brown, 'was in 1597, the year of the Midsummer Night's Dream'.[28] If sixteenth-century England could scarcely afford to buy the bread it needed, how much less could it afford to buy all the animal

27 E. Kerridge, The Agricultural Revolution (1967), p. 194.
28 E. H. Phelps-Brown and Sheila V. Hopkins, 'Seven Centuries of the Price of Consumables Compared with Builders' Wage-Rates', Economica, n.s., vol. xxiii (1956), reprinted in Carus-Wilson, ed., Essays in Economic History, vol. II (1962), p. 189.

products for which the farmer who had converted to the new system of husbandry was obliged to find a market! The growing export trade alleviated this problem without solving it. For the export trade absorbed no larger a share of his animal products than it had done two centuries before. And without markets for his animal products commensurate with the supply created by this prolific system of husbandry the unfortunate reforming farmer was bound to find himself running an admirably efficient business which did everything but make money.

In this plight he was lost. The new system would not work without all its constituent parts. In the Midlands, for example, Dr Kerridge finds that the new system 'married the livestock to the soil and extracted the greatest possible cereal and animal produce from the farm whilst continuously improving its fertility'.[29] And it was in the Midlands, after all, that the enclosure commissioners found most of the evidence of disturbance of established ways that they encountered. Presumably their evidence, if it means anything at all, means that when sixteenth-century farmers did attempt to do something new it involved them in keeping more animals. Consequently, a farmer who tried to withdraw from the system by cutting down his stock of animals and thereby eliminating the immediate cause of loss, soon found that he could not keep the arable in good heart without fallowing it. And if he tried to fallow the arable whilst maintaining his grass he next found that he had created for himself a monstrous hybrid which combined the disadvantages of the infield – outfield system with the drawbacks of the open-field system. Once the fallow was restored the old constraints, and with them the old practices, were bound to return.

What does all this mean if not that to look for radical changes in farming methods in the sixteenth century is to look in vain? Change is continuous in human affairs. No period, however stable it may appear to be, is unmarked by the sheer passage of time. But the idea of a caesura in the succession of events, a breach of continuity marking the rapid emergence of a world which was modern instead of medieval, makes no more sense in the farming history of the fifteenth and sixteenth centuries than it does in the history of the politics and institutions of these centuries.

In some respects the pace of change had undoubtedly quickened. The England that roared with laughter at Bottom and agonized over Hamlet, which prayed in the rhythms of Cranmer's Book of Common Prayer and heard the bible story told in the language of the Authorised Version, had travelled farther in a century than, perhaps, it ever had done before. But the economic realities had not changed to anything like the same extent, except in the sense that they had turned back upon the promising developments of the previous century and restored the throttling constraints of the century before that.

The time for radical reform, in the sense of the widespread diffusion of

29 Kerridge, *Agricultural Revolution*, p. 202.

techniques of farming which were not necessarily unknown to previous generations of improvers, called for a combination of changes in farming costs and market demand which were more profound than anything that the fifteenth century had managed to produce and were very conspicuously different from anything that the sixteenth or indeed the thirteenth century had achieved. An immense literature, both contemporary and modern, has obfuscated the issues by concentrating our attention upon what was said by men who could make themselves heard and felt, and persuading us to take what was said or done by such men more seriously than it deserves to be taken, or to take it seriously in a different sense, perhaps, from the sense in which it was meant to be taken.

In this respect sixteenth-century government reaction to the enclosure lobby bears a marked resemblance to fourteenth-century government re-action to the wages lobby that became so powerful after the Black Death. In both cases the government acted to check the development of a movement which apparently threatened the tranquillity of the realm and possibly the incomes of politically influential sections of the community. In both cases legislation was followed by litigation. And the immense, indeed unprecedented, activity that took place seems to imply that the response reflected the importance of the problem. In both cases closer examination of the problem reveals that it was not the problem it seemed to be. In the fourteenth century, when wages did in fact rise, prices rose more or less in proportion to them for more than a generation after the advent of the Black Death, thus protecting most of those who stood to lose by the rise in wages from the untoward consequences that might otherwise have ensued.[30] In the sixteenth century those who acceded to the passage of the enclosure legislation did not use it, and those who needed protection did not need protection from the threat of enclosure.

These are, perhaps, unfathomable problems. But they are problems that belong to the world of politics. They are not problems about what went on in the countryside. If we mean to find out about what went on in the countryside we must turn elsewhere than to politics for enlightenment. And if we mean to find out about what went on in the sixteenth-century countryside we shall do better, perhaps, to turn back to the thirteenth century for enlightenment than to look forward, as so many writers have been tempted to do, in an attempt to explain sixteenth-century changes in terms of seventeenth-century reforms and eighteenth-century achievements.

[30] Bridbury, 'The Black Death'.